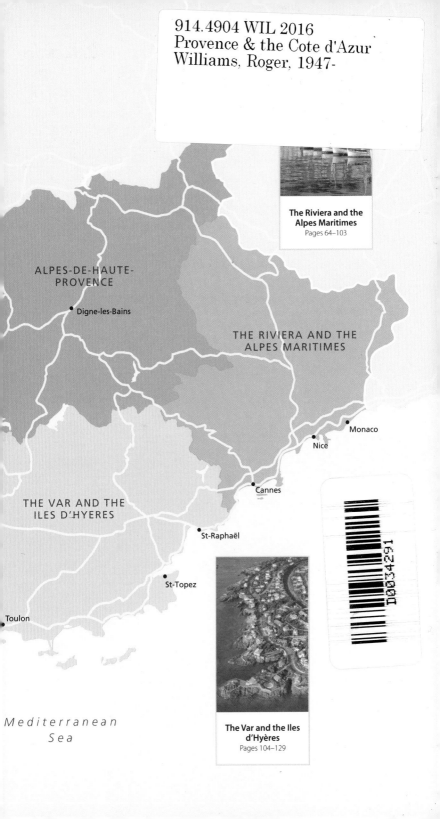

The Riviera and the Alpes Maritimes
Pages 64–103

ALPES-DE-HAUTE-
PROVENCE

Digne-les-Bains

THE RIVIERA AND THE
ALPES MARITIMES

Monaco

Nice

Cannes

THE VAR AND THE
ILES D'HYERES

St-Raphaël

St-Topez

Toulon

The Var and the Iles d'Hyères
Pages 104–129

Mediterranean
Sea

EYEWITNESS TRAVEL

PROVENCE
& THE CÔTE D'AZUR

EYEWITNESS TRAVEL

PROVENCE
& THE CÔTE D'AZUR

Main Contributor **Roger Williams**

DK

LONDON, NEW YORK,
MELBOURNE, MUNICH AND DELHI
www.dk.com

Project Editor Jane Simmonds
Art Editor Jane Ewart
Senior Editor Fay Franklin
Editors Tom Fraser, Elaine Harries, Fiona Morgan
Designers Claire Edwards, Pippa Hurst, Malcolm Parchment

Contributors
John Flower, Jim Keeble, Martin Walters

Photographers
Max Alexander, John Heseltine, Kim Sayer, Alan Williams

Illustrators
Stephen Conlin, Richard Draper, Steve Gyapay,
Chris D Orr Illustration, John Woodcock

Printed and bound in China

First American edition, 1995

15 16 17 18 10 9 8 7 6 5 4 3 2 1

Published in the United States by
DK Publishing, 345 Hudson Street,
New York, New York 10014

**Reprinted with revisions 1995, 1996, 1997, 1999, 2000, 2001, 2002, 2003,
2004, 2006, 2008, 2010, 2012, 2014, 2016**

Copyright 1995, 2016 © Dorling Kindersley Limited, London
A Penguin Random House Company

A catalog record for this book is available from the Library of Congress.

ISSN 1542 1554
ISBN 978-1-4654-3764-8

Floors are referred to throughout in accordance with French usage; ie the "first floor"
is the floor above ground level.

**The information in this
DK Eyewitness Travel Guide is checked regularly.**
Every effort has been made to ensure that this book is as up-to-date as possible
at the time of going to press. Some details, however, such as telephone numbers,
opening hours, prices, gallery hanging arrangements and travel information are
liable to change. The publishers cannot accept responsibility for any consequences
arising from the use of this book, nor for any material on third party websites, and
cannot guarantee that any website address in this book will be a suitable source of
travel information. We value the views and suggestions of our readers very highly.
Please write to: Publisher, DK Eyewitness Travel Guides, Dorling Kindersley,
80 Strand, London, WC2R 0RL, UK, or email: travelguides@dk.com.

Front cover main image: Lavender field outside Abbaye de Sénanque, Vaucluse

◄ Hilltop village of Gourdes, Vaucluse

ANTOINE MA 508

Contents

How to Use This Guide **6**

Poppy field outside the town of
Sisteron *(see p182)*

Introducing
Provence

Discovering Provence **10**

Putting Provence on the
Map **16**

Busy Pampelonne beach to the south of
fashionable St-Tropez *(see p122)*

Marseille fisherman and his catch

Provence Area by Area

The imposing Tarascon's château by the Rhône *(see p144)*

Goat cheese in chestnut leaves

Travellers' Needs

One of the perfumes of Provence

Fondation Maeght outside St-Paul de Vence *(see pp80–81)*

Survival Guide

Typical Provençal countryside between Grasse and Castellane

HOW TO USE THIS GUIDE

This guide will help you get the most from your stay in Provence. It provides both expert recommendations and detailed practical information. *Introducing Provence* maps the region and sets it in its historical and cultural context. *Provence Area by Area* describes the important sights, with maps, photographs and detailed illustrations. Suggestions for food, drink, accommodation, shopping and entertainment are in *Travellers' Needs*, and the *Survival Guide* has tips on everything from the French telephone system to getting to Provence and travelling around the region.

Provence Area by Area

In this guide, Provence has been divided into five separate regions, each of which has its own chapter. A map of these regions can be found inside the front cover of the book. The most interesting places to visit in each region have been numbered and plotted on a *Regional Map*.

Each area of Provence can be quickly identified by its colour coding.

1 Introduction

The landscape, history and character of each region is described here, showing how the area has developed over the centuries and what it has to offer the visitor today.

A locator map shows the region in relation to the whole of Provence.

2 Regional Map

This gives an illustrated overview of the whole region. All the sights are numbered and there are also useful tips on getting around by car and public transport.

Features and story boxes highlight special or unique aspects of a particular sight.

3 Detailed information on each sight

All the important towns and other places to visit are described individually. They are listed in order, following the numbering on the Regional Map. Within each town or city, there is detailed information on important buildings and other major sights.

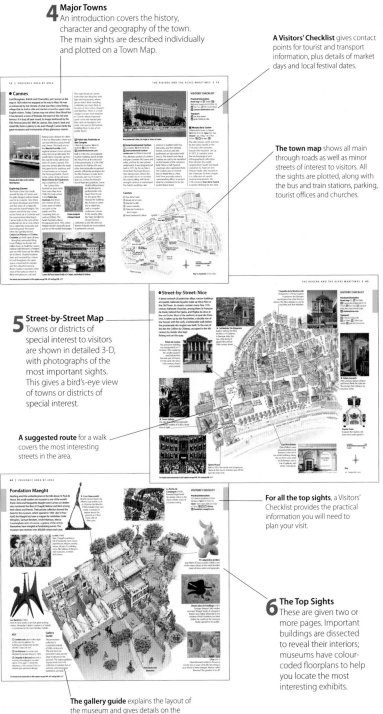

4 Major Towns
An introduction covers the history, character and geography of the town. The main sights are described individually and plotted on a Town Map.

A Visitors' Checklist gives contact points for tourist and transport information, plus details of market days and local festival dates.

The town map shows all main through roads as well as minor streets of interest to visitors. All the sights are plotted, along with the bus and train stations, parking, tourist offices and churches.

5 Street-by-Street Map
Towns or districts of special interest to visitors are shown in detailed 3-D, with photographs of the most important sights. This gives a bird's-eye view of towns or districts of special interest.

A suggested route for a walk covers the most interesting streets in the area.

For all the top sights, a Visitors' Checklist provides the practical information you will need to plan your visit.

Fondation Maeght

6 The Top Sights
These are given two or more pages. Important buildings are dissected to reveal their interiors; museums have colour-coded floorplans to help you locate the most interesting exhibits.

The gallery guide explains the layout of the museum and gives details on the arrangement and display of the collection.

INTRODUCING PROVENCE

DISCOVERING PROVENCE

The following tours have been designed to include as many of Provence's highlights as possible, with a minimum amount of travelling. First come a pair of two-day tours of the region's most popular cities, Nice and Avignon; either can be followed individually or as part of a week-long tour. These are followed by three seven-day tours of the region. The first covers the Côte d'Azur, with its beaches, dramatic scenery and exceptional art museums. The second takes in the major

sites along the banks of the River Rhône from Orange to the Camargue, including some of France's best-preserved Roman and medieval monuments. The third, designed specifically for drivers, covers many of the most iconic landscapes and villages of Provence. All have extra suggestions for extending trips to 10 days. Pick one or mix and match, but before setting out, be sure to check the listing of events *(pp36–9)* and perhaps adjust a tour so as not to miss any of the fun.

Nice
Stylish umbrellas and sun loungers lined up along the shore at the promenade des Anglais Beach Club.

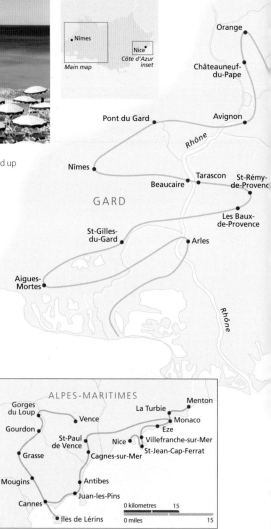

A Week on the Côte d'Azur

- Wander through the morning market in **Nice**, and visit the delightful Musée Matisse.

- Tour the spectacular Villa Ephrussi de Rothchild at **St-Jean-Cap-Ferrat**, and watch the sun set over the Riviera from **Eze**.

- Marvel at the sea life in **Monaco's** Musée Océanographique; see the Roman "trophy" at **La Turbie**.

- Delve into contemporary art at **St-Paul de Vence**, and visit Renoir's home in **Cagnes-sur-Mer**.

- Discover the joyful Picassos in **Antibes**, and relax on the beach at fashionable **Juan-les-Pins.**

- Take in the glamour of **Cannes** and the tranquillity of the **Iles de Lérins**.

◄ *Entrance to the port of Marseille, 1754, by Joseph Vernet*

Vaison-la-Romaine
Sitting on the river Ouvèze, this attractive stone-and-red-roof town has fascinating Roman remains including a theatre still used for the town's summer festival, a hilltop Haute Ville and some of Provence's most chic pavement cafés for relaxing in after a day of sightseeing.

A Week Along the Rhône

- Enjoy **Marseille's** iconic *bouillabaisse* in the scenic Vieux Port.
- Test the acoustics in **Orange's** ancient theatre, and the wines at **Châteauneuf-du-Pape**.
- Tour the medieval Palais des Papes in **Avignon**.
- Marvel at the **Pont du Gard**, and the Roman monuments in **Nîmes**.
- Visit the places Van Gogh painted in **St-Rémy**; enjoy breathtaking views from the citadel of **Les Baux-de-Provence**.
- Explore the walled city of **Aigues-Mortes** on the edge of the **Camargue**.
- Discover the ancient and medieval master-pieces of **Arles**, France's "Little Rome".

A Week in Classic Provence

- Take in the arty charms of **Aix**, the former capital of Provence and birthplace of Paul Cézanne.
- Tour through the beautiful Provençal villages and land-scapes of the **Petit Luberon**.
- Shop for antiques in **L'Isle-sur-la-Sorgue**, and wonder at the mysterious **Fontaine-de-Vaucluse**.
- Discover the vine-clad landscapes and wines grown under the **Dentelles de Montmirail**; seek out the Roman relics of chic **Vaison-la-Romaine**.
- Visit the striking *village perché* of **Gordes**; inhale the lavender at the 12th-century **Abbaye de Sénanque**; and stroll through **Roussillon's** dramatic ochre quarries.

0 kilometres 20
0 miles 20

Key
— A Week Along the Rhône
— A Week in Classic Provence
— A Week on the Côte d'Azur

2 Days in Nice

Nice has a fascinating historic centre, a wealth of museums and a stunning waterfront.

- **Arriving** Nice Airport is 7 km (4.5 miles) from the city. Buses link it with the centre.
- **Moving on** The journey from Nice to Avignon on a TGV train is just under 3 hours.

See pp84–9 for information on sights in Nice.

Day 1

Morning Start with a stroll through Nice's bustling Italianate Old Town: don't miss the **Cathédrale Ste-Réparate** with its glazed tile dome and the art-filled **Chapelle du la Miséricorde**. Take in the heady colours and fragrances of the market in the **cours Saleya**, then make your way up to the summit of the **Colline du Château** gardens for the best view over the Baie des Anges.

Afternoon Visit the elegant district of Cimiez to discover the life and work of one-time Nice resident Henri Matisse at the **Musée Matisse**. Stop by the serene **Monastery of Notre-Dame**, where the artist is buried, then see the **Musée Chagall**, filled with colourful paintings of biblical themes.

Day 2

Morning Explore two different aspects of Nice: start in the 17th century (when the city was part of Italy) at the ornate Baroque **Palais Lascaris**, with its prize collection of antique musical instruments. Then leap ahead four centuries at the striking **Musée d'Art Moderne et d'Art Contemporain**, set amid an outdoor sculpture garden.

Afternoon Stroll along the famous **promenade des Anglais** and consider lunch and a swim at one of the seaside bathing establishments. Or pay a visit to Nice's history museum, the **Villa Masséna** next door

Blue lounge chairs lined up along the promenade in Nice

to the famed **Hotel Négresco**. In the evening, enjoy a drink or dinner in the lively **cours Saleya**.

> **To extend your trip…**
> Take a scenic day trip on the **Train des Pignes** *(p185)* and visit **Entrevaux** *(p191)*.

2 Days in Avignon

A lively city on the Rhône river, Avignon is home to the Palais des Papes and excellent museums.

- **Arriving** Marseille has the nearest international airport (88 km/54 miles); direct TGV trains run from the airport to Avignon in only 54 minutes.

See pp170–72 for information on sights in Avignon.

Day 1

Morning Plunge straight into Avignon's glory days on a tour of the **Palais des Papes**, the biggest medieval palace in the world. Afterwards, visit the nearby **Cathédrale Notre-Dame-des-Doms**, with the tombs of two popes and the hilltop gardens of the **Rocher des Doms**.

Afternoon Discover the rich Gothic art patronized by the papal court at the **Musée du Petit Palais**, then walk along Avignon's famous bridge, the **Pont St-Bénézet**. Afterwards stroll the atmospheric medieval lanes of rue du Roi-René and rue des Teinturiers.

Day 2

Morning Visit the city's two outstanding art museums, the **Musée Calvet** and **Musée Angladon**, then relax and watch the world go by at a café in bustling **place de l'Horloge**.

Afternoon Take the bus over the Rhône to **Villeneuve-lès-Avignon** *(p134)*. Climb one of its towers (**Fort St-André** or the **Tour de Philippe le Bel**) for wonderful views over Avignon. See the masterpiece of the Avignon School of painting, Enguerrand Quarton's *Coronation of the Virgin*, in the **Musée Pierre de Luxembourg**, then visit the monastery it was painted for: the vast **Chartreuse du Val-de-Bénédiction**.

> **To extend your trip…**
> Make a day trip to **Nîmes** *(pp136–7)* and the majestic **Pont du Gard** *(p135)*.

Dining alfresco on rue des Teinturiers alongside the river Sorgue, Avignon

The Jardin Botanique Exotique at 19th-century Villa Val Rahmeh, Menton

A Week on the Côte d'Azur

- **Duration** 7 days – with suggestions for extending it to a 10-day tour.
- **Airport** Arrive and depart from Nice Côte d'Azur airport.
- **Transport** Lignes d'Azur buses go everywhere; trains serve coastal towns. Hire a car in Cannes to head inland.

Day 1: Nice
Pick a day from the city itinerary on p12.

Day 2: St-Jean-Cap-Ferrat, Villefranche-sur-Mer, Eze
Take the tour of the Villa Ephrussi de Rothschild and its spectacular gardens *(p90)* at **St-Jean-Cap-Ferrat** *(p89)*, then follow the beautiful path that starts just east of the port of St-Jean-Cap-Ferrat. Relax on the free beach at **Villefranche-sur-Mer** *(p92)*; wander through the town's skein of medieval lanes and sit in one of its buzzing waterfront cafés. Then head up to **Eze** *(p92)*, a stunning *village perché* to watch the sun set over the Riviera.

Day 3: Monaco, La Turbie and Menton
Discover the astonishing sea creatures in the Musée Océanographique in **Monaco** *(pp94–8)*, and visit its Palais Princier, for a peek into the lives of the Grimaldis, Europe's oldest ruling family. Head up the slopes above Monaco to **La Turbie** *(p93)*, famous for its ancient Trophée d'Auguste, erected in honour of Augustus. Descend to **Menton** *(pp102–3)* for a walk through its tropical gardens and a look at the Musée Jean Cocteau. In the evening, head back to Monaco and stop for a drink in **Monte-Carlo's** *(pp96–7)* glamorous Café de Paris and perhaps try your luck in Europe's most famous casino.

Day 4: St-Paul de Vence and Cagnes-sur-Mer
Contemporary art reigns at charming **St-Paul de Vence** *(p79)*, in the exquisite **Fondation Maeght** *(pp80–81)*, in the town's many galleries and the Colombe d'Or *auberge*. Next, aim for **Cagnes-sur-Mer** *(p82)*, for the eclectic Château Musée Grimaldi and the moving Musée Renoir, the Impressionist's last home.

Day 5: Antibes and Juan-les-Pins
Wander through the streets of old **Antibes** *(p76)*, ogle the billionaires' yachts in the marina and take in the excellent Musée Picasso housed in a waterfront castle. Stroll past the glamorous villas of Cap d'Antibes, and spend a lazy afternoon on the beach in **Juan-les-Pins** *(p76)*.

Day 6 : Cannes and the Iles de Lérins
Discover the two sides of **Cannes** *(pp72–3)*: the swanky Croisette, with its world-famous hotels and the Palais des Festivals, and the old town, with its bustling Marché Forville. The market is a great place to pick up a picnic for a trip to one of the **Iles de Lérins** *(pp74–8)*: choose between peaceful, monastic St-Honorat or larger Ste-Marguerite, with its links to the Man in the Iron Mask.

> **To extend your trip…**
> Visit the Roman ruins of **Fréjus** *(p129)* 36 km (22 miles) west of Cannes and the chic resort of **St-Tropez** *(pp122–6)*; the following day head to **Hyères** *(p119)* 51 km (32 miles) from Cannes to sail to the car-free island of **Porquerolles** *(p118)*.

Roman statuary at the Musée d'Art Classique de Mougins

Day 7: Mougins, Grasse, Gorges du Loup, Gourdon, Vence
Start in **Mougins** *(p70)*, famed for its great restaurants. Admire the works of former resident Picasso in the Musée de la Photographie and visit the captivating Musée d'Art Classique. Discover how perfume is made in **Grasse** *(p70)* at the Musée International de la Parfumerie, then drive the dramatic **Gorges du Loup** *(p69)*, stopping off at the breathtaking village of **Gourdon** *(p69)* and the delightful town of **Vence** *(p78)* before returning to Nice.

> **To extend your trip…**
> Go north from Grasse 64 km (40 miles) to **Castellane** *(p190)* to explore the even more spectacular **Gorges du Verdon** *(pp188–9)*.

A Week Along the Rhône

- **Duration** 7 days – with additional suggestions to extend it to 10 days.
- **Airports** Arrive at and depart from Marseille Provence Airport.
- **Transport** This tour can be made using a combination of trains and buses, although hiring a car would allow more flexibility.

Day 1: Marseille

A day is just enough to scratch the surface of **Marseille** (pp154–6). Start in the picturesque Vieux Port, with its morning fish market and the Abbaye de St-Victor. Enjoy the spectacular views from Notre-Dame-de-la-Garde, and visit the Palais Longchamp, with its fine arts collection. Stroll the Canebière before tucking into *bouillabaisse* for dinner.

Diners enjoying *bouillabaisse* at the Miramar Restaurant, Marseille's Vieux Port

To extend your trip...
Take a boat trip and swim in Marseille's dramatic **Les Calanques** (p157). Visit the wine town of **Cassis** (p157).

Day 2: Orange and Châteauneuf-du-Pape

Take the train to **Orange** (pp165–7) to visit its incomparable Roman Théâtre Antique, scene of summer theatre and dance festivals, and the well-preserved Arc de Triomphe. In the afternoon, head south to **Châteauneuf-du-Pape** (p168) for a tasting of the famous wines before dinner.

Day 3: Avignon

Pick a day from the city itinerary on p12.

To extend your trip...
Hire a car and take a day trip to **Fontaine-de-Vaucluse** (p169) 33 km (20 miles) east of Avignon; the hill town of **Gordes** (p173), **Abbaye de Sénanque** (p168) and **Roussillon** (p173) are nearby.

Day 4: Pont du Gard, Nîmes, Beaucaire and Tarascon

Cross the Rhône to visit antiquity's most beautiful aqueduct – the majestic **Pont du Gard** (p135), before moving on to the city it served, **Nîmes** (pp136–7). Don't miss the amphitheatre, Les Arènes, the Maison Carrée – a well-preserved Roman temple – and the Castellum, where the aqueduct's water was distributed. Head back to the Rhône, where the medieval castles of **Beaucaire** (p143) (famous for its bullfights) and **Tarascon** (p144) (known for its Tarasque and Souleïado fabrics) face each other across the river.

Day 5: St-Rémy-de-Provence and Les Baux-de-Provence

St-Rémy-de-Provence (p144) is one of Provence's most attractive towns, and was frequently painted by Van Gogh. Take a walk out to the Clinique St-Paul to see some views painted by Van Gogh, and the nearby ruins of Greco-Roman Glanum. Next, head into the mini-mountain chain of **Les Alpilles** (p145) and the citadel of **Les Baux-de-Provence** (p146), once the medieval setting of the troubadour Court of Love; the views are wonderful.

Day 6: St-Gilles-du-Gard and Aigues Mortes

Along with its iconic white horses, black bulls and pink flamingoes, the **Camargue** (pp140–43) has several fascinating historic sites. Begin at **St-Gilles-du-Gard** (p143) and the magnificent Romanesque façade of the Abbaye de St-Gilles, then head south to explore the unique 13th-century walled crusader town of **Aigues-Mortes** (pp138–9).

Day 7: Arles

France's "Little Rome", **Arles** (pp148–9) boasts both an ancient theatre and amphitheatre, the Thermes de Constantin and the intriguing Musée de l'Arles Antique. Also visit the cloisters of the church of St-Trophime, Les Alychamps cemetery and the Espace Van Gogh, with exhibits relating to the painter's sojourn in Arles.

To extend your trip...
Uncover the history of the Carmargue in the **Musée Camarguais** (p143); spot birds at the **Parc Ornithologique du Pont-de-Gau** (p142) and visit the Romany pilgrimage church at lively **Saintes-Maries-de-la-Mer** (p142).

Roman sarcophagus or tombs showing boar hunters, Musée de l'Arles Antique, Arles

A Week in Classic Provence

- **Duration** 7 days – or 10 with the additional trips.
- **Airports** Arrive and depart from Marseille Provence Airport.
- **Transport** Hiring a car is the best option. Although much of this itinerary is technically possible by bus, infrequent connections will make getting around difficult.

Brantes and Mont Ventoux, north Luberon Mountains

Day 1: Aix-en-Provence

Today a cosmopolitan university city and venue of a famous music festival, **Aix** (pp152–3) was once the capital of Provence. Stroll through the historic centre, with its elegant 17th- and 18th-century hôtels and fountains. Don't miss the Cathédrale St-Sauveur, with its triptych of *The Burning Bush*, the adjacent Musée des Tapisseries, with a unique collection of secular Beauvais tapestries, and the luxurious 17th-century villa, the Pavillon de Vendôme.

Day 2: More Aix and the Montagne Ste-Victoire

Aix is also synonymous with Paul Cézanne: see his paintings in the Musée Granet, and visit his evocative studio, which has been left unchanged. Take a scenic drive around Cézanne's beloved Montagne Ste-Victoire, which he painted many times, and have a drink at his favourite Café des Deux Garçons.

Day 3: Abbaye de Silvacane, Petit Luberon, Cavaillon

Some of Provence's most beautiful landscapes and villages are in the Petit Luberon, north of Aix. Stop at the 12th-century Cistercian **Abbaye de Silvacane** (p151), then take the driving tour (pp174–5), starting in **Lourmarin** and continuing through the delightful villages of **Bonnieux, Lacoste, Ménerbes and Oppède-le-Vieux**. End up in **Cavaillon** (p174), famous for melons; stay overnight to visit its exceptional morning market.

Day 4: L'Isle-sur-la-Sorgue, Fontaine-de-Vaucluse and Carpentras

Wander through pretty **L'Isle-sur-la-Sorgue** (p169), with its canals and weekend antiques market. Just upriver, visit the source of the Sorgue at the **Fontaine-de-Vaucluse** (p169), along with its paper mill and Musée d'Histoire 1939–45. Continue on to **Carpentras** (p168), which has a 14th-century synagogue and a cathedral.

Day 5: The Dentelles de Montmirail and Vaison-la-Romaine

The Dentelles de Montmirail mountains are among Provence's most beautiful landscapes. Take the scenic drive (p163), starting in **Beaumes-de-Venise**, famous for its dessert wine, and carrying on to **Vacqueyras** and **Gigondas**, home to a famous

A weekend antiques fair in L'Isle-sur-la-Sorgue, the "Venice of Provence"

red wine. In chic **Vaison-la-Romaine** (p162), visit the boutiques of the Haute Ville.

> **To extend your trip…**
> Spend a day exploring **Mont Ventoux** (p164), 32 km (20 miles) from Vaison – by car, bicycle or on foot.

Day 6: Gordes, Abbaye de Sénanque and Roussillon

Head back south through the **Dentelles** (p163), pausing in the old Huguenot village of **Malaucène**, and **Le Barroux**, for the views from its château. Next comes the striking **Gordes** (p173), a *village perché*. Visit the nearby 12th-century **Abbaye de Sénanque** (pp168–9) and finish in **Roussillon** (p173), taking a stroll through its ochre quarries.

Day 7: Apt, La Tour d'Aigues and Pertuis

Charming **Apt** (p176) has a fascinating cathedral; learn about Apt's famous crystallized fruits at the Musée de l'Aventure Industrielle. Go through the Parc Naturel Régional du Luberon; stop at **La Tour d'Aigues** (p177) for the Renaissance château and ceramics museum, then at **Pertuis** (p177) to see its Gothic Eglise St-Nicolas before heading back to Marseille.

> **To extend your trip…**
> Head 42 km (26 miles) east from Apt to **Forcalquier** (p186). Spend two days in the Alpes-de-Haute Provence.

Putting Provence on the Map

Provence is situated in the sun-blessed southeast corner of France, edged to the south by the Mediterranean. Its most illustrious stretch of coastline, roughly from Menton to Bandol, is also known as the Côte d'Azur, although the nearer to Italy it gets the more likely it is to be referred to as the Riviera. To the east are Italy and the Alps, to the west, the Rhône river. The region covers an area of over 30,000 sq km (18,650 sq miles) with a population of about 4.9 million.

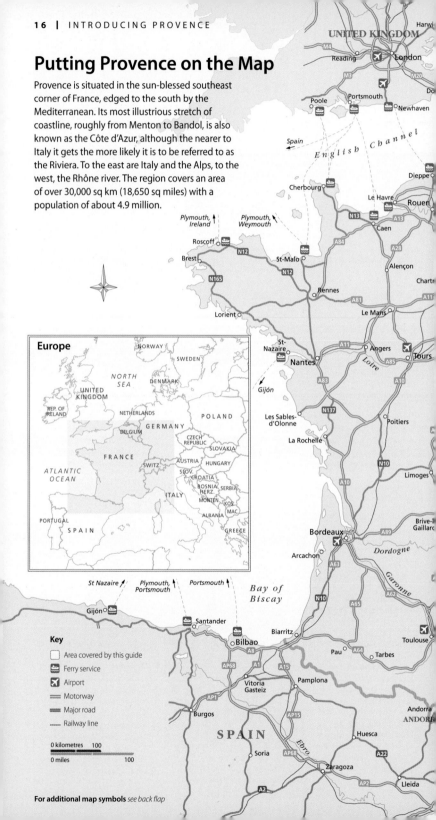

Key

- ☐ Area covered by this guide
- 🛳 Ferry service
- ✈ Airport
- ═ Motorway
- ▬ Major road
- ─── Railway line

0 kilometres   100
0 miles   100

For additional map symbols *see back flap*

A PORTRAIT OF PROVENCE

In a comparatively short time, Provence has changed its face. A few generations ago it was, to the French, a place of indolent southern bumpkins. To foreigners, it was an idyllic spot, but one reserved, it seemed to many, for the rich or artistic. Now, Provence, more than any other region, is where the French would choose to live and work, and its holiday routes buzz with both local and international traffic all year round.

The high-tech industry based here can attract top-flight staff, not just from France but from all over the world.

Still, Provence remains an essentially rural region. At its edges, it has a lively Latin beat: almost Spanish among the *gardians* of the Camargue in the west, Italian in Nice to the east. The rest of the region is mostly traditional and conservative. Only in games of *pétanque* or discussions about European bureaucracy does the talk become animated. But, once engaged in conversation, Provençals are the most generous and warmest of hosts. There is an all-pervading Frenchness, of course, which means that people are polite and punctilious.

Shopkeepers always greet you as you enter, but open and close on the dot. Lunch, in Provence, is sacrosanct.

Traditions are important to the people of Provence. Local crafts are not quaint revivals, but respected, time-honoured occupations. Festivals, such as La Bravade in St-Tropez, have been taking place for the last 450 years. Artists who came here for the light and the scenery found other inspirations, too. Picasso himself learned the potter's art at the wheel of a Provençal craftsman. Homes will have hand-turned local chestnut or oak furniture, *terre rouge* clay pots, Moustiers *faïence*, Biot glassware and furnishings using the traditional *indiennes* patterns of Arles and Nîmes.

Locals enjoying a leisurely game of *pétanque* at Châteauneuf-du-Pape

◀ Basilique de Notre-Dame-de-la-Garde in Marseille

A traditional bakery in Ville-sur-Auzon, in Vaucluse

The home is run as it has been for generations. Provençal kitchens, at the heart of family life, are famous. Combining simplicity with bounty, they mix the aroma of herbs with the generosity of wine. In the envious and admiring eyes of visitors, they are the epitome of taste.

Tradition and Customs

Good taste is inbred. In rural communities, the familiarity of the weather, the seasons and the harvests are sources of constant discussion. Gardens, full of fruit trees, vegetables and flowers, are a matter of pride. Even city-dwellers know how the best produce should be grown, and may well have access to a country relation's plot. Market stalls are beautifully laid out and carefully scrutinized and, no matter how abundant the fruit, the vegetables or the wine, they are all grist for debate.

There are still heated discussions fuelled by the latest developments imposed by the European Union, whose legislation, farmers say, has in the past had a detrimental effect on productive Provençal land, when for example ancient vineyards were grubbed up and landowners' wealth sent into rapid decline.

The harvest cycle is close to the gods, whose benificence can affect the crops as surely as any EU bureaucrat. As Catholic as the rest of France, the people of Provence are also touched with a mystic sense that has been influenced by Mithraism and

A colourful fruit and vegetable market

Islam, as well as by pagan gods. Religious beliefs are so well mixed that it is often difficult to separate them. Carnival and Corpus Christi extend Easter, which has more importance here than in many other parts of Europe. Christmas, too, is an elaborate affair. The rituals begin as early as 4 December, St Barb's day, with the planting of grains of wheat, a pagan symbol of renewal and rebirth.

Superstitions linger in the countryside. An egg, salt, bread and matches, humble representations of elemental concepts, may be given to a newborn baby, while carline thistles may be seen nailed to front doors for good luck.

Landscape and People

Provence has a typically Mediterranean landscape: the mountains drop down to the sea; communities perch on crags or cling to remote hillsides. It is little wonder that traditions live on here. For centuries, too, it was a place for outlaws from France, who could assume new identities here and carry on with their lives. Perhaps as a result, strangers

Harvesting linden blossoms to make *tilleul* infusion

The dramatic, isolated crags of Les Pénitents des Mées, in Alpes-de-Haute-Provence

were not to be trusted, and remained outsiders forever. A seemingly trivial slight might spark a feud which could last for generations. There are still villages today where one family does not speak to another, even though each has long forgotten why. This attitude, and its tragic implications, was finely portrayed by Yves Montand, with Gérard Depardieu as the shunned outsider, in Claud Berri's films of Marcel Pagnol's *Jean de Florette* and *Manon des Sources*. The more cosmopolitan coast is the territory of *film noir*. Here, the tradition of silence and family ties has not always been beneficial. Jean-Paul Belmondo and Alain Delon romanticized it in *Borsalino;* Gene Hackman revealed its dark underside in *The French Connection*.

In 1982, the Antibes-based English novelist Graham Greene published an exposé of corruption in Nice. In 1994, Yann Piat, anti-drugs campaigner and member of parliament, was assassinated in Hyères.

Peillon, a perched village in Provence

The fact that Piat was a woman made no difference to her enemies, ironic in a region where women have not been treated as equals. Alphonse Daudet noted the Provençal male's "incurable contempt" for women, however, the Queen of Arles is elected for her virtues as an upholder of the traditional Provençal values. It was also this region that nurtured the 20th century's icon of French womanhood, Brigitte Bardot. Furthermore, the town of Aix-en-Provence has had a female mayor since 2001.

There are great rewards for the visitor who can appreciate the many facets of Provence – its traditions as well as its beauty and glamour. But, the more often you return, the more you will realize, as have some of the world's greatest artists and writers, that part of the endless allure of Provence lies within the very secrets that it refuses to surrender.

The Natural History of Provence

A fascinating array of insects, birds, animals and flowers flourish in the varied habitats available in Provence, from the Mediterranean to coastal wetlands, rocky gorges and the remote peaks of the Alpes Maritimes. The area has the mildest climate in France: hot, mainly dry summers, and warm, mild winters near the coast. In early spring the myriad flowers are at their best, while numbers of unusual birds are at their highest in late spring. Many of the wilder areas have been made into reserves, often with routes marked out for exploration.

Mont Ventoux's lower slopes are flower-covered in the spring *(see p164)*.

The Luberon *(see pp174–6) is* a huge limestone range, rich in orchids, such as this military orchid. It is also a hunting ground for birds of prey.

Les Alpilles' limestone ridge *(see p145)* attracts birds of prey, including Bonelli's eagles, Egyptian vultures and eagle owls, as well as this more mild-mannered bee-eater.

• Orange

Carpentras •

• Avignon

Vaucluse

Rhône

• Arles

Bouches-du-Rhône and Nîmes

The Camargue, at the delta of the river Rhône, is one of Europe's most important wetlands *(see pp140–41)*. Water birds that thrive here include purple herons and the greater flamingo. Lizards, such as this ocellated lizard, can also be seen.

• Marseille

The Côte Bleue is rich in marine life, such as octopuses, in the deeper waters.

The Montagne Ste-Victoire is a limestone range that attracts walkers and climbers. It was one of Cézanne's favourite subjects.

The Plaine de la Crau is 50,000 ha (193 sq miles) of stony plains and steppe-like grasslands southeast of Arles, home to birds like this hoopoe, and the rare pin-tailed sandgrouse.

Les Calanques *(see p157)* are narrow inlets bounded by cliffs. The rocky slopes are home to woodland birds such as owls.

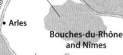

The Parc National du Mercantour is one of the finest Alpine reserves *(see p101)*, containing wildlife such as this marmot, and chamois, ibex and mouflon (wild sheep). It is also good walking country.

The Haute Provence Geological Reserve near Digne *(see p184)* has a spectacular collection of giant ammonites embedded in rock.

The Cime de la Bonette *(see p183)* is a lofty pass where chamois roam.

The Gorges du Verdon area, between the Alps and the Mediterranean, is a beautiful nature reserve with a dramatic canyon at its centre *(see pp188–9)*. A footpath along the canyon floor allows detailed examination of the rock formations, rare plants and birds.

Barcelonnette •

Alpes-de-Haute-Provence

Digne-les-Bains •

Var

Verdon

The Gorges de la Vésubie *(see p99)* has viewpoints from which to spot migrating birds such as swallows.

The Préalpes de Grasse, known for their dramatic gorges, lie to the east of the Alpes Maritimes.

The Riviera and the Alpes Maritimes

Nice •

The Var and the Iles d'Hyères

• Fréjus

The Massif de l'Esterel's *(see p128)* high rocky coves and scrubland are home to various species of snakes.

In the Massif des Maures *(see pp120–21)*, dense woods contain bee-eaters, woodchat shrikes and hoopoes. They also provide sanctuary for the rare Hermann's tortoise.

Toulon

The Massif de la Ste-Baume has many broadleaved trees that are vividly coloured in autumn.

Key

▢ National park
▢ Regional natural park
▢ Protected site
▢ Reserve

0 kilometres   25

0 miles   25

The Iles d'Hyères *(see pp118–19)*, scattered a ferry ride away from the most southerly point of Provence, are best known for their abundant sea life, including fish such as this wrasse. Geckos and rare birds like the great spotted cuckoo can be seen.

Perched Villages

Some of the most attractive architectural features of Provence are the *villages perchés* or perched villages. They rise like jagged summits on the hilltops where they were built for safety in the political turmoil of the Middle Ages. From their lofty heights they kept vigil over the hinterland as well as the coast. They were built around castle keeps and wrapped in thick ramparts, a huddle of cobbled streets, steps, alleys and archways. Few were able to sustain their peasant communities beyond the 19th-century agrarian reforms, and a century of poverty and depopulation followed. Today many of the villages have been restored by a new generation of artists, craftworkers and holiday-makers.

The mountainous site of Peillon *(see p99)* is typical of the way perched villages blend organically with the landscape.

PLACE CHARLES DE GAULLE

RUE DE LA POURTOUNE

RUE DE

RUE DES DORIERS

RUE DES BAUQUES

MONTÉE DE L'ÉGLISE

RUE GRANDE

COURTINE ST PAUL

BASTION ST REMY

REMPART

St-Paul de Vence

Many of the key features of this typical village perché have been preserved. The medieval ramparts were completely reinforced by Francis I in the 16th century. Today it is again besieged – as one of France's most popular tourist sights (see p79).

Complicated entrances confused invaders and provided extra security against attack.

The church was always the focal point of the village.

Side entrances were never obtrusive or elaborate, but were usually small and, as in Eze *(see p92)*, opened onto narrow, winding lanes. Sometimes there were more gates or abrupt turns within the walls to confuse attacking soldiers, making the town easier to defend.

Castles and keeps *(donjons)*, and sometimes fortified churches, were always sited with the best viewpoint in the village, and provided sanctuary in times of crisis. Many, like the castle at Eze *(see p92)*, were often attacked and are now in ruins.

The church sustained the religious life of the community. As in Les Baux *(see p146)*, it was usually built near the keep of the castle, part of a central core of communal buildings, and was often fortified. The bell would be rung to warn of impending attack.

Fountains were essential to the village, often being the sole source of water. Many, like this one in Vence *(see p78)*, were elaborately embellished.

The arcades lent support to the buildings in the narrow, winding streets, as here in Roquebrune *(see p102)*. They also gave shelter from sun and rain.

Fountain

Arched and stepped streets

A narrow gateway was easily secured.

Ramparts and bastions provided solid defences.

The ramparts surrounded the entire village with thick stone walls, often with houses built into them. The defences, like those of St-Paul de Vence *(see p79)*, were strengthened in the 16th century under Francis I and by Vauban, Louis XIV's military architect. Today they offer superb views.

Main gates were always narrow so they could be closed off and defended in times of attack. Some gates had the additional protection of portcullises. Peille *(see p99)* in the Alpes Maritimes is a typical Medieval village, full of narrow, cobbled streets, which also helped defend the village.

Rural Architecture in Provence

Traditional architectural features are reminders of how influential the weather is on living conditions in rural Provence. Great efforts are made to ease the biting gusts of the Mistral and the relentless heat of the summer sun. Thick stone walls, small windows and reinforced doors are all recognizable characteristics. Traditional farmhouses were built entirely from wood, clay, stone and soil, all locally found materials. Rows of hardy cypress trees were planted to act as a windbreak on the north side; plane and lotus trees provided shade to the south.

Bories *(see p173)* are drystone huts built using techniques dating back to 2,000 BC.

The Provençal Mas

Found across rural Provence, the mas *is a low, squat stone farmhouse. Protection and strength are vital to its construction – walls are made of compact stone blocks and the wooden doors and shutters are thick and reinforced. Outbuildings often included a cellar, stables, a bread oven and dovecote.*

Canal roof tiling, or *tuiles romaines,* is typical of the south.

Roughly cut stone bricks are used to make the walls.

Dovecot

Chimneys are stone-built, low and squat, and lie close to the roof.

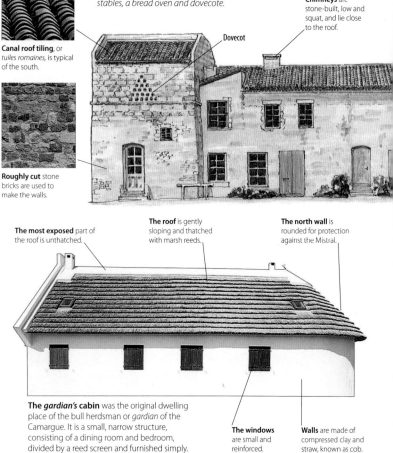

The most exposed part of the roof is unthatched.

The roof is gently sloping and thatched with marsh reeds.

The north wall is rounded for protection against the Mistral.

The *gardian's* cabin was the original dwelling place of the bull herdsman or *gardian* of the Camargue. It is a small, narrow structure, consisting of a dining room and bedroom, divided by a reed screen and furnished simply.

The windows are small and reinforced.

Walls are made of compressed clay and straw, known as cob.

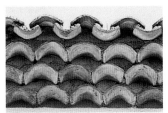

The tiled roofs are gently sloping and are influenced by Roman design, with a decorative frieze *(génoise)* under the eaves. The tiles are made of thick, red terracotta and curved in shape – a double or triple layer of tiles are set in mortar and protrude beyond the wall.

Windows are built on three sides of the *mas* but none on the north to avoid the Mistral's full blast. They are kept small to prevent the winter winds coming in, but large enough to let light in.

Interlocking clay tiles form canals, allowing rainwater to run down and drain off the roof.

The Mistral winds blow so fiercely that the *mas* was often built facing the southeast to minimize the wind's impact. Roofs are built low to the ground, covering the living quarters and annexes. The gentle slope prevents the tiles blowing and sliding off.

The walls are rendered smooth with plaster.

Stone ice houses were built near the *mas* and used for storage during the winter months. Blocks of ice were cut and put in the huts, insulated with hay.

Ironwork Bell Towers

Wrought-iron bell towers have been a speciality in Provence since the 16th century. Their light, open framework allows strong winds to blow through and the sound of the bells to carry for miles. The design and complexity depends on the size and purpose of the building. These examples illustrate the skills of craftsmen across the region.

Highly ornate bell tower in Aix

The bell tower of St-Jérôme in Digne-les-Bains

The Hôtel de Ville bell tower in Orange

Notre-Dame's bell tower in Sisteron

Architectural Styles in Provence

From the imperial grandeur of Roman constructions to the modern domestic designs of Le Corbusier, Provence has a magnificent array of architectural styles. The Middle Ages saw a flourishing of great Romanesque abbeys and churches and from the 16th to the 18th centuries, as prosperity increased, châteaux and town houses were built. With the expansion of towns in the 19th century came an increase in apartment blocks and public buildings to accommodate the fast-growing population. Today, successful restoration has taken place, but often in haste. The demands of tourism have taken their toll, particularly on the coast, resulting in some ugly developments.

An 18th-century fountain in Pernes-les-Fontaines

Roman Architecture (20 BC–AD 400)

The quality of Roman archi-tecture is illustrated by the many extant amphitheatres, triumphal arches and thermal baths found across the region, all built with large blocks of local limestone.

Ornate high-relief

The triumphal arch of Glanum *(see pp144–5)* is the original entrance to the oldest Roman city in Provence. Carvings on the outer arch show Caesar's victory over the Gauls and Greeks.

Doric columns on second storey

Both storeys have 60 arcades

Nîmes Arènes, built in the 1st century AD *(see p136)*

Nîmes' well-preserved Maison Carrée *(see p136)*

Roman Architecture (11th–12th Centuries)

The high point of Provençal architecture came after the Dark Ages. It was a combination of Classical order and perfection, inspired by Roman design and new styles from northern and southern Europe. This style is characterized especially in religious buildings by elegant symmetry and simplicity.

Multiple arches

Elaborate religious carvings

This church entrance in Seyne *(see p182)* is an example of 13th-century Romanesque architecture. The slight point of the multiple arches hints at a move away from strict Romanesque purity.

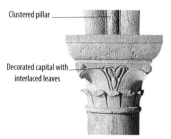

Clustered pillar

Decorated capital with interlaced leaves

Capital from the Abbaye du Thoronet *(see p112)*

The Abbaye de Sénanque, founded in 1148 *(see pp168–9)*

Late Middle Ages
(13th–16th Centuries)

Feuding and religious wars led to people withdrawing to towns, protected by fortified walls and gates. Communication between houses was often by underground passages. Streets were roughly paved and water and sewage were carried away by a central gutter.

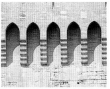

Tour de la Campana in the Palais des Papes *(see pp48–9)*

Street in St-Martin-Vésubie *(see p99)* showing central gutter

Aigues-Mortes *(see pp138–9)* was built by Louis IX in the 13th century, according to a strict grid pattern. This strategically placed fort overlooks both sea and land.

Crenellation or battlements

Portcullis used against invaders

Classical Architecture
(17th–18th Centuries)

The severity and order of the Classical style was relieved by elaborate carvings on doorways and windows. Gardens became more formal and symmetrical.

The 17th-century Barbentane château, fronted by formal gardens *(see p134)*

Tablet with symbol of authority

Carved Regency doorway

Refined stone

Neo-Classical pillar

The Musée des Tapisseries in Aix *(see p152)* has elaborately carved wooden entrance doors.

Pavillon de Vendôme detail, Aix-en-Provence *(see p153)*

Modern Architecture
(1890–Present Day)

The magnificent hotels and villas of the *belle époque* have given way to more utilitarian housing and public buildings. But the numerous modern art galleries represent the highest standards of 20th-century architecture.

Le Corbusier's Cité Radieuse *(see p156)*

Rounded pavilion

Cupola above a round corner tower

The palatial Négresco hotel in Nice *(see p88)*

The Musée d'Art Moderne et d'Art Contemporain in Nice *(see p89)* is made up of square towers, linked by glass passageways.

Artists of Provence

Provence inspired many of the most original 19th- and 20th-century painters. They were attracted by the luminescent quality of the light here, and the consequent brilliance of the colours. Cézanne, who was a native, and Van Gogh, a convert, were both fired by the vibrant shades of the landscape. The Impressionists Monet and Renoir came early, and followers included Bonnard, Signac and Dufy. The two giants of 20th-century painting, Matisse and Picasso, both settled here. The artistic tradition is kept alive by small galleries in almost every town, as well as major museums throughout the region.

Jean Cocteau (1889–1963) spent many years on the coast and created his museum in Menton *(see p103)*. *Noce imaginaire* (1957) is one of his murals from the Salle des Mariages.

Victor Vasarely (1906–97) restored the château in Gordes. His Kinetic and Op Art can be seen in Aix-en-Provence *(see p153)*.

Vincent Van Gogh (1853–90) painted Van Gogh's Chair (1888) in Arles *(see pp148–50)*. His two years here and in St-Rémy *(see pp144–5)* were his most prolific.

Regions of Provence

Orange
Sisteron
Digne-les-Bains
Avignon
Gordes
Nîmes
Arles
Area of main map
Menton
Aix-en-Provence
Martigues
Marseille
St-Raphaël
St-Tropez
Toulon

Paul Cézanne (1839–1906), in his desire to scour the "depth of reality", often painted his native Aix *(see pp152–3)*.

Mougins

Val

Le Cannet
Golfe-Ju

Paul Signac (1863–1935) came to St-Tropez in 1892, painting it in his palette of rainbow dots *(see pp122–6)*.

Cannes

Pointe Croisette

Félix Ziem (1821–1911), born in Burgundy, was a great traveller. He adored Venice, and found the same romantic inspiration by the canals of Martigues *(see p151)*, where he painted *La Camargue, Coucher de Soleil*.

0 kilometres   5

0 miles   5

Pablo Picasso (1881–1973) created this goat-like jug, Cabri (1947), while in Vallauris, where he learned the potter's craft. It is now in the Musée Picasso, Antibes *(see p77)*.

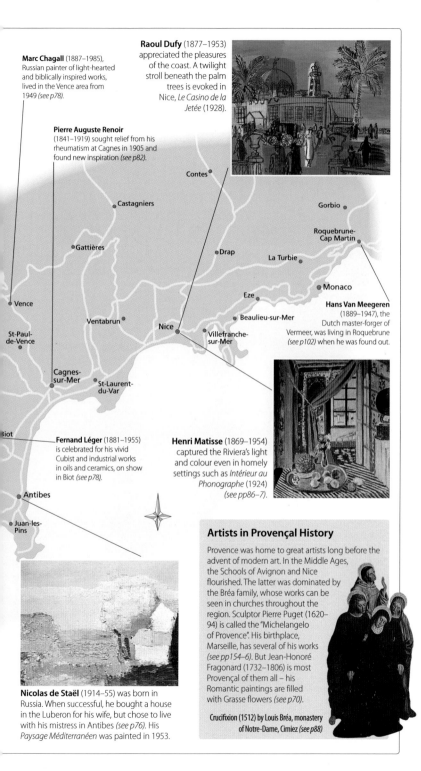

Marc Chagall (1887–1985), Russian painter of light-hearted and biblically inspired works, lived in the Vence area from 1949 *(see p78)*.

Raoul Dufy (1877–1953) appreciated the pleasures of the coast. A twilight stroll beneath the palm trees is evoked in Nice, *Le Casino de la Jetée* (1928).

Pierre Auguste Renoir (1841–1919) sought relief from his rheumatism at Cagnes in 1905 and found new inspiration *(see p82)*.

Contes

Castagniers

Gorbio

Roquebrune-Cap Martin

Gattières

Drap

La Turbie

Monaco

Eze

Vence

Ventabrun

Nice

Beaulieu-sur-Mer

Hans Van Meegeren (1889–1947), the Dutch master-forger of Vermeer, was living in Roquebrune *(see p102)* when he was found out.

St-Paul-de-Vence

Villefranche-sur-Mer

Cagnes-sur-Mer

St-Laurent-du-Var

Biot

Fernand Léger (1881–1955) is celebrated for his vivid Cubist and industrial works in oils and ceramics, on show in Biot *(see p78)*.

Henri Matisse (1869–1954) captured the Riviera's light and colour even in homely settings such as *Intérieur au Phonographe* (1924) *(see pp86–7)*.

Antibes

Juan-les-Pins

Artists in Provençal History

Provence was home to great artists long before the advent of modern art. In the Middle Ages, the Schools of Avignon and Nice flourished. The latter was dominated by the Bréa family, whose works can be seen in churches throughout the region. Sculptor Pierre Puget (1620–94) is called the "Michelangelo of Provence". His birthplace, Marseille, has several of his works *(see pp154–6)*. But Jean-Honoré Fragonard (1732–1806) is most Provençal of them all – his Romantic paintings are filled with Grasse flowers *(see p70)*.

Nicolas de Staël (1914–55) was born in Russia. When successful, he bought a house in the Luberon for his wife, but chose to live with his mistress in Antibes *(see p76)*. His *Paysage Méditerranéen* was painted in 1953.

Crucifixion (1512) by Louis Bréa, monastery of Notre-Dame, Cimiez *(see p88)*

Writers in Provence

The Nobel Laureate Frédéric Mistral (1830–1914) was the champion of the Provençal language, but better known are the local writers who have captured the Provençal character: Alphonse Daudet, Jean Giono, Emile Zola and Marcel Pagnol. French writers such as Dumas and Hugo used Provençal backdrops for their fiction; foreign writers also found inspiration in the region.

1920 Consumptive New Zealand short story writer Katherine Mansfield recuperates in Menton *(see pp102–3)* and writes *Miss Bull* and *Passion* among other pieces.

1895 Jean Giono is born in Manosque *(see p186)*. Work like *The Man who Planted Trees* evokes the region.

Alphonse Daudet

1892 The last part of *Thus Spake Zarathustra* by German Friedrich Nietzsche is published. He devised it after traversing the path in Eze *(see p92)* which was later named after him.

Frédéric Mistral

An early edition of *The Count of Monte Cristo*

1869 Alphonse Daudet publishes *Collected Letters from my Windmill*, set in a windmill at Fontvieille *(see p147)*.

1904 Poet Frédéric Mistral declared joint winner of the Nobel Prize.

1844 Alexander Dumas publishes *The Count of Monte Cristo*, set in the Château d'If, Marseille *(see p156)*.

1870 Death in Cannes of Prosper Mérimée, author of *Carmen*, Bizet's opera.

1840	1855	1870	1885	1900	1915

1840	1855	1870	1885	1900	1915

1862 *Les Misérables* by Victor Hugo is published. The early chapters are set in Digne-les-Bains *(see p184)*.

1887 Journalist Stéphen Liégeard introduces the term, *Côte d'Azur*.

1907 Provençal poet, René Char, is born in L'Isle-sur-la-Sorgue.

1868 Edmond Rostand, author of *Cyrano de Bergerac* (1897) is born in Marseille *(see pp154–6)*.

1919 Edith Wharton, American author of *The Age of Innocence*, visits Hyères *(see p119)*. A street is named after her.

Edith Wharton

Early Writers

For centuries, troubadour ballads and religious poems, or *Noels*, formed the core of literature in Provence. While certain unique individuals stand out, it was not until 1854, with Mistral's help, that Provençal writers found their own "voice".
1327 Petrarch *(see p49)* falls in unrequited love with Laura de Noves in Avignon, inspiring his *Canzonière* poems.
1555 Nostradamus, from St-Rémy, publishes *The Prophecies*, which are outlawed by the Vatican.
1764 Tobias Smollett "discovers" Nice. (He published his book, *Travels through France and Italy*, in 1766.)
1791 Marquis de Sade, the original sadist, publishes *Justine*, written while imprisoned in the Bastille.

Petrarch's Laura de Noves

Somerset Maugham

1926 British author W Somerset Maugham buys the Villa Mauresque, Cap Ferrat, and writes *Cakes and Ale* (1930).

Emile Zola

1885 *Germinal* published by Emile Zola, boyhood friend of Cézanne, as part of his 20-novel cycle, *The Rougon-Macquarts* (1871–93), set partly round Aix.

1931 Briton Aldous Huxley writes *Brave New World* in Sanary-sur-Mer *(see p116)*, the setting for *Eyeless in Gaza* (1936).

1933 Thomas Mann, who wrote *Death in Venice* (1913), flees Germany for Sanary *(see p116)* with his two sons and his brother Heinrich.

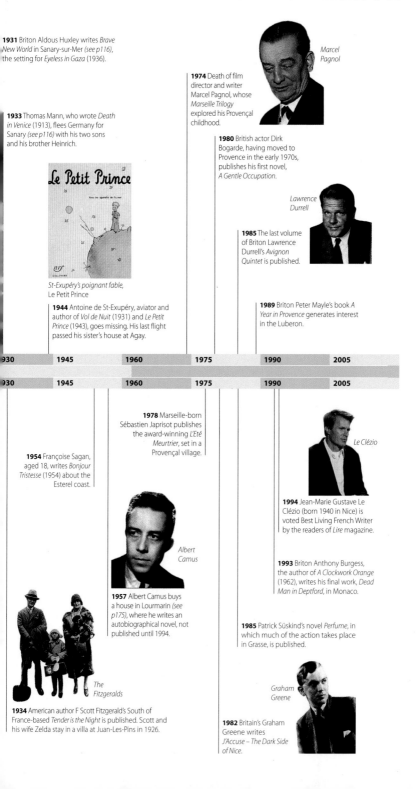

Marcel Pagnol

1974 Death of film director and writer Marcel Pagnol, whose *Marseille Trilogy* explored his Provençal childhood.

1980 British actor Dirk Bogarde, having moved to Provence in the early 1970s, publishes his first novel, *A Gentle Occupation*.

Lawrence Durrell

1985 The last volume of Briton Lawrence Durrell's *Avignon Quintet* is published.

Le Petit Prince

St-Exupéry's poignant fable, Le Petit Prince

1944 Antoine de St-Exupéry, aviator and author of *Vol de Nuit* (1931) and *Le Petit Prince* (1943), goes missing. His last flight passed his sister's house at Agay.

1989 Briton Peter Mayle's book *A Year in Provence* generates interest in the Luberon.

930	1945	1960	1975	1990	2005
930	1945	1960	1975	1990	2005

1978 Marseille-born Sébastien Japrisot publishes the award-winning *L'Eté Meurtrier*, set in a Provençal village.

Le Clézio

1954 Françoise Sagan, aged 18, writes *Bonjour Tristesse* (1954) about the Esterel coast.

1994 Jean-Marie Gustave Le Clézio (born 1940 in Nice) is voted Best Living French Writer by the readers of *Lire* magazine.

Albert Camus

1993 Briton Anthony Burgess, the author of *A Clockwork Orange* (1962), writes his final work, *Dead Man in Deptford*, in Monaco.

1957 Albert Camus buys a house in Lourmarin *(see p175)*, where he writes an autobiographical novel, not published until 1994.

1985 Patrick Süskind's novel *Perfume*, in which much of the action takes place in Grasse, is published.

The Fitzgeralds

Graham Greene

1934 American author F Scott Fitzgerald's South of France-based *Tender is the Night* is published. Scott and his wife Zelda stay in a villa at Juan-Les-Pins in 1926.

1982 Britain's Graham Greene writes *J'Accuse – The Dark Side of Nice*.

The Beaches of Provence

From the untamed expanses of the Rhône delta to the hot spots of the Riviera, via the cliffs and coves of the Var, the coastline of Provence is extremely varied. Resort beaches around the towns of the Riviera, such as Menton, Nice and Monte-Carlo, are crowded and noisy in the height of summer. They often charge a fee, but are usually well-kept and offer good watersports facilities. It is, however, possible to seek out quieter corners away from the crowds if you know where to look.

The Côte d'Azur beaches offer warmth and sunshine all year long, as advertised in this 1930s poster by Roger Broders.

The Camargue beaches *(see pp140–2)* at the mouth of the Rhône delta, are often deserted. The long, flat sands are ideal for horse riding, but there is a shortage of amenities.

The Côte Bleue is dotted with fishing ports and elegant summer residences. Pine trees line the beaches.

Arles

Salon de Provence

BOUCHES-DU-RHONE AND NIMES

Aix-en-Provence

Saintes-Maries-de-la-Mer

Camargue

Martigues

Carry-le-Rouet

Marseille

Côte Bleue

Aubagne

①

Les Calanques

②

Bandol ③

Sanary-sur-Mer

Cap Sicié

Les Calanques *(see p157)* are beautiful and dramatic fjord-like inlets situated east of Marseille. The sheer white cliffs, some 400 m (1,312 ft) high, drop vertically into the tempting, blue water.

Cap Sicié is a small peninsula that juts out from the Var mainland. It is famed for its strong winds and waves, ideal for experienced windsurfers.

Provence's Ten Best Beaches

① **Best sandy beach**
Plage de Piémanson, east of the Camargue, is remote enough for nudist bathing.

② **Best deep-sea diving**
The deep Calanques waters are ideal for exploring.

③ **Best sea fishing**
Bandol and Sanary-sur-Mer are charming resorts, where the tuna boats make their daily catch.

④ **Best small resort beach**
Le Lavandou offers all amenities on a small scale.

⑤ **Best trendy beach**
Tahiti-Plage in St-Tropez is the coast's showcase for fun, sun, fashion and glamour.

⑥ **Best family beaches**
Fréjus-Plage and the beach of St-Raphaël are clean, safe and have excellent facilities for families.

⑦ **Best star-spotter's beach**
Cannes' beautiful setting, with its scenic harbour, casino and stylish beaches, attracts the rich and famous.

⑧ **Best teen and twenties beach**
The all-night bars, cafés and nightclubs of Juan-les-Pins make this a lively resort.

⑨ **Best activity beach**
Watersports fanatics gather at the Ruhl-Plage in Nice for the jet-skiing and parasailing.

⑩ **Best winter beach**
Menton is the warmest resort on the Riviera and the sun shines all year round, ideal for relaxing winter holidays.

The Riviera is the most popular destination for sun-worshippers, with its big, traditional resorts and private golden beaches.

| 0 kilometres | 25 |
| 0 miles | 25 |

THE RIVIERA AND THE ALPES MARITIMES

Menton ⑩
Nice ⑨   Monaco
Grasse
Juan-les-Pins ⑧   Antibes
Cannes ⑦

Esterel *Riviera*

THE VAR AND THE ILES D'HYERES

Fréjus ⑥
Brignoles
St-Raphaël
St-Tropez ⑤
Cavalaire-sur-Mer
Toulon   Le Lavandou ④
Hyères
Iles d'Hyères

Côte Varoise

The Côte Varoise has a beach to suit all tastes, offering popular family resorts, small fishing ports and excellent snorkelling.

The Esterel coast stretches from Cannes to St-Raphaël. Its most striking features are the red cliffs and rocks, deep ravines and secluded coves.

PROVENCE THROUGH THE YEAR

Provence is at its prettiest in spring, when flowers bring livelihoods to perfume-makers and pleasure to passers-by. It can also be surprisingly cold as this is when the Mistral blows its strongest.

Summer fruit and vegetables are both abundant and beautiful, filling the local markets. The midsummer heat is added to by the fires of St Jean and the Valensole plains are striped with lavender, the indelible colour of the region. To entertain the thousands of holidaymakers, July and August are filled with music festivals. Come autumn, vineyards turn to copper and the grapes are harvested. Snows blanket the mountains from December and skiers take to the slopes. Throughout the year, every town and village celebrates with a *fête*, often with traditional costume and lively activities. For information, contact the local tourist office (*see p237*).

Women in traditional costume at the Feria de Paqûes in Arles

Spring

By the time March begins, lemons have already been harvested and the almond blossom has faded. Pear, plum and apricot blossom brightens the landscape and the first vegetables of spring are ready for the markets: asparagus, beans and green artichokes known as *mourre de gats*. By May, fruit markets are coloured with the first ripe cherries and strawberries of the year.

Southern mountain slopes warm to the sunshine and come alive with alpine flowers but the northern slopes remain wintery. Broom turns hillsides deep yellow and bees start to make honey from the sweet-smelling rosemary flowers. Flocks of sheep begin the journey of transhumance up to the summer pastures, and on the vast plains maize, wheat and rape push their way up through the softening earth.

March
Festin des Courgourdons (*last Sun*), Nice (*see pp88–9*). Folklore and sculpted gourd *fête*.

April
Procession aux Limaces (*Good Friday*), Roquebrune-Cap-Martin (*see p102*). The streets are lit with shell lamps and a parade of locals dressed as disciples and legionnaires recreate the entombment of Christ.
Printemps de Châteauneuf-du-Pape – Salon des Vins (*early April*), Châteauneuf-du-Pape (*see p168*). Spring wine festival displaying products of local wine growers.
Fête de la St-Marc (*end April*), Châteauneuf-du-Pape (*see p168*). Wine contest. (The year's vintage is blessed on the 1st weekend in August.)
Feria de Paqûes (*Easter*), Arles (*see pp148–50*). Arletans turn out in their traditional costume for a *feria*. The *farandole* is danced to the accompaniment of the *tambourin* drum and *galoubet* flute to mark the beginning of the famous bullfighting season.

May
Fête des Gardians (*1 May*), Arles (*see pp148–50*). The town is taken over by the *gardians* or cowboys who look after the Camargue cattle herds.
Pèlerinage des Gitans avec Procession à la Mer de Sainte Sarah (*24–25 May*), Stes-Maries-de-la-Mer (*see pp228–9*).
Festival International du Film (*two weeks in May*), Cannes (*see pp72–3*). The most prestigious annual film festival.
La Bravade (*16–18 May*), St-Tropez (*see p228*).
Fête de la Transhumance (*late May–early June*), St-Rémy (*see p144*). Celebrates the ancient custom of moving sheep to higher ground for the summer.
Grand Prix Automobile de Formule 1 (*weekend after Ascension*), Monaco (*see p98*). The only Grand Prix raced on public roads laps up an impressive 3,145 km (1,954 miles).
Feria (*Pentecost*), Nîmes (*see pp136–7*). The first major bullfighting event of the year takes place at Les Arènes.

Bullfighting at the Feria de Nîmes in Les Arènes, the Roman amphitheatre in Nîmes

Average Daily Hours of Sunshine

Hours

12 —
9 —
6 —
3 —
0 —

Jan Feb Mar Apr May Jun Jul Aug Sep Oct Nov Dec

Sunshine Chart
The summer months are guaranteed to be hot, with the intensity climaxing in July. Even in the winter, coastal towns can have up to 150 hours of sunshine a month, but be warned: it is often the icy Mistral that blows the clouds away in early spring.

Summer

The Côte d'Azur is essentially a playground in summer, particularly in August when the French take their holidays. Rafters take to the rivers and scuba divers explore the varied sealife. For laid-on entertainment, there are music festivals throughout the region.

Three national celebrations are also manifest: fireworks and bonfires brighten the skies on the **Fête de St-Jean** (June 24). **Bastille Day** (July 14) is celebrated with fireworks while **Assumption Day** (August 15) is a time for great feasting.

June
Fête de la Tarasque (last w/e), Tarascon (see p144). According to local legend, the Tarasque monster once terrorized the region. An effigy of the monster is paraded through the town.
Festival International d'Art Lyrique (June & July), Aix-en-Provence (see pp152–3). Extensive programme of classical music concerts and opera is staged in the courtyard theatre of the Archbishop's Palace.

July
Festival de la Sorgue (weekends in July), Fontaine-de-Vaucluse & l'Isle-sur-la-Sorgue (see p169). Concerts, boat races and floating markets on the river Sorgue.
Festival d'Avignon (mid- to late July), Avignon (see p229).
Chorégies d'Orange (all month), Orange. This long-established

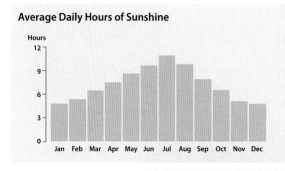

Celebrating the Fête de St-Jean with fireworks over Marseille harbour

The legendary Tarasque

opera season is held in the acoustically perfect Roman theatre (see pp166–7).
Jazz à Juan (mid- to late July), Juan-les-Pins (see p76). One of the area's top jazz festivals.
Jazz à Toulon (mid-July–early Aug), Toulon (see p116–17). Free concerts in different squares every day throughout the town.
Recontres Internationales de la Photographie (Jul–Sep), Arles (see pp148–50). The National School of Photography was set up in 1982 as a result of this festival, and each year the town is transformed into a photographic arena.

August
Corso de la Lavande (first weekend), Digne-les-Bains (see p229).
Véraison Festival – A Medieval Celebration (early Aug), Châteauneuf-du-Pape (see p168). A medieval market comes alive with 200 actors, music,

dancing, jousting and wine wagons open for tasting.
Fête du Jasmin (first week-end), Grasse (see pp70–71). Floats, music and dancing in the town.
Procession de la Passion (5 Aug), Roquebrune-Cap-Martin (see p102). Over 500 locals take part in staging Christ's passion, enacted since the Virgin saved the town from plague in 1467.
Le Festival de Musique (all month), Menton (see pp102–3). Chamber music in the square.

Holiday-makers on the crowded beaches of the Côte d'Azur

Average Monthly Rainfall

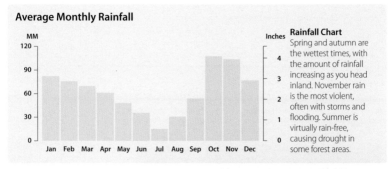

Rainfall Chart
Spring and autumn are the wettest times, with the amount of rainfall increasing as you head inland. November rain is the most violent, often with storms and flooding. Summer is virtually rain-free, causing drought in some forest areas.

Autumn

When summer is over, it is time for the *vendange*, the grape harvest. In the Camargue, rice is ready to be brought in. Walnuts are picked and, in the Maures, sweet chestnuts are collected. The woods also yield rewards for mushroom hunters, while in Vaucluse and the Var truffles are harvested from oak woods and sold on the market stalls, notably at Richerenches.

The hunting season begins in November. Small birds, such as thrushes, and ducks fall from flight into the pot and wild boar are bagged, their feet kept as talismans. Sheep are brought down to their winter pastures.

A grape picker at work during the autumn harvest

On the hunt for truffles in the woods of Haute Provence

September

Fête des Prémices du Riz *(early Sep)*, Arles *(see pp148–50)*. This festival of the rice harvest coincides with the last Spanish-style bullfights of the year.

Féria des Vendanges *(second week)*, Nîmes *(see pp136–7)*. An enjoyable combination of wine, dancing and bullfights.
Festival de la Navigation de Plaisance *(mid-Sep)*, Cannes *(see pp72–3)*. Yachts from around the world meet in the harbour. **Fête du Vent** *(mid-Sep)*, Marseille *(see pp154–6)*. Kites from all over the world decorate the sky for two days on the Plages du Prado.

October

Fête de Sainte Marie Salomé *(Sunday nearest 22 Oct)*, Stes-Maries-de-la-Mer. A similar festival to the Gypsy Pilgrimage held in May *(see pp228–9)* with a procession through the town's streets to the beach and the ritual blessing of the sea.
Foire Internationale de Marseille *(end of Sep–early Oct)*, Marseille *(see pp154–6)*. Thousands of visitors pour into the city to enjoy the annual fair. Various activities and sports are organized with crafts, music and folklore entertainment from over 40 different countries.

November

Fête du Prince (Fete Nationale) *(19 Nov)*, Monaco *(see pp94–8)*. The second smallest independent state in Europe celebrates its national day with a firework display over the harbour. **Festival International de la Danse** *(biennial, late-Nov or early Dec)*, Cannes *(see pp72–3)*. A festival of contemporary dance and ballet with an impressive programme of international performances.

Performers at the Festival International de la Danse in Cannes

Average Monthly Temperature

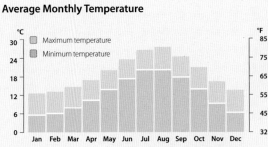

Temperature Chart
The Mistral has a substantial effect on the temperature. During the winter and early spring, it can drop 10°C (18°F) in only a few hours. The summer heat can be uncomfortable, but the evenings cool down and are perfect for sitting outside.

Winter

There is an old saying in Provence used to describe winter: "*l'hiver a ges d'ouro,*" "winter has no hours". It is a time to open the jams of the summer, to make the geese and duck *confits* and to turn the olive harvest into oil.

Snow soon cuts off mountain passes and, at weekends, locals and visitors take to the many ski resorts, warmed by juniper or wild strawberry liqueurs.

Christmas is heralded by the sale of *santons*, the figurines used to decorate Provence's distinctive cribs. Epiphany is another important festival, when the Three Kings are fêted with crown-shaped pastries.

December

Foire aux Santons (*all month*), Marseille (*see pp154–6*). The largest fair honouring the symbolic clay figures that are an integral part of Christmas.
Fête du Millesime – Vin de Bandol (*early December*), Bandol (*see p116*). Every wine-grower in the town has their own stand and there is free wine-tasting. A different theme is chosen every year with activities and much merriment.
Noël and midnight mass (*24 Dec*), Les Baux-de-Provence (*see pp146–7*). A traditional festive feast of the shepherds before mass.

January

Rallye de Monte-Carlo (*late Jan, pp96–7*). A major event in the motor sporting calendar.
Festival du Cirque (*end of month*), Monaco (*see p98*). Circus shows from around the globe.

Relaxing in the winter sun in the Alpes-de-Haute-Provence

February

Fête du Citron, (*late Feb–early Mar*), Menton (*see pp102–3*). Floats and music fill the town during the lemon festival.
Fête du Mimosa (*third Sunday*), Bormes-les-Mimosas (*see pp120–21*).

The annual festival in celebration of the medieval perched village's favourite flower.
Carnaval de Nice, (*all month*), Nice. France's largest pre-Lent festival (*see p228*).

Public Holidays

New Year's Day (1 Jan)
Easter Sunday and Monday
Ascension (sixth Thursday after Easter)
Whit Monday (second Monday after Ascension)
Labour Day (1 May)
VE Day (8 May)
Bastille Day (14 Jul)
Assumption Day (15 Aug)
All Saints' Day (1 Nov)
Remembrance Day (11 Nov)
Christmas Day (25 Dec)

The Taj Mahal re-created at the Fête du Citron in Menton

THE HISTORY OF PROVENCE

Few regions of France have experienced such a varied and turbulent history as Provence. There is evidence, in the form of carvings, tools and weapons, of nomadic tribes and human settlements from 300,000 BC. The introduction of the vine, so important today, can be credited to the Phoenicians and Greeks who traded along the coast. Perhaps more crucially, Provence was the Romans' "Province" and few regions of their vast empire have retained such dramatic buildings; the theatre at Orange, the arenas of Arles and Nîmes, the Pont du Gard and the imposing trophy of La Turbie are all testimony to past Roman power.

The Middle Ages proved a stormy period of feuding warlords and invasions; the many fortified hilltop villages that characterize the region were a desperate attempt at defence. The papacy dominated the 14th century, and the magnificent palace the popes built in Avignon remains today. The arts flourished too, especially under King René in his capital of Aix. After his death in 1480, Provence lost its independence and its history became enmeshed with that of France. Religious war took its toll and the Great Plague of Marseille killed tens of thousands in 1720.

A beguiling climate and improved transport in the 19th century began to attract artists and foreign nobility. Tiny fishing villages grew into glamorous Riviera resorts. The allure remains for millions of tourists while economic investment means it is also a boom area for the technology industry.

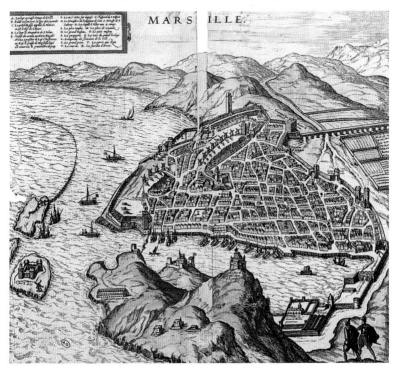

A 16th-century map of Marseille and its harbour

◀ Detail of an illuminated 13th-century manuscript showing a troubadour playing to a royal audience

Ancient Provence

Rock carvings, fragments of paintings and remains from primitive settlements suggest that Provence was first inhabited a million years ago. Carvings in the Grotte de l'Observatoire in Monaco and the decorated Grotte Cosquer near Marseille are among the oldest of their kind in the world. Nomadic tribes roamed the land for centuries, notably the Celts from the north and the Ligurians from the east. Not until the arrival of the Phoenicians and the Greeks did trade flourish in a more structured way and Provençal society become more stable.

"Double Head" Carving
This stone figure (3rd century BC) probably decorated a Celtic sanctuary.

The *bories* at Gordes date back to 3,500 BC.

Celtic Doorway
(3rd century BC) The niches in the pillars held the embalmed heads of Celtic heroes.

The Grotte des Fées at Mont de Cordes contain prehistoric carvings often associated with modern astrological symbols.

The Foundation of Marseille

When Greek traders arrived in 600 BC, their captain, Protis, attended a feast in honour of the local chief's daughter, Gyptis. She chose Protis as her husband. The chief's dowry to Protis and Gyptis was the strip of land on which Marseille grew.

St-Blaise, once a heavily fortified Greek trading centre, has only minimal remains.

The Grotte Cosquer, with paintings dating to 30,000 BC, is accessible only from the sea.

Wine jars, bound for Greece from 1,000 BC onwards, were found in Les Calanques near Marseille.

1,000,000 BC Earliest human presence in Provence at Grotte de l'Observatoire in Monaco; use of bone as a tool

400,000 BC
Fire first used in Nice

60,000 BC Neanderthal hunters on the Riviera

1,000,000 BC		5000	4500	4000	350

30,000 BC Appearance of *Homo sapiens* (modern man); cave painting at Grotte Cosquer

3,500 BC First *borie* villages

Cave painting from Grotte Cosquer

Vallée des Merveilles
About 36,000 carvings date from 2,000 BC. Among them are strange, witch-like figures known as orants.

Where to See Ancient Provence

Many museums, such as the Musée Archéologique, Nîmes (see p136), have excellent collections of ancient artifacts. The well-preserved *bories* in the Luberon (see p173) illustrate early village communities; the Grotte de l'Observatoire in Monaco (see p98) is an example of an even more primitive settlement.

Borie Village at Gordes
These dry-stone dwellings (see p173) have for centuries been used by nomadic shepherds.

The Vallée des Merveilles carvings suggest that nearby Mont Bégo was a focus for worship.

Grotte de l'Observatoire
Skeletons uncovered here have characteristics linking them with southern African tribes.

The Grotte de l'Observatoire in Monaco yielded evidence of symbolic human burials from prehistoric times.

The "Fairy Stone", *Péiro de la fado* in Provençal, is the only true pre-historic dolmen in Provence.

Standing Stone
Prehistoric stelae, like this carved stone from the Luberon, are scattered throughout Provence.

Ancient Sites of Provence

Most sites lie along the coast, but there are some pockets of settlement inland near Tende, in the Luberon, and in the Vallée des Merveilles (see p101), which stands at about 2,500 m (8,200 ft).

2,500–2,000 BC Carvings at Vallée des Merveilles

Hannibal crossing the Alps

380 BC Celtic invasions of Provence

| 3000 | 2500 | 2000 | 1500 | 1000 | 500 BC |

2,000 BC Tombs carved at Cordes

600 BC Greek traders settle at St-Blaise. Founding of Marseille

218 BC Hannibal passes through region to reach Italy

Gallo-Roman Provence

The Romans extended their empire into Provence towards the end of the 2nd century BC. They enjoyed good relations with the local people and within 100 years created a wealthy province. Nîmes and Arles became two of the most significant Roman towns outside Italy; colonies at the Site Archéologique de Glanum and Vaison-la-Romaine flourished. Many fine monuments remain and museums, for instance at Vaison-la-Romaine, display smaller Roman treasures.

Christ's followers are reputed to have brought Christianity to the region when they landed at Les-Saintes-Maries-de-la-Mer in AD 40.

Pont Julien (3 BC)
This magnificently preserved triple-arched bridge stands 8 km (5 miles) west of Apt.

Two temples, dedicated to the emperor Augustus and his adopted sons, Caius and Lucius, date from 20 BC.

Marble Sarcophagus (4th century)
The Alyscamps in Arles (see p150), once a vast Roman necropolis, contains many carved marble and stone coffins.

Triumphal Arch at Orange
Built in about 20 BC this is, in spite of much crude restoration, one of the best preserved Roman triumphal arches. Carvings depict the conquest of Gaul and sea battle scenes.

The fortified gate is thought to have been built by Greeks, who occupied Glanum from the 4th century BC.

Roman Glanum

The impressive ruined site at Glanum reveals much earlier Roman and Greek settlements. This reconstruction shows it after it was rebuilt in AD 49 (see p145).

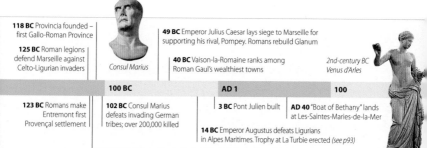

118 BC Provincia founded – first Gallo-Roman Province

125 BC Roman legions defend Marseille against Celto-Ligurian invaders

Consul Marius

49 BC Emperor Julius Caesar lays siege to Marseille for supporting his rival, Pompey. Romans rebuild Glanum

40 BC Vaison-la-Romaine ranks among Roman Gaul's wealthiest towns

2nd-century BC Venus d'Arles

100 BC	AD 1	100

123 BC Romans make Entremont first Provençal settlement

102 BC Consul Marius defeats invading German tribes; over 200,000 killed

3 BC Pont Julien built

AD 40 "Boat of Bethany" lands at Les-Saintes-Maries-de-la-Mer

14 BC Emperor Augustus defeats Ligurians in Alpes Maritimes. Trophy at La Turbie erected (see p93)

121 BC Foundation of Aquae Sextiae, later to become Aix-en-Provence

Les-Stes-Maries-de-la-Mer
Mary Magdalene, Mary Salome and Mary Jacobe reputedly sailed here in AD 40. The town where they landed is named in their honour and continues to attract pilgrims (see p142).

Where to See Gallo-Roman Provence

Arles (see pp148–50) and Nîmes (see pp136–7), with their amphitheatres and religious and secular buildings, offer the most complete examples of Roman civilization. Orange (see p165) and Vaison-la-Romaine (see p162) contain important monuments, and the Pont du Gard (see p135) and Le Trophée d'Auguste (see p93) are unique.

Théâtre Antique d'Orange
Built into a hill, this Roman theatre would have held up to 7,000 spectators (see pp166–7).

Cryptoportico
The foundations of Arles' forum, these horseshoe-shaped underground galleries were probably used as grain stores (see p150).

The baths occupied three rooms, each used for bathing at a different temperature.

The Forum, the commercial centre of the Roman town, was surrounded by a covered gallery.

Jewellery from Vaison-la-Romaine
1st-century AD jewellery was found in excavations of the Roman necropolis.

Roman Flask
Well-preserved ancient Roman glassware and everyday items have been found in many areas of Provence.

---

300 Arles reaches height of its prestige as a Roman town

300

413 Visigoths seize Languedoc

400

476 Western Roman Empire collapses

500

Abbaye St-Victor, founded in AD 416, in Marseille

Medieval Provence

With the fall of the Roman Empire, stability and relative prosperity began to disappear. Although Provence became part of the Holy Roman Empire, the local counts retained considerable autonomy and the towns became fiercely independent. People withdrew to hilltops to protect themselves from attack by a series of invaders, and *villages perchés (see pp24–5)* began to develop. Provence became a major base for Christian Crusaders, intent on conquering Muslim territories in Africa and Asia.

The Great Walls, finally completed in 1300, 30 years after Louis IX's death, were over 1.6 km (1 mile) long and formed an almost perfect rectangle.

St-Trophime Carving
The monumental 12th-century portal at St-Trophime in Arles *(see p148)* is adorned with intricate carvings of saints and scenes from the Last Judgment.

Louis IX's army consisted of 35,000 men plus horses and military equipment.

Louis IX

St Martha and the Tarasque
This 9th-century legend proved the strength of Christianity. The saint is said to have lured the Tarasque dragon to its death, using hymns and holy water *(see p144)*.

The Seventh Crusade
Hoping to drive the Muslims out of the Holy Land, Louis IX (St Louis) of France set sail from his new port, Aigues-Mortes (see pp138–9), in 1248. It was a spectacular occasion, with banners waving and his army singing hymns.

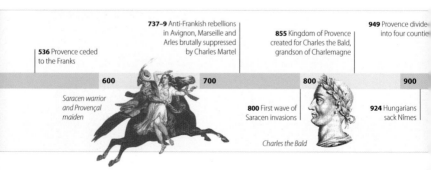

536 Provence ceded to the Franks

737–9 Anti-Frankish rebellions in Avignon, Marseille and Arles brutally suppressed by Charles Martel

855 Kingdom of Provence created for Charles the Bald, grandson of Charlemagne

949 Provence divided into four counties

| 600 | 700 | 800 | 900 |

Saracen warrior and Provençal maiden

800 First wave of Saracen invasions

924 Hungarians sack Nîmes

Charles the Bald

Troubadour Ivory (c. 1300)
The poetry of Provençal troubadours tells how knights wooed virtuous women through patience, courtesy and skill.

Where to See Medieval Provence

The highlights are undoubtedly the Romanesque abbeys and churches, especially the "three sisters": Silvacane (see p151), Le Thoronet (see p112) and Sénanque (see p168). Fortified villages perchés, such as Gordes (see p173) and the spectacular 11th-century citadel at Les Baux-de-Provence (see p146), testify to the unrest and horrific violence that scarred this period of Provence's history.

Notre-Dame-de-Beauvoir Chapel At the top of a path from Moustiers (see p190), the chapel has a fine Romanesque porch and nave.

Les Pénitents des Mées
These are said to be 6th-century monks turned to stone for gazing at Saracen women (see p185).

1500 ships set sail for the Holy Land on 28 August 1248.

Silvacane Abbey (1175–1230)
This beautiful, austere Cistercian abbey was Provence's last great Romanesque abbey.

St Christopher Fresco The Tour Ferrande in Pernes-les-Fontaines (see p168) contains religious frescoes from 1285. They are among the oldest in France.

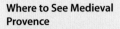

974 Saracens defeated at La Garde-Freinet

Seal of Simon de Montfort

1213 Battle of Muret: de Montfort defeats count of Toulouse and King of Aragon

1209 French military leader Simon de Montfort marches on Provence

1246 Charles of Anjou marries Béatrice, heiress of Provence, to become Count of Provence

1248 Louis IX embarks on Seventh Crusade from Aigues-Mortes

1000	**1100**	**1200**	**1300**

1032 Provence becomes part of Holy Roman Empire

1096–1099 First Crusade

1186 Counts of Provence declare Aix their capital

1187 Remains of St Martha discovered at Tarascon

1295 Death of Guiraut Riquier, the "Last Troubadour"

1274 Papacy acquires Comtat Venaissin

1112 Raymond-Bérenger III, Count of Barcelona, marries the Duchess of Provence

1125 Provence shared between Barcelona and Toulouse

1280 Relics of Mary Magdalene found at St-Maximin-la-Ste-Baume

Papal Avignon

When the papacy temporarily abandoned war-torn Italy, Avignon became the centre of the Roman Catholic world. From 1309 until 1377 seven French popes ruled unchallenged. When a new Italian pope, Urban VI, was elected, the French cardinals rebelled. In 1378 they chose a rival pope, Clement VII, thus causing a major schism that lasted until 1403. During the 14th century the papal court in Avignon became a wealthy centre for both learning and the arts, extending its influence across the region.

The Palais Vieux (1334–42), built by Benedict XII in typically austere Cistercian style, is more of a fortress than a church.

Benedict XII's cloister

Grand Tinel

Consistory Hall

Papal Throne
The Pope's Room in the Palais des Papes contains copies of the original 14th-century furniture, like this carved wooden throne.

Prophets Fresco (1344–5)
Matteo Giovanetti from Viterbo was the principal fresco-master of Clement VI. His realism contrasts with earlier medieval artists.

Great Courtyard

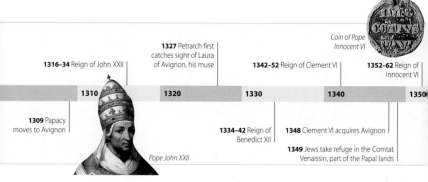

Coin of Pope Innocent VI

1327 Petrarch first catches sight of Laura of Avignon, his muse

1316–34 Reign of John XXII

1342–52 Reign of Clement VI

1352–62 Reign of Innocent VI

1310   1320   1330   1340   1350

1309 Papacy moves to Avignon

Pope John XXII

1334–42 Reign of Benedict XII

1348 Clement VI acquires Avignon

1349 Jews take refuge in the Comtat Venaissin, part of the Papal lands

THE HISTORY OF PROVENCE | **49**

Death of Clement VI
Clement VI came to Avignon to "forget he was pope". In 1348 he bought the town for 80,000 florins and built the splendid Palais Neuf.

Pope's Room

Stag Room Frescoes
The hunting scenes are a reminder that monastic life was not only about learning and prayer.

Stag Room

The Great Chapel, covering 780 sq m (8,400 sq ft), contains the restored papal altar.

The Palais Neuf was built by Clement VI in 1342–52.

Great Audience Hall

Palais Des Papes
The maze of corridors and rooms in the Palais des Papes (see p172), built over 18 years (1334–52), were richly decorated by skilled artists and craftsmen introduced from Italy. The building's scale is overwhelming.

Where to see Papal Provence

Avignon is surrounded by evidence of religious and aristocratic splendour. With the presence of the wealthy papacy – a kind of miniature Vatican – abbeys, churches and chapels flourished. The Musée du Petit Palais *(see p172)* in Avignon contains examples of work by the artists who were encouraged to work at the papal court.

Villeneuve Charterhouse
Innocent VI established this, the oldest charterhouse in France, in the 1350s *(see p134)*.

Châteauneuf-du-Pape
John XXII's early 14th-century castle became the popes' second residence. The keep and walls still stand today *(see p168)*.

Petrarch (1304–74) The great Renaissance poet Petrarch considered papal Avignon to be a "sewer" and a place of corruption.

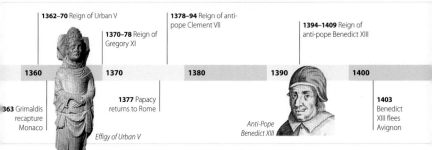

1362–70 Reign of Urban V

1370–78 Reign of Gregory XI

1378–94 Reign of anti-pope Clement VII

1394–1409 Reign of anti-pope Benedict XIII

| 1360 | 1370 | 1380 | 1390 | 1400 |

363 Grimaldis recapture Monaco

1377 Papacy returns to Rome

Effigy of Urban V

Anti-Pope Benedict XIII

1403 Benedict XIII flees Avignon

René and the Wars of Religion

The end of the 15th century saw the golden age of Aix-en-Provence *(see pp152–3)*, then Provence's capital. Under the patronage of King René, art and culture flourished and the Flemish-influenced Avignon School was formed. After René's death, Provence was annexed by the French king, Louis XI. Loss of independence and subsequent involvement with French politics led to brutal invasions by Charles V. The 16th-century Wars of Religion between "heretic" Protestants and Catholics resulted in a wave of massacres, and the wholesale destruction of churches and their contents.

Detail of the Triptych
René's favourite château at Tarascon *(see p144)* on the Rhône is realistically painted.

King René, himself a poet, painter and musician, was a great influence on Provençal culture.

Nostradamus
Born in St-Rémy *(see pp144–5)*, the physician and astrologer is best known for his predictions, *The Prophecies* (1555).

Massacres of Protestants and Catholics
The religious wars were brutal. Thousands of Protestants were massacred in 1545, and 200 Catholics died in Nîmes in 1567.

Burning Bush Triptych
Nicolas Froment's painting (1476) was commissioned by King René. The star of the Cathédrale de St-Sauveur, Aix, it depicts a vision of the Virgin and Child surrounded by the eternal Burning Bush of Moses.

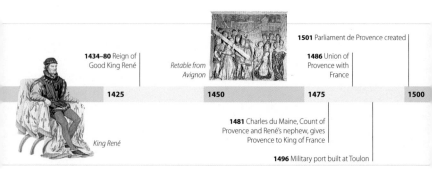

1434–80 Reign of Good King René

Retable from Avignon

1501 Parliament de Provence created

1486 Union of Provence with France

1425   **1450**   **1475**   **1500**

1481 Charles du Maine, Count of Provence and René's nephew, gives Provence to King of France

King René

1496 Military port built at Toulon

The Annunciation
The Master of Aix, one of René's artistic circle, painted this Annunciation. Dark symbolism, including the owl's wings of the angel Gabriel, undercuts this usually joyful subject.

Where to See 15th- and 16th-century Provence

Architecture from this period can be seen today in the fine town houses and elegant streets of Aix *(see pp152–3)* and Avignon *(see pp170–2)*. The Musée Granet, also in Aix, contains several interesting examples of religious paintings. A collection of period furniture is exhibited in the Musée Grobet-Labadié in Marseille *(see p155)*.

The Bush, burning but unconsumed, was a pagan and Christian symbol of eternal life.

Holy Roman Emperor, Charles V, by Titian
Between 1524 and 1536, Charles V (Charles I of Spain) attacked Provence frequently as part of his war against France.

Château at Tarascon
This 13th-century château *(see p144)* was partly rebuilt by Louis II of Anjou and then completed by King René, his son.

The saints John the Evangelist, Catherine of Alexandria and Nicolas of Myra are behind Queen Jeanne.

Rhinoceros Woodcut by Albrecht Dürer
In 1516, Marseille's Château d'If *(see p156)* was briefly home to the first rhinoceros to set foot in Europe. It was in transit as a gift for the Pope, but died later in the journey.

Moses is seen receiving the word of God from an angel.

Queen Jeanne, René's second wife, is shown kneeling in adoration.

1525 Jews in Comtat Venaissin forced to wear yellow hats	**1577** First soap factory in Marseille		**1598** Edict of Nantes signals end of Wars of Religion
	1545 Massacre of Protestants in Luberon villages		
1525	**1550**	**1575**	**1600**
1524 Invasion of Charles V	**1562** Wars of Religion commence	*Protestant martyrdom*	

Classical Provence

Provence in the 17th and 18th centuries saw a decrease in regional allegiance and growth of national awareness. Towns grew and majestic monuments, town houses *(hôtels)* and châteaux proliferated. But despite economic development in the textile industry and the growth of the ports of Toulon and Marseille, the period was bleak for many, culminating in the devastating plague of 1720. The storming of the Bastille in Paris in 1789 sparked popular uprisings and revolutionary marches on Paris.

Pavillon de Vendôme
Jean-Claude Rambot made the Atlantes for this building (1667) in Aix *(see pp152–3).*

The death toll
was over 100,000 in the last plague in Europe.

Boat-building in Toulon
Toulon, a strategic port, was famous for its boat-building. Galley slaves, chained to their oars, were a great tourist attraction in the 17th century.

Corpses were hauled in carts to mass graves.

Santon Crib Scene
The *santon* ("little saints" in Provençal) cribs were first made after the Revolution, when the churches were shut. They soon became a very popular local craft.

The Great Plague
Vue du Cours pendant la Peste by Michel Serre depicts the 1720 plague in Marseille, brought by a cargo boat from Syria. Over half of Marseille's population died. All contact with the city was banned and huge walls were built to halt the epidemic, but it still spread as far as Aix, Arles and Toulon.

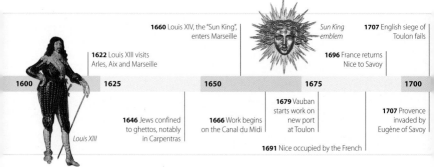

1660 Louis XIV, the "Sun King", enters Marseille

1622 Louis XIII visits Arles, Aix and Marseille

Sun King emblem

1707 English siege of Toulon fails

1696 France returns Nice to Savoy

1600 **1625** **1650** **1675** **1700**

1646 Jews confined to ghettos, notably in Carpentras

1666 Work begins on the Canal du Midi

1679 Vauban starts work on new port at Toulon

1707 Provence invaded by Eugène of Savoy

1691 Nice occupied by the French

Louis XIII

Napoleon Seizes Toulon
Junior officer Napoleon Bonaparte first made his name when he took Toulon from occupying English troops in 1793.

Cours Belsunce, built in 1670 in the Italian style, was lined with trees and Baroque palaces.

Monks, led by the devout Jean Belsunce, the Bishop of Marseille, gave succour to the dying.

Marshal Sébastien Vauban
Louis XIV's brilliant military architect, Vauban, fortified towns and ports including Toulon and Antibes.

Moustiers Faïence
Brought to France from Italy in the 17th century, traditional faïence features pastoral scenes in delicate colours.

Where to See Classical Provence

Avignon (see pp170–2) and Aix (see pp152–3) have period town houses with fine doorways and staircases. Jewish synagogues and remains of Jewish enclaves can be found in Cavaillon (see p174), Forcalquier (see p186) and Carpentras (see p168). The 18th-century Jardin de la Fontaine in Nîmes (see pp136–7) can still be visited.

Pharmacy at Carpentras
The 18th-century Hôtel-Dieu (hospital) houses a chapel and a pharmacy containing faïence apothecary jars.

Fontaine du Cormoran
The best known of the 36 fountains in Pernes-les-Fontaines is the 18th-century carved Cormoran fountain.

1713 Treaty of Utrecht cedes Orange to France

1718 Nice becomes part of new Kingdom of Sardinia

1720 Great Plague strikes Marseille and spreads throughout Provence

The Great Plague, Marseille

1725

1771 Aix parliament suppressed

1750

1779 Roman mausoleum at Aix demolished

1787 Provençal silk harvest fails

1789 Storming of the Bastille, Paris; Provençal peasants pillage local châteaux and monasteries

1775

1791 Avignon and Comtat Venaissin annexed to France

1793 Breaking of siege of Toulon catapults Napoleon Bonaparte to fame

1800

1792 Republicans adopt Rouget de Lisle's army song: *La Marseillaise*

The Belle Époque

From the start of the 19th century, the beguiling climate, particularly the mild winters, of coastal Provence attracted foreign visitors, from invalids and artists to distinguished royalty and courtesans. Railways, grand hotels, exotic gardens, opulent villas and the chic promenade des Anglais in Nice were built to meet their needs. Queen Victoria, the Aga Khan, King Leopold of Belgium and Empress Eugénie – Napoleon III's wife and doyenne of Riviera royalty – all held court. Artists and writers came in droves to revel in the light and freedom.

Homage à Mistral
Frédéric Mistral created the Félibrige group in 1854 to preserve Provençal culture.

Printing in Marseille
Cheap labour, ample paper supplies and good communications fostered the development of printing.

Belle époque **decor** featured gilt, ornate chandeliers and marble.

High society included famous courtesans as well as their rich and royal lovers.

Grasse Perfume
More modern methods of cultivation and distillation played an important role in the expanding 19th-century perfume-making industry.

Monte-Carlo Casino Interior

From being the poorest European state in 1850, Monaco boomed with the opening of the first Monte-Carlo casino in 1856, as seen in Christian Bokelmann's painting. The fashionable flocked to enjoy the luxury and glamour, while fortunes were won and lost (see pp96–8).

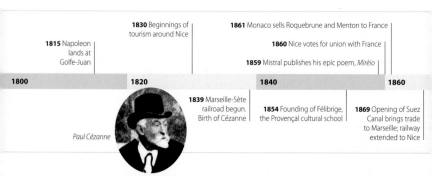

1815 Napoleon lands at Golfe-Juan

1830 Beginnings of tourism around Nice

1839 Marseille-Sète railroad begun. Birth of Cézanne

Paul Cézanne

1854 Founding of Félibrige, the Provençal cultural school

1859 Mistral publishes his epic poem, *Mirèio*

1860 Nice votes for union with France

1861 Monaco sells Roquebrune and Menton to France

1869 Opening of Suez Canal brings trade to Marseille; railway extended to Nice

1800   **1820**   **1840**   **1860**

Vineyard blight
Ravaged by phylloxera, vines in Provence and across France were replaced by resistant American root stocks.

Where to See Belle Époque Provence

Although many have been destroyed, villas and hotels built in the extravagant *belle époque* style still survive on the Côte d'Azur. The Négresco in Nice *(see pp88–9)* is especially fine. Other period pieces include the Cathédrale Orthodoxe Russe, also in Nice, and, on St-Jean-Cap-Ferrat, the Ephrussi de Rothschild Villa and Gardens *(see pp90–91)*. In Beaulieu the Villa Grecque Kérylos, Rotunda and gardens are typical of the era *(see p92)*.

Tourism
By the late 19th century, sun and sea air were considered beneficial to health.

InterContinental Carlton, Cannes
Built in 1911, this ostentatious Riviera landmark is still an exclusive hotel *(see p73)*.

Van Gogh's Provence
Van Gogh produced turbulent works in the Clinique St-Paul in St-Rémy *(see pp144–5)*.

Monte-Carlo Opéra
Charles Garnier designed this opera house *(see pp96–7)*, as well as the Casino.

Casino tables were sometimes draped in black mourning when a gambler succeeded in breaking the bank with a major win.

1879 Monte-Carlo Opéra opens

Casino at Monte-Carlo

1909 Earthquake centred on Rognes in the Bouches-du-Rhône causes widespread damage.

1880

1900

1920

1888–90 Van Gogh works in Provence

1904 Mistral wins Nobel prize for Literature for *Mirèio*

Provence at War

After the economic drain caused by World War I, Provence enjoyed increasing prosperity as the tourist industry boomed. While much of the interior remained remote and rural, the vogue for sea-bathing drew crowds to resorts such as Cannes and Nice from the 1920s onwards. Provence continued to build on its image as a playground for the rich and famous, attracting visitors from Noël Coward to Wallis Simpson. The 1942–44 German occupation brought an end to the glamorous social life for many, and some towns, including St-Tropez and Marseille, were badly damaged by Germans and Allies.

Tourism
As swimming in the sea and sunbathing became fashionable pursuits, resorts along the Riviera attracted many new visitors. In the 1930s a nudist colony opened on the Ile du Levant.

Monaco Grand Prix
This race around the principality's streets was started on the initiative of Prince Louis II in 1929. It is still one of the most colourful and dangerous Formula 1 races.

Precious ammunition and arms were dropped from Allied planes or captured from the Nazis.

Antoine de Saint-Exupéry
France's legendary writer-pilot disappeared on 31 July 1944 while on a reconnaissance flight *(see p33)*.

La Résistance

After 1942 the Résistance (or maquis after the scrubland that made a good hiding place) was active in Provence. The fighters were successful in Marseille and in preparing the coastal areas for the 1944 Allied invasion.

1925 Coco Chanel arrives on the Riviera

1930 Novelist D H Lawrence dies in Vence

Coco Chanel

1920

1925

1930

1930 Pagnol begins filming *Marius, Fanny* and *César* trilogy in Marseille

1924 Scott and Zelda Fitzgerald spend a year on the Riviera

1928 Camargue National Park created

F Scott Fitzgerald

Marcel Pagnol (1905–74)
Pagnol immortalized Provence and its inhabitants in his
plays, novels and films, depicting a simple, rural life *(see p33)*.

Where to See 1920s to 1940s Provence

The now slightly seedy suburbs of Hyères *(see p119)* retain evidence of graceful living after World War I. Toulon harbour's bristling warships *(see pp116–17)* are a reminder of the French navy's former power. The activities of the Résistance are well documented in the Musée d'Histoire 1939–45 in Fontaine-de-Vaucluse *(see p169)*.

Les Deux Garçons, Aix
This still chic café was frequented by Winston Churchill and Jean Cocteau among others *(see pp152–3)*.

Many who joined the Résistance had scarcely left school. Training was often only by experience.

Allied Landings
On 14 August 1944, Allied troops bombarded the coast between Toulon and Marseille and soon gained ground.

La Citadelle, Sisteron
Rebuilt after the Allied bombing in 1944, the impressive citadel has displays on its turbulent history *(see p182)*.

Marseille Exhibition
The 1922 exhibition was an invitation to enjoy the cosmopolitan delights of Marseille.

1942 Nazis invade southern France; French fleet scuttled in Toulon harbour

1943 *Maquis* resistance cells formed

1940 Italians occupy Menton

1935

1940

1939 Cannes Film Festival inaugurated, but first festival delayed by war

1944 American and French troops land near St-Tropez; liberation of Marseille

Liberation of Marseille

Post-War Provence

Paid holidays, post-war optimism, and the
St-Tropez sun cult all made the Riviera the magnet
it has remained for holiday-makers. The region still
offers a rich variety of produce – olive oil, wine, fruit,
flowers and perfume – though industry, especially
in the high-tech sector, grows apace. The environment
has suffered from over-development, pollution and
forest fires. The 1960s saw massive North African
immigration, and today unemployment creates
racial and political tension.

Port-Grimaud
The successful "Provençal Venice",
a car-free leisure port, was built by
François Spoerry in 1966 in regional
village style *(see p127)*.

Bus Stop by Philippe Starck
The modern architecture of
Nîmes typifies many bold
projects in the region.

Beach at Nice
Though many are pebbly, the
Riviera beaches still attract
dedicated sun-worshippers.

Fires
The devastating forest
fires that ravage the
region are fought by
planes that scoop up
sea water.

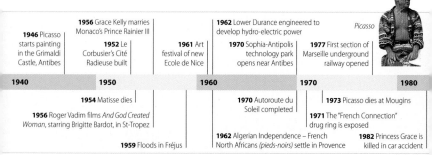

1946 Picasso
starts painting
in the Grimaldi
Castle, Antibes

1956 Grace Kelly marries
Monaco's Prince Rainier III

1952 Le
Corbusier's Cité
Radieuse built

1961 Art
festival of new
Ecole de Nice

1962 Lower Durance engineered to
develop hydro-electric power

1970 Sophia-Antipolis
technology park
opens near Antibes

Picasso

1977 First section of
Marseille underground
railway opened

1940	1950	1960	1970	1980

1954 Matisse dies

1956 Roger Vadim films *And God Created
Woman*, starring Brigitte Bardot, in St-Tropez

1959 Floods in Fréjus

1970 Autoroute du
Soleil completed

1962 Algerian Independence – French
North Africans *(pieds-noirs)* settle in Provence

1973 Picasso dies at Mougins

1971 The "French Connection"
drug ring is exposed

1982 Princess Grace is
killed in car accident

THE HISTORY OF PROVENCE | 59

Winter Sports
Skiing has become increasingly popular *(see p100)*. Isola 2000, near Nice, a purpose-built, futuristic resort, was built in 1971.

Colombe d'Or café
Once an artists' haunt, this is now one of St-Paul de Vence's chic celebrity venues *(see p79)*.

Where to See Modern Provence

Some of the most striking modern architecture includes Le Corbusier's Cité Radieuse in Marseille *(see p156)*, the Musée d'Art Moderne et d'Art Contemporain in Nice *(see p89)* and the Norman Foster-designed Carré d'Art in Nîmes *(see p136)*. Large-scale rebuilding programmes in towns such as Marseille *(see pp154–6)*, St-Tropez *(see pp122–6)* and Ste-Maxime *(see p127)* have concentrated on new buildings that blend well with the existing ones.

St-Tropez
Successful post-war restoration means it is often difficult to tell new buildings from old.

Fondation Maeght
The building reflects the modern use of traditional Provençal style and materials *(see pp80–1)*.

Cannes Film Festival
First held in 1946, the festival (see p72) *has become the world's annual film event, a glamorous jamboree of directors, stars and aspiring starlets.* And God Created Woman, *starring Brigitte Bardot, became a* succès de scandale *in 1956.*

Brigitte Bardot   Kim Novak

1992 Floods in ison-la-Romaine

1998 Jacques Médecin dies in Uruguay, self-exiled after a year in jail in France

1990 Jacques Médecin, Mayor of Nice, flees to Uruguay to avoid trial for corruption and tax arrears

2001 TGV Méditerranée link with Paris launched

2002 Euro replaces Franc as legal tender

2005 Prince Rainier III dies and is succeeded by his only son, Prince Albert II

2009 J M G Le Clézio wins the Nobel Prize for Literature

Prince Albert II

2013 EU designates Marseille as European Capital of Culture

2011 Prince Albert II marries Charlene Wittstock

TGV train

| 1990 | 2000 | 2010 | 2020 |

PROVENCE
AREA BY AREA

Provence at a Glance

From natural wonders and historic architecture to the cream of modern art, Provence is a region with something for everyone. Even the most ardent sun-worshipper will be tempted into the cool shade of its treasure-filled museums and churches. Visitors who come in the footsteps of the world's greatest artists will be equally dazzled by the wild beauty of the Gorges du Verdon and the Camargue. In a region packed with delights, those shown here are among the very best.

Papal Avignon's medieval architectural splendour *(see pp170–71)*

The beautifully preserved Roman theatre at Orange *(see pp166–7)*

Orange

Carpentras

VAUCLUSE

Avignon

Cavaillon

Manosque

Arles

Salon de Provence

Pertuis

BOUCHES-DU-RHONE AND NIMES

Aix-en-Provence

Martigues

Marseille

Aubagne

Wildlife in its natural habitat in the Camargue *(see pp140–41)*

0 kilometres 25

0 miles 25

The massive basilica of St-Maximin-la-Ste-Baume, housing relics of St Mary Magdalene *(see pp114–15)*

◀ The stunning town of Moustiers-Ste-Marie, Alpes-de-Haute-Provence

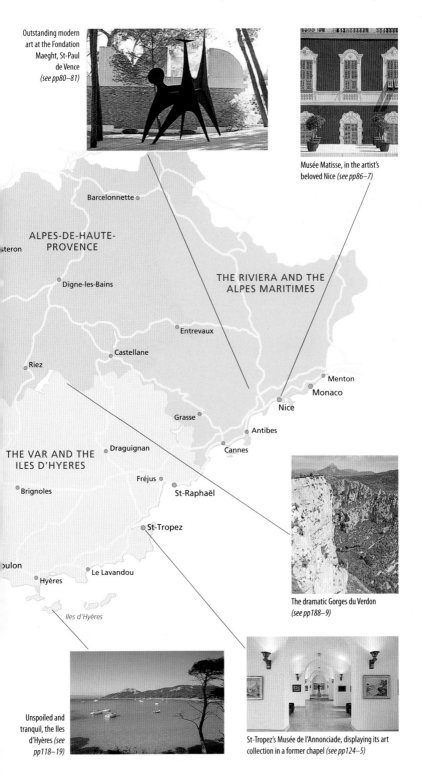

Outstanding modern art at the Fondation Maeght, St-Paul de Vence *(see pp80–81)*

Musée Matisse, in the artist's beloved Nice *(see pp86–7)*

Barcelonnette

ALPES-DE-HAUTE-PROVENCE

steron

Digne-les-Bains

THE RIVIERA AND THE ALPES MARITIMES

Entrevaux

Castellane

Riez

Menton

Monaco

Nice

Grasse

Antibes

THE VAR AND THE ILES D'HYERES

Draguignan

Cannes

Brignoles

Fréjus

St-Raphaël

St-Tropez

The dramatic Gorges du Verdon *(see pp188–9)*

oulon

Le Lavandou

Hyères

Iles d'Hyères

Unspoiled and tranquil, the Iles d'Hyères *(see pp118–19)*

St-Tropez's Musée de l'Annonciade, displaying its art collection in a former chapel *(see pp124–5)*

THE RIVIERA AND THE ALPES MARITIMES

The French Riviera is, without doubt, the most celebrated seaside in Europe. Just about everybody who has been anybody for the past 100 years has succumbed to its glittering allure. This is the holiday playground of kings and courtesans, movie stars and millionaires, where the seriously rich never stand out in the crowd.

There is a continual complaint that the Riviera is not what it used to be, that the Cannes Film Festival is mere hype, that grand old Monte-Carlo has lost all sense of taste and that Nice isn't worth the trouble of finding a parking space. But look at the boats in Antibes harbour, glimpse a villa or two on Cap Martin, or observe the baubles on the guests at the Hôtel de Paris in Monte-Carlo; money and class still rule.

The Riviera is not just a millionaire's watering hole: a diversity of talent has visited, seeking patrons and taking advantage of the luminous Mediterranean light. This coast is irrevocably linked with the life and works of Matisse and Picasso, Chagall, Cocteau and Renoir. It lent them the scenery of its shores and the rich environment of hill villages like St-Paul de Vence. This village has echoed to the voices of such luminaries as Bonnard and Modigliani, F Scott Fitzgerald and Greta Garbo. Today, its galleries still spill canvases on to its medieval lanes.

The Alpes Maritimes, which incorporates the principality of Monaco, is renowned for its temperate winter climate. The abundance of flowers here attracted the perfume industry and the English – who created some of the finest gardens on the coast. Inland, the mountainous areas of Provence offer a range of skiing activities in superb mountain scenery, and a chance to try traditional Alpine food.

Relaxing on the promenade des Anglais, Nice

◀ Cannes Old Town, known locally as Le Suquet, overlooking the harbour

Exploring the Riviera and the Alpes Maritimes

The rocky heights of the pre-Alps lie in tiers, running east to west and tumbling down to the Riviera's dramatic, Corniche-hemmed coast. On bluffs and pinnacles, towns and villages keep a watchful eye on the distant blue sea. Towards the Italian border, the Alpine ridges run from north to south, cut by torrents and gorges which provide snowy winter slopes for skiers. Much of the higher ground is occupied by the Parc National du Mercantour *(see p101)*, home of the ibex and the chamoix. Its jewel is the prehistoric Vallée des Merveilles, less than two hours from the contrasting bustle of the Riviera.

Getting Around

The A8 from Italy runs inland, parallel to the coast. Between this highway and the sea, from Nice to Menton, are three corniches. The Grande Corniche follows the Roman road, Julia Augusta, via La Turbie. The Moyenne Corniche passes through Eze, and the Corniche Inférieure visits all coastal resorts. The inland roads are narrow and winding, so allow more time for your journey. Grasse and Cannes are linked by a regular bus service, and bikes can be hired at some railway stations. Other bus links are also good. The largest airport in the region and second busiest in France, is at Nice, west of the city.

Expensive yachts in the colourful harbour at Antibes

Sights at a Glance

Saint-Étienne-de-Tinée

Auron

Entraunes

Valberg · Bel

Guillaumes

LE PY

Var

GORGES DU CIANS

PUGET-THÉNIERS ②

Digne-les-Bains

Tou sur-

Roquest

Mont Cheiron

Sisteron

Le Logis-du-Pin

GOURDON

St-Vallier-de-Thiey

Grottes de St-Cézaire

GRASSE ⑤

③ ST-CÉZAIRE-SUR-SIAGNE

MOUGINS

CANNES

Draguignan

La Napo

0 kilometres   10

0 miles   10

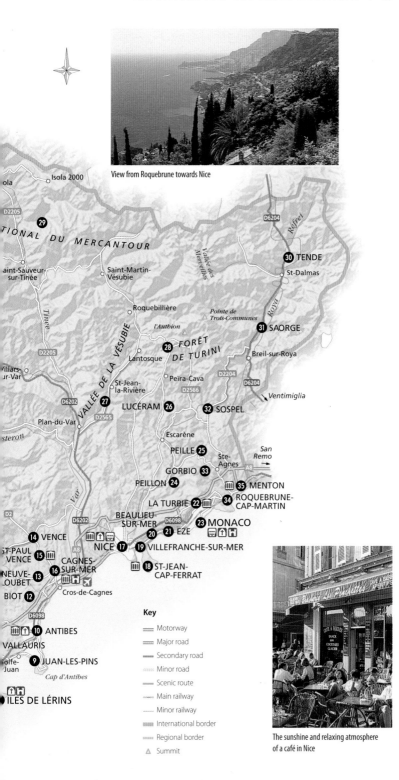

View from Roquebrune towards Nice

Isola 2000

ola

D2205

29

TIONAL DU MERCANTOUR

aint-Sauveur-
sur-Tinée

Saint-Martin-
Vésubie

Roquebillière

l'Authion

VALLÉE DE LA VÉSUBIE

28 FORÊT
DE TURINI

Lantosque

D2205

Villars-
ur-Var

St-Jean-
la-Rivière

Peïra-Cava

27 LUCÉRAM **26**

D2565

D6202

Plan-du-Var

steron

Escarène

PEILLE **25**

GORBIO **33**

PEILLON **24**

D2

BEAULIEU-
SUR-MER

D6202

14 VENCE

ST-PAUL
VENCE **15**

CAGNES-
SUR-MER

EUVE-
OUBET **13**

16

Cros-de-Cagnes

BIOT **12**

D6098

10 ANTIBES

VALLAURIS

iolfe-
Juan

9 JUAN-LES-PINS

Cap d'Antibes

ILES DE LÉRINS

Tinée

Thée

Var

Vallée des
Merveilles

D6204

Réfret

30 TENDE

St-Dalmas

Pointe de
Trois-Communes

31 SAORGE

Breil-sur-Roya

D2204

D6204

D2566

32 SOSPEL

Ventimiglia

Roya

Ste-
Agnes

San
Remo

A8

35 MENTON

34 ROQUEBRUNE-
CAP-MARTIN

LA TURBIE **22**

23 MONACO

D6098

20 **21** EZE

17 NICE

19 VILLEFRANCHE-SUR-MER

A8

18 ST-JEAN-
CAP-FERRAT

Key

═══ Motorway

═══ Major road

── Secondary road

┅┅┅ Minor road

── Scenic route

─·─· Main railway

── Minor railway

▬▬▬ International border

▬▬▬ Regional border

△ Summit

The sunshine and relaxing atmosphere
of a café in Nice

Impressive upstream view of the upper Gorges du Cians

❶ Gorges du Cians

Road map E3. ✈ Nice. 🚌 Touët-sur-Var. Nice, Touët-sur-Var, Valberg. 🛈 Pl du Quartier, Valberg (04 93 23 24 25).

Among the finest natural sights in the region, these gorges are a startling combination of deep red slate and vivid mountain greenery. They follow the course of the river Cians, which drops 1,600 m (5,250 ft) in 25 km (15 miles) from Beuil to Touët-sur-Var. At Touët, through a grille in the floor of the church nave, you can see the torrent below.

Approaching from the lower gorges, olives give way to scrubland. It is not until Pra d'Astier that the gorges become steep and narrow: at their narrowest, the rock walls entirely obliterate the sky. Higher still up the gorge, you may spot saffron lilies in June.

At the upper end of the gorges, overlooking the Vallée du Cians, is the 1,430-m (4,770-ft) eyrie of Beuil. Now a military sports centre, it was first fortified by the counts of Beuil, members of the aristocratic Grimaldi family *(see pp82–3)*. They lived here until 1621, despite staff revolt: one count had his throat cut by his barber and another was stabbed by his valet. The last, Hannibal Grimaldi, was tied to a chair and strangled by two Muslim slaves. Stones from their château were used to build the Renaissance chapel of the White Penitents in the 1687 Eglise St-Jean-Baptiste.

❷ Puget-Théniers

Road map E3. 🏠 1,920. 🚌
🛈 RD 6202 (04 93 05 05 05).
🌐 provence-val-dazur.com

This attractive village lies at the foot of a rocky peak, nestling at the confluence of the Roudoule and the Var beneath the ruins of a château that belonged to the Grimaldi family *(see pp82–3)*. The old town has some fine medieval houses with overhanging roofs, but the chief attraction is the 13th-century parish church Notre-Dame de l'Assomption. The delightful altarpiece, *Notre-Dame de Bon Secours* (1525), is by Antoine Ronzen. Inside the entrance, the altarpiece of the Passion (1520–25) – the masterpiece of the church – is by Flemish craftsmen, working with the architect and sculptor Matthieu d'Anvers.

Beside the main road, the statue of a woman with her hands tied is called *L'Action Enchaînée*, by Aristide Maillol (1861–1944). It commemorates the local revolutionary, Louis-Auguste Blanqui. He was born in the town hall in 1805 and became one of the socialist heroes of the

L'Action Enchaînée, in Puget-Théniers square

Paris Commune in 1871. A year later he was imprisoned for life and served seven years, having already spent 30 years in jail.

❸ St-Cézaire-sur-Siagne

Road map E3. 🏠 3,850.
🛈 3 rue de la République (04 93 60 84 30). 🗓 Tue & Sat.
🌐 saintcezairesursiagne.fr

Dominating the steep-sided Siagne valley, St-Cézaire has been inhabited since pre-Roman times. The walls and gates of the village are reminders of its feudal past. At its heart is the 13th-century Eglise Paroissiale Notre-Dame de Sardaigne, which houses a Gallo-Roman tomb discovered nearby – a fine example of Provençal Romanesque design. From the medieval part of the village, there is a magnificent viewpoint. To the northeast of the village are the **Grottes de St-Cézaire-sur-Siagne** – iron-rich caves filled with beautiful rock crystallization. Dramatic stalactites and stalagmites have formed on the cave ceilings and floors,

Antoine Ronzen's altarpiece *Notre-Dame de Bon Secours* (1525), Puget-Théniers

creating enchanting shapes, reminiscent of flowers, animals and toadstools. If touched, the stalactites become remarkably resonant, but leave this to the guide. Red oxide in the limestone gives a rich colour to the caves' chambers: the Fairies' Alcove, Great Hall, Hall of Draperies and Organ Chamber, all connected by narrow underground passages, one of which ends abruptly, 40 m (130 ft) below ground, at the edge of an abyss.

Grottes de St-Cézaire-sur-Siagne
1481 route des Grottes. **Tel** 04 93 60 22 35. **Open** Feb–mid-Nov: daily. obligatory. **grottes-saintcezaire.com**

Inside the remarkable Grottes de St-Cézaire-sur-Siagne

The village of Gourdon, on the edge of a rocky cliff

❹ Gourdon

Road map E3. 421.
1 pl Victoria (08 11 81 10 67).
gourdon06.fr

For centuries, villages were built on hilltops, surrounded by ramparts. Gourdon is a typical *village perché (see pp24–5)*, its shops filled with regional produce, perfume and local art. From the square at its precipitous edge, there is a spectacular view of the Loup valley and the sea with Antibes and Cap Roux in the distance.

There are good views, too, from the gardens of the **Château de Gourdon**, built in the 12th century by the seigneurs du Bar, overlords of Gourdon, on the foundations of what was once a Saracen fortress. Its vaulted rooms are remnants of Saracen occupation. The terrace gardens were laid out by André Le Nôtre when the château was restored in the 17th century. There are three distinct gardens – the Jardin à l'Italienne, the Jardin de Rocaille (or Provençal Gardens) and the Jardin de l'Apothicaire with its own centrally located sundial. Although the château is still privately owned and not open to the public, visitors can take a guided tour of the gardens in groups of ten or more by appointment.

Château de Gourdon
Tel 04 93 09 68 02. **Open** Apr–Sep by reservation for groups of 10 or more. **chateau-gourdon.com**

Journey in the Gorges du Loup

The village of Gourdon is on the edge of the Gorges du Loup, the most accessible of many dramatic gorges running down to the coast. The route up to the Gorges du Loup begins at Pré-du-Loup, just east of Grasse, and leads to Gourdon. From Gourdon, the D3 goes up into the gorge and offers the best views, turning back down the D6 after 6.5 km (4 miles).

Descending on the left bank, the road passes the great pothole of Saut du Loup and the Cascades des Demoiselles, where the river's lime carbonate content has partly solidified the vegetation. Just beyond is the 40-m (130-ft) Cascade de Courmes, which has a treacherously slippery stairway under it.

The D2210 continues to Vence, passing via Tourrettes-sur-Loup, an art and craft centre on a high plateau. The 15th-century church has a triptych by the Bréa School and a 1st-century altar dedicated to the Roman god Mercury.

The 40-m (130-ft) Cascade de Courmes

❺ Grasse

Road map E3. 🔼 52,000. 🚍 ℹ️ Pl du cours Honoré Cresp (04 93 36 66 66). 🚌 Sat. 🖥️ **grasse.fr**

Once known for its leather tanning industry, Grasse became a perfume centre in the 16th century. The tanneries have vanished, but three major perfume houses are still here. Today, perfume is mainly made from imported flowers, but each year, Grasse holds a Jasmine festival *(see p37)*. The best place to discover the history of perfume is the **Musée International de la Parfumerie**. It also displays *bergamotes*, decorated scented *papier-mâché* boxes. At **Molinard** there is also a museum and visitors can create their own perfume.

Grasse became fashionable after 1807–8 when Princess Pauline Bonaparte recuperated here. Queen Victoria often wintered at the Grand Hotel.

Artist Jean-Honoré Fragonard (1732–1806) was born here and the walls of the **Villa-Musée Fragonard** are covered with his son's murals. The artist's *Washing of the Feet* hangs in the 12th-century **Ancienne Cathédrale Notre-Dame-du-Puy**, in the old town. The cathedral also houses three works by Rubens. The **Musée d'Art et d'Histoire de Provence** has Moustiers ware. 18th–19th century Provençal costumes and jewellery can be seen at the **Musée Provençal du Costume et du Bijou**.

🏛️ **Musée International de la Parfumerie**
2 blvd du Jeu de Ballon. **Tel** 04 97 05 58 11. **Open** daily (Oct–Mar: Wed–Mon). **Closed** public hols. 🈂️ ♿ 🈳

🏛️ **Molinard**
60 blvd Victor Hugo. **Tel** 04 93 36 01 62. **Open** daily (Oct–May: Mon–Sat). **Closed** 1 Jan, 25 Dec. 🈂️

🏛️ **Villa-Musée Fragonard**
23 blvd Fragonard. **Tel** 04 97 05 58 00. **Open** daily (Oct–May: Wed–Mon). **Closed** public hols, Nov. 🈂️ 📷 by appt. 🈳

🏛️ **Musée d'Art et d'Histoire de Provence**
2 rue Mirabeau. **Tel** 04 97 05 58 00. **Open** daily (Oct–May: Wed–Mon). **Closed** public hols, Nov. 🈂️ 📷 by appt. 🈳

Exterior of the Musée International de la Parfumerie in Grasse

❻ Mougins

Road map E3. 🔼 18,200. 🚍 ℹ️ 39 place des Patriotes (04 92 92 14 00). 🖥️ **mougins-tourisme.com**

This old hilltop town *(see pp24–5)*, huddled inside the remains of 15th-century ramparts and fortified Saracen Gate, is one of the finest in the region. Mougins is a smart address: it has been used by royalty and film stars as well as Yves St Laurent and Picasso, who spent his last years in a house opposite the Chapelle de Notre-Dame-de-Vie.

Mougins is also one of the smartest places in France to eat. Among its many high-class restaurants, is stylish gastronomic restaurant **La Place de Mougins** *(see p209)*.

The **Musée de la Photographie** has a fine permanent collection of Picasso's photographs. The eclectic collection at the **Musée d'Art Classique de Mougins** includes works by Picasso, Cézanne, Andy Warhol and Damien Hirst. The **Eco'Parc Mougins** some 5 km (3 miles) south of Mougins, features exhibitions and interactive displays on science and nature.

🏛️ **Musée de la Photographie**
Porte Sarrazine. **Tel** 04 93 75 85 67. **Open** daily (Feb–Dec). **Closed** Jan.

🏛️ **Musée d'Art Classique de Mougins**
32 rue Commandeur. **Tel** 04 93 75 18 65. **Open** daily. 🈂️

🏛️ **Eco'Parc Mougins**
772 chemin de Font de Currault, autoroute A8. **Tel** 04 93 46 00 03. **Open** Wed, Sat, Sun. **Closed** 1 Jan, 25 Dec. 🈂️ ♿ 🈳

Jacques-Henri and Florette Lartigue, Musée de la Photographie, Mougins

The Perfumes of Provence

For the past 400 years, the town of Grasse has been the centre of the perfume industry. Before that it was a tannery town, but in the 16th century, Italian immigrant glove-makers began to use the scents of local flowers to perfume soft leather gloves, a fashion made popular by the Queen, Catherine de' Médici. Enormous acres of lavender, roses, jonquils, jasmine and aromatic herbs were cultivated. Today, cheaper imports of flowers and high land prices mean that Grasse focuses on the creation of scent. The power of perfume is evoked in Patrick Süskind's disturbing novel, *Perfume*, set partly in Grasse, in which the murderous perfumer exploits his knowledge of perfume extraction to grisly effect.

Picking early morning jasmine

Jasmine waiting to be processed

Creating a Perfume
Essences are extracted by various methods, including distillation by steam or volatile solvents, which separate the essential oils. *Enfleurage* is a costly and lengthy method for delicate flowers such as jasmine and violet. The blossoms are layered with lard which becomes impregnated with scent.

Steam distillation is one of the oldest extraction processes originally developed by the Arabs. It is now used mainly for flowers such as orange blossom. Flowers and water are boiled together in a still and the essential oils are extracted by steam in an *essencier*, or oil decanter.

Vast quantities of blossoms are required to create the essence or "absolut" perfume concentrate. For example, almost a ton of jasmine flowers are needed to obtain just one litre of jasmine essence.

The best perfumes are created by a perfumer known as a "nose" who possesses an exceptional sense of smell. The nose harmonizes fragrances rather like a musician, blending as many as 300 essences for a perfume. Today, scents can be synthesized by using "head-space analysis" which analyzes the components of the air above a flower.

❼ Cannes

Lord Brougham, British Lord Chancellor, put Cannes on the map in 1834 when he stopped there on his way to Nice. He was so entranced by the climate of what was then a tiny fishing village that he built a villa and started a trend for upper-class English visitors. Today, Cannes may not attract blue blood but it has become a town of festivals, the resort of the rich and famous. It is busy all year round, its image reinforced by the Film Festival *(see p36)*. With its casinos, fairs, beach, boat and street life, there is plenty to do, even though Cannes lacks the great museums and monuments of less glamorous resorts.

Relaxing deck chairs on the seafront, Hôtel Martinez

Exploring Cannes

The heart of the city is built around the Bay of Cannes and the palm-fringed seafront boulevard de la Croisette. Here there are luxury boutiques and hotels and fine views of La Napoule Bay and the Esterel heights. The eastern end of the bay curves out to Pointe de la Croisette and the summertime Palm Beach Casino, built on the ruins of the medieval Fort de la Croix, which has a nightclub, restaurant and swimming pool. The town's other two gaming houses, **Casino Les Princes** and **Casino Croisette**, are both open all year.

Brougham persuaded King Louis-Philippe to donate two million francs to build the Cannes harbour wall. Between La Pantiero and rue Félix Faure are the *allées* de la Liberté. Shaded by plane trees and surveyed by a statue of Lord Brougham, this open space is ideal both for boules and the colourful morning flower market. It provides a fine view of the harbour, which is filled with pleasure craft and

fishing boats. Behind the *allées* is the rue Meynadier, where you can buy delicious pasta, bread and cheese. This leads you to the **Marché Forville**. Fresh regional produce turns up here every day except Monday. The small streets meander up from the *marché* to the old Roman town of Canoïs Castrum. This area was named after the reeds that grew by the seashore, and is now known as Le Suquet. The Provençal Gothic church in the centre of the old town, **Notre-Dame de l'Espérance**, was completed in 1648.

The Cannes Film Festival has been held here every May since 1946. The main venue is the **Palais des Festivals**, but there are cinemas all over town, some of which are open to the public and film screening starts as early as 8:30am. The beach has been a focus for paparazzi since 1953, when Brigitte Bardot's beautiful pout put her on the world's front pages.

Famous handprint of Roman Polanski

The main hotels in Cannes have their own beaches with bars and restaurants, where prices match their standing. Celebrities are most likely to be seen at the Carlton, Majestic and Martinez. There is a small charge to enter most beaches in Cannes, where imported sand covers the natural pebbles, and sun-loungers cost extra. Just next to the festival building there is also a free public beach.

🎭 Palais des Festivals et des Congrès

1 blvd de la Croisette. **Tel** 04 92 99 84 00. ℹ️ 04 92 99 84 22.
🌐 palaisdesfestivals.com

Built in 1982, this unmistakably modern building stands beside the Vieux Port at the west end of the promenade. It is the chief venue for the *Palmes d'Or* and other internationally recognised awards sufficiently prestigious for the film business to take them seriously, and much business goes on, so that the festival is not all hype and publicity. Some 78,000 official tickets are distributed to professionals only. Apart from its use for the great Film Festival, the building also houses a casino and a nightclub, and is a regular conference venue. In the nearby *allée* des Stars, handprints of such famous celebrities as the film director Roman Polanski are immortalized in pavement cement.

Cannes Old Town, known locally as Le Suquet, overlooking the harbour

InterContinental Carlton, the height of luxury at Cannes

🏛 Musée de la Castre
Château de la Castre, Le Suquet.
Tel 04 93 38 55 26. **Open** Tue–Sun.
Closed 1 Jan, 1 May, 1 & 11 Nov,
25 Dec. 🅿 🗖 by appt. ♿

The old Cannes castle, erected
by the Lérins monks in the
11th and 12th centuries,
houses this museum. Set up
in 1877, it contains some
fine archaeological and
ethnographical collections
from all over the world,
ranging from South Sea Island
costumes to Asian art and
African masks. Also housed in
the Cistercian St-Anne chapel
is a collection of superb
musical instruments. The
11th-century **Tour de la Castre**
is worth climbing for the view.

🏨 InterContinental Carlton
58 la Croisette. **Tel** 04 93 06 40 06.
🆆 intercontinental-carlton-
cannes.com See Where to Stay p198.

This ultimate symbol of comfort
and grace contains 343 rooms and
suites, and has its own private
sandy beach. It was designed and
built in 1911 by the architect,
Henri Ruhl. The huge Rococo-
style dining room, where the
colonnades rise to an ornately
decorated ceiling with finely
wrought cornices, is unchanged.
The hotel's wedding-cake
exterior is studded with tiny
balconies, and the window
frames, cornices and attic
pediments are decorated with
stucco. The hotel's twin black
cupolas are said to be modelled
on the breasts of the notorious
Belle Otéro, a half-Spanish
courtesan who captivated Ruhl.
The Carlton was so revered
that in World War II, a *New
York Times* journalist asked a
commanding officer to protect
what he considered to be the
world's finest hotel.

Cannes

① Palais des Festivals et
   des Congrès
② InterContinental Carlton
③ Musée de la Castre

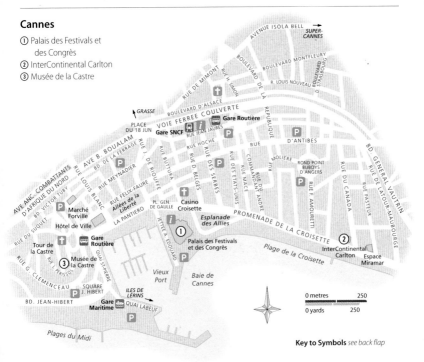

Key to Symbols see back flap

❽ Iles de Lérins

Although only a 15-minute boat ride from the glitter of Cannes, the Iles de Lérins reflect a contrasting lifestyle, with their forests of eucalyptus and Aleppo pine and their tiny chapels. The two islands, separated only by a narrow strait, were once the most powerful religious centres in the south of France. St-Honorat is named after the Gallo-Roman, Honoratus, who visited the smaller island at the end of the 4th century and founded a monastery. Some believe that Ste-Marguerite was named after his sister, who set up a nunnery there. Its fort is well known as the prison of the mysterious 17th-century Man in the Iron Mask, who spent 11 years here.

★ **Fort Ste-Marguerite**
Built under Richelieu and strengthened by Vauban in 1712, its ground floor has a maritime museum.

Ile Ste-Marguerite

Port for ferries to and from Cannes

Etang du Batéguier

Allée des Eucalyptus

Chapelle St-Michel

Ile St-Honorat

Chapelle St-Sauveur

St Honorat et les Saints de Lérins
This icon of St Honorat can be found in the Abbaye de Lérins.

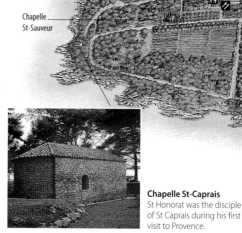

Chapelle St-Caprais
St Honorat was the disciple of St Caprais during his first visit to Provence.

The Man in the Iron Mask
The mystery man was imprisoned in Fort Royal from 1687 to 1698, then moved to the Bastille, where he died in 1703.

Remains on Ste-Marguerite
Excavations on the coast near the fort have revealed houses, mosaics, wall paintings and ceramics which date back to around the 3rd century BC.

Allée du Grand Jardin

Route de la Convention
Both the islands have many paths leading through the densely wooded interior as well as round the coast.

Chapelle St-Cyprien

La Chapelle de la Trinité

Abbaye de Lérins
The old church and monks' quarters were incorporated in the 19th-century building.

★ Monastère Fortifié
Built in 1073 by Abbot Aldebert, to protect the monks from Saracen pirates, this "keep" gives views as far as Esterel.

0 metres	1000
0 yards	1000

⑨ Juan-les-Pins

Road map E4. 🚂 76,770. 🚗 🚌
ℹ️ Palais des Congres, 60 chemin des Sables (04 22 10 60 01).
🌐 antibesjuanlespins.com

To the east of Cannes is the hammerhead peninsula of Cap d'Antibes, a promontory of pines and coves where millionaires' mansions grow. Just next door is one of the finest beaches in the area tucked in the west side of the cape in Golfe-Juan, where Napoleon came ashore from Elba in 1815. This is a 20th-century resort, promoted by American railroad heir Frank Jay Gould, who attracted high society in the 1920s and 1930s when writers F Scott Fitzgerald and Ernest Hemingway stayed here.

Today, in the high season, it is filled with a young crowd. The area at the junctions of boulevards Baudoin and Wilson is filled with bars. Action centres round the 1988 casino, the Palais des Congrés, and Penedé Gould pine grove, which gives shelter to the International Jazz à Juan Festival (see p37) in July.

A glimpse of nightlife in one of the vibrant streets of Juan-les-Pins

⑩ Antibes

Road map E3. 🚂 76,770 (Commune of Antibes). 🚗 🚌 🚂 ℹ️ 42 ave Robert Soleau (04 22 10 60 10).
🛒 Mon–Sun (daily Jul & Aug).
🌐 antibesjuanlespins.com

Originally the ancient Greek trading post of Antipolis, Antibes became heavily fortified over the centuries, notably by Vauban in the 17th century, who built the main port and Fort Carré, where Napoleon was allegedly temporarily imprisoned.

The old town is pleasant, with a picturesque market place in

Spectacular pleasure yachts in Antibes harbour

cours Masséna. The town's high points include the 12th-century towers of the church and Grimaldi castle on the site of Antipolis. The **Cathédrale Notre-Dame**, which took over the town's watchtower as a belfry, has a wooden crucifix from 1447, a 16th-century Christ and a fine Louis Bréa altarpiece depicting the Virgin Mary.

The Château Grimaldi nearby houses the **Musée Picasso**, which displays over 50 drawings, paintings, and ceramics created by the artist when he used the museum as a studio during 1946.

The exceptional modern art collection includes works by Ernst, Modigliani, Léger, Miró and Nicolas de Staël in the last two years of his life.

Further south, the **Musée d'Histoire et d'Archéologie** in the fortified Bastion St-André houses Greek and Etruscan finds, including a 3rd-century BC inscription to the spirit of Septentrion, a boy who danced at the Antipolis theatre.

Marineland leisure park, north of Antibes, includes a shark-filled aquarium and other attractions such as polar bears and whales.

🐋 Marineland
306 ave Mozart. **Tel** 04 93 33 49 49.
Open Feb–Dec: daily. 🚻 ♿ 📷 🚫
🌐 marineland.fr

🏛 Musée Picasso
Château Grimaldi, Place Mariejol.
Tel 04 93 95 85 98. **Open** Tue–Sun.
Closed 1 Jan, 1 May, 1 Nov, 25 Dec.
🚻 ♿ 📷 ✉️ 📷

🏛 Musée d'Histoire et d'Archéologie
Bastion St-André. **Tel** 04 93 95 85 98.
Open Tue–Sun. **Closed** 1 Jan, 1 May, 1 Nov, 25 Dec. 📷 ♿ 📷

⑪ Vallauris

Road map E3. 🚂 31,000. 🚌 ℹ️ 67 ave George Clemenceau (04 93 63 82 58) & Golfe-Juan Vieux Port (04 93 63 73 12).
🛒 Mon–Sat. 🌐 vallauris-golfe-juan.fr

In summer, the wares of potters spill on to the avenue of this pottery capital. Picasso revitalized this industry, the history of which is traced in the **Musée de la Ceramique**, together with a collection of contemporary pieces. In the square is Picasso's sculpture *L'Homme au Mouton* (1943). *La Guerre et la Paix* (1952) is on the ceiling of the **Musée National Picasso**, which is located in the Romanesque chapel of the Château de Vallauris.

🏛 Musée de la Ceramique
Pl de la Libération. **Tel** 04 93 64 71 83.
Open Wed–Mon. **Closed** 1 Jan, 1 May, 1 & 11 Nov, 25 Dec. 📷

🏛 Musée National Picasso
Pl de la Libération. **Tel** 04 93 64 71 83.
Open Wed–Mon. **Closed** 1 Jan, 1 May, 1 & 11 Nov, 25 Dec. 📷 📷

78-year-old Pablo Picasso with a man-sized dalmatian companion

Pablo Picasso (1881–1973)

Picasso, the giant of 20th-century art, spent most of his later life in Provence, inspired by its luminous light and brilliant colours. He came first to Juan-les-Pins in 1920, and returned to Antibes in 1946 with Françoise Gilot. He was given a studio in the seafront Grimaldi palace, where, after wartime Paris, his work became infused with Mediterranean light and joyful images. No other artist has succeeded with so many art forms, and the Antibes collection is a taste of his versatility. He died at Mougins, aged 92.

Violin and Sheet of Music (1912), now in Paris, is a Cubist collage from the period when Picasso experimented with different forms.

Les Demoiselles d'Avignon (1907), now in New York, was the first Cubist painting. Its bold style shocked the art world of the day.

La Joie de Vivre (1946), is one of Picasso's main works from the Antibes period, using favourite mythological themes. He is the bearded centaur playing the flute, and Françoise Gilot is the Maenad who dances while two fauns leap about and a satyr plays a panpipe.

The Goat (1946), also in Antibes, is one of his best-known images. In 1950 he made his famous goat sculpture using a wicker basket as the ribcage.

L'Homme au Mouton (1943) was sculpted in an afternoon. It stands in the main square of Vallauris, also home of *La Guerre et la Paix* (1951).

⑫ Biot

Road map E3. 🗺 10,300. 🚉 🚌
i 46 rue St-Sébastien (04 93 65 78 00).
🏛 Tue. 🌐 **biot-tourisme.com**

The picturesque village of Biot, which has 12 themed walks (available at the tourist office), was the main pottery town in the region until Pablo Picasso revived the industry in Vallauris after World War II. Today, Biot is renowned for its bubble-flecked glasswork, with eight glassworks, including **La Verrerie de Biot** where visitors can marvel at master craftsmen at work.

Biot was once the domain of the Knights Templar *(see p127)*, and some fortifications remain, such as the 1566 Porte des Migraniers (grenadiers). The church has two fine 16th-century works: *L'Ecce Homo*, attributed to Canavesio, and *La Vierge au Rosaire*, attributed to Louis Bréa.

The **Musée National Fernand Léger** contains many of the artist's vibrant works.

🏛 **Musée National Fernand Léger**
316 chemin du Val-de-Pome. **Tel** 04 92 91 50 30. **Open** Wed–Mon.
Closed 1 Jan, 1 May, 25 Dec. 🏛 🏛 🌐 **musee-fernandleger.fr**

🏛 **La Verrerie de Biot**
Chemin des Combes. **Tel** 04 93 65 03 00.
Open daily. **Closed** 1 & 15–27 Jan, 25 Dec. 🏛 🏛 🏛
🌐 **verreriebiot.com**

Detail of Léger mosaic from the eastern façade of the museum, Biot

⑬ Villeneuve-Loubet

Road map E3. 🗺 15,000. *i* 16 ave de la Mer (04 92 02 66 16). 🏛 Wed & Sat. 🌐 **villeneuve-tourisme.com**

This old village is dominated by a restored medieval castle built by Romée de Villeneuve. It is also where the celebrated chef, Auguste Escoffier, (1846–1935) was born. The man who invented the *bombe Néro* and *pêche Melba* was *chef de cuisine* at the Grand Hotel, Monte-Carlo before he was persuaded to become head chef at the Savoy in London. The **Musée Escoffier de l'Art Culinaire**, in the house of his birth, contains many showpieces

Chef Auguste Escoffier, born in Villeneuve-Loubet

in almond paste and icing sugar, and over 1,800 menus, dating back to 1820. Each summer, the town celebrates Escoffier with a gastronomic festival.

🏛 **Musée Escoffier de l'Art Culinaire**
3 de la rue Escoffier. **Tel** 04 93 20 80 51. **Open** daily. **Closed** Nov, 24 & 31 Dec, pub hols. 🏛 🏛
🌐 **fondation-escoffier.org**

⑭ Vence

Road map E3. 🗺 19,500. 🚌 *i* 8 place du Grand-Jardin (04 93 58 06 38).
🏛 Tue & Fri. 🌐 **vence-tourisme.fr**

A delightful old cathedral town on a rocky ridge, Vence has long attracted artists. The English writer D H Lawrence died here in 1930.

The old town is entered by the Porte de Peyra (1441), beside the place du Frêne, named after its giant ash tree planted to commemorate the visits of King François I and Pope Paul III. The 16th-century castle of the lords of Villeneuve, seigneurs of Vence, houses the museum and the **Fondation Emile Hugues**, named after an illustrious former mayor.

The cathedral, one of the smallest in France, stands by the site of the forum of the Roman city of Vintium. Vence was a bishopric from the 4th to the 19th centuries. Its notable prelates included Saint Véran (d AD 492), and Bishop Godeau (1605–72). The 51 oak and pear choir stalls are carved with satirical

The Creation of Biot Glassware

Biot is the capital of glass-blowing on the coast. Local soils provide sand for glass-making, and typical Biot glass is sturdy, with tiny air bubbles (known as *verre à bulles*). The opening of Léger's museum led to an increased interest in all local crafts, and to the arrival of the Verrerie de Biot workshop in 1956. This revived old methods of making oil lamps, carafes and narrow-spouted *porrons*, from which a jet of liquid can be poured straight into the mouth.

figures. Marc Chagall designed the mosaic of *Moses in the Bulrushes* in the chapel (1979).

Henri Matisse *(see pp86–7)* decorated the **Chapelle du Rosaire** between 1947 and 1951 to thank the Dominican nuns who nursed him through an illness. The stations of the cross are reduced to black lines tinted with stained glass.

Fondation Emile Hugues
Château de Villeneuve. **Tel** 04 93 58 15 78. **Open** Tue–Sun. **Closed** 1 Jan, 1 May, 25 Dec.
museedevence.com

Chapelle du Rosaire
Ave Henri Matisse. **Tel** 04 93 58 03 26. **Open** Tue & Thu: am; Mon–Thu & Sat: pm **Closed** mid-Nov–mid-Dec, public hols.

⑮ St-Paul de Vence

Road map E3. 3,500. Vence and Nice. 2 rue Grande (04 93 32 86 95). **saint-pauldevence.com**

This classic medieval *village perché (see pp24–5)* was built behind the coast to avoid Saracen attack. Between 1543 and 1547, it was re-ramparted, under François I, to stand up to Savoy, Austria and Piedmont. A celebrity village, it was first "discovered" by Bonnard, Modigliani and other artists of the 1920s. Since that time, many of the rich and famous literati and glitterati have flocked to St-Paul de Vence. Most famously, these personalities slept, dined, and, in the case of Yves Montand and Simone Signoret, had their wedding reception at the

Simone Signoret and Yves Montand in St-Paul de Vence

Colombe d'Or *auberge (see p210)*. Today the *auberge* has one of the finest 20th-century private art collections, built up over the years thanks to the owner's friendship with artists and sometimes in lieu of payment of bills. The priceless dining-room décor includes paintings by such world-famous artists as Miró, Picasso and Braque. In the Romanesque and Baroque church, there is a painting, *Catherine of Alexandria*, attributed to Claudio Coello. There are also

gold reliquaries and a fine local 13th-century enamel Virgin. The **Musée d'Histoire Locale** nearby features waxwork costumed characters and a tableaux of scenes from the town's rich past, and the old castle keep adjacent is now used as the town hall. Just in front of the museum, the 17th-century White Penitants chapel was decorated by Belgian artist Jean-Michel Folon.

The main street runs from the 14th-century entrance gate of Porte Royale and past the Grande Fontaine to Porte Sud. This gives on to the cemetery, a resting place for Chagall, the Maeghts and many locals. It also offers wonderful views.

Just outside St-Paul de Vence, on La Gardette Hill, is Josep Lluis Sert's striking concrete and rose **Fondation Maeght** *(see pp80–81)*, one of Europe's finest modern art museums.

Musée d'Histoire Locale and Chapelle Folon
Pl de la Mairie. **Tel** 04 93 32 41 13. **Open** daily. **Closed** 1 Jan, Nov, 25 Dec.

Entrance to Chapelle du Rosaire in Vence, decorated by Henri Matisse

Fondation Maeght

Nestling amid the umbrella pines in the hills above St-Paul de Vence, this small modern art museum is one of the world's finest. Aimé and Marguerite Maeght were Cannes art dealers who numbered the likes of Chagall, Matisse and Miró among their clients and friends. Their private collection formed the basis for the museum, which opened in 1964. Like St-Paul itself, the Maeght has been a magnet for celebrities: Duke Ellington, Samuel Beckett, André Malraux, Merce Cunningham and, of course, a galaxy of the artists themselves have mingled at fundraising events. The museum now receives over 200,000 visitors each year.

★ **Cour Giacometti**
Slender bronze figures by Alberto Giacometti, such as *L'Homme Qui Marche I* (1960), inhabit their own shady courtyard or appear about the grounds as if they have a life of their own.

La Vie (1964)
Marc Chagall's painting is full of humanity: here is love, parenthood, religion, society, nature; all part of a swirling, circus-like tableau of dancers and musicians, acrobats and clowns.

Les Renforts (1963)
One of many works of art that greet arriving visitors, Alexander Calder's creation is a "stabile" – a counterpart to his more familiar mobiles.

KEY

① **Cowled roofs** allow indirect light to filter into the galleries. The building was designed by Spanish architect Josep Lluis Sert.

② **Les Poissons** is a mosaic pool designed by Georges Braque in 1963.

③ **Chapelle St-Bernard** was built in memory of the Maeghts' son, who died in 1953, aged 11. Above the altarpiece, a 12th-century Christ, is a stained-glass window by Braque.

Gallery Guide

The permanent collection is comprised entirely of 20th-century art. The only items on permanent view are the large sculptures in the grounds. The indoor galleries display works from the collection in rotation but, in summer, only temporary exhibitions are held.

La Partie de Campagne (1954)
Fernand Léger lends his unique vision to the classic artistic scene of a country outing.

VISITORS' CHECKLIST

Practical Information
623 chemin Gardettes, St-Paul-de-Vence. **Tel** 04 93 32 81 63.
Open 10am–6pm daily (Jul–Sep: to 7pm). 🌐 💻 📖 Library.
W fondation-maeght.com

★ Labyrinthe de Miró
Joan Miró's *l'Oiseau Lunaire* (1968) is one of the many statues in this multi-levelled maze of trees, water and gargoyles.

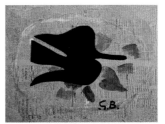

Oiseau dans le Feuillage (1961)
Georges Braque's bird nestles amongst "foliage" made of newsprint. Braque was highly influential in the creation of the Fondation, but died before he could see the museum finally opened to the public.

L'Eté (1917)
Pierre Bonnard settled in Provence for the last 22 years of his life, becoming a close friend of Aimé Maeght. Matisse called Bonnard "the greatest of us all".

Main entrance and information

Pierre-Auguste Renoir's studio at Les Collettes

⑯ Cagnes-sur-Mer

Road map E3. 🚆 47,156. 🚌 🚐
ℹ 6 blvd Maréchal Juin (04 93 20 61 64). 📅 Tue–Sun. 🌐 cagnes-tourisme.com

There are three parts to Cagnes-sur-Mer: Cros-de-Cagnes, the fishing village and beach; Cagnes-Ville, the commercial centre; and Haut-de-Cagnes, the upper town.

Haut-de-Cagnes is the place to head for. This hill-top town is riven with lanes, steps and vaulted passages. It is dominated by the **Château-Musée Grimaldi** but also has some fine Renaissance houses and the church of St-Pierre, where the Grimaldis are entombed.

East of Cagnes-Ville is Les Collettes, built in 1907 among ancient olive trees by Pierre-Auguste Renoir (1841–1919). He came here, hoping that the climate would relieve his rheumatism and stayed for the rest of his life. A picture of Renoir in his last year shows him still at work, a brush tied to his crippled hand.

Now the **Musée Renoir** at Les Collettes is almost exactly as it was when the artist died. In the house are 14 of Renoir's paintings, as well as works by his friends Bonnard and Dufy. Renoir's beloved olive groves are the setting for the bronze *Venus Victrix* (1915–16).

🏛 **Musée Renoir**
Chemin des Collettes.
Tel 04 93 20 61 07. **Open** Wed–Mon.
Closed 1 Jan, 1 May, 25 Dec.
🎨 ♿ 📷

Château-Musée Grimaldi

In the Middle Ages the Grimaldi family held sway over many of the Mediterranean coastal towns. The castle that towers over Haut-de-Cagnes was built by Rainier in 1309 as a fortress-prison; in 1620 his descendant, Jean-Henri, transformed it into the handsome palace which shelters behind its dramatic battlements. Mercifully, the château survived the worst ravages of the Revolution and later occupation by Piedmontese troops in 1815. It now houses an eclectic mixture of museums, from olives to modern art.

Second floor

Stairs to the tower

The chapel contains a wealth of religious ornamentation, both ancient and modern.

★ **Donation Suzy Solidor**
This 1930s chanteuse was painted by 244 artists during her lifetime. The 40 works on display include portraits by Jean Cocteau (*above*) and Kisling (*above right*).

Gallery Guide

The olive tree museum is on the ground floor, along with exhibits about life in the medieval castle. The Suzy Solidor collection is displayed in a former boudoir on the first floor. Selections from the permanent collection of modern Mediterranean art, as well as temporary exhibitions, are on the first and second floors.

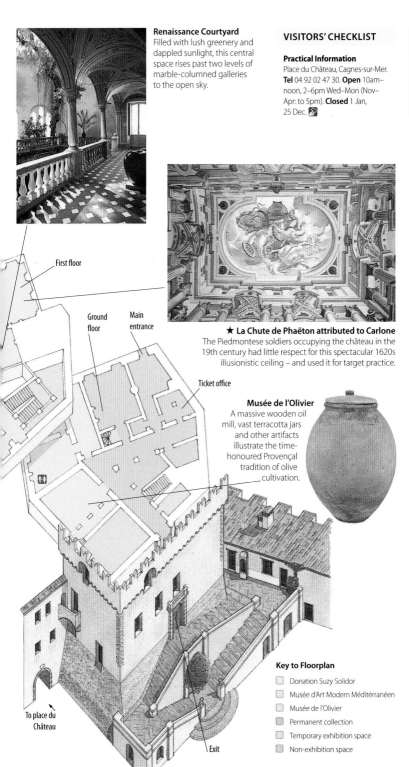

Renaissance Courtyard
Filled with lush greenery and dappled sunlight, this central space rises past two levels of marble-columned galleries to the open sky.

First floor

Ground floor

Main entrance

Ticket office

★ La Chute de Phaëton attributed to Carlone
The Piedmontese soldiers occupying the château in the 19th century had little respect for this spectacular 1620s illusionistic ceiling – and used it for target practice.

Musée de l'Olivier
A massive wooden oil mill, vast terracotta jars and other artifacts illustrate the time-honoured Provençal tradition of olive cultivation.

To place du Château

Exit

Key to Floorplan
- Donation Suzy Solidor
- Musée d'Art Modern Méditérranéen
- Musée de l'Olivier
- Permanent collection
- Temporary exhibition space
- Non-exhibition space

⓱ Street-by-Street: Nice

A dense network of pedestrian alleys, narrow buildings and pastel, Italianate façades make up Vieux Nice or the Old Town. Its streets contain many fine 17th-century Italianate churches, among them St-François-de-Paule, behind the Opéra, and l'Eglise du Jésus in the rue Droite. Most of the seafront, at quai des Etats-Unis, is taken up by the Ponchettes, a double row of low houses with flat roofs, a fashionable walk before the promenade des Anglais was built. To the east of this lies the Colline du Château, occupied in the 4th century by Greeks who kept fishing nets on the quay.

★ **Cathédrale Ste-Réparate**
Built in 1650 by the Nice architect J-A Guiberto in Baroque style, this has a fine dome of glazed tiles and an 18th-century tower.

Palais de Justice
This awesome building was inaugurated on 17 October 1892, replacing the smaller quarters used before Nice became part of France. On the same site was a 13th-century church and convent.

★ **Cours Saleya**
The site of an enticing vegetable and flower market, it is also a lively area at night.

Opera House
Built in 1855, the ornate and sumptuous *Opéra de Nice* has its entrance just off the quai des Etats-Unis.

RUE DE LA BOUCHER

RUE F GAL

RUE COLONNA D'ISTRIA

RUE DU MARCHE

RUE DE LA PREFECT

PLACE DU PALAIS

PLAC PIER GAUT

RUE RAOUL

RUE ALEXANDRE MARI

BOSIO

RUE L GASSIN

COL

RUE ST-F DE PAULE

Chapelle de la Miséricorde
Designed in 1740 by Guarino Guarinone, this Baroque masterpiece has a fine Rococo interior. The Nice altarpieces are by Louis Bréa and Jean Miralhet.

★ Palais Lascaris
18th-century statues of Mars and Venus flank the staircase. The *trompe l'oeil* ceiling is by Genoese artists.

Tourist Train
It passes the market, old town and castle gardens.

Les Ponchettes
One of Nice's most unusual architectural features is the row of low white buildings along the seafront once used by fishermen, now a mix of galleries and ethnic restaurants.

0 metres 100
0 yards 100

Key
— Suggested route

Nice: Musée Matisse

Henri Matisse (1869–1954) first came to Nice in 1916, and lived at several addresses in the city before settling in Cimiez for the rest of his life. His devotion to the city and its "clear, crystalline, precise, limpid" light culminated, just before his death in 1954, with a bequest of works. Nine years later they formed the museum's core collection, sharing space with archaeological relics in the Villa des Arènes, next to the Cimiez cemetery, which holds the artist's simple memorial. Since 1993 the entire villa, complete with its new extension, has been devoted to celebrating his life, work and influence.

★ **Nu Bleu IV** (1952)
The celebrated "cut-outs" were made in later life when Matisse was bedridden.

Matisse in his Studio (1948)
The museum's photographic collection offers a unique insight into the man and his work. Robert Capa's picture shows him drafting the murals for the Chapelle du Rosaire at Vence (see pp78–9).

First floor

Ground floor

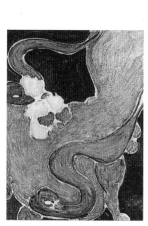

★ **Fauteuil Rocaille**
A gilded Rococo armchair, painted by Matisse in 1946, is among many of his personal belongings that are on display in the museum.

Main entrance

Gallery Guide

The ground and first floors display works from the museum's permanent collection, from which items are sometimes loaned out to other museums. The subterranean wing is used for exhibitions devoted to Matisse and his contemporaries.

Key to Floorplan

☐ Permanent collection
☐ Temporary exhibition space

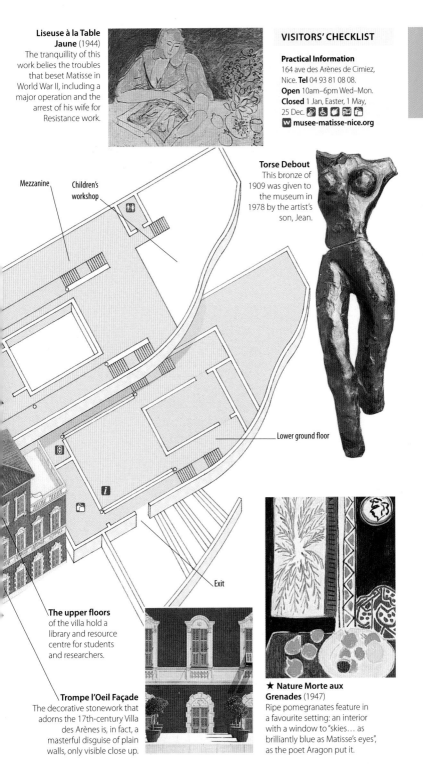

Liseuse à la Table Jaune (1944)
The tranquillity of this work belies the troubles that beset Matisse in World War II, including a major operation and the arrest of his wife for Resistance work.

VISITORS' CHECKLIST

Practical Information
164 ave des Arènes de Cimiez, Nice. **Tel** 04 93 81 08 08.
Open 10am–6pm Wed–Mon.
Closed 1 Jan, Easter, 1 May, 25 Dec.
w musee-matisse-nice.org

Torse Debout
This bronze of 1909 was given to the museum in 1978 by the artist's son, Jean.

Mezzanine

Children's workshop

Lower ground floor

Exit

The upper floors of the villa hold a library and resource centre for students and researchers.

Trompe l'Oeil Façade
The decorative stonework that adorns the 17th-century Villa des Arènes is, in fact, a masterful disguise of plain walls, only visible close up.

★ Nature Morte aux Grenades (1947)
Ripe pomegranates feature in a favourite setting: an interior with a window to "skies… as brilliantly blue as Matisse's eyes", as the poet Aragon put it.

Exploring Nice

Nice is France's largest tourist resort and fifth biggest city. It has the second busiest airport in France and more banks, galleries and museums than anywhere else outside the capital. Each year, Nice hosts a lavish pre-Lent carnival, ending with a fireworks display and the Battle of the Flowers *(see p228)*. The city has its own dialect and its own cuisine of *socca*, chickpea pancakes, but the ubiquitous pizza ovens lend a rich Italian flavour.

Beach and promenade des Anglais, one of the major attractions of Nice

A glimpse of the city

Nice lies at the foot of a hill known as the Château, after the castle that once stood there. The flower and vegetable market (Tue–Sun) in the Cours Saleya is a shoppers' paradise. The fashionable quarter is the Cimiez district, on the hills

overlooking the town, where the old monastery of **Notre-Dame** is worth a visit. Lower down, next to the **Musée Matisse** *(see pp86–7)*, are the remains of a Roman amphitheatre and baths. Artifacts are on show at the nearby archaeological museum.

The city's most remarkable feature is the 19th-century promenade des Anglais, which runs right along the seafront. It was built in the 1820s, using funds raised by the English colony. Today it is a pleasant 5-km (3-mile) highway. Until World War II, Nice was popular with aristocrats. Queen Victoria stayed here in 1895, and in 1912, Tsar Nicholas II built the onion-domed **Cathédrale Orthodoxe**

Russe (closed for renovation) in St-Philippe. At the heart of the city, the promenade du Paillon is a strip of parkland with a central waterway that runs from the old town, through the centre to the promenade des Anglais. It also hosts arts projects, sports events and includes a children's park.

🏨 Hotel Négresco

37 promenade des Anglais. **Tel** 04 93 16 64 00. *See Where to Stay (see p198).*
This palatial hotel was built in 1912 for Henri Négresco, once a gypsy-violin serenader, who went bankrupt eight years later. In the *salon royale* hangs a Baccarat chandelier made from 16,000

Ornate statue at the fountain in place Masséna

Nice

① Hotel Négresco
② Villa Masséna
③ Musée Chagall
④ Cathédrale Ste-Réparate
⑤ Palais Lascaris
⑥ Musée d'Art Moderne et d'Art Contemporain (MAMAC)

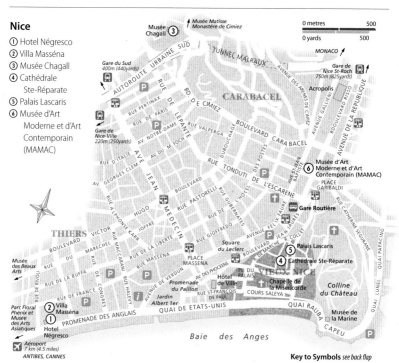

For hotels and restaurants in this region see pp198–201 and pp208–217

stones. The infamous American dancer Isadora Duncan spent her last months here in 1927. She died tragically outside the hotel when her trailing scarf caught in the wheel of her Bugatti and broke her neck.

🏛 Villa Masséna

65 rue de France. **Tel** 04 93 91 19 10. **Open** Wed–Mon. **Closed** 1 Jan, Easter, 1 May, 25 Dec.

This 19th-century Italianate villa belonged to the great-grandson of Napoleon's Nice-born Marshal. Its Empire-style main hall has a bust of the Marshal by Canova. Among its exhibits are religious works, paintings by Niçois primitives, white-glazed faïence pottery *(see p190)* and Josephine's gold cloak.

🏛 Musée Chagall

36 ave Dr Ménard. **Tel** 04 93 53 87 20. **Open** Wed–Mon. **Closed** 1 Jan, 1 May, 25 Dec. 📷 ♿ ✎ 🖼 in summer. **w** musee-chagall.fr

This museum houses the largest collection of Marc Chagall's work. There are 17 canvases from his Biblical Message series, including five versions of *The Song of Songs.*

Russian Orthodox cathedral in St-Philippe

Three stained-glass windows depict the *Creation of the World,* and the large mosaic reflected in the pool is that of the prophet Elijah.

🏛 Cathédrale Ste-Réparate

3, place Rossetti. **Tel** 08 92 70 74 07 for guided tours. **Open** daily. ✎

This 17th-century Baroque building has a handsome tiled dome. The interior is lavishly decorated with plasterwork, marble and original panelling.

🏛 Palais Lascaris

15 rue Droite. **Tel** 04 93 62 72 40. **Open** Wed–Mon. **Closed** 1 Jan, Easter, 1 May, 25 Dec. 🖼

This salon of this stuccoed 17th-century palace has a *trompe l'oeil* ceiling, said to be by Carlone. The palace now houses a museum of musical instruments.

🏛 Musée des Arts Asiatiques

405 promenade des Anglais. **Tel** 04 92 29 37 00. **Open** Wed–Mon. **Closed** 1 Jan, 1 May, 25 Dec. ♿ ✎ 🖼

This museum has outstanding examples of ancient and 20th-century art from across Asia in Kenzo Tange's uncluttered white marble and glass setting.

🏛 Musée des Beaux-Arts

33 ave des Baumettes. **Tel** 04 9215 28 28. **Open** Tue–Sun. **Closed** 1 Jan, Easter, 1 May, 25 Dec. ♿ ✎ 🖼 📷 **w** musee-beaux-arts-nice.org

Once home to a Ukranian princess, this 1878 villa houses a collection begun with a donation by Napoleon III. Three centuries of art cover work by Jules Chéret, Carle Van Loo, Van Dongen, and Impressionists and Post-Impressionists such as Bonnard, Dufy and Vuillard.

🏛 Musée d'Art Moderne et d'Art Contemporain (MAMAC)

Place Yves Klein. **Tel** 04 97 13 42 01. **Open** Tue–Sun. **Closed** 1 Jan, Easter, 1 May, 25 Dec. ♿ ✎ 🖼 📷

Housed in a strikingly original building with marble-faced towers and glass passageways, the collection reflects the history of the *avant-garde,* including Pop Art by Andy Warhol and work by Ecole de Nice artists such as Yves Klein.

Amazing hillside view over St-Jean-Cap-Ferrat

⑱ St-Jean-Cap-Ferrat

Road map F3. 👥 1,913. ✈ Nice. 🚌 Beaulieu-sur-Mer. 🚌 St-Jean-Cap-Ferrat. 🛈 5/59 ave Denis Séméria (04 93 76 08 90). **w** saintjeancapferrat-tourisme.fr

The Cap Ferrat peninsula is a playground for the rich, with exclusive villas, luxury gardens and fabulous yachts in the St-Jean marina.

King Léopold II of Belgium started the trend in the 19th century, when he built his Les Cèdres estate on the west side of the cape, overlooking Villefranche. Later residents have included the Duke and Duchess of Windsor, David Niven and Edith Piaf. High hedges and gates protect these villas, but one of the finest, housing the **Musée Ephrussi de Rothschild** *(see pp90–91),* is open to the public.

There is a superb view from the little garden of the 1837 lighthouse at the end of the cape. A pretty walk leads around the Pointe St-Hospice, east of the port at **St-Jean-Cap-Ferrat**, a former fishing village with old houses fronting the harbour.

For a fee, you can enjoy one of the town's two private beaches: **Plage de Passable** or **Plage de Paloma**. Both offer sun loungers, water sports and boat excursions.

🚩 Plage de Passable

Chemin de Passable. **Tel** 04 93 76 06 17. **Open** daily (Easter–Sep). 📷 ♿ 🖼

🚩 Plage de Paloma

1 route de Saint Hospice. **Tel** 04 93 01 64 71. **Open** daily (Easter–Sep). 📷 ♿ 🖼

Yves Klein's *Anthropométrie* (1960) in the Musée d'Art Contemporain

St-Jean-Cap-Ferrat: Ephrussi de Rothschild Villa and Gardens

Béatrice Ephrussi de Rothschild (1864–1934) could have led a life of indolent luxury, but her passions for travel and fine art, combined with an iron will, led to the creation of the most perfect "dream villa" of the Riviera, Villa Ile-de-France. Despite interest shown by King Léopold II of Belgium for the land, she succeeded in purchasing it and later supervised every aspect of the villa's creation. It was completed in 1912 and, although she never used it as a primary residence, Béatrice hosted garden parties and soirées here until 1934. The villa remains a monument to a woman of spirit and vision.

★ **Fragonard Room**
The fine collection of working drawings by Jean-Honoré Fragonard (1732–1806) includes this sketch, wryly named *If he were as faithful to me.*

Béatrice, Aged 19
Her meek appearance belies a woman who, a contemporary once observed, "commands flowers to grow during the Mistral".

①

Béatrice's Boudoir
Béatrice's writing desk is a beautiful piece of 18th-century furniture by cabinetmaker Jean-Henri Riesener (1734–1806).

KEY

① **The State Room** looks out on to the French garden, combining the pleasures of a sea breeze with the comfort of elegant surroundings.

② **First-floor apartments**

Villa Ile-de-France
Béatrice christened her villa following a pattern established by another villa she owned named "Rose de France". Its stucco walls are coloured in a lovely shade of rose pink.

Covered Patio
Combining Moorish and Italian elements, this airy space rises the full height of the villa. The marble columns, mosaic flooring and diffused light complement the Renaissance religious works on the walls.

Entrance to villa and assembly point for guided tours

Cabinet des Singes
Béatrice's love of animals is epitomized by this tiny room. Its wooden panels are painted with monkeys dancing to the music of the diminutive 18th-century Meissen monkey orchestra.

↗To ticket office and car park

★ **Gardens**
The main garden is modelled on a ship's deck – Béatrice employed extra staff to wander around in sailors' uniforms. There are nine themed gardens, including Japanese and Florentine gardens.

★ **State Room**
Like every room in the villa, the decor here is lavish, with wood ornamentation from the Crillon in Paris, Savonnerie carpets, and chairs upholstered in 18th-century Savonnerie tapestries.

⓭ Villefranche-sur-Mer

Road map F3. 🏔 5,795. 🚋 🚌
ℹ️ Jardin François Binon (04 93 01 73 68). 🗓 Wed, Sat, Sun.
🌐 **villefranche-sur-mer.com**

This unspoilt town overlooks a beautiful natural harbour, deep enough to be a naval port, with a lively waterfront lined by bars and cafés.

Chapelle St-Pierre on the quay, once used for storing fishing nets, was renovated in 1957, when Jean Cocteau added lavish frescoes. Steep lanes climb up from the harbour, turning into tunnels beneath the tightly packed buildings. The vaulted rue Obscure has provided shelter from bombardment as recently as World War II. The Baroque **Eglise St-Michel** contains a 16th-century carving of St Rock and his dog and a 1790 organ.

Within the 16th-century Citadelle de St-Elme are the chapel, open-air theatre and museums.

🏛 **Chapelle St-Pierre**
4 quai Amiral Courbet. **Tel** 04 93 76 90 70. **Open** Wed–Mon. **Closed** mid-Nov–mid-Dec, 25 Dec. 🎫

⓮ Beaulieu-sur-Mer

Road map F3. 🏔 3,800. 🚋 🚌
ℹ️ Pl Clemenceau (04 93 01 02 21). 🗓 daily. 🌐 **beaulieusurmer.fr**

Hemmed in and protected by a rock face, this is one of the Riviera's warmest resorts in winter, with two beaches: the Baie des Fourmis and, by the port, Petite Afrique. The casino,

Fishing in the natural harbour at Villefranch-sur-Mer

formal gardens and the Belle Epoque Rotunda, now a conference centre and museum, add to Beaulieu's old-fashioned air. Among its hotels is La Réserve, founded by Gordon Bennett, the owner of the *New York Herald*. As a stunt, in 1871, he sent journalist H M Stanley to rescue the Scottish missionary and explorer Dr Livingstone, who was looking for the source of the Nile.

Beaulieu-sur-Mer is the site of the **Villa Grecque Kérylos**. Built by archeologist Théodore Reinach, it resembles an ancient Greek villa. Authentic techniques and precious materials were used to create lavish mosaics, frescoes and inlaid furniture. There are also numerous original Greek ornaments, and an antique sculpture gallery.

🏛 **Villa Grecque Kérylos**
Impasse Gustave Eiffel. **Tel** 04 93 01 01 44. **Open** daily. 🎫 🏛
🌐 **villa-kerylos.com**

⓯ Eze

Road map F3. 🏔 2,574. 🚋 🚌
ℹ️ Pl Général de Gaulle (04 93 41 26 00). 🗓 Sun. 🌐 **eze-tourisme.com**

Eze, a dramatic *village perché* (*see pp24–5*) is a cluster of ancient buildings some 429 m (1,407 ft) above the sea. The **Jardin Exotique**, built around the ruins of a 14th-century castle, offers stunning views as far as Corsica.

Flower-decked, car-free streets lead to an 18th-century church. Its bust of Christ is made from olive wood that survived the terrible fires that raged close by in 1986.

🌿 **Jardin Exotique**
Rue du Château. **Tel** 04 93 41 10 30. **Open** daily. **Closed** Christmas week. 🎫

Steps of the elegant Belle Epoque Rotunda (1886), Beaulieu-sur-Mer

❷ La Turbie

Road map F3. ⛰ 3,200. 🚌 ℹ️ 2 pl
Detras (04 93 41 21 15). 🔄 Thu.
🌐 ville-la-turbie.fr

High above Monte-Carlo is one
of the finest views on the Riviera,
reached by a stretch of the
Grande Corniche that crosses
ravines and tunnels through
mountains. The village of La
Turbie, scented with bougain-
villea, has two medieval gate-
ways. Its oldest houses, dating
from the 11th–13th centuries,
are on the Roman Via Julia.

View of Trophée d'Auguste from the village of La Turbie

🏛 Musée du Trophée d'Auguste

18 cours Albert 1er. **Tel** 04 93 41 20 84.
Open Tue–Sun. **Closed** 1 Jan,
1 May, 1 & 11 Nov, 25 Dec.
🔲 🔲 🔲 ♿ 📷 by appt. 📷
🌐 la-turbie.monuments-
nationaux.fr

The most spectacular
feature of La Turbie
is the Trophée
d'Auguste, a huge
Roman monument,
built out of white local
stone, which marked
the division between
Italy and Gaul. Its
construction was ordered in
6 BC by the Roman Senate to

Monument detail,
Trophée d'Auguste

honour Augustus's victory in
13 BC over 44 fractious Ligurian
tribes. The original trophy was
50-m (164-ft) tall and had niches
with statues of each of
the campaign's victors.
There were stairs
leading to all parts of
the structure.

When the Romans
left, the trophy was
gradually dismantled.
In the 4th century,
St Honorat chipped
away at the monu-
ment because it had
become the object of
pagan worship. Later
it served both as a fort and as
a stone quarry. It was partly

destroyed on the orders of Louis
XIV, who feared it would fall into
enemy hands during the invasion
of Provence by Savoy in 1707.
Restoration was first begun in
1905, and continued in 1923
by an American, Edward Tuck.
Today, the triumphal inscription
of Roman victory has been
restored to its original position.

A small museum on the site
documents the history of the
trophy, with fragments of the
monument, pieces of sculpture,
inscriptions, drawings and a
small-scale model.

The spectacular panorama
from the terraces of the trophy
takes in Cap Ferrat and Eze.
Monaco, at 480 m (1,575 ft)
below, seems breathtakingly
close, like an urban stage set
seen from a seat in the gods.

Among visitors impressed
with La Turbie and its trophy,
was the poet Dante (1265–
1321), and his comments are
inscribed on a plaque in rue
Comte-de-Cessole. From the
end of this street there is a fine
view of the monument.

🛐 Eglise St-Michel-Archange

Open daily. ♿
The 18th-century Nice Baroque
church was built with stones
plundered from the trophy.
Inside there is an altar of multi-
coloured marble and a
17th-century onyx and agate
table, which was used for
communion. Its religious
paintings include two
works by the Niçois artist
Jean-Baptiste Van Loo,
a portrait of St Mark
attributed to Veronese, and
a Piéta from the Bréa School.

Trophée d'Auguste

*This triumphal monument had
a square podium, a circular
colonnade and a stepped cone
which was surmounted by the
statue of Augustus.*

**6-m (20-ft) statue of
Emperor Augustus**

**The original
colonnade** included
niches for the statues
of Augustus's
campaign generals.

The inscription records
the names of the
44 tribes subjugated
by Augustus, with a
dedication to the
emperor.

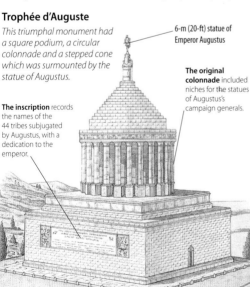

㉓ Monaco

If you come to Monaco by car, you may well travel in on the Moyenne Corniche, one of the world's most beautiful coastal highways. Arriving amid the skyscrapers of present-day Monaco, it is hard to imagine its turbulent history, much of it centred on Monaco-Ville. The palace, cathedral and museums are all in this old part of town, set on the Rock, a sheer-sided, flat-topped finger of land extending 792 m (2,600 ft) into the sea. First a Greek and later a Roman colony, it was bought from the Genoese in 1309 by François Grimaldi. In spite of family feuds and at least one political assassination, the Grimaldis, whose crest shows two sword-waving monks, remain the world's oldest ruling monarchy.

Modern Monaco
Lack of space has led to vertical building, and a striking skyline of skyscrapers and apartment blocks.

Palais Princier
The Grimaldis have ruled from here since the 14th century. The palace dates from the 16th–17th centuries but its towers are Genoese of 1215. The constitution insists it is guarded by French *carabiniers. (See p98).*

KEY

① **Museum of Vieux Monaco**

② **Monaco Top Cars Collection**, is an automobile museum displaying Prince Rainier III's private collection of more than one hundred antique cars.

Cathédrale
This Neo-Romanesque construction in cream-coloured stone sits on a rocky spur. Among its treasures are two early 16th-century screens by Bréa, *La Pietà* and *St-Nicolas. (See p98).*

Musée Océanographique
Erected on a sheer cliff, high above the Mediterranean, Monaco has one of the best aquaria in Europe. It is also used as a scientific research institute. *(See p98).*

VISITORS' CHECKLIST

Practical Information
Road map F3. 🚶 35,000. ℹ️ 2a blvd des Moulins (00 377 92 16 61 16). 🗓️ daily. 🎪 Festival du Cirque (Jan); Grand Prix (May); Fête Nationale (19 Nov).
ⓦ visitmonaco.com

Transport
✈️ 15 km (9 miles) SW Nice.
🚉 Pl Ste Dévote (08 36 35 35 35)

Théâtre du Fort Antoine
This ancient fort has been converted into a theatre which shows a wide range of productions in summer.

Typical Old Town Villa
Hidden in a labyrinth of passages are fountains, tiny squares and elegant façades.

The Royal Family

Monaco was ruled from 1949 by the businesslike Prince Rainier Louis Henri Maxence Bertrand de Grimaldi. He was the 26th ruling prince, a descendant of the Grimaldi who, disguised as a monk, entered the Monaco fortress in 1297. At that time the territory extended to Antibes and Menton. Prince Rainier's wife, the former film star Grace Kelly, whom he married in 1956, died tragically in 1982. Their son, Albert, inherited the $200 million throne on Rainier's death in 2005. In July 2011, Albert married former Olympic swimmer and model Charlene Wittstock in a civil ceremony, held in the throne room of the Palais Princier.

Prince Rainier III and Grace Kelly at their engagement party in 1956

Monaco: Monte-Carlo

The dramatic heights of Monte-Carlo are the best-known area of Monaco. People flock to the annual car rally in January and many of the world's greatest singers perform here in the opera season. Monte-Carlo is named after Charles III, who opened the first casino in 1856, to save himself from bankruptcy. Such was his success that in 1883 he abolished taxation. Although Queen Victoria thought Monte-Carlo a den of iniquity, her view was not shared by other aristocrats, including Edward VII, who were regular visitors. The stunning Casino and Opera House were built by Charles Garnier, architect of the Paris Opéra. Between Monaco-Ville and Monte-Carlo lies La Condamine, a shopping and commercial centre surrounding the luxury yachts.

View of Monte-Carlo
It is worth pausing at La Turbie *(see p93)* to admire the panorama.

Jardin Exotique
Plants normally grown in balmy climates flourish here, and its grottoes housed prehistoric animals and humans 200,000 years ago *(see p98)*.

La Condamine
The quays are pleasant yacht-watching promenades laid out by Albert I. The current prince added a water sports pool, and it is also a popular setting for funfairs.

KEY

① Palais Princier

② La Turbie

③ Eglise Ste-Dévote

④ Hôtel Hermitage

⑤ Centre de Congrès

Le Brasserie du Café de Paris
Ladies' man Edward VII was a
regular visitor to this renovated
belle époque triumph. The dessert
crêpe suzette was named after
one companion.

②

③

④

⑤

Salle Garnier
Designed by Charles Garnier
in 1878, this was where ballet
innovators such as Diaghilev and
Nijinsky congregated.

Casino
In a 3-day gambling spree
in 1891, Charles Deville
Wells turned £4,000
into a million francs,
inspiring the song, *The
Man Who Broke the Bank at
Monte-Carlo (see p98).*

Exploring Monaco

After the Vatican, Monaco is the world's smallest sovereign state. It covers 1.95 sq km (0.75 sq miles), about half the size of New York City's Central Park. Its inhabitants, 20 per cent Monégasque citizens, pay no taxes and enjoy the world's highest per capita income. Monégasque, a Ligurian language derived from Provençal French and Genoese Italian, is reflected in street names, such as *piaca* for place, *carrigiu* for rue, but the official language is French. The euro is used here and most of France's laws apply. Monaco's road network is complex, so drivers should plan routes with care.

Renowned French marine explorer Jacques Cousteau

Monaco Grand Prix, one of the major attractions of Monte-Carlo

🏰 Palais Princier

Pl du Palais. **Tel** 00 377 93 25 18 31. **Open** Apr–Oct: daily. 🖼

Monaco's seat of government is an attractive castle-palace, protected by cannons donated by Louis XIV, and sentries who change daily at 11:55am. The interior features priceless furniture and frescoes.

🏛 Museum of Vieux Monaco

2 rue Emile de Loth. **Tel** 00 377 93 50 57 28. **Open** Jun–Sep: Wed–Fri.

The museum houses a range of exhibits such as paintings, ceramics, furniture and costumes, demonstrating the heritage of Monaco. An initiative taken by the representatives of the old Monégasque families to preserve their national identity, the place allows visitors to catch a glimpse of daily life in the old days.

🎰 Casino

Pl du Casino. **Tel** 00 377 98 06 21 75. **Open** from 2pm daily. ♿
W casino-montecarlo.com

Renovated in 1878 by Charles Garnier *(see p55)*, the casino sits on a terrace with superb views of Monaco. Its interior is still decorated in *belle époque* style. Roulette is played in the opulent Salon Europe, blackjack in the Salons Privés. American games are played in the Sun Casino.

🏛 Nouveau Musée National de Monaco

Villa Sauber, 17 ave Princesse Grace. **Tel** 00 377 98 98 91 26. Villa Paloma, 56 blvd du Jardin-Exotique. **Tel** 00 377 98 98 48 60. **Open** daily. **Closed** 1 Jan, Grand Prix, 19 Nov, 25 Dec. 🖼 📷
W nmnm.mc

Two spectacular villas house this museum charting the cultural, historical and artistic heritage of the Principality. The Villa Sauber, a fine example of *belle époque* architecture, hosts entertainment exhibits. Villa Paloma, with its beautiful Italian garden, shows modern and contemporary art, architecture and design.

⛪ Cathédrale

Ave St-Martin. **Tel** 00 377 93 30 87 70. **Open** daily. ♿

The 12th-century church of St-Nicolas was replaced by this 19th-century Neo-Romanesque building in La Turbie stone. Its old altarpiece, by Louis Bréa, is by the ambulatory, with its tombs of princes and bishops. The much-mourned Princess Grace is buried here.

🏛 Musée Océanographique

Ave St-Martin. **Tel** 00 377 93 15 36 00. **Open** daily. **Closed** 1 Jan, Grand Prix, 25 Dec. 🖼 ♿ 📷 📷 Cinema.
W oceano.mc

Founded by Prince Albert I in 1910, this clifftop museum has an aquarium filled with rare marine plants and animals, a collection of shells, coral and pearls, and a life-sized model of a giant squid. Marine explorer Jacques Cousteau was director here for 30 years until 1988. The roof terrace offers superb views.

🌴 Jardin Exotique

62 blvd du Jardin Exotique. **Tel** 00 377 93 15 29 80. **Open** daily. **Closed** 19 Nov, 25 Dec. 🖼 📷 ♿ restricted.
W jardin-exotique.mc

A vast array of magnificent tropical and sub-tropical plants grow here. The adjoining **Grotte de l'Observatoire**, is where prehistoric animals lived 200,000 years ago. The **Musée d'Anthropologie Préhistorique**, accessible via the gardens, displays prehistoric tools, figurines and bones.

Roulette tables in the Salle Europe of the Casino

㉔ Peillon

Road map F3. ㊐ 1,449. ℹ 4 carriera
Centrale (06 24 97 42 25)
🆆 **tourismepaca.fr**

At a level of 373 m (1,225 ft), this
pretty *village perché* is said by
locals to mark the extremity of the
inhabited world. Its streets are
stepped and narrow, with houses
that have scarcely changed since
the Middle Ages. There is an attractive cobbled square with fine
views, and the 18th-century parish
church has an unusual octagonal
lantern. But most impressive of
all are Giovanni Canavesio's frescoes in the Chapelle des Pénitents
Blancs. Peillon is ideally placed
for woodland walks leading to
both Peille and La Turbie.

Ancient arch across a narrow street
in Peillon

㉕ Peille

Road map F3. ㊐ 2,343. 🚌 ℹ 15 rue
Centrale (04 93 82 14 40). 🆆 **peille.fr**

Peille is a charming medieval
village with a view from its war
memorial across the Peillon Valley
and as far as the Baie des Anges.
Behind the village looms the
vast Pic de Baudon, rising to
1,264 m (4,160 ft).

The town is full of cobbled
alleys and covered passages.
At the end of place A-Laugier,
beyond a Gothic fountain, two
arches beneath a house rest on
a Romanesque pillar.

The Counts of Provence were
lords of the castle, and the 12th-
century church of Ste-Marie has a
picture of Peille in the Middle Ages.
There is also a fine 16th-century

The Gorges de la Vésubie in the pine-forested Vallée de la Vésubie

altarpiece by Honoré Bertone.
The Hôtel de Ville is in the domed
18th-century former Chapelle
de St-Sébastien, and there is a
museum in rue de la Turbie.

㉖ Lucéram

Road map F3. ㊐ 1,234. 🚌
ℹ Maison de Pays, Pl Adrien Barralis
(04 93 79 46 50). 🆆 **luceram.com**

In the midst of this pretty, Italianate
village is the tiled roof of the 15th-
century Eglise Ste-Marguerite, which
contains art by Nice's Primitive
masters, notably Louis Bréa, the
artist of the 10-panelled altarpiece,
who made Lucéram a centre for
religious painting. Other treasures
include a silver statue of the
Tarascon dragon and Ste Marguerite
(*see p144*). The church is the setting
for a Christmas service, where
shepherds, accompanied by
flutes and tambourines, bring
lambs and fruit as offerings.

Italian-style houses in Lucéram, set
between two ravines

㉗ Vallée de la Vésubie

✈ Nice. 🚌 St-Martin-Vésubie.
ℹ Hotel de Ville, St-Martin-Vésubie
(04 93 03 60 10). 🆆 **vesubie-
mercantour.com**

Some of the most attractive
landscape around Nice can be
uncovered and enjoyed in the
valley of the river Vésubie, with
its dense pine forests, alpine
pastures, peaks and cascades. The
river rises high in the snowy Alps
near the Italian border, courses
past Roquebillière to the west of
the Parc National du Mercantour
(*see p101*) and dives through the
Gorges de la Vésubie before
entering the river Var, 24 km
(15 miles) north of Nice airport.

The Vésubie is created from
the Madone de Fenestre and the
Boréon torrents, which meet at
St-Martin-Vésubie. This popular
summer mountaineering centre
is surrounded by waterfalls,
summits and lakes. In its fine
17th-century church is a
12th-century statue of Notre-
Dame-de-Fenestre. Each year
this statue is carried to the
Chapelle de la Madone de
Fenestre, 12 km (8 miles) to the
east, for a three-month stay.

The Gorges de la Vésubie
begins at St-Jean-la-Rivière, and
there is a spectacular panorama
at la Madonne d'Utelle, above
the fortified village of Utelle.
In places, the dramatic gorge,
etched with coloured rock,
runs up to 244 m (800 ft) deep.
Sadly, the road beside it has few
stopping places from which to
admire the view.

Skiing in the Alpes d'Azur

Provence offers a wide range of skiing activities in the Alpes d'Azur. Around one hour from the coast, in breathtaking mountain scenery, there are more than 20 resorts, with over 250 ski-runs. The *après-ski* includes ice-skating, riding on snowmobiles and a chance to sample traditional Alpine food such as delicious melted cheese *raclette*. In summer, Auron and Isola 2000, resorts in the Parc National du Mercantour, offer swimming, cycling and horse-riding in dramatically contrasting surroundings to the Côte d'Azur.

Snowbound Valberg, a winter resort since 1935

Auron

Altitude 1,600 m (5,250 ft) – 2,100 m (6,890 ft).
Location 97 km (60 miles) from Nice via RN 202 and D 2205.
Ski Runs 43 runs – 9 black, 15 red, 16 blue, 3 green.
Ski Lifts 20 including 8 chair lifts and 3 cable cars.

Isola 2000

Altitude 2,000 m (5,250 ft) – 2,310 m (7,584 ft).
Location 90 km (56 miles) from Nice via RN 202, D 2205 and D 97.
Ski Runs 42 runs – 3 black, 11 red, 21 blue, 7 green.
Ski Lifts 22 including 2 cable cars and 9 chairlifts. Funicular railway.

Valberg

Altitude 1,500 m (4,921 ft) – 2,100 m (6,890 ft).
Location 86 km (51 miles) from Nice via RN 202, CD 28, CD 202 or CD 30.
Ski Runs 56 runs – 6 black, 28 red, 10 blue, 12 green.
Ski Lifts 23 including 6 chair lifts.

Climbing a frozen waterfall, or "frozen fall climbing", in one of the many alpine resorts

Getting ready for a few hours of snow-shoe trekking

Alpine Activities

	Auron	Isola 2000	Valberg
Cross-country skiing	●	●	●
Disabled skiing	●	●	
Horse riding	●	●	●
Horse-driven buggy rides	●	●	
Ice circuit driving		●	
Ice skating		●	●
Kart Cross on ice		●	
Mono-skiing		●	
Night skiing		●	●
Skijoring		●	
Ski jumping		●	
Ski school	●	●	●
Ski touring	●	●	
Snowboarding	●	●	●
Snow scooter circuits		●	
Snow-shoe trekking	●	●	●
Speed ski school		●	
Aquatic centre/pool, sauna and Jacuzzi	●	●	●

Snowboarding in the alpine resort of Isola 2000

28 Forêt de Turini

Road map F3. 🚌 l'Escarène, Sospel.
🚌 Moulinet, Sospel. 🛈 La Bollène
(04 93 03 60 54).

Between the warm coast and the chilly Alps, from the Gorges de la Vésubie to the Vallée de la Bévéra, lies this humid, 3,497-sq km (1,350-sq mile) forest. Beech, maple and sweet chestnut thrive here, and pines grow to great heights. At the forest's north-eastern edge is the 1,889-m (6,197-ft) mountain of l'Authion, site of heavy fighting in the German retreat of 1945. Casualties are recorded on a war memorial.

The neighbouring Pointe des Trois-Communes, at 2,082 m (6,830 ft), offers superb views of the pre-Alps of Nice and the peaks of the Mercantour national park.

29 Le Parc National du Mercantour

Road map E2 & F2. 🚌 Nice.
🚌 St Etienne de Tinée, Auron.
🛈 Maison du Parc (04 93 02 42 27).
🌐 **mercantour.eu**

Scoured by icy glaciers and bristling with rocky summits, this sparsely populated park covers 70,000 ha (270 sq miles). Among its unusual wildlife are the chamois, the ibex and the *mouflon*, a sheep which originated in Corsica. Sometimes visible in the mornings is the marmot, a rodent which is prey to golden eagles, and the exotic lammergeier, a bearded vulture with orange-red feathers and black wings. There are also many brightly coloured butterflies and alpine flowers.

Tower at Tende

30 Tende

Road map F2. 🏔 2,200. 🚌 🛈 103 ave 16 Sep 1947 (04 93 04 73 71).
♻ Wed. 🌐 **tendemerveilles.com**

Sombre Tende once guarded the mountain pass connecting Pied-mont and Provence, now bypas-sed by a tunnel. Its tall, green schist buildings appear piled on top of each other. Only a wall

Walkers above Lake Allos, Parc National du Mercantour

remains of the castle of Lascaris' feudal lords, near the cemetery above the town. Tende's unusual towers include that of the 15th-century church of **Notre-Dame-de-l'Assomption**. Lions support the pillars around the Renaissance doorway and there are green schist columns inside.

The **Vallée des Merveilles**, the most spectacular part of Mercantour national park, can be visited with a guide. For information, contact the tourist office at Tende or St-Dalmas.
The most direct route starts from Lac des Mesches car park. A two-and-a-half-hour walk leads to Lac Long and Le Refuge des Merveilles. The Mont Bégo area has 36,000 engravings, dating from 2,000 BC, carved into the rock face. They reveal a Bronze Age culture of shepherds and farmers.
In Tende, the **Musée des Merveilles** is worth a visit. Southeast of Tende, there are fine paintings in the church at La Brigue. Jean Canavesio's 15th-century frescoes of *La Passion du Christ,* and the lurid *Judas pendu* are in the nearby **Chapelle Notre-Dame-des-Fontaines**.

🏛 Musée des Merveilles

Ave du 16 Septembre 1947. **Tel** 04 93 04 32 50. **Open** daily (Oct–Jun: Wed–Mon). **Closed** public hols, 2 weeks mid-Mar & mid-Nov. ♿ 📷

31 Saorge

Road map F3. 🏔 450. 🚌 🛈 La Mairie, Avenue Docteur Joseph Davéo (04 93 04 51 23). 🌐 **saorge.fr**

Saorge is the prettiest spot in the Roya Valley. Set in a natural amphitheatre high over the river, its slate-roofed houses are tiered between narrow alleys, in the style of a typical stacked village or *village empilé*.

Olive-wood carvings are traditional, and carved lintels date many houses to the 15th century, when Saorge was a stronghold. It was taken by the French under Masséna in 1794.

Churches range from the dank 15th-century St-Sauveur with an Italian organ to the Baroque church of the Franciscan monas-tery and the octagonal tower and Renaissance frescoes of **La Madone-del-Poggio** (open during European Heritage days only).

View of Saorge from the Franciscan monastery terrace

32 Sospel

Road map F3. 3,650. 📷 🚌
ℹ️ 19 ave Jean Medecin (04 93 04
15 80). 🗓️ Thu, Sun. 🌐 sospel-
tourisme.com

This charming resort has a
13th-century toll tower, which
was restored after bomb
damage in World War II, when
the town's bravery earned it the
Croix de Guerre. Fort St-Roch,
built in 1932 as protection
against a possible Italian
invasion, has a museum with
exhibits on the Maginot line.
The church of St-Michel
contains one of François Bréa's
best works, and has a lovely
façade, as does the Palais Ricci.
The interior of the White
Penitent chapel is magnificent.

🏛️ **Musée Maginot de la Seconde
Guerre Mondiale**
Fort St-Roch. **Tel** 04 93 04 00 70.
Open Apr–Jun & Sep: Sat, Sun & public
hols pm; Jul & Aug: Tue–Sun pm. 🎟️

Impressive *trompe l'oeil* façades of houses
in Sospel

33 Gorbio

Road map F3. 1,300. 🚌 ℹ️ La
Mairie, 30 rue Garibaldi (04 92 10 66 50).

More than a thousand species
of flowers have been identified
in the sunny Gorbio valley, which
produces vegetables, as well as
fruit, wine and oil. Until the last
century the area was entirely
supported by its olive production.
Often shrouded in mist in the
mornings, Gorbio itself is a
village perché (see pp24–5), with
sea views. The old Malaussène
fountain stands by the entrance
to the narrow cobbled lanes,
and an elm tree in the square
was planted in 1713. The church

Early morning Gorbio, surrounded by olive groves

has a conical belfry, a typical
feature of the region. Each June a
procession marks the Penitents'
ritual, when the village lanes
twinkle with the lights from oil
lamps made from snail shells.
A good hour's walk from
Gorbio is Ste-Agnès, at 671 m
(2,200 ft) it is the highest *village
perché* on the coast.

34 Roquebrune-Cap-Martin

Road map F3. 12,800. 🚌 🚌
ℹ️ 218 ave Aristide Briand (04 93 35
62 87). 🗓️ Wed. 🌐 roquebrune-
cap-martin.com

Roquebrune is said to have
the earliest feudal **château** in
France, the sole example of the
Carolingian style. Built in the
10th century by Conrad I, Count
of Ventimiglia, to ward off
Saracen attack, it was later
remodelled by the Grimaldis
(see p95). Wealthy Englishman
Sir William Ingram, one of the
first wave of tourist residents,

View of Château Grimaldi de Roquebrune,
overlooking Cap Martin

bought the château in 1911
and added a mock medieval
tour anglaise.
At the turn of the century,
Cap Martin was the Côte d'Azur's
smartest resort, attracting the
era's glitterati. Empératrice
Eugénie, wife of Napoléon III,
wintered here. Winston Churchill,
Coco Chanel and Irish poet W B
Yeats also visited. Architect Le
Corbusier, who drowned off the
cape in 1965, has a coastal path
named after him.
A number of important prehistoric remains have been found
around Roquebrune, some in caves
such as the **Grotte du Vallonet**.
Just outside the village, on the
Menton road, is the *olivier millénaire*,
one of the oldest olive trees in
the world, which is believed to
be at least 1,000 years old.
Every August since 1467, in
gratitude for being spared from
the plague, Roquebrune's
inhabitants take part in scenes
from the Passion *(see p37)*.

🏰 **Château Grimaldi de
Roquebrune**
Pl William Ingram **Tel** 04 93 35 07 22.
Open daily. **Closed** Fri (Nov–Dec),
public hols. 🎟️

35 Menton

Road map F3. 29,670. 📷 🚌
ℹ️ Palais de l'Europe, 8 ave Boyer
(04 92 41 76 76). 🗓️ Tue–Sun.
🌐 tourisme-menton.fr

Just a mile from the border,
Menton is the most Italian of
the French resorts. Tucked in by
mountains, it is a sedate town
with a Baroque square and a
promenade stretching towards
Cap Martin.

Menton has several fine tropical gardens, and citrus fruits thrive in a climate mild enough for the lemon festival in February (see p39). The **Palais de l'Europe** of the *belle époque* (1909), once a casino, now a cultural centre, is beside the **Jardin Biovès**. The **Jardin Botanique Exotique** has tropical plants and is in the grounds of Villa Val Rahmeh. Above the town is the **Jardin des Colombières** designed by artist and writer Ferdinand Bac (1859–1952). This private garden reputedly has France's oldest carob tree and can be visited in the summer by appointment.

The jetties offer good views of the old town, and steps lead to Parvis St-Michel, a fine square paved with the Grimaldi coat of arms, where summer concerts are held. To the left side are the twin towers of the Baroque **Basilica St-Michel**, its main altarpiece by Manchello (1565). Behind the marina is Garavan where New Zealand writer Katherine Mansfield lived, in the Villa Isola Bella, from 1920–22.

🏛 Musée des Beaux-Arts

Palais Carnolès, 3 ave de la Madone. **Tel** 04 93 35 49 71. **Open** Wed–Mon. **Closed** public hols. 🅿

The 17th-century palace, now Menton's main art museum, was once the summer residence of the princes of Monaco. It has paintings by Graham Sutherland (1903–80), an honorary citizen, 13th- to 18th-century Italian, French and Flemish art, and works by Utrillo and Dufy.

🏛 Salle des Mariages

Mairie de Menton, Pl Ardoino. **Tel** 04 92 10 50 00. **Open** Mon–Fri. **Closed** public hols. 🅿

Jean Cocteau decorated this room in 1957 with colourful images of a fisherman and his bride, and the less happy story of Orpheus and Eurydice, and Provençal motifs such as using a fish for a fisherman's eye.

🏛 Musée Jean Cocteau – Collection Severin Wundermun

2 quai de Monléon. **Tel** 04 89 81 52 50. **Open** Wed–Mon. **Closed** 1 Jan, 1 May, 1 Nov, 25 Dec. 🅿

W museecocteaumenton.com

Cocteau supervised the conversion of this former 17th-century fort into his museum. He designed the mosaic on the ground floor, and donated his first tapestry and other pieces.

🏰 Cimetière du Vieux-Château

Rue du Vieux-Château. **Tel** 04 93 57 95 99.

Each terrace of this former castle site accommodates a separate faith. Webb Ellis, inventor of rugby, is buried here, as is Rasputin's assassin, Prince Youssoupov.

🏛 Musée de Préhistoire Régionale

Rue Loredan Larchey. **Tel** 04 93 35 84 64. **Open** Wed–Mon. **Closed** public hols.

The museum's fine local history and archaeological pieces include the skull of 30,000-year-old "Grimaldi Man".

Jean Cocteau (1889–1963)

Born near Paris in 1889, Cocteau spent much of his very public life around the Côte d'Azur. A man of powerful intellect and great élan, he became a member of the Académie Française in 1955. Among other talents, Cocteau was a dramatist (*La Machine Infernale, 1934*); the writer of *Les Enfants Terribles* (1929), and a surrealist film director. *Orphée* (1950) was partly shot against the barren landscape at Les Baux (see p146). He died before his museum opened in 1967.

Mosaic at the entrance of the Musée Jean Cocteau in Menton

View over Menton from Ferdinand Bac's Jardin des Colombières

THE VAR AND THE ILES D'HYÈRES

The Var is a region of rolling lands, rocky hills, thick forests and swathes of vineyards. To the north, Provençal villages are thinly scattered by mountain streams, on hilltops and in valleys; to the south, a series of massifs slope down to the coast making this stretch of the Côte d'Azur the most varied and delightful shore in France.

Through the centre of the Var, dividing it roughly into two sections, runs the A8 autoroute. To the south of this artery the influence of the sea is unmistakable. Toulon, the departmental capital, occupies a fine deep-water harbour that is home to the French Mediterranean fleet. Beyond it are the pleasant resorts of Bandol and Sanary, where Jacques Cousteau first put scuba-diving to the test. To the east are the sandy beaches beneath the great slab of the Massif des Maures. The Var's most famous resort, St-Tropez, facing north in the crook of a bay, lies in a glorious landscape of vineyards. Beyond it, just past Fréjus, the first Roman settlement in Gaul, the land turns blood red in the twinkling inlets and coves below the beautiful Corniche de l'Esterel, which heads east towards the Riviera. The more remote areas to the north of the autoroute have always provided a retreat from the bustling activity of the coast. This is where the Cistercians built their austere Abbaye du Thoronet. Today visitors escape inland from the summer traffic around St-Tropez to the sparsely populated Haut Var, where towns seem to grow from tufa rock.

Highlights include wines from the Côtes de Provence, and fresh tuna from quayside restaurants. Music enthusiasts should spare time to hear both the organ at St-Maximin-la-Ste-Baume, Provence's finest Gothic building, and the string quartets at the festival in the hill towns near Fayence. Visitors can also go walking, sailing and sunbathing, and enjoy a rich collection of museums and architecture.

Sunrise over the boats in St-Tropez harbour

◀ The meandering Corniche de l'Esterel, St-Raphaël

Exploring the Var and the Iles d'Hyères

The Var *département* covers about 6,000 sq km (2,300 sq miles). It combines a stunning coastline sprinkled with red cliffs, delightful bays and the Iles d'Hyères, which spill out from its southernmost point, with dramatic chains of hills, rising up behind the coast and further inland. The slopes of the Massif des Maures and the Haut Var are home to a fascinating array of flora and fauna, as well as to the many producers of Côtes-de-Provence wines.

View of the Abbaye du Thoronet

Sights at a Glance

Key

═══ Motorway
═══ Major road
─── Secondary road
┄┄┄ Minor road
─── Scenic route
╺╾╺ Main railway
─── Minor railway
═══ Regional border
△ Summit

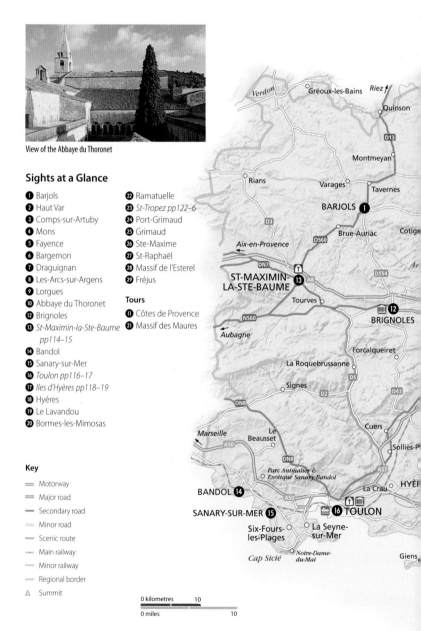

For additional map symbols *see back flap*

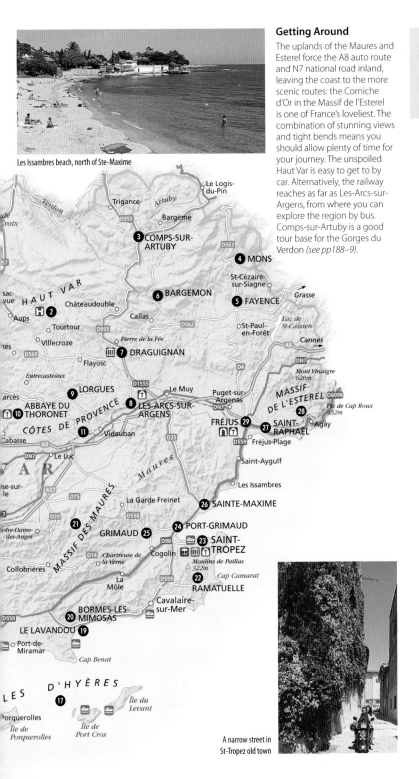

Les Issambres beach, north of Ste-Maxime

Getting Around

The uplands of the Maures and Esterel force the A8 auto route and N7 national road inland, leaving the coast to the more scenic routes: the Corniche d'Or in the Massif de l'Esterel is one of France's loveliest. The combination of stunning views and tight bends means you should allow plenty of time for your journey. The unspoiled Haut Var is easy to get to by car. Alternatively, the railway reaches as far as Les-Arcs-sur-Argens, from where you can explore the region by bus. Comps-sur-Artuby is a good tour base for the Gorges du Verdon (see pp188–9).

A narrow street in
St-Tropez old town

A traditional flute-maker at work in Barjols

❶ Barjols

Road map D4. 🏔 3,135. 🚌 *i* Blvd Grisolle (04 94 77 20 01). 🛍 Sun.
🌐 ot-barjols.provenceverte.fr

Once renowned for its seething tanneries, Barjols lies peacefully among woods and fast-flowing streams. In 1983, after almost 400 years, the leather industry finally folded. The many abandoned factories have become bustling artisans' studios.

Today, it is these local craftsmen who bring manufacturing acclaim to the area. Two traditional Provençal instruments, the three-holed flute (*galoubet*) and the narrow drums (*tambourins*), were still made in Barjols until recently.

These instruments resound each January at the annual *fête* of St-Marcel, the town's patron saint. About every four years the ceremony includes the slaughter and roasting of an ox in the square. This is followed by a colourful "tripe dance" inside and outside the 11th-century church of Notre-Dame-de-l'Assomption, where St-Marcel's relics can be seen. The ceremony commemorates the survival of the town after a siege in 1350. For information about roastings contact the tourist office.

Of the many stone fountains dotted around the town, the most famous is the mossy *Champignon* in place Capitaine Vincens. It stands under what is reputed to be the largest plane tree in Provence. Between the church and the old tanneries are the restored buildings of the old quartier du Réal. Exotic porticoes, particularly on the Renaissance Hôtel de Pontevès, add spice to some otherwise drab streets.

❷ Haut Var

Road map D3. 🛬 Toulon-Hyères, Nice. 🚊 Les Arcs. 🚌 Aups. *i* Pl Frédéric Mistral, Aups (04 94 84 00 69).
🌐 aups-tourisme.com

The most remote and unspoiled lands of the Var are situated between Barjols and Comps-sur-Artuby, up towards the Gorges du Verdon (*see pp188–9*). Much of the land near here has been taken over by the military.

Aups, set among undulating hills on the plateau edge, is the region's centre. Epicureans may be drawn by the local honey, olive oil and the truffle market each Thursday morning in winter. It is an attractive town with a grand old square and castle ruins. The 15th-century St-Pancrace church has a Renaissance doorway. Also worth a visit is the **Musée Simon Segal**, which is housed in a former Ursuline convent. The museum contains works by Segal and Paris painters, as well as local scenes.

About 5 km (3 miles) north-west on the D9 is the village of Moissac-Bellevue. Many of its buildings date from the 16th and 17th centuries and its church was mentioned in a papal edict of 1225.

View of Entrecasteaux château near Cotignac, Haut Var

South from Aups is Villecroze. The town is set against a natural backdrop of caves on three levels, which local lords in the 16th century turned into dwellings, known as the **Grottes Troglodytiques**. The arcaded streets and the keep of the feudal castle give the town a medieval flavour. A short drive from Villecroze leads up to the hill village of Tourtour, a smaller, prettier and more popular place. Renowned French expressionist painter Bernard Buffet lived his last days here. Two of his creations – large, metal-built insect sculptures are still displayed in the village.

The valley town of Salernes lies in the opposite direction, 10 km (6 miles) west on the D51. Smoke pumps from the

Troglodyte dwellings in Villecroze

The 110 m (361 ft) Artuby bridge spanning the Canyon du Verdon

kilns of its 15 ceramic factories. Salernes is one of the best-known Provençal tile-making centres, noted for *tomettes* – hexagonal terracotta floor-tiles.

Cotignac, west of Salernes, is an echo of Villecroze, with a cave-pocked cliff behind it. Behind the *mairie*, a river springs from the rocks and beyond is an open-air theatre.

The region's most intriguing château is **Entrecasteaux**, 15 km (8 miles) east of Cotignac. The 17th-century castle is filled with the present owner's 17th- to 18th-century collection of paintings, artifacts, tapestries and furniture. The garden, by Le Nôtre, is publicly owned.

🏛 Musée Simon Segal
Rue Albert Premier, Aups. **Tel** 04 94 70 00 07. **Open** Jun–Sep: Wed–Mon.

🏚 Grottes Troglodytiques
Villecroze. **Tel** 04 94 70 63 06. **Open** Apr–Jun: Fri–Mon; Jul–Sep: daily. 🅿

🏰 Château d'Entrecasteaux
83570 Entrecasteaux.
Tel 04 94 04 43 95. **Open** Sun–Fri.
Closed Oct–Easter. 🅿 🅿
W chateau-entrecasteaux.com

❸ Comps-sur-Artuby

Road map D3. 🚗 338. 🚌 **ℹ** La Mairie, Ave de Charnay (04 94 76 92 91).

The eastern approach to the Gorges du Verdon *(see pp188–9)* passes through Comps-sur-Artuby. The village nestles at the foot of a rock topped by the 13th-century chapel of **St-André**, which has been restored. From the church there are grand views of the Artuby Gorges.

To the east lies Bargème, a village of steep streets and hollyhocks with a population of just 86. At 1,094 m (3,589 ft) it is the highest community in the Var. The village itself is closed to all traffic.

Dominating Bargème is a large, partially ruined but nevertheless remarkably well preserved 14th-century castle. Also worth a visit is the 13th-century Romanesque **Eglise St-Nicolas** which contains a carved, wooden altarpiece depicting Saint Sebastian.

❹ Mons

Road map E3. 🚗 885. 🚌
ℹ Pl St Sébastien (04 94 76 39 54).

Dramatically situated on a rock-spur, Mons, with its tiny lanes and overhanging arches, has an almost magical appeal. The place St-Sébastien looks out across the entire coast, from Italy to Toulon.

Originally a Celtic-Ligurian settlement, its Château-Vieux quarter dates from the 10th century, but it was mainly built by Genoese who repopulated the village after ravages by the plague in the 14th century. The first families came in 1461 from Figounia near Ventimiglia; their legacy is the local dialect, *figoun*, which still survives thanks to the unusually isolated position of the village. Nearby is the *roche taillée*, a Roman aqueduct carved from solid rock. There are also many dolmens in the surrounding area.

One of the quiet streets of the picturesque village of Mons

Truffles

This richly flavoured and treasured fungal delicacy of the Var is traditionally sniffed out by trained pigs. The golfball-sized truffles are collected during the winter, when they are at their most fragrant, from underground near the roots of oak trees. Local markets specialize in truffles when they are in season, though their rarity means that they tend to be very expensive.

A trained pig hunting for truffles

View over Bargemon's terracotta rooftops to the wooded hills beyond

❺ Fayence

Road map E3. 🏔 5,500. 🚌
i Pl Léon Roux (04 94 76 20 08).
🛒 Tue, Thu, Sat. **w** ville-fayence.fr

The hillside town of Fayence is the largest between Draguignan and Grasse and is an international centre for local crafts as well as gliding. Dominated by a wrought-iron clock tower, it still has a few remains of its 14th-century defences including a Saracen-style gate.

The **Eglise St-Jean-Baptiste** was built in the 18th century with a baroque marble altar (1757) by a local mason, Dominique Fossatti. Its terrace offers a sweeping view over the town's glider airfield.

On the hillside opposite, in the community of Tourettes, there is a striking château. Part

modelled on the Cadet school in St Petersburg, it was constructed in 1824 for General Alexandre Fabre, who once worked as a military engineer for Tsar Alexander I of Russia. He originally intended to make the building a public museum, but failed to finish the task and so it remains private.

There are a number of attractive villages nearby. Among the best are Callian and Montauroux to the east and Seillans, 5 km (3 miles) to the west, where the German-born painter Max Ernst (1891–1976) chose to spend his last years. The prestigious Musique en Pays de Fayence festival in October brings string quartets who perform in some of the charming local churches.

❻ Bargemon

Road map E3. 🏔 1,550. 🚉 Les Arcs.
🚌 *i* Ave Pasteur (04 94 47 81 73).
🛒 Thu. **w** ot-bargemon.fr

This medieval village, fortified in AD 950, has three 12th-century gates and a tower from the mid-16th-century. The village is laid out around a number of squares with fountains, shaded by plane trees.

The angels' heads on the high altar of the 15th-century church, **St-Etienne**, now the Musée-Galerie Honoré Camos, are attributed to the school of Pierre Puget, like those in the **Chapelle Notre-Dame-de-Montaigu** above the town. The chapel also contains an oak-wood carving of the Virgin brought here in 1635. The **Fossil and Mineral Museum** on rue de la Résistance displays over 3,000 pieces.

❼ Draguignan

Road map D4. 🏔 38,317. 🚌 *i* 2 ave Lazare Carnot (04 98 10 51 05). 🛒 Wed, Sat. **w** tourisme-dracenie.com

During the day, the former capital of the Var *département* has the busy air of a small market town. At night, however, the only sign of life is groups of young people in the place des Herbes. Baron Haussmann, planner of modern Paris, laid out

Traditional Pottery and Crafts

Cotignac, Aups and Salernes are at the centre of an exciting revitalization of Provençal crafts, which includes weaving, pottery, stone and wood carving. A regional speciality is hand-crafted domestic pottery made using traditional techniques and designs, as well as local clays in a wonderful variety of colours. Examples of all these crafts can be found in small shops and studios, or craft fairs and local markets. There are good buys to be had, but do shop around to avoid being unknowingly overcharged.

A Provençal potter at work

Draguignan's 19th-century boulevards. At the end of his plane-tree-lined allées d'Azémar, there is a Rodin bust of the prime minister Georges Clemenceau (1841–1929) who represented Draguignan for 25 years.

The main interest lies in the pedestrianized old town. Its 24-m (79-ft) clockless clock tower, built in 1663, stands on the site of the original keep and there is a good view from its wrought-iron campanile. The **Eglise St-Michel**, in the place de la Paroisse, contains a statue of St Hermentaire, first bishop of Antibes. In the 5th century he slew a local dragon, giving the town its name.

Draguignan has two good local museums. The **Musée des Arts et Traditions Provençales** is concerned with the region's

St Hermentaire slaying the dragon

social and economic history. It occupies buildings that date back to the 17th century. Regional country life is illustrated using reconstructed kitchens and barns. Exhibits include beautiful hand-painted wooden horses. The **Musée Municipal d'Art et d'Histoire** shows local and regional archaeology as well as eye-catching collections of both ceramics and furniture. The adjoining library houses a lavishly illuminated 14th-century manuscript of the *Roman de la Rose*, considered to be the most important book of courtly love *(see p146)* in France (by appointment only).

Northwest of the town on the D955 is the enormous prehistoric dolmen Pierre de la Fée, or Fairy Stone *(see p43)*.

🏛 **Musée des Arts et Traditions Provençales**
15 rue Joseph-Roumanille. **Tel** 04 94 47 05 72. **Open** Tue–Sat, Sun pm. **Closed** 1 May, 25 Dec. 🅿 🎦 ♿ ltd.

🏛 **Musée Municipal d'Art et d'Histoire**
9 rue de la République. **Tel** 04 98 10 26 85. **Open** Tue–Sat. **Closed** public hols. ♿

Pierre de la Fée, the giant dolmen outside Draguignan

❽ Les-Arcs-sur-Argens

Road map D4. 🚶 7,153. 🚃 🚌
ℹ Place du Général de Gaulle (04 94 73 37 30). 🛍 Thu.
🌐 **tourisme-dracenie.com**

Wine centre for the Côtes de Provence *(see pp112–3)*, Les Arcs has a medieval quarter, Le Parage, based around the 13th-century Château de Villeneuve. The **Eglise St-Jean-Baptiste** (1850), in the rue de la République, contains a screen by Louis Bréa (1501).

East of Les Arcs on the D91 is the 11th-century Abbaye de Ste-Roseline, which was named

after Roseline de Villeneuve, daughter of Arnaud de Villeneuve, Baron of Arcs. Legend has it that when Roseline's father stopped her while taking food to the poor, her provisions turned into roses. She entered the abbey in 1300 and later became its abbess.

The Romanesque **Chapelle Ste-Roseline** contains the well-preserved body of the saint in a glass shrine. There is also a famous Chagall mosaic *(see p31)*.

🔼 **Chapelle Ste-Roseline**
RD 91, Les Arcs-sur-Argens. **Tel** 04 94 73 37 30. **Open** Tue–Sun pm. **Closed** Jan, mid-Mar, public hols. ♿

Mosaic by Marc Chagall (1887–1985) in the Chapelle Ste-Roseline

❾ Lorgues

Road map D4. 🗺 9,341. 🚌
ℹ️ 12 rue du 8 mai (04 94 73 92 37).
📅 Tue. 🌐 lorgues-tourisme.fr

Nestling on a slope beneath oak and pine woodland, Lorgues is surrounded by vineyards and olive groves. Its old town was fortified in the 12th century. Today, two 14th-century gates and city wall remains can be seen. The town centre's handsome square is shaded by a large plane tree. Lorgues has many 18th-century municipal buildings and monuments and one of France's longest plane-tree avenues.

In the centre of town is the stately **Collégiale St-Martin**, consecrated in 1788. Its organ, dating from 1857, is the finest example of the work of the Augustin Zeiger factory, Lyon. Also on display is a marble Virgin and Child (1694) which came from the Abbaye du Thoronet and is attributed to the school of Pierre Puget.

❿ Abbaye du Thoronet

Road map D4. 83340 Le Thoronet.
Tel 04 94 60 43 90. **Open** daily.
Closed 1 Jan, 1 May, 1 & 11 Nov, 25 Dec. 🚫 🔊 📷 📱

Founded in 1146, Le Thoronet was the first Cistercian building in Provence. Lost in deep woodland, it occupies a typically remote site. Along

Graceful cloisters on the north side of the Abbaye du Thoronet

with the two Romanesque abbeys of Sénanque (see pp168–9) and Silvacane (see p151), it is known as one of the three "Cistercian sisters" of Provence.

The cool geometry of the church, cloister, dormitory and chapter house reflects the austerity of Cistercian principles. Only the bell tower breaks with the order's strict building regulations: instead of wood, it is made of stone, to enable it to withstand the strong Provençal winds.

Dilapidated by the 1400s, the abbey was finally abandoned in 1791. Its restoration, like that of many medieval Provençal buildings, was instigated by Prosper Mérimée, Romantic novelist and Napoleon III's Inspector of Historic Monuments, who visited in 1834.

Just beside the abbey is the modern Monastère de Bethléem, home to Cistercian nuns.

⓫ Côtes de Provence Tour

The Côtes de Provence wine-growing region reaches from the Haut Var to the coast. Dozens of roadside vineyards offer tastings and a chance to buy. This rural route suggests a few accessible and well-regarded producers, starting at the Maison des Vins in Les Arcs. Here you can find out about local wines, plot your own route, buy wine from the producers, and even book to stay at a vineyard. The tour passes a few interesting towns en route. For more information on the region's wines, *see pages 206–7*.

⑥ Entrecasteaux
From Entrecasteaux, dominated by its huge 17th-century château, follow signs for Les Saigues to find Château Mentone.

L Saigu

Château Mentone

D50

⑥

D31

Tips for Drivers

Tour length: 100 km (62 miles).
Stopping-off points: The Maison des Vins should be your first stopping point – it is open all day. Around the route motorists should have no difficulty in spotting places to stop and sample, though many of the wine producers close between noon and 2pm. The Lac de Carcès makes a good place for a picnic. *(See also pp250–51.)*

D562 Argens D562

⑤

D13

Domaine de l'Abbaye

D79

④ **Le Thoronet**
The Domaine de l'Abbaye vineyard is named after Le Thoronet's beautiful abbey.

D13

⑤ **Carcès**
As you head north, the Lac de Carcès is on the left in a steep valley. The town's castle remains and gardens are worth seeing.

Key

▬▬▬ Tour route
═══ Other roads

La Gayole sarcophagus, dating from the 2nd or 3rd century, in the Musée du Pays Brignolais

⑫ Brignoles

Road map D4. 🔼 16,881. 🚌
ℹ️ Carrefour de l'Europe (04 94 72 04 21). 🛒 Sat. 🌐 **ot-brignoles. provenceverte.fr**

Bauxite mines have stained the Brignoles countryside red: vital to the region's economy, over a million tonnes of metal are mined here annually. The medieval town remains above it all, quiet and empty for most of the year. An unexpected delight is the **Musée du Pays Brignolais** in a 12th-century castle that was built as a summer retreat for the Counts of Provence. The eclectic collection includes La Gayole marble sarcophagus, which is carved with images in both the pagan and Christian traditions; a boat made of cement designed by J Lambot (1814–87), who gave the world reinforced concrete; and a collection of votive offerings. St Louis, bishop of Toulouse and patron of Brignoles, was born in a palace beside the Eglise St-Sauveur in 1274. The church has a 12th-century portico and a side entrance in the rue du Grand Escalier.

🏛️ **Musée du Pays Brignolais**
2 place des Comtes de Provence. **Tel** 04 94 69 45 18. **Open** Apr–Sep: Wed–Sun; Oct–Mar: Wed–Sat. **Closed** 1 Jan, Easter, 1 May, 1 Nov, 25 Dec. ♿ 🌐 **museebrignolais.com**

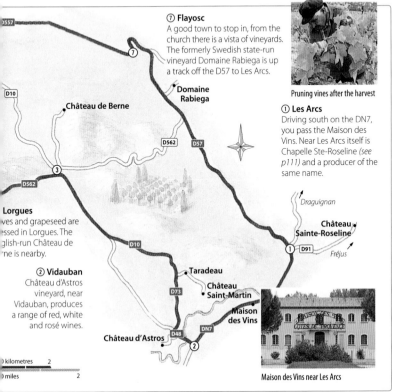

⑦ Flayosc
A good town to stop in, from the church there is a vista of vineyards. The formerly Swedish state-run vineyard Domaine Rabiega is up a track off the D57 to Les Arcs.

Pruning vines after the harvest

① Les Arcs
Driving south on the DN7, you pass the Maison des Vins. Near Les Arcs itself is Chapelle Ste-Roseline (see p111) and a producer of the same name.

D557

⑦

Domaine Rabiega

D10

Château de Berne

D562 D57

③

D562

Lorgues
...ves and grapeseed are ...essed in Lorgues. The ...glish-run Château de ...ne is nearby.

D10

② Vidauban
Château d'Astros vineyard, near Vidauban, produces a range of red, white and rosé wines.

Taradeau

D73

Château Saint-Martin

Maison des Vins

Château d'Astros

D48 DN7

②

Draguignan

Château Sainte-Roseline

① D91

Fréjus

0 kilometres 2

0 miles 2

Maison des Vins near Les Arcs

⓭ St-Maximin-la-Ste-Baume

Surrounded by hills and vineyards, St-Maximin-la- Ste-Baume is dominated by the basilica Ste-Marie-Madeleine and its attached monastery. According to Provençal tradition, the basilica was built on the site of the tombs of St Mary Magdalene and of St Maximin, legendary first bishop of Aix *(see pp152–3)*. The saints' remains, hidden from the Saracens *(see pp46–7)*, were rediscovered in 1279. The building, started 16 years later by Charles II, Count of Provence, is the region's finest example of Gothic architecture.

Sarcophagus of St Cedonius
This is one of four 4th-century saints' sarcophagi in the crypt, which was once the burial vault of a Roman villa.

★ **Relics of St Mary Magdalene**
This bronze gilt reliquary (1860) holds the skull of St Mary Magdalene. Although pilgrim popes and princes took away other parts of her body, the majority of her relics can still be found here.

★ **Ronzen's Retable** (1517–1520)
Antoine Ronzen's wood retable and surrounding panels include the first picture of the Papal Palace in Avignon *(see pp48–9)*.

KEY

① **The apse** was completed in the early 14th century. The present Baroque-style arrangement was finished in 1697.

② **Stairs to crypt**

③ **Former refectory**

★ **Organ**
One of the finest in France, with 2,962 pipes, the organ was built between 1772 and 1774 by Jean-Esprit Isnard. Napoleon's brother Lucien saved it in the Revolution by having the *Marseillaise* played on it whenever a visiting official arrived to dismantle the organ for its metal.

Basilica Entrance
The western side of the basilica has three matching wooden doors. They feature studied carving that contrasts sharply with the surrounding façade, which appears to have been crudely chopped off. When work stopped on the building in 1532, this part was left unfinished.

VISITORS' CHECKLIST

Practical Information
Road map D4. **i** Place de l'Hôtel de Ville. **Tel** 04 94 59 84 59. Basilica and Monastery: **Open** 8:30am–6pm daily (except during services). **†** 6pm Sat, 10:30am Sun; call 04 94 78 00 19 for details of weekday services. **&** basilica only. **w** lesamisdela basilique.fr

Hôtel de Ville
The town hall, planned and constructed between 1750 and 1779, was formerly the pilgrims' hostelry.

Milestone
Discovered along the Roman Aurelian Way *(see p129)*, this 1st-century milestone is now on display at the entrance to the cloisters.

Cloisters
The cloisters are at the centre of the Royal Monastery, so called because the French kings were its priors. The Domincan friars left in 1957 and it is now a hotel-restaurant.

Boats in the colourful, palm-fringed harbour at Sanary-sur-Mer

⑭ Bandol

Road map C4. 🏔 7,745. 🚃 🚌
ℹ Allée Alfred Vivien (04 94 29 41 35).
🛒 daily. 🆆 **bandoltourisme.fr**

Tucked away in a bay, this cheerful resort has a tree-lined promenade, casino and yachting harbour. The shelter of encircling hills makes for excellent grape-growing conditions. Indeed, Bandol has produced superb wines since 600 BC.

⑮ Sanary-sur-Mer

Road map C4. 🏔 16,200.
🚌 Ollioules-Sanary. 🚃 ℹ Maison du Tourisme, 1 quai du Levant (04 94 74 01 04). 🛒 Wed.
🆆 **sanary-tourisme.com**

In the agreeable, clear blue waters of Sanary-sur-Mer, the diver Jacques Cousteau's experiments to develop the modern aqualung took place. Diving and fishing (mainly for tuna and swordfish) are still popular pursuits in this delightful resort, where rows of pink and white houses line the bay. Its name derives loosely from St-Nazaire; the lovely local 19th-century church took the saint's name in its entirety. Dating from about 1300, the

One of the popular wine labels of Bandol

landmark medieval tower in the town still contains the cannon that saw off an Anglo-Sardinian fleet in 1707. It is now part of a hotel. Sanary-sur-Mer has enticed visitors for many years. Once the home of the British writer Aldous Huxley (1894–1963), it was a haven between the wars for innumerable other authors. Bertolt Brecht (1898–1956) and Thomas Mann (1875–1955) fled here from Nazi Germany.

To the east of Sanary, the coast becomes dramatic and rocky. By the peninsula's extremity at the Cap Sicié is the **Notre-Dame-du-Mai** chapel, which was built in the 17th century. A pilgrimage destination full of votive offerings, its stepped approach offers a wonderful panorama over the coast and surrounding hills.

Outside town, the **Parc Animalier & Exotique Sanary-Bandol** has wildlife and tropical plants.

🏰 Parc Animalier & Exotique Sanary-Bandol
131 ave Pont d'Aran, Sanary-sur-Mer.
Tel 04 94 29 40 38. **Open** Feb–Oct: daily; Nov–Jan: Wed, Sat & Sun.
Closed public hols am. 🐾 ♿ 📷
🆆 **zoaparc.com**

⑯ Toulon

Road map D4. 🏔 167,168. ✈ 🚉
🚌 ⛴ ℹ 12 place Louis Blanc (04 94 18 53 00). 🛒 Tue–Sun.
🆆 **toulontourisme.com**

Tucked into a fine natural harbour, Toulon is home to France's Mediterranean fleet. In the old town, or along the quays of the Darse Vieille, the *matelots* and the bars reinforce the maritime connection.

In Roman times, Toulon was renowned for its sea snails *(murex)* which, when boiled, produced an imperial-quality purple dye. During the reign of Louis XIV, Pierre Puget (1620–94) was in charge of the port's decoration. Two of his best-known works now support the town-hall balcony. These are

Ornate Baroque entrance to the Musée de la Marine

Strength and *Tiredness*, his 1657 carved marble figures of Atlantes.

The port was extensively damaged in World War II by the Allies and Nazis. Today, much of the town is under restoration. Toulon has a large opera house and several interesting museums, including the **Musée des Arts Asiatiques** located in the Villa Jules Verne, which has been entirely re-designed to house it.

🏛 Musée National de la Marine

Place Monsenergue. **Tel** 04 22 42 02 01. **Open** Wed–Mon (Jul-Aug daily). **Closed** 15 Dec–Jan. 🌐 🛈 restricted. 🅿

Imposing statues of Mars and Bellona decorate the grand entrance, once the gateway to the 17th-century city arsenal that stretched for more than 240 ha (595 acres) behind it.

Inside, the museum boasts two vast model galleons, *La Sultane* (1765) and *Duquesne* (1790), used for training. Some figureheads and ships' prows are on show, as are two wooden figures that were carved by Pierre Puget, and various 18th-century naval instruments.

🏛 Musée d'Art de Toulon

113 blvd du Maréchal Leclerc. **Tel** 04 94 36 81 01. **Open** Tue–Sun pm only. **Closed** public hols. 🛈 limited.

A permanent collection of traditional and contemporary Provençal paintings makes up the core of this small but illuminating museum. Works by international artists are often included in the first-floor temporary exhibitions.

🏛 Musée du Vieux Toulon

69 cours Lafayette. **Tel** 04 94 92 29 23. **Open** Tue–Sat pms. **Closed** public hols. This quaint museum features the young Napoleon and his

endeavours in the defence of Toulon, as well as old weapons and a number of historical sketches by Puget.

⛪ Cathédrale Ste-Marie-de-la-Seds

Place de la Cathédrale. **Tel** 04 94 92 28 91. **Open** daily.

Directly inland from the town hall, in the Darse Vieille, is the city's 11th-century cathedral. It was treated to a Classical face-lift and extended in the 1600s.

Inside, there are works by Puget and Jean Baptiste Van Loo (1684–1745), as well as a spectacular Baroque altar.

Place Victor Hugo and the opera house in Toulon

Toulon

① Musée National de la Marine
② Musée d'Art de Toulon
③ Musée du Vieux Toulon
④ Cathédrale Ste-Marie-de-la-Seds

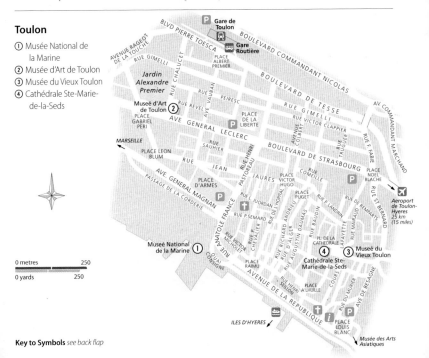

⑰ Iles d'Hyères

The Iles d'Hyères, also known as the Golden Isles, are three unspoilt islands, found 10 km (6 miles) off the Var coast – Porquerolles, Le Levant and Port-Cros. Their history has been chequered due to their important strategic position: occupiers have included Greeks, Romans and Saracens, as well as ruthless pirates. Today the French Navy uses much of Le Levant. Porquerolles, the largest island, is partly cultivated with vineyards, but also has expanses of pine forest and *maquis*. Both Porquerolles and Port-Cros are national parks, protected for their woodlands (including holm oak, strawberry tree and myrtle), rare birds and rich underwater habitats.

Locator Map

Port-Cros Marine Life

The wooded slopes of the island shelve down into unpolluted sea, where colourful fish swim among beds of Neptune grass. A ready-planned swimming route makes exploration easy.

Fort du Moulin, over-looking Port-Cros harbour

Sponge alga
Codium bursa

Mermaid's cup
Acetabularia mediterranea

Bath sponge
Spongia officinalis

Neptune grass
Posidonia oceanica

Peacock's tail
Padina pavonia

Sea peacock
Thalassoma pavo

Saupe *Sarpa salpa*

Sea urchins, *Paracentrotus lividus*

Black goby
Gobius niger

Moray eel
Muraena helena

Port-Cros Harbour
The tiny, palm-fringed harbour and village of Port-Cros nestle in a sheltered bay to the northwest of the island.

VISITORS' CHECKLIST

Practical Information
Road map D5. 🛈 Porquerolles (04 94 58 33 76).

Transport
✈ Toulon-Hyères. 🚆 Hyères. 🚌 Hyères. ⛴ from Hyères (Tour Fondu) to Porquerolles daily (every 30 mins in summer); from Hyères and Le Lavandou to Port-Cros and Le Levant daily (Nov–Mar: 3–4 times a week).

Scuba diving off the coast of Port-Cros

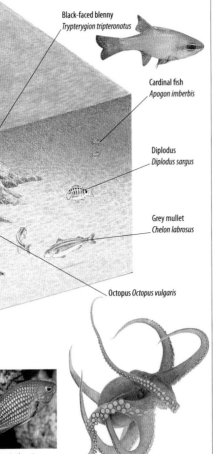

Black-faced blenny
Trypterygion tripteronotus

Cardinal fish
Apogon imberbis

Diplodus
Diplodus sargus

Grey mullet
Chelon labrosus

Octopus *Octopus vulgaris*

Damsel fish, *Chromis chromis*

⑱ Hyères

Road map D4. 🛆 57,000. ✈ Toulon-Hyères. 🚆 🚌 ⛴ 🛈 Rotunde du Park Hotel, Ave de Belgique (04 94 01 84 50). 🛒 Tue, Thu & Sat in city centre; Mon, Wed, Fri & Sun in neighbourhoods. 🌐 hyeres-tourisme.com

Hyères is one of the most agreeable towns on the Côte d'Azur, and the oldest of the south of France winter resorts. The town lies at the centre of well-cultivated land that provides fresh fruit and vegetables all year. It has three leisure ports, 25-km (16-miles) of sandy beach and a peninsula facing the Iles d'Hyères.

The new town was called Hyères-les-Palmiers. A palm-growing industry was established here in 1867, soon becoming the largest in Europe. The industry is still important and thousands of palms line the new town boulevards.

Hyères' main church is **St-Louis** in Place de la République. Romanesque and Provençal Gothic, it was completed in 1248. From place Massillon, rue St-Paul leads past the 11th-century **Eglise St-Paul**, full of 17th-century ex-votos. The road continues to the ruined 12th-century Château St-Bernard, which has good views. In the gardens is the Cubist-inspired **Villa de Noailles** (1924), built by Robert Mallet-Stevens for the Vicomte de Noailles. **Jardin Olbius Riquier** has a petting zoo and exotic plants.

🛆 Jardin Olbius Riquier
Ave Ambroise Thomas. **Tel** 04 94 00 78 65. **Open** daily. ♿

Façade of a house in Hyères built in Moorish architectural style

Beach at Le Lavandou overlooked by hotels and exclusive villas

⓳ Le Lavandou

Road map D4. 🚠 5,236. 🚌 🚢
ℹ️ Quai Gabriel Péri (04 94 00 40 50).
🗓️ Thu. 🅦 ot-lelavandou.fr

An embarkation port for the nearby Iles d'Hyères, Le Lavandou is a fishing village now almost entirely given over to tourism. This is due to its twelve sandy beaches, each with a different coloured sand.

It is a centre for water sports and offers moorings for luxury yachts. Full of bars, nightclubs and restaurants, Le Lavandou is a favourite of younger, less well-heeled visitors.

It takes its name not from the lavender fields in the surrounding hills, but from a *lavoir* (wash-house) depicted in a painting of the town by Charles Ginoux dating from 1736. During the last century, when it was no more than a fishing village, Le Lavandou was popular with artists. The most famous, though not so well known outside France, was Ernest Reyer (1823–99), a composer and music critic after whom the main square is named. From this square there is a view over the Iles du Levant and Port-Cros.

Much of nearby Brégançon is in the hands of the military and the French president has a summer residence there.

⓴ Bormes-les-Mimosas

Road map D4. 🚠 7,845. 🚌 Hyères.
ℹ️ 1 place Gambetta (04 94 01 38 38).
🗓️ Wed. 🅦 bormeslesmimosas.com

Bormes is a medieval hill village on the edge of the Dom Forest, bathed in the scent of oleander and eucalyptus and topped with a flower-lined walk around its castle. "Les

Rue Rompi-Cuou, one of the steep, old streets in Bormes-les-Mimosas

㉑ Tour of the Massif des Maures

The ancient mountain range of Maures takes its name from the Provençal *maouro*, meaning dark or gloomy, for the Massif is carpeted in sweet chestnuts, cork trees, oaks and pines with a deeply shaded undergrowth of myrrh and briar, though forest fires have reduced some of it to scrubland. Lying between Hyères and Fréjus, the Massif is nearly 60-km (40-miles) long and 30-km (18-miles) wide. This tour is a simple route that takes you through the wild and often deserted heart of the Massif, through dramatic countryside ranging from flat valley floors covered in cork trees to deep valleys and lofty peaks. A few of the roads are steep and winding.

③ Village des Tortues
Keep bearing left on the D75 for the "Tortoise Village", which has saved France's only remaining species of wild tortoise.

Gonfaron

④ Notre-Dame-des-Anges
Beside this priory and its chapel full of votive offerings, is the highest summit in the Massif at 780 m (2,559 ft).

Tips for Drivers

Tour length: 75 km (47 miles)
Stopping-off points: Collobrières is a pleasant lunchtime stop. Allow time to visit Chartreuse de la Verne (04 94 48 08 00 for opening times), which is reached up narrow, steep roads. *(See also pp250–51.)*

← Toulon

⑤ Collobrières
This riverside village with its hump-backed bridge is famed for its *marrons glacés*. Nearby forests supply bottle corks.

Farm workers at Collobrières

For additional map symbols *see back flap*

Mimosas" was not added to its name until 1968, a century after the plant was first introduced to the south of France from Mexico. A pretty and popular village, Bormes serves a marina of more than 800 berths. Plummeting streets such as Rompi-Cuou lead to lively cafés and coastal views.

A statue of St Francis di Paola stands in front of the attractive 16th-century **Chapelle St-François**, commemorating the saint's timely arrival during a plague outbreak in 1481. The 18th-century church of **St-Trophyme** has restored 18th-century frescoes. The works of local painter Jean-Charles Cazin (1841–1901) are well represented in the **Musée d'Arts et Histoire**.

Musée d'Arts et Histoire
103 rue Carnot. **Tel** 04 94 71 56 60.
Open Tue–Sun.

Ramatuelle village enclosed by wooded slopes and vineyards

㉒ Ramatuelle

Road map E4. 2,166. Pl de l'Ormeau (04 98 12 64 00). Thu & Sun. **ramatuelle-tourisme.com**

Surrounded by vineyards, this attractive hilltop village was called "God's Gift" (Rahmatu 'llah) by the Saracens who left behind a gate, now well-restored, in its fortifications, as well as a penchant for figs. It is one of three particularly quaint villages on the St-Tropez peninsula (with Grimaud and Gassin). Gérard Philipe (1922–59), the leading young French actor during the 1950s, is buried here. Theatre and jazz festivals take place here annually.

Nearby, Les Moulins de Paillas (322 m, 940 ft), offers a fine panorama, as does Cap Camarat, with its lighthouse, at the tip of the peninsula, 5 km (3 miles) east of Ramatuelle.

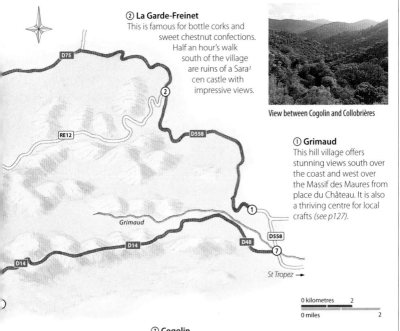

② La Garde-Freinet
This is famous for bottle corks and sweet chestnut confections. Half an hour's walk south of the village are ruins of a Saracen castle with impressive views.

View between Cogolin and Collobrières

① Grimaud
This hill village offers stunning views south over the coast and west over the Massif des Maures from place du Château. It is also a thriving centre for local crafts (see p127).

St Tropez →

0 kilometres 2
0 miles 2

⑥ Chartreuse de la Verne
Inhabited since the 12th century, this restored hilltop charterhouse is surrounded by chestnut woods.

⑦ Cogolin
Visitors can see the rugs for which the town is known being handmade at Manufacture des Tapis in Cogolin (see p221).

Key
━━ Tour route
═══ Other roads

㉓ Street-by-Street: St-Tropez

Clustered around the old port and nearby beaches, the centre of St-Tropez, partly rebuilt in its original style after World War II (*see p56*), is full of fishermen's houses. In the port itself, traditional fishing boats are still to be seen moored side-by-side with sleek luxury cruisers of all shapes and sizes. Behind the port-side cafés of the quai Jean-Jaurès, the narrow, bustling streets are packed with boutiques and restaurants. The town is overlooked by the church's wrought-iron bell tower in the centre and the citadel just outside.

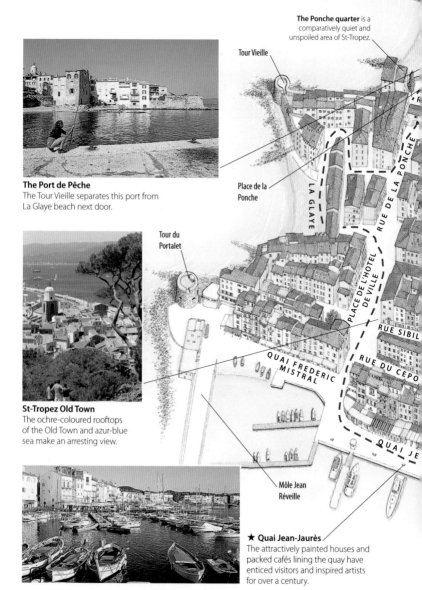

La Fontanette beach leads to a coastal walk with views over Ste-Maxime.

The Ponche quarter is a comparatively quiet and unspoiled area of St-Tropez.

Tour Vieille

Place de la Ponche

LA GLAYE

RUE DE LA PONCHE

PLACE DE L'HOTEL DE VILLE

RUE SIBIL

RUE DU CEPO

The Port de Pêche
The Tour Vieille separates this port from La Glaye beach next door.

Tour du Portalet

QUAI FREDERIC MISTRAL

QUAI JE

St-Tropez Old Town
The ochre-coloured rooftops of the Old Town and azur-blue sea make an arresting view.

Môle Jean Réveille

★ Quai Jean-Jaurès
The attractively painted houses and packed cafés lining the quay have enticed visitors and inspired artists for over a century.

View from the Ramparts of the Citadel
The hilltop citadel, situated east of St-Tropez, offers spectacular views over the rooftops of the town and beyond.

VISITORS' CHECKLIST

Practical Information
Map E4. 4,525. Quai Jean-Jaurès (08 92 68 48 28). Tue & Sat. Bravades: 16–18 May, 15 Jun.
sainttropeztourisme.com

Transport
Gare Routière (04 94 56 25 74).

★ Eglise Notre-Dame de l'Assomption
Its bust of St Torpès features in the bravade (see p228).

Open Window on the Harbour at St-Tropez (1925–6)
Charles Camoin's painting is now in the Annonciade.

RUE FONTANETTE

RUE DES PECHEURS

REMPARTS

To the citadel

RUE D'AUMAVE

RUE DE LA CITADELLE

RUE DU CLOCHER

L'EGLISE

RUE VICTOR LAUGIER

MARTIN

To place des Lices

QUAI SUFFREN

Statue of Pierre André de Suffren

To Musée de l'Annonciade (see pp124–5)

Key

— Suggested route

0 metres 50
0 yards 50

Musée de l'Annonciade

This innovative gallery opened in 1955 in the former Chapelle de l'Annonciade by the old port in St-Tropez. Built in 1568, the building was converted into a museum by architect Louis Süe (1875–1968), funded by art collector Georges Grammont. The collection began with the paintings of Paul Signac and the other artists who followed him to St-Tropez, and now contains many stunning Post-Impressionist works from the late 19th and early 20th centuries. In 1961, 65 valuable works were stolen from the museum, but were recovered and restored a year later.

Le Rameur (1914)
This bold Cubist work is by Roger de la Fresnaye.

★ **St-Tropez, la Place des Lices et le Café des Arts**
This painting (1925) is one of several that Charles Camoin made of St-Tropez's famous square after he followed Paul Signac and settled in the town.

★ **L'Orage** (1895)
Paul Signac's atmospheric work vividly depicts the onset of a storm in St-Tropez harbour.

Temporary exhibition room

Gallery Guide

Exhibition space is too limited for all works to be permanently on view, so the display changes frequently. An exhibition room holds temporary displays linked with the permanent collection.

★ **Nu Devant la Cheminée** (1919)
In this warm, intimate picture, characteristic of the artist, Pierre Bonnard uses delicate tones within a limited colour range to create an effect of light and shade.

Le Temps d'Harmonie
In this study (1893–5) for a larger work, Paul Signac departs from his more usual Pointillist technique, using simple, fluid lines.

Balcony

VISITORS' CHECKLIST

Practical Information
2 rue de l'Annonciade, Place Grammont, St-Tropez. **Tel** 04 94 17 84 10. **Open** Wed–Mon. **Closed** 1 Jan, Ascension, 1 May, 17 May, Nov, 25 Dec. 🅿 🚻 📷 ♿ ground floor only.

La Nymphe (1930)
This Classically influenced bronze sculpture, one of several excellent works by Aristide Maillol in the Annonciade, is a graceful evocation of ideal beauty.

Deauville, le Champ de Courses
Raoul Dufy's racecourse, painted in 1928, is typical of his interest in glamorous subjects.

18th-century main entrance

Key to Floorplan

- ☐ Ground floor
- ☐ Mezzanine
- ☐ First floor
- ◼ Non-exhibition space

Exploring St-Tropez

This exceptional resort has become a victim of its own charms – the August high season attracts about 80,000 hell-bent hedonists. Following their departure, however, the genuine, peaceful nature of the village still shines through. Surrounded by slopes covered with vineyards, looking out over the millpond bay of Golfe St-Tropez and protected by an imposing citadel, its situation remains inviolate. It does, however, face the northerly Mistral which thunders through the town for much of the winter, ensuring it remains a summer haunt.

Baroque-style Eglise Notre-Dame de l'Assomption

Paintings by local artists for sale on the quai Jean-Jaurès

A glimpse of the town

Activity is centred north of the Musée de l'Annonciade, beside the little port. Here, local artists sell their wares and people pass the time of day in the Café de Paris, le Gorille or Senequier (see p219).

The pretty, pastel-painted houses lining the quai Jean-Jaurès can be viewed at their best from the harbour breakwater, the Môle Jean Réveille. These buildings were among the town's sights that inspired Paul Signac (1863–1935) to start painting in St-Tropez. Many other artists followed, all well represented in the Annonciade (see pp124–5).

The old town, just behind the waterfront, is marked by the tower of the Eglise Notre-Dame de l'Assomption. To its north lies the Hôtel de Ville and the Tour Suffren, home of the former local lords. Admiral Pierre André de Suffren (1726–88), "terror of the English", is commemorated by a statue on the quay. Behind the quai Suffren is the place des Lices, a large square crowded with cafés.

Out to the east, beyond the old Ponche quarter and the unspoiled fishing port nearby, lies the 16th-century hexagonal citadel. With fine views from the ramparts, it contains the Musée Naval de St-Tropez. Further east, is La Madrague where Brigitte Bardot used to live. And God Created Woman, the 1959 film shot in St-Tropez starring Bardot, started the celebrity rush to the town.

🏛 **Musée de l'Annonciade**
See pp124–5.

🏛 **Eglise Notre-Dame de l'Assomption**
Rue de l'Eglise. **Open** Tue–Sun am.
This 19th-century Baroque church contains several busts

of saints, including one of St Torpès after whom St-Tropez is named. Beheaded for his Christianity, his body was put in a boat with a dog and a cockerel and the boat landed here in AD 68. Every year, his bust is carried through the town in the 16 May bravade.

The impressive hilltop citadel east of St-Tropez

🏛 **Musée de la Citadelle**
Forteresse. **Tel** 04 94 97 59 43. **Open** reopened following renovations; call for the latest opening times. 📷

Located in the dungeon of the citadel keep, to the east of the town, the Musée de la Citadelle houses temporary exhibitions on the history of St-Tropez and the navy.

🏛 **Maison des Papillons**
9 rue Etienne Berny. **Tel** 04 94 97 63 45.
Open Mon–Sat pm. **Closed** 1 Jan, 1 & 17 May, Ascension, 15 Aug, 1 Nov, 25 Dec. 📷

Hidden in a narrow medieval lane is this amazingly complete collection of butterflies found in France, as well as rare specimens from the Amazon.

Fishing boats and luxury cruisers docked at quai Jean-Jaurès

㉔ Port-Grimaud

Road map E4. 🗺 150. 📮 **ℹ** Les Terrasses, Rue de l'Amarrage (04 94 55 43 83). 📅 Thu & Sun. 🕸 grimaud-provence.com

This beautiful port village was dreamed up entirely by the renowned Alsace architect François Spoerry (1912–98). In 1962 he bought up the marshy delta lands of the River Giscle west of the Golfe St-Tropez. Four years later, work began on a mini-Venice of 2,500 canal-side houses with moorings covering 90 ha (222 acres). There are now three "zones", a marina and a beach. Its church, **St-François-d'Assise**, in the place d'Eglise, contains some stained glass by Victor Vasarély (1908–97) and offers a sweeping view of the port from the top of its tower.

The whole port is free of traffic and the *coche d'eau* offers a water-taxi service. A major tourist attraction, Port-Grimaud brings in about one million visitors a year.

View of Port-Grimaud from the Eglise de St-François-d'Assise

㉕ Grimaud

Road map E4. 🗺 2,700. 📮 **ℹ** 679 route nationale (04 94 55 43 83). 📅 Thu. 🕸 grimaud-provence.com

The medieval, fortified, traffic-free *village perché (see pp24–5)* of Grimaud has a long history dating back to the Gallo-Roman days. During the 11th century, its steep summit allowed Grimaud to dominate the Gulf of St-Tropez (also known as the Golfe de Grimaud) and control access to the town from the North and Maures mountains. Contrary to popular belief, Grimaud has no connection to the ubiquitous Grimaldi family. Rather it can be associated with the much older Grimaldo family. The castle of Grimaud dates from the 11th century and was reduced to ruins in the Wars of Religion between Catholics and Protestants *(see pp50–51)*.

The view of the coast from its heights made it an ideal vantage point from which to watch for further invasion.

Once called rue Droite, the rue des Templiers is the town's oldest street, lined with arcades designed to be battened down in case of attack. Legend has it that the Knights Templar stayed in Grimaud, but this fact has not been historically attested. In the same street is the pure Romanesque 12th-century church of St-Michel.

One of the popular beaches at Ste-Maxime on a sunny day

㉖ Ste-Maxime

Road map E4. 🗺 13,900. 📮 St-Tropez, St-Raphaël. **ℹ** promenade Aymeric Simon-Lorière (08 76 20 83 83). 📅 daily.

Facing St-Tropez across the neck of the Gulf, Ste-Maxime is protected by hills. Its year-round clientele reaches saturation point in summer. The attractions of this smart resort are its port, promenade, good sandy beaches, watersports, nightlife, fairs and casino.

Ste-Maxime was once protected by the monks of Lérins, who named the port after their patron saint and put up the defensive Tour Carrée des Dames which now serves as the **Musée de la Tour Carrée**. The church opposite contains a 17th-century green marble altar that was brought from the former Carthusian monastery of La Verne in the Massif des Maures.

🏛 **Musée de la Tour Carrée**
Place Mireille de Germond. **Tel** 04 94 96 70 30. **Open** Wed–Sun. **Closed** 1 Jan, 1 May, 25 Dec, Feb. 📷

Grimaud, dominated by the castle ruins

ⓩ St-Raphaël

Road map E4. 🏔 34,716. 🚉 🚌
ℹ Quai Albert Premier (04 94 19 52 52).
🏛 Tue–Sun. **w saint-raphael.com**

This staid and sensible family resort dates to Roman times when rich families came to stay at a spot near the modern seafront casino. Napoleon put the town on the map when he landed here in 1799 on his return from Egypt, and 15 years later when he left St-Raphaël for exile on Elba.

Popularity came when the Parisian satirical novelist Jean-Baptiste Karr (1808–90) publicized the town's delights. In the old part is the 12th-century church of St-Raphaël and the **Musée Archéologique**, which contains Greek amphorae and other underwater finds.

🏛 Musée Archéologique
Place de la Vieille Eglise. **Tel** 04 94 19 25 75. **Open** Tue–Sat. **Closed** public hols.

Tourist poster of St-Raphaël from the 19th century

㉘ Massif de l'Esterel

Road map E4. ✈ Nice. 🚉 🚌 Agay, St-Raphaël. ℹ Quai Albert Premier, St-Raphaël (04 94 19 52 52) & 86 ave de Cannes, Mandelieu-La Napoule (04 93 93 64 78).

The Esterel, a mountainous volcanic mass, is a wilderness compared to the popular coast. Although it rises to no more than 620 m (2,050 ft), and a succession of fires have laid waste its forests, its innate ruggedness and the dramatic colours of its porphyry

Château de la Napoule, now an art centre

rocks remain intact. Until the mid-1800s, it was a refuge for highwaymen and escaped prisoners from Toulon. Here, after being fêted on arrival in St Raphaël, Napoleon and his coach were robbed of all their valuables while on their way out of town heading to Paris.

The north side of the massif is bounded by the DN7 which runs through the Esterel Gap, following the Roman Aurelian way from Cannes to Fréjus. To reach Mont Vinaigre, at the Testanier cross-roads 11 km (7 miles) from Fréjus, follow the road leading to the Malpey ranger station. Park there and do the final 45 minutes on foot. This is the highest point on the massif, and there is a fine panorama from the Alps to the Massif des Maures.

On the seaward side of the massif the D1089 from St-Raphaël twists along the top of startlingly red cliffs to Agay. This resort has the best anchorage on the coast. It is famous for its red porphyry, from which the Romans cut columns for their Provençal monuments. Be aware that there is only one paved road (mostly one-way) to reach Agay and no access to return to the seafront between Agay and Theoule.

Round the bay is Pointe de Baumette where there is a memorial to French writer and World War II aviator, Antoine de St-Exupéry (see p33). The road continues to Anthéor and the Pointe de l'Observatoire. Just before here, a left turn leads to the circuit of the Cap Roux and Pic de l'Ours.

The coast road continues through a series of resorts to the start of the Riviera, at La Napoule. Here there is a 14th-century château refurbished by American sculptor Henry Clews (1876–1937), who left work scattered about the estate. The château is now an art centre, the **Fondation Henry Clews**. The pedestrian route leading inland to the Col Belle-Barbe from the coast passes on the right a turn to the 452-m (1483-ft) Pic du Cap Roux. An hour's walk to the top is rewarded by a sweeping view of the coast.

Inland from Col Belle-Barbe over the Col du Mistral up to the Col des Trois Termes, the path then twists south to Col Notre-Dame. A 45-minute walk leads to the dramatic 496-m (1,627-ft) Pic de l'Ours. Between here and the coast is the 323-m (1,060-ft) Pic d'Aurelle, which also provides an impressive vista.

🏛 Fondation Henry Clews
1 blvd Henry Clews, Mandelieu-La Napoule. **Tel** 04 93 49 95 05. **Open** daily; Nov–Feb: Mon-Fri pm. **Closed** 25 Dec. 🏛 🎫 📷 Apr–Sep 📷 **w chateau-lanapoule.com**

Remaining timber on the fire-ravaged Massif de l'Esterel

㉙ Fréjus

Road map E4. 🏔 52,344. 🚉 St Raphaël.
🚌 ℹ 249 rue Jean-Jaurès (04 94 51
83 83). 🛒 Tue, Wed, Fri, Sat & Sun.
🌐 frejus.fr

Visibly, though not ostentatiously,
wealthy in history, Fréjus is one
of the highlights of the coast.
The oldest Roman city in Gaul, it
was founded by Julius Caesar in
49 BC and greatly expanded by
Augustus. Lying on the Aurelian
way – a huge road built in the
reign of Augustus from Rome to
Arles – it covered 40 ha (100 acres),
had a population of 30–40,000
and, as a port, was second in
importance only to Marseille.

Although substantial sections
of the Roman city were deci-
mated by the Saracens in the
10th century, a few parts
of their walls remain,
including a tower of
the western Porte
des Gaules. The
opposite eastern
entrance, the Porte de
Rome, marks one end
of a 40-km (25-mile)
aqueduct, the ruins of which
amble alongside the DN7 towards
the Siagnole river near Mons.

**Mosaic in the Musée
Archéologique in Fréjus**

Just to the north of here the
remains of the semicircular, 1st-
century theatre can be viewed.
In their midst, performances are
still held. The praetorium or
Plateforme – military headquarters that formed the eastern
citadel – lie to the south. North
of the Porte des Gaules, on the
road to Brignoles, stands the
large 1st–2nd-century **Arènes**,
built to hold 6,000 spectators,
now used for music.

The spectacular **Cathédrale
St-Léonce et Cloître** houses a
Musée Archéologique with
finds from all around Fréjus. The
Chapelle Notre-Dame, decorated
by Cocteau, and Musée d'Histoire
Locale are also well worth a visit.

South of the town
is the Butte
St-Antoine citadel,
which once
overlooked the
harbour. The canal
linking the harbour
to the sea began
silting up in the 10th
century; by the 1700s
it was entirely filled in,
forming Fréjus-Plage. A little
over 2 km (1 mile) from the
town's centre, this modern

Well in the centre of the Cathedral
cloisters at Fréjus

resort stretches along a sandy
beach towards St-Raphaël.
North of the Arènes is a Buddhist
Pagoda commemorating
Vietnamese soldiers who died
serving in the French army.

🏛 **Arènes de Fréjus**
Rue Vadon. **Tel** 04 94 51 34 31.
Open Apr–Sep: Tue–Sun; Oct–May:
Tue–Sat. **Closed** public hols.

⛪ **Cathédrale St-Léonce**
58 rue du Cardinal Fleury. **Tel** 04 94
51 26 30. **Open** daily. Cloisters: daily
(Oct–May: Tue–Sun). **Closed** Mon
(winter), public hols. 🚫 cloisters.
🎟 📷 🌐 **cathedrale-frejus.
monuments-nationaux.fr**

Cathedrale St-Léonce et Cloître

*The fortified cathedral and the
marble-columned cloister date from
the 12th century, while the 5th-century
baptistry is one of the oldest in France.*

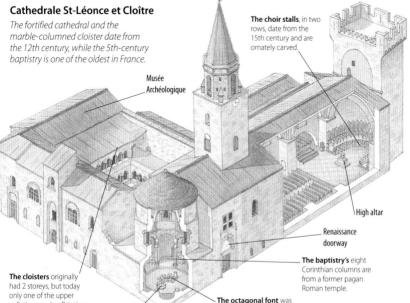

The choir stalls, in two
rows, date from the
15th century and are
ornately carved.

Musée
Archéologique

High altar

Renaissance
doorway

The baptistry's eight
Corinthian columns are
from a former pagan
Roman temple.

The cloisters originally
had 2 storeys, but today
only one of the upper
galleries remains. Paintings
cover the ceilings.

Earthenware basin

The octagonal font was
originally used only to
baptize adults.

BOUCHES-DU-RHÔNE AND NÎMES

This southwestern corner of Provence has a feel that's unique in the region. It is the land of Van Gogh, brightly patterned materials and beaches of shifting sands. Its wildest point is the Camargue in the Rhône delta, a place of light and colour, lived in for centuries by gypsies and by cowboys who herd the wild horses and bulls.

Many inland towns reflect the region's Greek and Roman past. The Greeks first settled in France circa 600 BC and founded Marseille, now a cosmopolitan cultural centre and the country's second largest city. The Romans, who arrived after them, built the theatre at Arles and the amphitheatre at Nîmes, and left the remains of Classical houses at the archaeological site of Glanum. The skeleton of a Roman aqueduct runs beween a spring at Uzès to a water tower at Nîmes, a great feat of engineering best seen at Pont du Gard.

"A race of eagles" is how Frédéric Mistral, the Provençal writer *(see p32)* described the Lords of Baux, bloodthirsty warriors who ruled in the Middle Ages from an extraordinary eyrie in Les Baux-de-Provence. This former fief was paradoxically famous as a Court of Love *(see p146)* during the 13th century. Louis IX (Saint Louis) built the fortified city of Aigues-Mortes for the Crusaders. In the 15th century, Good King René *(see pp50–51),* held his court in the castle of Tarascon and in Aix-en-Provence, the ancient capital of Provence. Aix's university, founded by René's father in 1409, is still the hub of this lively student town.

The area provides great walks and stunning scenery, particularly in the Alpilles and around Marseille. The films and books of Marcel Pagnol *(see 157)* and the stories of Daudet *(see p147),* which have influenced perceptions of Provençal people and life, are set in this region. The Camargue maintains a unique collection of flora and fauna, providing, in addition to fine vistas, superb horse riding and bird-watching.

Produce on display in the colourful food market, Aix-en-Provence

◀ Hiking in the Sormiou *calanque,* one of the many inlets between Marseille and Cassis

Exploring Bouches-du-Rhône and Nîmes

At the mouth of the Rhône lie the flat, wetland marshes and sand dunes of the Camargue wildlife reserve. Further inland, cities such as Aix-en-Provence, Arles and Nîmes are awash with ancient architecture. Northeast of Arles, the herb-covered chain of the Alpilles rises from the surrounding plains to the heady heights of Les Baux, and there are some stunning walks through the mountains. St-Rémy-de-Provence makes a good base for exploring the Alpilles. Popular coastal towns are Marseille and the scenic port of Cassis. A short car or boat trip away lie Les Calanques, deep, narrow inlets set between pine trees and white cliffs.

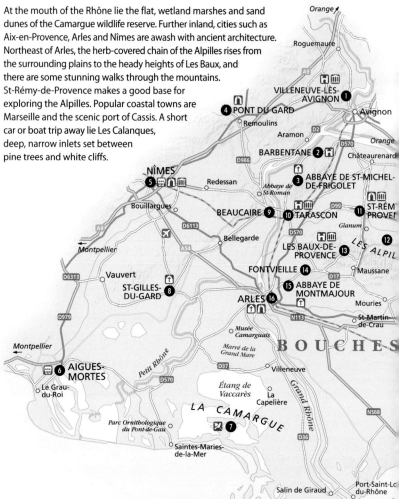

Atlantes grace the doorway of the Pavillon de Vendôme in Aix

For additional map symbols *see back flap*

Sights at a Glance

1. Villeneuve-lès-Avignon
2. Barbentane
3. Abbaye de St-Michel-de-Frigolet
4. Pont du Gard
5. *Nîmes pp136–7*
6. *Aigues-Mortes pp138–9*
7. *La Camargue pp140–3*
8. St-Gilles
9. Beaucaire
10. Tarascon
11. St-Rémy-de-Provence
12. Les Alpilles
13. Les Baux-de-Provence
14. Fontvieille
15. Abbaye de Montmajour
16. *Arles pp148–50*
17. Martigues
18. Salon-de-Provence
19. Abbaye de Silvacane
20. *Aix-en-Provence pp152–3*
21. *Marseille pp154–7*
22. Aubagne
23. Les Calanques
24. Cassis

View across the harbour of Fort St-Jean, Marseille

Getting Around

If you have a car, the auto-routes are fast and bypass slow traffic in the towns. The A8 autoroute which leads along the Riviera meets the Paris-Marseille A7 Autoroute du Soleil 17 km (11 miles) west of Aix, while the A9 Languedocienne heads west through Nîmes towards Spain. The main towns are all linked by trains and buses, though bus services tend to be poor outside towns. Arles and Aix-en-Provence make particularly good bases for getting around. Boat trips are organized from Arles and Stes-Maries-de-la-Mer in the Camargue, where a good way to see the countryside is to hire the native horses.

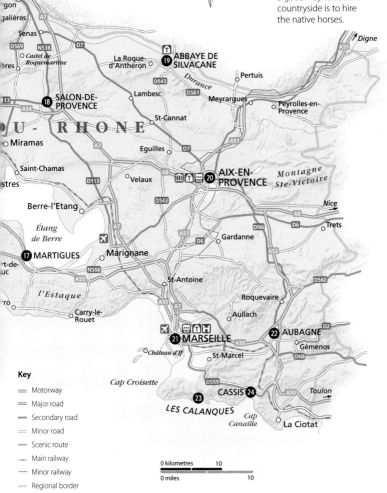

Key

- ▬▬ Motorway
- ▬▬ Major road
- ▬▬ Secondary road
- ▬▬ Minor road
- ▬▬ Scenic route
- ▬▬ Main railway
- — Minor railway
- ▬▬ Regional border

0 kilometres 10
0 miles 10

Part of the Chartreuse du Val-de-Bénédiction, Villeneuve

❶ Villeneuve-lès-Avignon

Road map B3. 🚗 12,735. 🚉 Avignon. 🚌 🛈 1 pl Charles David (04 90 25 61 33). 🛍 Thu & Sat. 🖥 **tourisme-villeneuvelezavignon.fr**

This town arose beside the Rhône, opposite Avignon (see pp170–71), and the connecting bridge, Pont St-Bénézet, was guarded by the **Tour de Philippe le Bel**, built in 1307. Its rooftop terrace, 176 steps up, gives a fine panorama of the papal city. Even better is the view from the two giant 40-m (130-ft) round towers at the entrance to the impressive 14th-century **Fort St-André**, which enclosed a small town, monastery and church.

Between these two bastions lies the 14th-century Eglise-Collégiale Notre-Dame. In the **Musée Pierre de Luxembourg** is *The Coronation of the Virgin*

(1453) by Enguerrand Quarton, regarded as the best work of the Avignon School. This work was painted for the abbot of the **Chartreuse du Val-de-Bénédiction**, which was founded by Innocent VI in 1356. There are three cloisters and a chapel dedicated to St John the Baptist decorated with frescoes by Giovanetti da Viterbo. The building is now used as a cultural centre.

🏛 **Fort St-André**
Tel 04 90 25 45 35. **Open** daily. **Closed** 1 Jan, 1 May, 1 & 11 Nov, 25 Dec. 🅿️ 🖥 **fort-saint-andre.monument-nationaux.fr**

🏛 **Musée Municipal Pierre de Luxembourg**
Rue de la République. **Tel** 04 90 27 49 66. **Open** Tue–Sun. **Closved** Jan, 1 & 11 Nov, 25 Dec. 🅿️

🏛 **Chartreuse du Val-de-Bénédiction**
Rue de la République. **Tel** 04 90 15 24 24. **Open** daily. **Closed** 1 Jan, 1 May, 1 & 11 Nov, 25 Dec. 🅿️ 🎫 in summer. 🚫 in summer. 🖥 in winter. 🏠 🖥 **chartreuse.org**

❷ Barbentane

Road map B3. 🚗 4,067. 🚉 Avignon, Tarascon. 🚌 🛈 3 rue des Pénitents (04 90 90 85 86). 🖥 **barbentane.fr**

Members of Avignon's Papal court liked to build summer houses in Barbentane, beside the Rhône 10 km (6 miles) south of the city. One such, opposite the 13th- to 15th-century Notre-Dame-de-Grace, was the handsome Maison des Chevaliers, which was

owned by the Marquises of Barbentane. Only the 40-m (130-ft) Tour Anglica remains of the town's 14th-century castle. Just outside the medieval quarter is the Château de Barbentane, a finely decorated Italianate mansion, built in 1674 by the Barbentane aristocracy who still own and reside in it.

In the town is the 16th- to 17th-century **Moulin de Mogador**, which was used as an oil mill and now hosts dinners.

Façade of the 17th-century Château de Barbentane

❸ Abbaye de St-Michel de Frigolet

Road map B3. **Tel** 04 90 95 70 07. **Open** 8am–6pm daily. Phone to reserve for groups. 🎫 3pm Sun. 🅿️ 🖥 **frigolet.com**

The abbey is situated south of St-Michel de Frigolet, in the La Montagnette countryside. A cloister and small church date from the 12th century, but in 1858 a Premonstratensian abbey was founded and one of the most richly decorated churches of that period was built. The whole interior is colourfully painted, with stars and saints on the pillars and ceiling. After a brief period of exile in Belgium at the beginning of the 20th century, the monks returned to Frigolet. The word *frigolet* is Provençal for thyme.

The ceiling of the abbey church of St-Michel de Frigolet

❹ Pont du Gard

Road map A3. 🚌 Nîmes. 🛈 Place des Grands Jours, Remoulins (04 66 37 22 34). **Open** daily. 🌐 ot-pontdugard.com

Begun around 19 BC, this bridge is part of an aqueduct which transported water from a spring near Uzès to Roman Nîmes *(see pp136–7)*. An underground channel, bridges and tunnels were engineered to carry the 20 million litre (4.4 million gallon) daily water supply 50 km (31 miles). The three-tiered structure of the Pont du Gard spans the Gardon valley and was the tallest aqueduct in the Roman empire.

The Pont du Gard, the tallest of all Roman aqueducts at 48 m (158 ft)

Its huge limestone blocks, some as heavy as 6 tonnes, were erected without mortar. The water channel, covered by stone slabs, was in the top tier of the three. Skilfully designed cutwaters ensured that the bridge has resisted many violent floods.

It is not known for certain how long the aqueduct remained in use but it may still have been functioning as late as the 9th century AD. The adjacent road bridge was erected in the 1700s. The **Site du Pont du Gard** has a museum (open daily in summer) tracing the aqueduct's history.

Trademark graffiti left by 18th-century masons on the stones

Protruding stones for supporting scaffolding during construction

The Remains of the Aqueduct

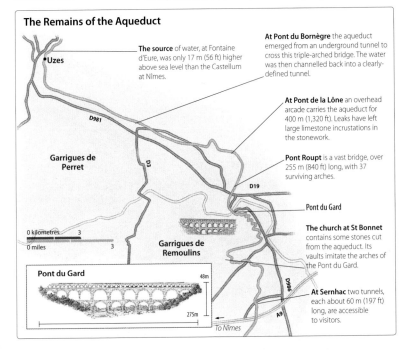

The source of water, at Fontaine d'Eure, was only 17 m (56 ft) higher above sea level than the Castellum at Nîmes.

At Pont du Bornègre the aqueduct emerged from an underground tunnel to cross this triple-arched bridge. The water was then channelled back into a clearly-defined tunnel.

At Pont de la Lône an overhead arcade carries the aqueduct for 400 m (1,320 ft). Leaks have left large limestone incrustations in the stonework.

Pont Roupt is a vast bridge, over 255 m (840 ft) long, with 37 surviving arches.

Pont du Gard

The church at St Bonnet contains some stones cut from the aqueduct. Its vaults imitate the arches of the Pont du Gard.

At Sernhac two tunnels, each about 60 m (197 ft) long, are accessible to visitors.

Uzès

Garrigues de Perret

Garrigues de Remoulins

D981

D3

D19

D986

A9

0 kilometres 3
0 miles 3

Pont du Gard

48m

275m

To Nîmes

❺ Nîmes

A magnificent carved black bull at the end of the avenue Jean-Jaurès highlights Nîmes' passion for bullfighting. Crowds fill Les Arènes, the Roman amphitheatre, for bullfights during the two annual *ferias (see pp36–8)*. Year round, the city's biggest draw is its fine Roman architecture, and it is a great city of the arts. The city's textile industry is famous for creating denim *(de Nîmes)*, worn by the Camargue cowboys. Most shops stock vividly coloured Provençal fabrics, known as *indiennes (see p221)*.

Exploring Nîmes

Roman veterans from Emperor Augustus's 31 BC Egyptian campaign introduced the city's coat of arms: a crocodile chained to a palm tree. Today, the logo is splashed on everything from bollards to road signs.

Nîmes' generous boulevards give it a wide-open feel. A renaissance of modern building, art and design, including the fine Carré d'Art, lends a touch of class. Some of the newer monuments, such as the Fontaine du Crocodile in place du Marché, are becoming as well known as Nîmes' most familiar landmark, the Castellum.

The city's coat of arms: a crocodile and palm tree

🏛 Les Arènes (L'Amphithéâtre)

Place des Arènes. **Tel** 04 66 21 82 56. **Open** daily. **Closed** Feria de Pentecôte, Feria des Vendanges & performance days. 🅿 ♿ restricted. 📷
🌐 arenes-nimes.com

The most dramatic of the city's Roman ruins is the 1st-century amphitheatre. At 130 m (427 ft) by 100 m (328 ft) and with seating for 22,000, it is slightly smaller than Arles' amphitheatre *(see p150)*. It was built as a venue for gladiatorial combat, and you can see a demonstration of their fighting technique. After Rome's collapse in AD 476, it became a fortress and knights' headquarters. Until its 19th-century restoration, it was used as home for 2,000 people in slum conditions. Today it is thought to be one of the best preserved of all Roman amphitheatres.

🏛 Porte d'Auguste

Blvd Amiral Courbet.
With a central arch 6 m (20 ft) high and 4 m (13 ft) wide, this gate was built to take horsemen and carriages, since the main road from Rome to Spain, the Domitian Way, passed through the middle of Nîmes.

An ancient inscription tells visitors that the city walls were built in 15 BC.

🏛 Musée du Vieux Nîmes

Pl aux Herbes. **Tel** 04 66 76 73 70. **Open** Tue–Sun. **Closed** 1 Jan, 1 May, 1 Nov, 25 Dec. 📷
The 17th-century Bishop's Palace just east of the cathedral houses this museum. The old-fashioned interior has been beautifully restored: the summer room has Directoire and Empire-style furnishings and Old Town views.

🏛 Carré d'Art (Musée d'Art Contemporain)

Pl de la Maison Carrée. **Tel** 04 66 76 35 85. **Open** Tue–Sun. 🅿 📷 ♿ 🌐
🖥 🌐 carreartmusee.com
On the opposite side of the square from the Maison Carrée, this modern, light-flooded art complex opened in 1993 and was designed by Norman Foster.

Modernist façade of Norman Foster's Carré d'Art

🏛 Maison Carrée

Pl de la Maison Carrée. **Tel** 04 66 21 82 56. **Open** daily. 🅿 🌐 arenes-nimes.com
The Maison Carrée ("square house") is the world's best-preserved Roman temple. Built by Marcus Agrippa, it is Hellenic with Corinthian columns around the main hall. Louis XIV's chief minister, Colbert, wanted it taken brick by brick to Versailles. A multimedia film – *Nemausus, the birth of Nîmes* – is shown inside the temple.

🏛 Musée Archéologique et Musée d'Histoire Naturelle (Musée de Nîmes)

13 bis blvd Amiral Courbet. **Tel** 04 66 76 74 80 (Archéologique); 04 66 76 73 45 (Histoire Naturelle). **Open** Tue–Sun. **Closed** 1 Jan, 1 May, 1 Nov, 25 Dec. 📷

The ground-floor gallery of this museum has a number of pre-Roman carvings, including busts of Gallic warriors, friezes and also contemporary objects. Upstairs, Gallo-Roman tools and household utensils give

The Roman amphitheatre, today used for bullfights at festival times

a good idea of life at the time. The pottery collection includes the pre-Roman Warrior of Grézan. The atmospheric chapel in this one-time Jesuits' College is used for temporary displays. The Natural History Museum also houses the city's planetarium.

🏛 Musée des Beaux-Arts
Rue Cité Foulc. **Tel** 04 66 28 18 32. **Open** Tue–Sun. **Closed** 1 Jan, 1 May, 1 Nov, 25 Dec. 🅿 🕭

A diverse collection in the Fine Art Museum includes paintings by Boucher, Rubens and Watteau. The ground floor displays a large Roman mosaic, *The Marriage of Admetus*, found in 1883 in Nîmes' former covered market.

🏛 Cathédrale Notre-Dame et St-Castor
Pl aux Herbes. **Tel** 04 66 67 67 00. **Open** daily & for services.

Nîmes' cathedral, in the centre of the Old Town, dates from the 11th century but was extensively rebuilt in the 19th century. The west front has a partly Romanesque frieze with scenes from the Old Testament.

🏛 Castellum
Rue de la Lampèze.
Between the Porte d'Auguste and the Tour Magne, set in the Roman wall, is the Castellum, a tower used for storing the water brought in from Uzès via the aqueduct at Pont du Gard *(see p135)*. The water was distributed in the town by means of a canal duct system.

🏛 Les Jardins de la Fontaine
Quai de la Fontaine. **Tel** 04 66 21 82 56 (Tour Magne). **Open** daily.
The city's main park lies at the end of the wide avenue Jean-Jaurès. It was named after an underground spring harnessed in the 18th century. The park's 2nd-century Temple of Diana, part of a complex of baths, is today in ruins. Benedictine nuns lived there during the Middle Ages and converted it into a church, which was sacked in the Wars of Religion *(see pp50–51)*.

At the summit of the 114-m (374-ft) Mont Cavalier stands the 34-m (112-ft) octagonal Tour Magne. Of all the towers originally set in Nîmes' Roman wall, this is the most remarkable. Dating from 15 BC, it is the earliest surviving Roman

building in France. There are 140 steps, worth climbing for a fine view of Mont Ventoux.

L'Obéissance Récompensée by Boucher, Musée des Beaux-Arts

Nîmes

1. Les Arènes
2. Porte d'Auguste
3. Musée du Vieux Nîmes
4. Carré d'Art
5. Maison Carrée
6. Musée Archéologique et Musée d'Histoire Naturelle
7. Musée des Beaux-Arts
8. Cathédrale Notre-Dame et St-Castor

Key to Symbols *see back flap*

❻ Aigues-Mortes

A lone, sturdy sentinel set among the salt marshes of the Camargue, Aigues-Mortes ("dead waters" in Provençal) looks today much as it must have done when it was completed, around 1300. Then, however, the Rhône had not deposited the silt which now landlocks the town. Canals transported the vast stone blocks to make its walls from the quarries of Beaucaire, and the town's founder, Louis IX, set sail from under the shadow of Tour de Constance on his crusade of 1248 *(see pp46–7)*. Only the Hundred Years' War saw its ramparts breached: now its gates are always open to the besieging armies of admiring visitors.

Tour de la Poudrière
was the arsenal, where weapons and gunpowder were stored.

Porte de l'Arsenal

RUE DE L'ARSENAL

RUE HOCHE

RUE HOCHE

RUE ROGER

SALENGRO

RUE E

RUE BAUDIN

BOULEVARD GAMBETTA

RUE D

King Louis IX
Saint Louis, as he was to become, built Aigues-Mortes as his only Mediterranean sea port. People had to be bribed to come and settle in this inhospitable spot.

Porte de la Reine
was named for Anne of Austria, who visited the town in 1622.

Tour de la Mèche or "wick tower" held a constant flame used to light cannon fuses.

Chapelle des Pénitents Blancs

Tour du Sel

★ The Ramparts
The 1,634-m (1-mile) long walls are punctuated by ten gates, six towers, arrow slits and overhanging latrines.

Chapelle des Pénitents Gris
Built around 1607, this chapel is still used by an order founded in 1400. Named for their grey cowls, they walk with their white-cowled former rivals in the Palm Sunday procession.

Porte de la Marine
This was the main portside gate. Ships were moored by the Porte des Galions, anchored to a vast metal ring known as an *organeau*.

Place St-Louis
This charming, leafy square, lined with cafés, is at the heart of town life. In its centre is a bronze statue of Saint Louis, on a base carved with the prows of crusader ships.

Porte des Galions

Porte de l'Organeau

Notre-Dame des Sablons,
"Our Lady of the Sands", was built before the town itself.

JEAN JACQUES ROUSSEAU

RUE THEAULON

RUE VICTOR HUGO

RUE P ROLLAND

RUE DENFERT ROCHEREAU

US BLANC

RUE MARCEAU

AMAIS

RUE ALSACE LORRAINE

PASTEUR

ST-LOUIS

RUE SADI-CARNOT

GRAND RUE JEAN JAURES

RUE AMIRAL COURBERT

UBLIQUE

orte de Gardette

Tour des Bourguignons
In the massacre of 1421 Gascons took the town from Burgundy. There were too many bodies to bury, so salted bodies were kept here.

Key
— Suggested route

0 metres   100
0 yards   100

★ **Tour de Constance**
This tower often held religious prisoners: first Catholic, then Calvinist, and then Huguenot women such as Marie Durand, freed in 1768 after 38 years.

⦿ The Camargue

This flat, scarcely habited land is one of Europe's major wetland regions and natural history sites. Extensive areas of salt marsh, lakes, pastures and sand dunes, covering a vast 140,000 ha (346,000 acres), provide a romantic and haunting environment for the wildlife. Native horses roam the green pastures and are ridden by the traditional cowboys of the region, the *gardians*, *(see p26)* who herd the black bulls. Numerous sea birds and wildfowl also occupy the region, among them flocks of greater flamingoes. North of the reserve, rice is cultivated in paddy fields. Many of the thousands of visitors confine their exploration to the road between Arles and Saintes-Maries-de-la-Mer, and miss the best of the wild flora and fauna.

Camargue Bulls
Periodically, the herds of black bulls are rounded up by the *gardians* to perform in local bullfights. The larger bulls are sold to Spain.

Camargue Birds

This region is a haven for bird spotters, particularly during the spring when migrant birds visit on their journey north. Resident birds include little egrets and marsh harriers. This is the only French breeding site of the slender-billed gull, and the red-crested pochard, rarely seen in Europe, also breeds here.

Little egret
(Egretta garzetta)

Collared pratincole
(Glareola pratincola)

Slender-billed gull
(Larus genei)

Marsh harrier *(Circus aeruginosus)*

Black-winged stilt
(Himantopus himantopus)

Red-crested pochard
(Netta rufina)

Map labels
Le Petit Rhône

D572

D570

Méjanes

PLAINE DE LA CAMARGUE

PETITE CAMARGUE

D570

P (i)

i **Centre de Ginès**

Stes-Maries-de-la-Mer

KEY

① **Parc Ornithologique du Pont-de-Gau** bird reserve *(see p142)* is where most birds in the Camargue live and where, twice a year, over 350 species of migrating birds stop off on their journey north or south.

② **Musée Camarguais** *(see p143)*.

③ **Information Centre for Nature Reserve**

Camargue Horses
These hardy animals are direct descendants of pre-historic horses. The foal's coat turns white between the ages of four and seven.

European Beavers

European beavers came close to extinction at the start of the 20th century, when they were hunted for their fur. These nocturnal animals were protected in 1905 and began to colonize the region in the 1970s.

0 kilometres 5

0 miles 5

VISITORS' CHECKLIST

Practical Information
Road map A4 & B4. ℹ️ Pont de Gau, near Stes-Maries-de-la-Mer (04 90 97 86 32). 🎉 Pèlerinage des Gitans (24–25 May, end Oct). 🌐 parc-camargue.fr

Transport
✈️ 90 km (56 miles) E Montpellier-Méditerranée. 🚉 🚌 Ave Paulin Talabot, Arles.

Greater Flamingoes

Some 10,000 pairs of these exotic, bright pink birds breed in the Camargue. They are often seen feeding on the marshes of the Etang de Vaccarès, although their main breeding ground is on the saltier lagoons towards the south.

de Rousty

D36B

Villeneuve

Le Grande Rhône

D36

ang du Vaccarès

③ ℹ️

La Capelière

PLAINE DE LA CAMARGUE

P

The Salt Industry

Flat, shallow lagoons fill with sea water, which then evaporates in the sun, leaving behind huge salt deposits. These expanses provide a rich feeding ground for waders such as avocets.

P

D36C

Salin de Giraud

Key

— Nature reserve boundary

– – Walking routes

– – Walking and cycling routes

Dune Vegetation

The sand dunes form a line between the lagoons and salt marshes and the sea. Among the many wild flowers that grow here is sea chamomile.

Exploring the Camargue

The unique character of the Camargue has given rise to unusual traditions. The native white horses and black bulls are ranched by *manadiers* and herded, branded and tended by the region's cowboys, or *gardians*, whose small, low, whitewashed houses dot the landscape. Local bullfights are advertised in Saintes-Maries-de-la-Mer, the main tourist centre of the region and chief place to stay, also renowned for its gypsy population. It has a sandy beach and offers watersports and boat trips. Tourist offices throughout the area provide information on walks, but the best views are from the 7-km (5-mile) footway and cycle path along the Digues-de-la-Mer (sea dyke) from the town. Several sights within the Camargue have been turned into museums and exhibitions of local life and natural history. Several ranches and activity centres organize rides and riding holidays.

A bloodless Camargue bullfight in Méjanes

A place of pilgrimage

The three Marys who gave Saintes-Maries-de-la-Mer its name are Mary Magdalene, Mary Jacobe (the Virgin Mary's sister) and Mary Salome, mother of the apostles James and John. Set adrift after the Crucifixion with, among others, their servant Sara, Saint Martha and her brother Lazarus, they landed here in their boat. They built a shrine to the virgin, and while the others went to spread the word of the gospel, Mary Jacobe, Mary Salome and Sara stayed behind.

In winter, the town is an unpretentious, low-rise resort. It overflows during the May and October festivals, when Mary Salome and Mary Jacobe are celebrated, their statues marched to the sea to be blessed. The larger festival is in May, when gypsies from all over the world come to pay homage to their patron saint, Sara, the black Madonna who lies in the crypt of the 9th-century **Eglise de Notre-Dame-de-la-Mer**. An effigy is also paraded through the streets. Afterwards there are bullfights, horse races and flamenco dances *(see pp228–9)*. The prominent church is also worth visiting for the view from its rooftop walkway.

Throughout the centre of the town are cheery restaurants with checked tablecloths, and shops selling patterned skirts, shirts and scarves, lucky charms and Romany souvenirs.

Still in the Saintes-Maries area, 4.5 km (3 miles) north of the centre on the banks of the Etang de Ginès, lies the **Parc Ornithologique du Pont-de-Gau**, with a vast range of Camargue birdlife *(see p140)*.

Eglise de Notre-Dame-de-la-Mer, in Saintes-Maries-de-la-Mer

⌂ Eglise de Notre-Dame-De-la-Mer

19 pl Jean XXIII. **Tel** 04 90 97 80 25. **Open** Apr–Nov & school hols: daily; Dec–Mar: Sat & Sun pm. ⌂ 6pm Mon–Sat (& 11am Wed), 10:30am Sun:

The church dates back to the 4th century, but has been destroyed and rebuilt due to excavations of the saints and its early (and valuable) relics. These are all on display here. The population of the village increases dramatically during the summer and the great pilgrimages. Over 200,000 pilgrims and visitors enter the "Door of Faith" every year. Pilgrims are welcomed and offered guided tours.

🏛 Ginès Information Centre

Pont-de-Gau. **Tel** 04 90 97 86 32. **Open** daily. **Closed** 1 Jan, 1 May, 25 Dec. 🖥 parc-camargue.fr

This information centre offers wonderful views over the flat lagoon. Photographs and documents chronicle the history of the Camargue and its diverse flora and fauna.

🐦 Parc Ornithologique du Pont-de-Gau

RD 570, Pont-de-Gau **Tel** 04 90 97 82 62. **Open** daily. **Closed** 25 Dec. 🐦 ⌂ 🖥 parcornithologique.com

Most of the birds that live in or migrate through the region are represented in this reserve. Huge aviaries house birds that might otherwise be hard to spot. Try to keep to the signposted paths to avoid damage or disturbance *(see p140)*.

🏛 Musée Camarguais

Parc Naturel Régional de Camargue, Mas du Pont de Rousty. (On the D570, 10 km south-west of Arles). **Tel** 04 90 97 10 82. **Open** Wed–Mon. **Closed** Jan, 1 May, 25 Dec. 🅿 ♿ 📷
🆆 parc-camargue.fr

A traditional Provençal *mas* or farmhouse *(see pp26–7)*, that only a short time ago was part of a farm raising cattle and sheep, has been converted to accommodate a fascinating museum of the Camargue. The main part of the museum is housed in a huge sheep barn, built in 1812 and skilfully restored. Displays, including video footage and slide shows, provide an excellent intro-duction to traditional life in the Camargue and to the unique plant and animal life of the Camargue delta. Among the many subjects covered are the lives of the Camargue cowboys, and the *grand* and *petit* Rhône rivers which once flowed far to the east past Nîmes. Many of the displays are focused on traditional life at the time of poet and champion of the Provençal language, Frédéric Mistral, *(see p32)*, a local man who won the Nobel Prize for literature in 1904.

A signposted 3.5-km (2-mile) nature trail leads out from the museum to the Marré de la Grand Mare and back again by a pleasant circular route. Examples of traditional *mas* husbandry are marked on the way. An observation tower at the end of the walk gives great views over the surrounding countryside.

Honey buzzard enclosure at the Pont-de-Gau bird sanctuary

The fine Romanesque façade of the abbey church at St-Gilles-du-Gard

❽ St-Gilles-du-Gard

Road map A3. 🚉 13,838. 🚌 Nîmes. ℹ 1 place F Mistral (04 66 87 33 75). 🗓 Thu & Sun. 🆆 **tourisme.saint-gilles.fr**

Called the "Gateway to the Camargue", St-Gilles is famous for its **Abbaye de St-Gilles.** In medieval times the abbey was vast. The building was damaged in 1562 during the Wars of Religion and all that remains are the west façade, chancel and crypt. The carved façade is the most beautiful in all Provence. It includes the first sculpture of the Passion in Christendom, from the late 12th century.

Founded by Raymond VI of Toulouse, the abbey church was the Knights of St John's first priory in Europe. It soon became one of the key destinations on the pilgrimage route to Santiago de Compostela in Spain and a port of embarkation for the Crusades *(see pp46–7)*. The crypt houses the tomb of Saint Gilles, a hermit who arrived by raft from Greece.

The belltower of the original abbey contains *La Vis*, a spiral staircase which is a master-piece of stonemasonry.

❾ Beaucaire

Road map B3. 🚉 16,000. 🚂 Tarascon. 🚌 ℹ 24 cours Gambetta (04 66 59 26 57). 🗓 Thu & Sun.
🆆 **ot-terredargence.fr**

The bullring in Beaucaire occupies the site of one of the largest fairs in Europe. Held

The unique troglodyte Abbaye de Saint-Roman near Beaucaire

every July for the past seven centuries, it attracted up to a quarter of a million people. A smaller version of the fair takes place today, with a procession through the town on 21 July.

It was inaugurated by Raymond VI in 1217, who enlarged the **Château de Beaucaire**. This was later used by the French kings to look down on their Provençal neighbours across the river. It was partly dismantled on the orders of Cardinal Richelieu but the triangular keep and enough of the walls remain to indicate its impressive scale. There is a Romanesque chapel within the walls, and medieval spectacles, including frequent displays of falconry.

The **Abbaye de St-Roman** is situated 5 km (3 miles) to the northwest of Beaucaire. Dating from the 5th century, it is the only troglodyte monastery in Europe.

🏰 Château de Beaucaire

Place Raymond VII. **Tel** 04 66 59 90 07. **Open** Wed–Mon. 🅿 📷

The legendary Tarasque, the terror of Tarascon

⑩ Tarascon

Road map B3. 13,600.
Ave de la République (04 90 91 03 52). Tue & Fri. **tarascon.fr**

The gleaming white vision of the **Château Royal de Provence** is one of the landmarks of the Rhône. Little is left of the glittering court of Good King René who finished the building his father, Louis II of Anjou, began early in the 15th century *(see pp50–51)*. Following René's death in 1480, Provence fell to France, and the castle became a prison until 1926. A drawbridge leads to the poultry yard and garrison quarters. Beside it rises the impressive main castle, centred on a courtyard from where two spiral staircases lead to royal apartments and other rooms in its sturdy towers. Prisoners' graffiti and some painted ceiling panels remain, but the only adornment is a handful of borrowed 17th-century tapestries which depict the deeds of Roman general Scipio (237–183 BC).

The **Collégiale Ste-Marthe,** nearby has a tomb in the crypt to the monster-taming saint. According to legend, St Martha *(see p46)* rescued the inhabitants from the Tarasque, a man-eating monster, half lion, half armadillo, which gave the town its name. The event is celebrated each June in the Fête de la Tarasque *(see p37)*.

In the old town is the 16th-century Cloître des Cordeliers where exhibitions are held. On the arcaded Rue des Halles is the 17th-century town hall, with a carved façade and balcony.

The fairy-tale Château de Tarascon, stronghold of Good King René

The traditional life of the area and its hand-printed fabrics is seen in the **Musée Souleïado**. The ancient textile industry was revived in 1938, under the name *Souleïado*, meaning "the sun passing through the clouds" in Provençal. In the museum are 40,000 18th-century woodblocks, many of them still used for the company's colourful prints.

L'Espace Tartarin is a museum devoted to the tall-story telling Provençal "hero" of three comic novels by Alphonse Daudet *(see p32)*.

🏠 **Château Royal de Provence**
Blvd du Roi René. **Tel** 04 90 91 01 93. **Open** daily. **Closed** 1 Jan, 1 May, 1 & 11 Nov, 25 Dec.
chateau.tarascon.fr

🏛 **Musée Souleïado**
39 rue Charles Deméry. **Tel** 04 90 91 50 11. **Open** Mon–Sat. **Closed** 1 Jan, 1 & 11 Nov, 25 Dec.

🏛 **L'Espace Tartarin**
55 bis blvd Itam. **Tel** 04 90 91 38 71. **Open** Apr–Nov: Mon–Sat. **Closed** 1 May, 1 & 11 Nov.

⑪ St-Rémy-de-Provence

Road map B3. 10,600. Avignon. Pl Jean-Jaurès (04 90 92 05 22). Wed & Sat. **saintremy-de-provence.com**

St-Rémy is ideal for exploring the Alpilles countryside which supplies the plants for its traditional *herboristeries*, or herb shops. In nearby Graveson, the **Musée des Arômes et du Parfum** displays implements of their craft.

St-Rémy's **Eglise St-Martin** contains an exceptional organ, which can be heard during the summer festival "Organa", or on Saturday recitals.

One of the town's most attractive 15th–16th-century mansions is now a museum. The **Musée des Alpilles** has a fine ethnographic collection. The well-known 16th-century physician and astrologer, Nostradamus, was born in a house in the outer wall of the avenue Hoche, in the old quarter of St-Rémy.

The **Musée Estrine Centre**, in the 18th-century Hôtel Estrine, houses modern and contemporary art. Temporary exhibits pay tribute to Van Gogh's relationship with St-Rémy. In May 1889, after he had mutilated his ear, Van Gogh arrived at the **Cloistre et Cliniques de St-Paul de Mausole**, which is situated between the town and Glanum. The grounds and the 12th-century monastery house a museum and culture centre in which an entire wing is dedicated to the painter's stay. You can visit a reconstruction of Van Gogh's room and the field that he painted 15 times.

Just behind the clinic is Le Mas de la Pyramide, a farmstead half-built into the rock. It was once a Roman quarry, but now houses an

Herbs and spices on sale in St-Rémy market, place de la République

The triumphal arch at the Site Archéologique de Glanum, built in the reign of Augustus, a 15-minute walk from the centre of St-Rémy

agricultural museum. The remains of the earliest Greek houses in Provence, from the 4th-century BC, are in **Site Archéologique de Glanum** *(see p44)*, a Greco-Roman town at the head of a valley in the Alpilles. Dramatic memorials, known as Les Antiques, still stand along the roadside – a triumphal arch from 10 BC, celebrating Caesar's conquest of the Greeks and Gaul, and a mausoleum dating from about 30 BC.

Musée des Arômes et du Parfum
Ancien chemin d'Arles, Graveson-en-Provence. **Tel** 04 90 95 81 72. **Open** daily. **Closed** 1 Jan, 1 May, 25 Dec. **W** museedesaromes.com

Musée des Alpilles
Place Favier. **Tel** 04 90 92 68 24. **Open** May–Sep: Tue–Sun; Oct–Apr: Tue–Sat. **Closed** 1 Jan, 1 May, 25 Dec.

Musée Estrine Centre
8 rue Estrine. **Tel** 04 90 92 34 72. **Open** Tue–Sun. **Closed** Dec–Mar. restricted. **W** musee-estrine.fr

Cloistre et Cliniques de St-Paul de Mausole
Chemin St-Paul. **Tel** 04 90 92 77 00. **Open** Mar–Dec: daily. **Closed** public hols. **W** saintpauldemausole.fr

Site Archéologique de Glanum
Rte des Baux. **Tel** 04 90 92 35 07. **Open** Apr–Aug: daily; Sep–Mar: Tue–Sun. **Closed** 1 Jan, 1 May, 1 & 11 Nov, 25 Dec. **W** glanum. monuments-nationales.fr

Les Alpilles

Road map B3. Arles, Tarascon, Salon-de-Provence. Les Baux-de-Provence, St-Rémy-de-Provence, Eyguières, Eygalières. St-Rémy-de-Provence (04 90 92 05 22).

St-Rémy-de-Provence is on the western side of the lime-stone massif of Les Alpilles, a 24-km (15-mile) chain between the Rhône and Durance rivers. A high point is **La Caume**, at 387 m (1,270 ft), reached from St-Rémy, just beyond Glanum.

East of St-Rémy, the road to Cavaillon runs along the north side of the massif, with a right turn to Eygalières. The painter Mario Prassinos

(1916–85) lived here. Just beyond the village is the 12th-century Chapelle St-Sixte.

The road continues towards Orgon where there are views across the Durance Valley and the Luberon. Orgon skirts the massif on the eastern side. A right turn leads past the ruins of Castelas de Roquemartine and Eyguières, a pleasant village with a Romanesque church. It is a two-hour walk to Les Opiés, a 493-m (1,617-ft) hill crowned by a tower. This forms part of the GR6 which crosses the chain to Les Baux, one of the best walking routes in Provence. From Castelas de Roquemartine the road heads back west towards Les Baux.

The chalky massif of Les Alpilles, "Little Alps", in the heart of Provence

A late 18th-century fresco showing the Baux warriors in battle against the Saracens in 1266

🔞 Les Baux-de-Provence

Road map B3. 🏛 470. 🚌 ℹ️ La Maison du Roy (04 90 54 34 39). 🌐 **lesbauxdeprovence.com**

Les Baux sits on a spur of the Alpilles (*bau* in Provençal means escarpment) and the historic **Château des Baux** has views across to the Camargue (*see pp140–43*). The most dramatic fortress site in Provence, it has nearly two million visitors a year, so avoid midsummer, or go early in the morning. The pedestrianized town has a car park beside the Porte Mage gate.

When the Lords of Baux built their fine citadel here in the 10th century, they claimed one of the three wise men, King Balthazar, as an ancestor and took the star of Bethlehem as their emblem. These fierce warriors originated the troubadour Courts of Love and wooed noble ladies with poetry and songs. This became the medieval convention known as courtly love and paved the way for a literary tradition.

The citadel ruins lie on the heights of the escarpment. Their entrance is via the 14th-century Tour-du-Brau. A plateau extends to the end of the escarpment, where there is a monument to the poet Charloun Rieu (1846–1924). In the town centre, two other museums of local interest are

Monument to poet Charloun Rieu

the **Fondation Louis Jou** and the **Musée des Santons**. Next door to the 12th-century Eglise St-Vincent is the Chapelle des Pénitents Blancs, decorated in 1974 by the local artist Yves Brayer. Just north of Les Baux lies the **Carrières de Lumières**.

🏰 Château des Baux

Tel 04 90 54 55 56. **Open** daily. 🌐 **chateau-baux-provence.com**
This majestic fortified castle offers breathtaking views of the surrounding region from Aix to Arles.

🏛 Fondation Louis Jou

Hôtel Brion, Grande Rue. **Tel** 04 90 54 34 17. **Open** by appt. 🈲
Medieval books are housed here, along with a collection of prints and drawings by Dürer, Goya and Jou, the local engraver after whom the museum is named.

🏛 Musée des Santons

La Maison du Roy. **Tel** 04 90 54 34 39. **Open** daily.

In the 16th-century old town hall, a Provençal crib scene has been created, representing the nativity at Les Baux. Handmade clay *santons* or figurines (*see p52*), representing saints and local figures, show the evolution of Provençal costume.

🏛 Carrières de Lumières

Route de Maillane. **Tel** 04 90 54 47 37. **Open** daily. 🈲🅿️🌐 **carrieres-lumieres.com**

Located on the D27 road to the north of Les Baux and within walking distance of the main car park in Les Baux is the Val d'Enfer or the Valley of Hell. This jagged gorge, said to be inhabited by witches and spirits, may have inspired some of Dante's poetry. It is also the site where bauxite was discovered in 1822 by the mineralogist Berthier, who named it after the town. It was in this big quarry that the Cathédrale d'Images

View of the citadel and village of Les Baux

or presently, the Carrières de Lumières was established. The imaginative slide show is projected not only onto the white limestone walls of the natural theatre, but also the floor and ceiling, creating a three dimensional effect. The 30-minute show is renewed each year. Accompanied by captivating music, it is an extraordinary audio-visual experience.

Les Baux's Chapelle des Pénitents, next to the Eglise St-Vincent

⑭ Fontvieille

Road map B3. 🗺 3,700. 🚍 🚉
🛈 Ave des Moulins (04 90 54 67 49).
🗓 Mon & Fri. 🌐 **fontvieille-provence.com**

Fontvieille is an agreeable country town in the flat fruit and vegetable lands of the irrigated Baux Valley. Halfway between Arles and Les Alpilles, the town makes an excellent centre from which to explore. Until the French Revolution in 1789, the town's history was bound up with the Abbaye de Montmajour. The oratories that stand at the four corners of the small town were erected in 1721 to celebrate the end of the plague (see pp52–3).

To the south on the D33, set on a stony hill is the Moulin de Daudet and further on at Barbegal are the remarkable remains of a Roman aqueduct.

⑮ Abbaye de Montmajour

Road map B3. Route de Fontvieille.
Tel 04 90 54 64 17. **Open** Apr–Sep: daily; Oct–Mar: Tue–Sun. **Closed** 1 Jan, 1 May, 1 & 11 Nov, 25 Dec. 🚻 ♿

Standing out like Noah's ark on Mount Ararat, 5 km (3 miles) northwest of Arles, this Benedictine abbey was built in the 10th century. At the time, the site was an island refuge in marshland. The handful of monks in residence spent all their spare time draining this area of marshland between the Alpilles chain and the Rhône.

The abbey was an imposing place, though all the Baroque buildings were destroyed by fire in 1726 and never restored. The original church is said to have been founded by Saint Trophime as a sanctuary from the Romans. It grew rich in the Middle Ages when thousands of pilgrims arrived at Easter to purchase pardons. After 1791, the abbey was broken up by two successive owners who bought it from the state. The

The cloisters and keep of the Abbaye de Montmajour

abbey was largely restored in the 19th century.

The **Eglise Notre-Dame** is one of the largest Romanesque buildings in Provence. Below, the 12th-century crypt has been built into the sloping hill. The cloister has double pillars ornamented with beasts and lies in the shadows of the 26-m (85-ft) tower, built in the 1360s. It is worth climbing the 124 steps to the tower platform to see the stunning view across to the sea. Also carved into the hillside is the atmospheric **Chapelle de St-Pierre**. It was established at the same time as the abbey and is a primitive place of worship. There are a number of tombs in the abbey grounds, but the principal burial area is the 12th-century **Chapelle Ste-Croix**. It lies not far to the east and is built in the shape of a Greek cross.

Daudet's Windmill

The Moulin de Daudet is one of the most famous literary landmarks in France. Alphonse Daudet was born in Nîmes in 1840 and made his name in Paris. The windmill is the setting of Daudet's *Letters from my Windmill*, stories about Provençal life, first published in 1860 and popular ever since. He observed the local characters and wrote about their lives with irony and pathos. He never actually lived in the mill, but made imaginative use of some of the resident miller's tales. When he stayed in Fontvieille he was a guest in the 19th-century Château de Montauban. He came to find respite from the capital, but returned there in order to write his stories. The mill cannot be visited, but there is a small museum located in the château dedicated to Daudet.

⑯ Street-by-Street: Arles

Many tourist sites in Arles bear the stamp of their Roman past, and all are within comfortable walking distance of the central place de la République. On its north side is the Hôtel de Ville, behind which is the place du Forum. This square is the heart of modern life in Arles. Another place to sit at a café and observe the Arlésiens is the boulevard des Lices, where the lively twice-weekly market is held. Some of the shops here and in nearby rue Jean-Jaurès sell bright Provençal fabrics. For museum-buffs, an inclusive ticket (*Passeport Avantage*) gives access to all the museums (except temporary exhibits) and monuments (except Abbaye de Montmajour).

Les Thermes de Constantin are all that remain of Constantine's Palace, built in the 4th century AD.

Musée Réattu
This museum on the banks of the Rhône houses 18th–19th-century and modern art, including this figure of *Le Griffu* (1952) by Germaine Richier.

Hôtel de Ville

Cryptoportico
These three, vaulted subterranean galleries, from the 1st century BC, were built as foundations for the forum. Access is via the Hôtel de Ville.

★ **Eglise St-Trophime**
This fine Romanesque church has a 12th-century portal of the *Last Judgment*, including saints and apostles.

L'Espace Van Gogh, a cultural centre

Roman Obelisk
An ancient obelisk with fountains at its base (one of which is shown here) stands in the place de la République. It came from the Roman circus across the Rhône.

| 0 metres | 100 |
| 0 yards | 100 |

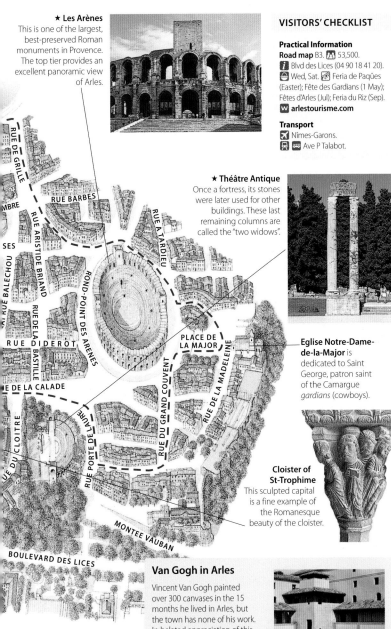

★ **Les Arènes**
This is one of the largest, best-preserved Roman monuments in Provence. The top tier provides an excellent panoramic view of Arles.

VISITORS' CHECKLIST

Practical Information
Road map B3. 🚇 53,500.
🛈 Blvd des Lices (04 90 18 41 20).
🏠 Wed, Sat. 🎪 Feria de Paques (Easter); Fête des Gardians (1 May); Fêtes d'Arles (Jul); Feria du Riz (Sep).
w arlestourisme.com

Transport
✈ Nîmes-Garons.
🚉 🚌 Ave P Talabot.

★ **Théâtre Antique**
Once a fortress, its stones were later used for other buildings. These last remaining columns are called the "two widows".

Eglise Notre-Dame-de-la-Major is dedicated to Saint George, patron saint of the Camargue *gardians* (cowboys).

Cloister of St-Trophime
This sculpted capital is a fine example of the Romanesque beauty of the cloister.

RUE DE GRILLE
RUE BARBES
RUE A. TARDIEU
RUE ARISTIDE BRIAND
RUE BALECHOU
ROND-POINT DES ARÈNES
SES
RUE DE LA BASTILLE
RUE DIDEROT
E DE LA CALADE
RUE PORTE DE LAURE
UE DU CLOITRE
PLACE DE LA MAJOR
RUE DU GRAND COUVENT
RUE DE LA MADELEINE
MONTEE VAUBAN
BOULEVARD DES LICES

Van Gogh in Arles

Vincent Van Gogh painted over 300 canvases in the 15 months he lived in Arles, but the town has none of his work. In belated appreciation of this lonely artist, the Hôtel-Dieu has been turned into L'Espace Van Gogh, with a library and exhibition space. Several sites are evocative of him, however; the Café Van Gogh in the place du Forum has been renovated to look as it did in his *Café du Soir*.

Courtyard of L'Espace Van Gogh, formerly known as Hôtel-Dieu

Key

— Suggested route

Exploring Arles

The city of Arles was a Greek site expanded by the Romans into a "little Rome". Here, on the most southerly crossing point on the Rhône, they built shipyards, baths, a racetrack and an arena. Then the capital of the three Gauls – France, Spain and Britain – Arles remains one of the most distinctive towns in Provence with fine relics from its Gallo-Roman past. Cars should be parked outside the narrow lanes of the old town.

Sarcophagi in the historic cemetary of Les Alyscamps

Roman mosaic of *Europa and the Bull*, in the Musée Départemental de l'Arles Antique

🏛 Les Arènes

Rond-point des Arènes. **Tel** 04 90 49 59 05. **Open** daily. **Closed** 1 Jan, 1 May, 1 Nov, 25 Dec & for bullfights and events. 🎫 📷 🆆 **arenes-arles.com**

The most impressive of the surviving Roman monuments, the amphitheatre is on the east side of the old town. It was the largest of the Roman buildings in Gaul. Slightly oval, it measures 136 m (446 ft) by 107 m (351 ft) and could seat 20,000. Mosaics decorated the floors of some internal rooms, the better to wash down after bloody affrays. Today Spanish and Provençal bullfights are held regularly in the arena.

Just to the southwest of the amphitheatre is the elegant Roman **Théâtre Antique**, which has 2,000 tiered seats arranged in a hemisphere.

🏛 Musée Départemental de l'Arles Antique

Presqu'île du Cirque Romain. **Tel** 04 13 31 51 03. **Open** Wed–Mon. **Closed** 1 Jan, 1 May, 1 Nov, 25 Dec. ♿ 🅿 🏪 🆆 **arles-antique.cg13.fr**

Arles became Christian after Constantine's conversion in AD 312. This museum displays fine examples of Romano-Christian sculpture, as well as local ancient artifacts and pagan art, including a copy of the Venus of Arles.

🏛 Cryptoportico

Place de la République. **Tel** 04 90 49 38 20. **Open** daily (mid-May–Oct). **Closed** 1 Jan, 1 May, 1 Nov, 25 Dec. 📷 🆆 **patrimoine-ville-arles.fr**

These huge subterranean galleries (*see p45*), ventilated by air shafts, were part of the forum's structure.

🏛 Les Alyscamps

Ave des Alyscamps. **Tel** 04 90 49 38 20. **Open** daily. **Closed** 1 Jan, 1 May, 1 Nov, 25 Dec. 📷 ♿

From Roman to late Medieval times, Les Alyscamps was one of the largest and most famous cemeteries in the Western world. Romans avoided it at night, making it an ideal meeting place for early Christians, led by St Trophime. Christians were often buried by the tomb of Genesius, a Roman servant and beheaded Christian martyr.

🏛 Eglise St-Trophime

Place de la République. **Tel** 04 90 96 07 38. **Open** daily. **Closed** 1 Jan, 1 May, 1 Nov, 25 Dec. 📷 cloisters. 📷 ♿ 🆆 **patrimoine-ville-arles.fr**

This is one of the most beautiful Romanesque churches in Provence. The portal and cloisters are decorated with biblical scenes. St Trophime, thought to be the first bishop of Arles in the early 3rd century, appears with St Peter and St John on the carved northeast pillar.

🏛 Les Thermes de Constantin

Rue du Grand-Prieuré. **Tel** 04 90 49 38 20. **Open** daily. **Closed** 1 Jan, 1 May, 1 Nov, 25 Dec. 📷

Built by the Roman emperor Constantine in 306 AD, these once vast public baths fell into ruin, but were partially restored by archaeologists, historians and architects at the end of the 19th century. The three remaining original buildings attest to the ingenuity of Roman engineering.

🏛 Musée Réattu

10 rue du Grand-Prieuré. **Tel** 04 90 49 37 58. **Open** Tue–Sun. **Closed** 1 Jan, 1 May, 1 & 11 Nov, 25 Dec. 📷 🆆 **museereattu.arles.fr**

The local artist Jacques Réattu (1760–1833) and his contemporaries form the basis of this collection. A Picasso donation and a photographic display are among 20th-century works.

View of Arles from the opposite bank of the Rhône

For hotels and restaurants in this region see pp198–201 and pp208–217

⓱ Martigues

Road map B4. 👥 48,200. 🚇 🚌
ℹ️ Rond-Point de l'Hôtel de Ville
(04 42 42 31 10). 🛍️ Thu & Sun.
🌐 **martigues-tourisme.com**

The Etang de Berre, situated between Marseille and the Camargue, has the largest petroleum refinery industry in France, which dominates the landscape. However, on the inland side of the Canal de Caronte is the former fishing port and artists' colony of Martigues, which still attracts a holiday crowd.

Martigues lies on both banks of the canal and on the island of Brescon, where the Pont San Sébastien is a popular place for artists to set up their easels. Félix Ziem (1821–1911) was the most ardent admirer of this "little Venice" *(see p30)*; his paintings and works by contemporary artists can be viewed in the **Musée Ziem**.

🏛️ Musée Ziem
Blvd du 14 Juillet. **Tel** 04 42 41 39 60.
Open Wed–Sun pm (Jul–Aug: daily).
Closed public hols.

Canal San Sébastien in Martigues, known as the Birds' Looking-Glass

⓲ Salon-de-Provence

Road map B3. 👥 44,500. 🚇
🚌 ℹ️ 56 cours Gimon (04 90 56 27 60). 🛍️ Wed & Sun.
🌐 **visitsalondeprovence.com**

Known for its olives (the olive oil industry was established in the 1400s) and soap, Salon-de-Provence is dominated by the castellated **Château de l'Empéri**. Once home of the archbishops

The 12th-century Cistercian Abbaye de Silvacane

of Arles, this now contains the Musée de l'Empéri, which has a large collection of militaria from Louis XIV to World War I.

The military tradition in the town is upheld by the French Air Force officers' college, La Patrouille Aérienne de France.

Near the château is the 13th-century **Eglise de St-Michel** and in the north of the old town is the Gothic **St-Laurent**, where the French physician and astrologer Nostradamus is buried. Nostradamus is Salon's most famous citizen. Here, in his adopted home, he wrote *Les Centuries*, his book of predictions, published in 1555. It was banned by the Vatican, as it foretold the diminishing power of the papacy. But his renown was widespread and in 1560 he was made Charles IX's physician.

Salon's four-day Gospel music festival in July echoes throughout the town, with concerts in the château, free street performances and song workshops.

🏰 Château de l'Empéri
Montée du Puech. **Tel** 04 90 44 72 80.
Open Tue–Sun. **Closed** 1 Jan, 1 May, 1 Nov, 24–25 Dec, 31 Dec. 🕵️

Nostradamus, astrologer and citizen of Salon

⓳ Abbaye de Silvacane

Road map C3. **Tel** 04 42 50 41 69.
Open Jun–Sep: daily; Oct–May: Tue–Sun. **Closed** 1 Jan, 1 May, 25 Dec. 🕵️
🏠 🌐 **abbaye-silvacane.com**

Like her two Cistercian sisters, Silvacane is a harmonious 12th-century monastery tucked away in the countryside. A bus from Aix-en-Provence runs regularly to Roque-d'Anthéron, the nearest village. The abbey was founded on the site of a Benedictine monastery, in a clearing of a "forest of reeds" *(silva canorum)*. It adheres to the austere Cistercian style, with no decoration. The church, with nave, two aisles and a high, vaulted transept, is solid, bare and echoing. The cloisters, arcaded like a pigeon loft, are 13th century and the refectory 14th century. Shortly after the refectory was built, all the monks left and the church served the parish. After the Revolution, it was sold as state property and became a farm until transformed back into an abbey.

⑳ Aix-en-Provence

Provence's former capital is an international students' town, with one of the region's most cosmopolitan streets of restaurants and bars, rue de la Verrerie. The university was founded by Louis II of Anjou in 1409 and flourished under his son, Good King René (see pp50–51).

Another wave of prosperity transformed the city in the 17th century, when ramparts, first raised by the Romans in their town of Aquae Sextiae, were pulled down, and the mansion-lined cours Mirabeau was built. Aix's renowned fountains were added in the 18th century.

The cours Mirabeau, grandest of Aix's boulevards

Exploring Aix

North of the cours Mirabeau, sandwiched between the **Cathédrale St-Sauveur** and the place d'Albertas, lies the town's old quarter. Sights include the **Musée des Tapisseries**, housed in the former Bishop's palace, and the splendid 17th-century Hôtel de Ville. Built around a courtyard by Pierre Pavillon from 1655–1670, it stands in a square now used as a flower market. Nearby is the 16th-century clock tower.

Just outside the old town are the ancient Roman baths, the **Thermes Sextius**, and nearby is the 18th-century spa complex.

Aix's finest street, the cours Mirabeau, is named after the orator and revolutionary Comte de Mirabeau. At its western end is the Fontaine de la Rotonde, a cast-iron fountain built in 1860. The north side is lined with shops, pâtisseries and cafés, the most illustrious being the 18th-century Les Deux Garçons (see p219). The south side is lined with elegant mansions: No. 4, Hôtel de Villars (1710); No. 10, the Hôtel d'Isoard de Vauvenargues (1710), former residence of the Marquis of

Entrecasteau who murdered his wife here; No. 19, Hôtel d'Arbaud Jouques (1730); No. 20, Hôtel de Forbin (1658); and Hôtel d'Espagnet at No. 38, once home to the Duchess of Montpensier, known as "La Grande Mademoiselle", niece of Louis XIII. South of the cours Mirabeau is the Quartier Mazarin built during the time of Archbishop Michel Mazarin. Aix's first Gothic church, St-Jean- de-Malte, now houses the **Musée Granet**.

The 17th-century Hôtel de Ville, with the flower market in front

⛪ Cathédrale St-Sauveur

34 pl des Martyrs de la Résistance. **Tel** 04 42 23 45 65. **Open** daily (timings vary, call ahead). 📷 for cloisters. 🌐 **cathedrale-aixenprovence-monument.fr**

The cathedral at the top of the old town creaks with history. The main door has solid walnut panels sculpted by Jean Guiramand (1504). On the right there is a fine 4th–5th-century baptistry, with a Renaissance cupola standing on 2nd-century Corinthian columns. These are from a basilica which stood here beside the Roman forum. The jewel of the church is the triptych of The Burning Bush (1476, see pp50–51) by Nicolas Froment. South of the cathedral are tiled Romanesque cloisters.

🏛 Musée des Tapisseries

Ancien Palais de l'Archeveche, 28 place des Martyrs de la Résistance. **Tel** 04 42 23 09 91. **Open** Wed–Mon. **Closed** Jan, 1 May, 25 & 26 Dec. 📷

Apart from magnificent 17th- and 18th-century Beauvais tapestries, the museum has costumes and stage designs from 1948 onwards, used in the annual Festival International d'Art Lyrique (see p37).

🏛 Musée Estienne de Saint-Jean (Vieil Aix)

17 rue Gaston de Saporta. **Tel** 04 42 91 89 78. **Open** phone for details. 📷
This eclectic collection includes furniture, a 19th-century crèche parlante and figures from the Corpus Christi parade commissioned by King René.

🏛 Muséum d'Histoire Naturelle

Parc Saint Mitre, 166 ave Jean Monnet. **Tel** 04 88 71 81 81. **Open** daily. 📷 📷 📷 🌐 **museum-aix-en-provence.org**
Located in the Parc Saint Mitre, the museum has some fascinating collections of mineralogy and palaeontology, including locally found dinosaur eggs.

🏛 Musée Granet

Pl St-Jean de Malte. **Tel** 04 42 52 88 32. **Open** Tue–Sun. **Closed** 1 Jan, 1 May, 25 Dec. 📷 📷 📷 🌐 **museegranet-aixenprovence.fr**

The city's main museum is in an impressive 17th-century former priory of the Knights of Malta.

Cézanne's studio, filled with his furniture and personal belongings

François Granet (1775–1849), a local artist, bequeathed his collection of French, Italian and Flemish paintings to Aix, including Ingres' *Portrait of Granet* and *Jupiter and Thetis*. There are also works by Granet and other Provençal painters, with eight canvases by Paul Cézanne, plus artifacts from Roman Aix.

🏛 Fondation Vasarely
1 ave Marcel Pagnol. **Tel** 04 42 20 01 09.
Open daily. **Closed** first 2 weeks Jan.
🎨 ♿ ground floor. 🎦 🎭 🔊
🖰 fondationvasarely.org

This series of innovative black-and-white metal hexagons was designed by the king of Op Art Victor Vasarely in the mid-1970s. Alongside his monumental works, the gallery's exhibitions promote art in the city at a national and international level.

🏠 L'Atelier de Cézanne
9 ave Paul Cézanne. **Tel** 04 42 21 06 53.
Open Apr–Sep: daily; Oct–Mar: Mon–Sat. **Closed** 1–3 Jan, 1 May, 25 Dec.
🎨 🎦 🔊 Apr–Sep. 🎭
🖰 atelier-cezanne.com

Ten minutes' walk uphill from the Cathédrale St-Sauveur is the house of renowned artist Paul Cézanne (*see p30*). The studio is much as he left it when he died in 1906. Not far from here you can see the scenic Montagne Ste-Victoire, a favourite subject of the painter.

🏛 Pavillon de Vendôme (Arts Décoratifs)
13 rue de la Molle or 32 rue Célony.
Tel 04 42 91 88 75. **Open** Wed–Mon.
Closed Jan, 1 May, 25 & 26 Dec. 🎭

One of Aix-en-Provence's grandest houses, built for Cardinal de Vendôme in 1667 and later enlarged, the main entrance is supported by two figures of Atlantes. The beautiful rooms are filled with Provençal furniture and portraits.

Aix-en-Provence

1 Cathédrale St-Sauveur
2 Musée des Tapisseries
3 Musée Estienne de Saint-Jean (Vieil Aix)
4 Musée Granet
5 Pavillon de Vendôme (Arts Décoratifs)

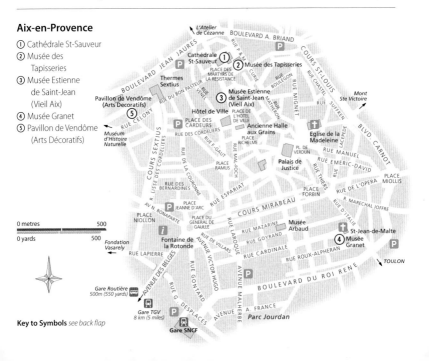

㉑ Marseille

France's premier port and oldest major city is in a surprisingly attractive setting, centred on the Vieux Port, which fishing boats enter between the guardian forts of St-Jean and St-Nicolas. On the north side are the commercial docks and the old town, rebuilt after World War II. People have lived here for 26 centuries, its mixture of cultures being so varied that Alexandre Dumas called it "the meeting place of the entire world".

Boats moored at Marseille's Vieux Port

Exploring Marseille

Inland, running from the end of the port, is La Canebière – cannabis walk – a big, bustling boulevard which stretches from former hemp fields down to the port where the hemp was made into rope.

At the top of La Canebière is the Neo-Gothic Eglise des Réformés. A left and a right turn lead to boulevard Longchamp, and a walk along its length brings you to the Palais Longchamp. This is not really a palace, but more an impressive folly in the form of a colonnade that fans out around a fountain and ends in two large wings. These wings support a natural history and a fine arts museum.

Behind the palace is the city's zoo. Beyond the grid of shopping streets to the south, the town rises towards the basilica of Notre-Dame-de-la-Garde, which provides an unparalleled view of the city. If you visit the morning fish market on the quai des Belges, you can delight in Marseille's famed *bouillabaisse* (see pp204–5) at one of the countless nearby fish restaurants. Just

behind the quai des Belges, at the back of St-Ferréol, is the Jardin des Vestiges, where remains of the ancient Greek settlement, dating from the 4th century BC, have been discovered.

🏛 La Vieille Charité

2 rue de la Vieille Charité. **Tel** 04 91 14 58 38. **Open** Tue–Sun. **Closed** public hols. 🅿 🏠 🖥 ♿ 🆆 vieille-charite-marseille.com

The old town's finest building is the Vieille Charité, a large, well-restored hospice designed by

Pierre Puget (1620–94), architect to Louis XIV. Begun in 1671, its original purpose was to house rural migrants. It is centred on a chapel, now used as an exhibition centre. The first floor has a rich collection of ancient Egyptian artifacts in the Musée d'Archéologie Méditerranéenne and the second floor displays African and Oceanic art.

🏛 Cathédrale de la Major

Place de la Major. **Tel** 04 91 90 52 87. **Open** Tue–Sun.

The old town descends on the west side to the Cathédrale de la Major, a Neo-Byzantine confection completed in 1893. Its crypt contains the tombs of the bishops of Marseille. Beside it, small and beautiful, is the 11th-century Ancienne Cathédrale de la Major, part of which was sacrificed in the building of the new cathedral. Inside are a reliquary altar of 1073 and a 15th-century altar.

🏛 Musée des Docks Romains

10 place Vivaux. **Tel** 04 91 55 36 00. **Open** Tue–Sun. **Closed** public hols. 🅿 🆆 musee-des-docks-romain. marseille.fr

During post-war rebuilding the Roman docks were uncovered. A small museum, mainly displaying large storage urns once used for wine, grain and oil, occupies the site of the docks, now buried in the foundations of a residential block.

🏛 Musée d'Histoire de Marseille

2 rue Henri Barbusse. **Tel** 04 91 55 36 00. **Open** Tue–Sun. **Closed** public hols. 🅿 🏠 🆆 musee-histoire.marseille.fr

Formerly located at the Centre Bourse, this renovated and

The Palais Longchamps, a 19th-century folly set around a fountain

expanded historical museum now sits on the archaeological site of the Jardin des Vestiges, which has been reclassified as Marseille's ancient sea port. Surrounded by the remains of the port, with its fortifications and docks dating from the 1st century, visitors can follow the paved Roman road leading to the entrance of the museum. The museum retraces the history of the city and its port, from prehistoric times to the present day, around the theme of navigation. There are ten maritime wrecks, including the hull of an important 3rd-century ship and seven ancient Greek and Roman vessels. Other interesting exhibits include medieval ceramics, a relief map of the city as it was in 1848 and sarcophagi unearthed at nearby excavations. A visit to the museum ends with displays on the latest developments in Marseille and predictions about the future of the city.

The Jardin des Vestiges, Greek ruins outside the Musée d'Histoire de Marseille

🏛 Musée Cantini
19 rue Grignan. **Tel** 04 91 54 77 75.
Open Tue–Sun. **Closed** public hols.
🖼 📷 Ⓦ musee-cantini.marseille.fr

The Musée Cantini is housed in the 17th-century Hôtel de Montgrand. Its collection of 20th-century art, donated along with the building by the sculptor Jules Cantini, includes Fauve, Cubist and Surrealist paintings.

Basilique de Notre-Dame-de-la-Garde in Marseille

🏛 Musée Borély – la Musée des Arts Décoratif, de la Mode et de la Faïence
Château Borély, 134 av Clôt Bey.
Tel 04 91 55 33 60. **Open** Tue–Sun.
Closed pub hols. 🖼 🦽 📷
Ⓦ musee-borely.marseille.fr

Château Borély, a masterpiece of 18th-century architecture, now houses an exhibition devoted to decorative arts and furniture, fashion from the 17th century to the present day, and earthenware and ceramics. Outdoor shows and concerts take place in the château's gardens.

🏛 Abbaye de St-Victor
Place St-Victor. **Tel** 04 96 11 22 60.
Open daily. 📷 for crypt.
Ⓦ saintvictor.net

Marseille's finest piece of religious architecture is St Victor's basilica, between Notre-Dame and the port. This religious fortress belonged to one of the most powerful abbeys in Provence. It was founded in the 5th century by a monk, St Cassian, in honour of St Victor, martyred two centuries earlier. There are crypts containing catacombs, sarcophagi and the cave of St Victor.

On 2 February St-Victor becomes a place of pilgrimage. Boat-shaped cakes are sold to commemorate the legendary arrival in Provence of the Stes-Maries (see p45).

🏛 Basilique de Notre-Dame-de-la-Garde
Rue Fort du Sanctuaire. **Tel** 04 91 13 40 80. **Open** daily. 🖼
Ⓦ notredamedelagarde.com

The basilica of Notre-Dame-de-la-Garde, which dominates the

VISITORS' CHECKLIST

Practical Information
Road map C4. 🗺 860,000.
ℹ 11 la Canebière (08 26 50 05 00). 🚆 Mon–Sat. 🎉 Fête de la Chandeleur (2 Feb).
Ⓦ marseille-tourisme.com

Transport
✈ 25 km (15 miles) NW Marseille. 🚋 🚌 pl Victor Hugo. 🚢 SNCM, 61 bd des Dames; Chateau d'If ferry, Quai des Belges.

south of the town at 155 m (500 ft), is a 19th-century Neo-Byzantine extravaganza. It is presided over by a golden Madonna on a 46-m (150-ft) bell tower. Much of the interior decoration is by the Düsseldorf School. Many come for the incomparable view over the city.

🏛 Musée Grobet-Labadié
140 blvd Longchamp. **Tel** 04 91 62 21 82. **Closed** for renovation (call for details). 🖼 📷 Ⓦ musee-grobet-labadie.marseille.fr

To the north of the city, at the top of boulevard Longchamp, is the finest house in Marseille, with one of the most unusual interiors in the region. It was built in 1873 for a Marseille merchant, Alexandre Labadié. The house and its collection were given to the city in 1919 by his daughter, Marie-Louise.

The Musée Grobet-Labadié has a fine furniture collection, tapestries, 17th–19th century paintings, and many objects of interest, including unusual musical instruments, among them silk and ivory bagpipes.

Detail of *The Flagellation of Christ*, in the Musée Grobet-Labadié

🏛 Palais Longchamp

Blvd de Montrichet. Musée des Beaux-Arts (left wing): **Tel** 04 91 14 59 30. **Open** Tue–Sun. **Closed** public hols. 🚫 ⓦ **musee-des-beaux-arts.marseille.fr** Museum d'Histoire Naturelle (right wing): **Tel** 04 91 14 59 50. **Open** Tue–Sun. **Closed** public hols. 🚫 ⓦ **museum-marseille.org**

This 19th-century palace is home to the Musée des Beaux-Arts and the Museum d'Histoire Naturelle, with its stuffed animal collection. The renovated Musée des Beaux-Arts contains works by local artists as well as paintings by French, Italian and Flemish old masters.

Le Sacrifice de Noé by Pierre Puget in the Musée des Beaux Arts

The Château d'If in the bay of Marseille, a prison in reality and fiction

🏰 Château d'If

Vieux Port. **Tel** 04 91 59 02 30. **Open** daily (Sep–Mar: Tue–Sun). 🚫 ∅ Feb–Nov.

Fact, fiction and legend mingle in this island castle in the bay of Marseille. Until the 16th century it was a barren island, only visited by local fishermen. On a trip to Marseille in 1516, François I decided to make it a fortress. It was built in 1529, and turned into a prison in 1540 until World War I. Famous inmates have included Alexander Dumas' fictional Count of Monte Cristo, the legendary Man in the Iron Mask *(see p75)* and the real

Comte de Mirabeau. In 1516, the first rhinoceros to set foot in Europe was brought ashore here, and drawn by Albrecht Dürer *(see p51)*.

🏢 Cité Radieuse

280 blvd Michelet. **Tel** 08 26 50 05 00 (for guided tour information).

Open Tue–Sat.

A landmark in modern architecture, the Cité Radieuse or Radiant City was opened in 1952. This vertical, concrete construction by Le Corbusier includes shops, social clubs, schools and crèches *(see p29)*.

Marseille

① La Vieille Charité
② Cathédrale de la Major
③ Musée des Docks Romains
④ Musée d'Histoire de Marseille
⑤ Musée Cantini
⑥ Abbaye de St-Victor

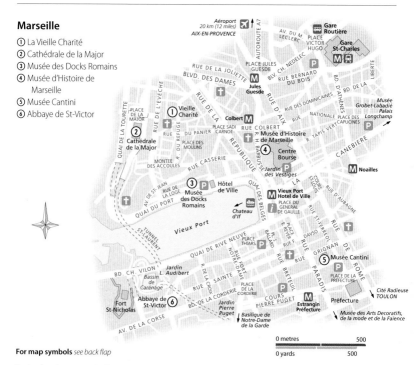

For hotels and restaurants in this region see pp198–201 and pp208–217

㉒ Aubagne

Road map C4. 45,700. 8 cours Barthelémy (04 42 03 49 98). Tue, Thu, Sat & Sun. **tourisme-paysdaubagne.fr**

Marcel Pagnol's life and work is the main attraction of this simple market town. It has a tradition of making ceramics and *santons (see p52).* The tableaux can be seen in the Petit Monde de Marcel Pagnol display on the Esplanade de Gaulle about 300 m from the tourist office.

Just outside the town is the headquarters of the French Foreign Legion, moved here from Algeria in 1962. The renovated headquarters has a **Musée de la Légion Etrangère** with memorabilia on display from a variety of campaigns ranging from Mexico to Indo-China and an extensive library.

Musée de la Légion Etrangère
Chemin de la Thuilière. **Tel** 04 42 18 12 41. **Open** 10am–12pm & 2–6pm Wed–Sun. **samle.legion-etrangere.com**

Poster for Pagnol's film *Angèle*

Marcel Pagnol

A plaque at No. 16 cours Barthélemy in Aubagne marks the birthplace of Pagnol, Provençal writer and film-maker. Born in 1895, his holidays were spent in the village of La Treille. His insights into rural Provence enriched tales such as *Jean de Florette* and *Manon des Sources.* The Office de Tourisme has a Circuit Marcel Pagnol, with road routes and walks which take in La Treille and other sites of Pagnol's inspiration.

㉓ Les Calanques

Road map C4. Marseille. Marseille, Cassis. Cassis. Cassis, Marseille. Cassis (08 92 39 01 03).

Between Marseille and Cassis the coast is broken up by *calanques* – enticing fjord-like inlets lying between vertical white cliffs. Continuing deep under the blue waters, they offer safe natural harbours and fascinating aquatic life, with glorious views from the high clifftops *(see also pp34–5).* Their precipitous faces provide a challenge to climbers. A major attraction of the area is the Parc national des Calanques, the only national park in Europe to inlcude land, marine and semi-urban areas. Opened in 2012, it has around 200 protected animal, plant and marine species.

From Cassis, it is possible to walk to the nearest *calanque*, Port-Miou. Beyond it lies Port-Pin, with occasional pine trees and a shady beach, but the most scenic is En-Vau, which has a sandy beach and needle-like rocks rising from the sea. On the western side, the Sormiou and Morgiou inlets can be approached by road.

In 1991, a cave was found with its entrance 100 m (350 ft) beneath the sea at Sormiou. It is decorated with pictures of prehistoric animals resembling the ancient cave paintings at Lascaux in the Dordogne. Bear in mind when visiting the area that the main car parks serving Les Calanques beaches are notorious for theft.

En-Vau, the most beautiful of Les Calanques, along the coast from Cassis

㉔ Cassis

Road map C4. 7,600. Quai des Moulins (08 92 25 98 92). Wed & Fri. **ot-cassis.com**

A favourite summer resort of artists such as Derain, Dufy and Matisse, Cassis is a lovely port, tucked into limestone hills. The Romans liked it, too, and built villas here, and when Marseille prospered in the 17th century a number of mansions were erected. It was also a busy fishing centre in the 19th century, and is still known for its seafood. The local delicacy is sea urchins, enjoyed with a glass of Cassis' reputed AOC white wine.

There is **Musée Municipal Méditerranéen**, with items dating back to the Greeks, some rescued from the seabed. It also shows Cassis to have been a substantial trading port up till World War II. There are paintings by Félix Ziem *(see p30)* and by other early 20th-century artists who were equally drawn to Cassis, like Winston Churchill, who learnt to paint here.

Apart from Les Calanques, there are three good beaches, notably the Plage de la Grande Mer. Between Cassis and La Ciotat are the red cliffs of Cap Canaille, with a 4-hour walk (one-way) along Route des Crêtes.

Musée Municipal Méditerranéen d'Art et Traditions Populaires
Place Baragnon. **Tel** 04 42 01 88 66. **Open** Wed–Sat. **Closed** public hols. restricted.

VAUCLUSE

Vaucluse is a land of vines and lavender, truffles and melons, which many know about through the books of the English expatriate and author Peter Mayle. His works depict village life in the Luberon, an idyllic countryside where Picasso spent his last years. Roussillon, set among ochre quarries, also became the topic of a book, when American sociologist Laurence Wylie experienced village life there in the 1950s.

The jewel of Vaucluse is the fortified riverside city of Avignon, home to the popes during their "Babylonian exile" from 1309–77, and now host to one of the great music and theatre festivals of France. The popes' castle at Châteauneuf-du-Pape is now a ruin, but the village still produces stupendous wines. The Rhône valley wine region is justly renowned, and its vineyards spread as far northeast as the slopes of the towering giant of Provence, Mont Ventoux.

The Roman legacy in Vaucluse is also remarkable. It is glimpsed in the great theatre and triumphal arch in Orange, and in the ruins of Vaison-la-Romaine which were not built over by successive civilizations. Carpentras was also a Roman town, but its claim to fame is its possession of France's oldest synagogue. The story of the Jews, who were given papal protection in Vaucluse, is one of many religious histories which can be traced through the region. Another is the Baron of Oppède's brutal crusade against the Vaudois heretics in 1545, when many villages were destroyed.

Near Oppède, at Lacoste, a path leads to the château of France's notorious libertine Marquis de Sade. Perhaps a more elevated writer was Petrarch, who lived in Fontaine-de-Vaucluse, where the Sorgue river emerges from a mysterious source.

A vine-covered house at Le Bastidon, near the Luberon

◀ Lavender fields in glorious bloom outside the 12th-century Abbaye de Sénanque

Exploring Vaucluse

Vaucluse, which takes its name from the Latin *vallis clausa* (closed valley), covers 3,540 sq km (2,200 sq miles). It is bordered by the Rhône in the west, the Durance in the south, and the foothills of the Alps to the east, and has a series of highland chains, dominated by the serene Mont Ventoux *(see p164)*. The extraordinary Dentelles pinnacles are in the west and to the south is the Vaucluse Plateau, where the river Sorgue flows in the beautiful and dramatic setting of Fontaine-de-Vaucluse.

Sights at a Glance

1 Bollène
2 Vaison-la-Romaine
4 Mont Ventoux
5 *Orange pp165–7*
6 Caderousse
7 Châteauneuf-du-Pape
8 Carpentras
9 Abbaye de Sénanque
10 Fontaine-de-Vaucluse
11 L'Isle-sur-la-Sorgue
12 *Avignon pp170–2*
13 Gordes
14 Roussillon
15 Cavaillon
17 Apt
18 Cadenet
19 Ansouis
20 Pertuis
21 La Tour d'Aigues

Tours

3 Dentelles
16 *Petit Luberon pp174–5*

The roofs and terraces of Gordes, crowned by the church and castle

Key

▬▬ Motorway
▬▬ Major road
▬▬ Secondary road
▬▬ Minor road
▬▬ Scenic route
▬▬ Main railway
— Minor railway
▬▬ Regional border

For additional map symbols *see back flap*

Night view across the Rhône to Avignon's famous bridge and Palais des Papes

Getting Around

The main highways, the A7 Autoroute du Soleil and its accompanying toll-free national road, the D907, travel down the Rhône valley to the west of the region. The main railway line follows these roads, stopping at the principal towns, and the TGV halts at Avignon. The other railway lines across Vaucluse are used for freight, so you may need to take a bus from Avignon to such places as Vaison-la-Romaine, Carpentras and Orange. Boat trips are organized on the Rhône at Avignon.

MONT VENTOUX **4**

alaucène D974

Bédoin

D164

Mormoiron D1

D974

Sault-de-Vaucluse

zan D942

Nesques

St Jean-de-Sault

Plateau de Saint Christal

Venasques

D943

D30

VAUCLUSE

D4

NTAINE-DE-UCLUSE

St Saturnin-lès-Apt

9 ABBAYE DE SÉNANQUE

des ries

13 GORDES

D943

14 ROUSSILLON

Coustellet

APT **17**

D900

Saignon

Oppède-le-Vieux

Ménerbes

Lacoste

Bonnieux

Luberon

Mourre Nègre 1125m

TIT

16 LUBERON

D943

Grand

Parc Naturel Régional de Luberon

D956

Digne-les-Bains

Lourmarin

Grambois

A51

CADENET **18**

19 ANSOUIS

Durance

D973

21 LA TOUR D'AIGUES

D973

20 PERTUIS

D96

0 kilometres   10

0 miles   10

Aix-en-Provence

A51

The Belvédère Pasteur garden in Bollène

❶ Bollène

Road map B2. 🏛 14,400. 🚘 🚌
ℹ Pl Reynaud de la Gardette
(04 90 40 51 45). 🅿 Mon.
🌐 **bollenetourisme.com**

Despite being spread along the A7 autoroute, Bollène is pleasant, with airy boulevards and walks beside the river Lez, where there is a camping site. The narrow streets of the old quarter lead to the 11th-century **Collégiale St-Martin**, with its timber saddleback roof and Renaissance doorway. Bollène became famous in 1882, when Louis Pasteur stayed here and developed innoculation against swine fever. The **Belvédère Pasteur** garden above the town has views over the Rhône valley to the Cévennes, the Bollène hydroelectric power station and Tricastin nuclear power plant. The town hosts a world music festival during the last two weeks of July.

Just north of Bollène is the ghost village of Barri. Its trogolodyte houses, presently under renovation, were hiding places in World War II.

❷ Vaison-la-Romaine

Road map B2. 🏛 6,429. 🚌 ℹ Pl du Chanoine Sautel (04 90 36 02 11).
🛒 Tue. 🌐 **vaison-ventoux-tourisme.com**

The pavement cafés in this attractive stone-and-red-roof town on the river Ouvèze are among Provence's most chic.

The modern town sits beside the Roman town, opposite the hilltop Haute-Ville on the other side of the river. Vaison is a smart address for Parisians' second homes and, judging by the opulent remains left by the Romans, it has long been sought after. The Romans lived with the native Celtic Vocontii and the population was around 10,000. Two sites have been excavated, divided by the avenue Général-de-Gaulle. The upper site, known as the Puymin Quarter, has a Roman theatre, still used for Vaison's summer festival in July, centred on dance. Its stage is cut out of rock, and the theatre seats up to 6,000. Many Roman remains come from the villa of a wealthy family, the House of the Messii, and an elegant, colonnaded public building, Pompey's Portico. The site is dotted with copies of original statues that are now kept in the **Musée Théo Desplans**, and include a powerful nude of Hadrian and his well-draped empress, Sabina. Many statues were designed to have their heads replaced whenever there was a change of local officials. Other remains include a communal six-seater latrine and a 3rd-century silver bust, which once stood in the hall of a patrician's house in La Villasse, the district on the other side of the avenue Général-de-Gaulle.

The Haute-Ville, which artists and craftspeople helped to re-populate, is reached by means of a Roman bridge, a single 56-ft (17-m) span used for more than 2,000 years until recent devastating floods necessitated huge repairs. Entrance is via a 14th-century fortified gate. The Romanesque church, built as a **cathedral**, has 7th-century columns in the apse, and a 12th-century cloister. A walk to the summit reveals the ruined castle the victorious Counts of Toulouse built here in 1160.

Mosaic in the museum at Vaison-la-Romaine

🏛 **Roman City**
Fouilles de Puymin and Musée Archeologique Théo Desplans, Pl du Chanoine Sautel. **Tel** 04 90 36 50 48.
Open daily. **Closed** Jan. 🌳 🏛 🚫 🔇 🌀

Grounds of Roman house with 3rd-century silver bust, Vaison-la-Romaine

❸ A Tour of the Dentelles

Dentelle means "lace", and the Dentelles de Montmirail is the name of the 15-km (9-mile) range of hills that form a lacework of delicate peaks. Not as high or rugged as they initially seem, the Dentelles have good paths and offer some of the most accessible, enjoyable mountain walks in Provence. The paths are bright with broom and flanked by pines, oaks and wild almond trees. When you have had your fill of the stunning scenery, enjoy fine Côtes du Rhône wines and delicious goat's cheese produced in the picturesque villages tucked into the folds of the Dentelles.

Muscat grapes outside Beaumes-de-Venise

① Vaison-la-Romaine
A chic town, favoured by wealthy Parisians, Vaison is built on separate Roman and medieval sites. Among its many attractions are the cathedral with its 6th-century sarcophagus of healer St Quenin, and a Romanesque chapel.

Gigondas vineyard

⑥ Gigondas
The local red wine is highly regarded and its producers include the master-chef Roux brothers. The Counts of Orange built the 14th-century château.

Dentelles de Montmirail

② Malaucène
This former Huguenot stronghold has a clock tower, originally built as a watchtower during the Wars of Religion *(see pp50–51)*.

③ Le Barroux
Surrounded by olive and apricot trees, this tiny village is overlooked by a 12th-century château, once a stronghold of the lords of Baux. It has fine views.

⑤ Vacqueyras
The home of the famous troubadour, Raimbaud, who died on a Crusade, this village has a church with a 6th-century baptistry.

④ Beaumes-de-Venise
This is a town of many restaurants, and the home of Muscat, the town's famous fortified sweet white dessert wine, which can be enjoyed with lunch or dinner.

Tips for Drivers

Tour length: 50 km (30 miles).
Stopping off points: The hilltop village of Crestet; Lafare, a hamlet leading to the 627-m (2057-ft) Rocher du Turc; and Montmirail, a 19th-century spa resort visited by Mistral. *(See also pp250–51.)*

Valréas · Crestet · Séguret · Lafare · Montmirail · Orange · Avignon

Key

🚌🚌 Tour route
--- Other roads

0 kilometres 2
0 miles 2

● Mont Ventoux

Road map C2. ✈ Avignon. ⛰ 3,000.
🚌 ℹ Ave de la Promenade, Sault-
en-Provence (04 90 64 01 21).
🔲 **ventoux- en-provence.com**

The "Giant of Provence" is the dominant feature west of the Alps, a limestone massif which reaches 1,912m (6,242 ft). It is easy to reach the car park at the top, unless there is deep snow, which can last until April. The snowline starts at 1,300 m (4,265 ft), but the limestone scree of its summit forms a year-round white cap.

Until 1973 there was a motor race on the south side of Mont Ventoux, to the top: speeds reached up to 145 km/h (90 mph). A car rally takes place in Bedoin in June. The roads have gradually improved and the worst hairpins are now ironed out, but the mountain roads are often included as a gruelling stage on the Tour de France. Britain's cyclist Tommy Simpson suffered a fatal heart attack here in 1967.

It takes around five hours to walk to the summit of Mont Ventoux. Petrarch (see p49) made the first recorded journey from Malaucène at dawn one day in May in 1336. As there were no roads then, it took him a great deal longer.

Summit of Mont Ventoux during the Mistral season

Engraving of rally motor car ascending Mont Ventoux (1904)

The mountain is often windy and its name comes from the French word (vent) for wind. When the northerly Mistral blows, it can almost lift you out of your boots. But the winds dry the moisture in the sky, painting it a deep blue colour and leaving behind clear vistas.

There are three starting points for a walking tour of the mountain: Malaucène, on the north slopes, Bedoin to the south and Sault to the east. Another direct route for hikers is from Brantes on the northeast side, up the Toulourenc valley. The first two towns both have tourist offices that organize guided hikes to see the sun rise

Monument to cycling hero Tommy Simpson

at the summit. The 21-km (13-mile) road from Malaucène passes the 12th-century Chapelle Notre-Dame-du-Groseau and the Source Vauclusienne, a deep pool tapped for an aqueduct by the Romans. The ski centre at Mt Serein is based 5 km (3 miles) from the summit. A viewing table at the peak helps to discern the Cévennes, the Luberon and Ste-Victoire. Descending, the road passes the Col des Tempêtes, known for its stormy weather. The ski centre of Le Chalet-Reynard is at the junction to Sault and les Gorges de la Nesque, and St-Estève has fine views over the Vaucluse.

Provençal Flowers

Because the temperature on Mont Ventoux drops between the foot and the summit by around 11° C (20° F), the vegetation alters from the lavender and peach orchards of the plain via the oak, beech and conifer woodlands to the arctic flowers towards the summit. June is the best month for flowers.

Early purple orchid
Orchis mascula

Alpine poppy
Papaver rhaeticum

Trumpet gentian
Gentiana clusii

For hotels and restaurants in this region see pp198–201 and pp208–217

❺ Orange

Road map B2. 🚂 30,000. 🚪 🚌
ℹ️ 5 cours Aristide Briand (04 90 34
70 88). 🚌 Thu. 🌐 **otorange.fr**

This historical town contains
two of the finest Roman
monuments in Europe. The
Théâtre Antique d'Orange is
known for its world-famous
concerts *(see pp166–7)*, while
the Arc de Triomphe celebrates
the honour of Tiberius and the
conquest of Rome after the
Battle of Actium. Orange is also
the centre for the Côtes du
Rhône vineyards and produce
such as olives, honey and
truffles. Around the 17th-
century Hôtel de Ville, streets
open on to peaceful, shady
squares with café terraces.

Side-chapel altar in the Ancienne
Cathédrale Notre-Dame, Orange

Roman Orange

When the first Roman army
attempted to conquer Gaul, it
was defeated near Orange with
a loss of 80,000 men in 105 BC.
When the army came back
three years later and triumphed,
one of the first monuments
built to show supremacy was
the 19-m (63-ft) Arc de Triomphe
on the via Agrippa between
Arles and Lyons, today little used.

The Old Town

Old Orange is centred around
the 17th-century town hall and
**Ancienne Cathédrale Notre-
Dame**, with its crumbling
Romanesque portal, damaged in
the Wars of Religion *(see pp50–51)*.
The theatre's wall dominates the
place des Frères-Mounet. Louis
XIV described it as "the greatest
wall in my kingdom". There is an

excellent view of the theatre, the
city of Orange and the Rhône
plain from **Colline St-Eutrope**.
This is the site of the remains of
the castle of the princes of Orange,
who gave the Dutch royal family
its title, the House of Orange,
through marriage. The family
also lent their name to states
and cities around the world.

🏛 Arc de Triomphe
Ave de l'Arc de Triomphe.
The monument, a UNESCO World
Heritage Site, has excellent
decorations devoted to war and
maritime themes. There is a mod-
ernistic quality, particularly visible
in the trophies above the side
arches. On the east face, Gallic
prisoners, naked and in chains,
broadcast to the world who was
in charge. Anchors and ropes
showed maritime superiority.
    When Maurice of Nassau
fortified the town in 1622 by
using Roman buildings as
quarries, the arch escaped this
fate by being incorporated into
the defensive walls as a keep.

🏛 Musée d'Art et d'Histoire
d'Orange
1 rue Madeleine Roch. **Tel** 04 90 51
17 60. **Open** daily. 🚫 🌐 **theatre-
antique.com**
The exhibits found in the
courtyard and ground floor reflect
the history of Orange. They include
more than 400 marble fragments
which, when assembled, proved
to be plans of the area, based on

Stone carving of a centaur in the Musée
d'Art et d'Histoire d'Orange

three surveys dating from AD 77.
Also in the museum are portraits
of members of the Royal House
of Orange and paintings by the
British artist, Sir Frank Brangwyn
(1867–1956). One room demons-
trates how printed fabrics were
made in 18th-century Orange.

🏛 L'Harmas de Fabre –
Museum National d'Histoire
Naturelle
Route d'Orange, Serignan du Comtat.
Tel 04 90 30 57 62. **Open** Apr–Oct.
Closed Wed (except Jul–Aug), Sat am,
Sun am. 🚫 🚫
At Sérignan-du-Comtat, 8 km
(5 miles) northeast of Orange is
L'Harmas, the estate of the ento-
mologist and poet Jean-Henri
Fabre (1823–1915). His collection
of insects and fungi, and the
surrounding botanical garden,
attract visitors worldwide.

Arc de Triomphe monument, representing Julius Caesar's conquests

Théâtre Antique et Musée d'Orange

Orange's Roman theatre, a UNESCO World Heritage site, is one of the best preserved in Europe. It was built at the start of the Christian era against the natural height of the Colline-St-Eutrope. Its stage doors were hollow so that actors could stand in front of them and amplify their voices; today other acoustic touches make it ideal for concerts. The *cavea*, or tiered semicircle, held up to 7,000 spectators. From the 16th to 19th centuries, the theatre was filled with squalid housing, traces of which can still be seen. A new roof has been built above the stage. A multimedia presentation of great moments in the theatre's history takes place in four grottoes behind the tiers of the amphitheatre.

Awning Supports
Still visible on the exterior walls are corbels which held the huge *velum*-bearing masts.

Roman Theatre
This reconstruction shows the theatre as it would have looked in Roman times. Today it owes its reputation to its exceptional stage wall, the only Roman stage wall to remain intact.

Main entrance

Night Concerts
Cultural events such as *Les Chorégies d'Orange*, a festival of opera, drama and ballet *(see p37)*, once frequented by Sarah Bernhardt, have been held here since 1869. The theatre is also a popular rock concert venue.

KEY

① **A canvas awning**, known as a *velum*, protected the theatregoers from sun or rain.

② **The stage curtain** *(aulaeum)* was lowered to reveal the stage, rather than raised. It was operated by machinery concealed beneath the floor of the stage.

③ **Side rooms**, or *parascaenia*, were where actors could rest, and props be stored, when not required on stage.

④ **Each strip** of *velum* awning could be rolled individually to suit the direction of the sunlight.

⑤ **Winched capstans** held and tightened the ropes supporting the *velum*.

The Great Wall
Built of red limestone, this massive construction is 103 m (338 ft) long, 36 m (117ft) high and over 1.8 m (5 ft) thick.

Emperor Augustus
This 3.5-m (11-ft) statue, with a hand raised in greeting, dominates the stage at the third level. At its base kneels a figure in breeches, possibly a defeated enemy. Other statues have been destroyed, but this copy was returned to the niche in 1951.

Stage Wall
The inner face of the stage wall *(Frons Scaenae)* still bears fragments of marble friezes and mosaics. A frieze of centaurs framed the royal doorway in the centre.

Marble Columns
The stage wall had three levels, the two upper levels with 76 marble columns, of which only two remain. The wall's many surfaces broke up sound waves, so that the actors could speak without their voices having an echo.

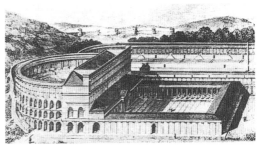

The Great Roman Temple
From 1925–37, excavations took place to the west of the theatre, where 22 houses had been pulled down. They unearthed a vast semicircle and ruins of a temple. Together with the theatre, they would have formed an *Augusteum*, an architectural unit devoted to the worship of Roman emperors.

Exterior of the Romanesque St-Michel church at Caderousse

❻ Caderousse

Road map B2. 🏛 2,700. 🚹 La Mairie, Rue Berbiguier (04 90 51 90 69). 🚌 Tue. 🌐 caderousse.fr

This bankside village lies at a point where Hannibal is said to have crossed the river Rhône with his elephants on his way to Rome in 218 BC. For centuries, Caderousse has endured the floods of the Rhône, and plaques on the town hall record the high levels of floodwater. By 1856, the villagers had had enough, and erected a dyke that is still in place. Its four entry points can close if floods should threaten again.

Caderousse has a Romanesque church, **St-Michel**, to which the Flamboyant Gothic chapel of St-Claude was added during the 16th century.

❼ Châteauneuf-du-Pape

Road map B3. 🏛 2,200. 🚌 🚉 Sorgues, then taxi. 🚹 Place du Portail (04 90 83 71 08). 🌐 ot-chateauneuf-du-pape.mobi

The best-known of the Côtes-du-Rhône wine labels takes its name from an unassuming yellowstone village on a small hill, given over to cellars and restaurants selling the products of the local growers entitled to the *appellation d'origine contrôlée*. The **Musée du Vin** traces the history and current state of the local viniculture.

At the top of the village are the ruins of the **Château des Papes**, mostly burned down in the 16th-century Wars of Religion. From the remaining walls there is a superb view of Avignon and the vineyard-lined clay fields where smooth stones deposited by the Rhône reflect the sun's heat onto 13 varieties

of grapes. The château was built in 1317 by John XXII, an Avignon pope who planted the first vineyards, but it took some 400 years for the wine's reputation to spread. Today, there are 350 Châteauneuf-du-Pape domaines. The nearby town of Pernes-les-Fontaines is known for its 40 fountains, in particular the 18th-century Fontaine du Cormoran. Until 1914, each of the fountains had an individual keeper.

🏛 **Musée du Vin – Maison Brotte**
Ave Pierre de Luxembourg, Châteauneuf-du-Pape. **Tel** 04 90 83 59 44. **Open** daily. **Closed** 1 Jan, 25 Dec. 🚻 restricted. 📷

❽ Carpentras

Road map B3. 🏛 29,500. 🚌 🚹 97 place 25 Août 1944 (04 90 63 00 78). 🚌 Fri. 🌐 carpentras-ventoux.com

As the capital of the Comtat Venaissin, this market town is in the centre of the Côtes-du-Ventoux wine region.

Boulevards encircle the old town, but the Porte d'Orange is the only surviving part of the medieval ramparts. In the Middle Ages, the town had a large Jewish community, and their 14th-century **synagogue** is the oldest in France, now used by some 100 families. While not openly persecuted under papal rule, many Jews changed faith and entered the **Cathédrale-St-Siffrein** by its 15th-century south door, the *Porte Juive*. The cathedral is in the centre of the old town, near a smaller version of Orange's Arc de Triomphe. In it are Provençal paintings and statues by local

sculptor Jacques Bernus (1650–1728). The *Hôtel-Dieu* has a fine 18th-century pharmacy, and there are regional costumes in the **Musée Comtadin-Duplessis**.

✡ **Synagogue**
Pl Maurice Charretier. **Tel** 04 90 63 39 97. **Open** Mon–Fri. **Closed** Jewish feast days.

⛪ **Cathédral St-Siffrein**
3 pl Saint-Siffrein. **Tel** 04 90 63 08 33. **Open** Tue–Sat. **Closed** Sun. ♿

🏛 **Musée Comtadin-Duplessis**
234 blvd Albin-Durand. **Tel** 04 90 63 04 92. **Open** Wed–Mon. **Closed** public hols, Oct–Mar. 📷

Pharmacy in the 18th-century *Hôtel-Dieu* at Carpentras

❾ Abbaye de Sénanque

Road map C3. **Tel** 04 90 72 05 86. **Open** Feb–mid-Nov: Mon–Sat & Sun pm; mid-Nov–Jan: pms only, by guided tour (in French). 🚻 📷 🌐 senanque.fr

The beautifully sited Abbaye de Sénanque, surrounded by a tranquil sea of lavender, is best approached from Gordes (*see p173*). Its monks are often to be seen in the fields.

Like the other abbeys that make up the Cistercian triumvirate in Provence (*see p47*), Sénanque is harmonious and

Châteauneuf-du-Pape vineyards

unadorned. It was founded in 1148 by an abbott and 12 monks, and the building of the serene north-facing abbey church started 12 years later.

Some roofs of the building are still tiled with limestone slates called *lauzes*, also used for making traditional stone dwellings known as *bories* (*see p173*). The abbey's simply designed interior has stone walls, plain windows and a barrel-vaulted ceiling.

Sénanque reached its zenith in the early 13th century, when the abbey owned several local farms. But new riches brought corruption in the 14th century, and by the 17th century, only two monks remained. In 1854 it was restored and housed Cistercian monks, some of whom remained there from 1926 to 1969. The present monks have been living there since 1988.

Fontaine-de-Vaucluse, where the Sorgue river begins

Serene Abbaye de Sénanque built in the 12th century

❿ Fontaine-de-Vaucluse

Road map B3. 🗾 600. 🚍 Avignon. *i* Residence Jean Garcin, Ave Robert Garcin (04 90 20 32 22). **w** oti-delasorgue.fr

The source of the Sorgue river is one of the natural wonders of Provence. It begins underground, with tributaries that drain the Vaucluse plateau, an area of around 2,000 sq km (800 sq miles). In the closed valley above the town, water erupts from an unfathomable depth to develop into a fully fledged river.

Beside the river is the **Moulin à Papier Vallis Clausa**, which produces handmade paper using a 15th-century method. It sells maps, prints and lampshades.

The underground museum, the **Eco-Musée du Gouffre**, features a speleologist's findings over 30 years of exploring Sorgue's dams, caves and waterfalls. The **Musée d'Histoire 1939–1945**, traces the fate of the Resistance during WWII and daily life under Occupation. The **Musée Bibliotheque Pétrarque** was the house where the poet lived for 16 years, and wrote of his love for Laura of Avignon.

🔲 **Moulin à Papier Vallis Clausa**
Chemin du Gouffre. **Tel** 04 90 20 34 14. **Open** daily. **Closed** 1–15 Jan, 25 Dec. 🅱️ 🅿️ **w** moulin-vallisclausa.com

🏛️ **Eco-Musée du Gouffre (Musée de Spéléologie)**
Chemin du Gouffre. **Tel** 04 90 20 34 13. **Open** Feb–15 Nov: daily. 🅿️ 🅱️ 🅾️ 🅰️

🏛️ **Musée d'Histoire Jean Garcin 1939–45**
Chemin de la Fontaine. **Tel** 04 90 20 58 35. **Open** Apr–Oct: Wed–Mon; Nov–Dec & Mar: Sat–Sun. **Closed** Jan, Feb, 1 May, 25 Dec. 🅿️ 🅱️

🏛️ **Musée Bibliotheque Pétrarque**
Rive gauche de la Sorgue. **Tel** 04 90 20 37 20. **Open** Apr–Oct: Wed–Mon. **Closed** 1 May, Nov–Mar. 🅿️

⓫ L'Isle-sur-la-Sorgue

Road map B3. 🗾 19,400. 🚍 🚍 *i* Pl de la Liberté (04 90 38 04 78). 🅰️ Mon, Thu, Sat, Sun (antiques). **w** oti-delasorgue.fr

A haunt for antique hunters at weekends, this attractive town lies on the river Sorgue, which once powered 70 watermills. Today, 14 idle wheels remain. The ornate 17th-century **Notre-Dame-des-Anges** is a major attraction. The tourist office is in an 18th-century granary, and the Musée du Jouet et de la Poupée Ancienne has displays of antique toys and dolls.

Water wheel near place Gambetta, l'Isle-sur-la-Sorgue

⑫ Street-by-Street: Avignon

Bordered to the north and west by the Rhône, the medieval city of Avignon is the chief city of Vaucluse and gateway to Provence. Its walls cover nearly 4.5 km (3 miles) and are punctuated by 39 towers and seven gates. Within the walls thrives a culturally rich city with its own opera house, university, several foreign language schools and numerous theatre companies. The streets and squares are often filled with buskers, and the Avignon festival in July, which includes theatre, mime and cabaret, has now become a major international event.

Chapelle St-Nicolas, named after the patron saint of bargemen, is a 16th-century building on a 13th-century base. Entrance is via Tour du Châtelet.

Porte du Rhône

★ Pont St-Bénézet
Begun in 1177 by shepherd boy Bénézet, this bridge is the subject of the famous rhyme *Sur le Pont d'Avignon*.

Hôtel des Monnaies
The façade of this former mint, built in 1619, bears the arms of Cardinal Borghese.

RUE FE

RUE DE LIMAS

RUE GRANDE FUSTERIE

RUE DES GROTTES

RUE DE LA BALAN

RUE ST-ETIENNE

RUE PETITE FUSTERIE

RUE RACINE

PLACE DE L'HORLOGE

Place de l'Horloge
The main square was laid out in the 15th century and is named after the Gothic clock tower above the town hall. Many of today's buildings date from the 19th century.

Key

— Suggested route

Musée du Petit Palais
The former episcopal offices house a museum of medieval and Renaissance Italian paintings and French works by the Avignon School, including this 1457 *Vierge de Pitié.*

BD DE LA LIGNE

ROCHES DES DOMS

PLACE DU PALAIS

RUE VICE LEGAT

RUE PEYROLLERIE

VISITORS' CHECKLIST

Practical Information
Road map B3. ⛟ 91,250.
ℹ 41 cours Jean-Jaurès (04 32 74 32 74). 🏛 Tue–Sun. 🎭 Le Festival d'Avignon *(see p37).*
Ⓦ avignon-tourisme.com

Transport
✈ 8 km (5 miles) Avignon-Caumont. 🚌 🚏 Blvd St-Roch; Gare TGV (pl de l'Europe, Courtine).

Rocher des Doms
These hillside gardens behind Notre-Dame-des-Doms are the site of earliest settlement.

★ Palais des Papes
Popes ruling in the 14th century built this grand, fortress-like palace *(see pp48–9).* The Chambre du Pape, here, has exquisite tiles.

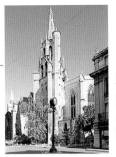

Eglise St-Pierre
This church was built during the 14th to early 16th centuries. The doors on its west façade were carved in 1551 by Antoine Valard. Inside is a fine 15th-century pulpit.

0 metres   100
0 yards   100

Exploring Avignon

Massive ramparts enclose one of the most fascinating towns in southern France. A quick stroll reveals *trompe l'oeil* windows and mansions such as King René's house in the rue du Roi-René. This street leads to the rue des Teinturiers, named after local dyers and textile-makers, where a bridge for pedestrians crosses the river Sorgue to the 16th-century Chapelle des Pénitents Gris.

Palais des Papes in Avignon glimpsed across the river Rhône

🏠 Palais des Papes

Pl du Palais. **Tel** 04 32 74 32 74.
Open daily (times vary). 🅿️ 🎫 📷
📱 📷 **W** palais-des-papes.com

These buildings *(see pp48–9)* give an idea of the grand life under the seven French popes who built a miniature Vatican during their rule here, lasting from 1309–77. They owned their own mint, baked a vast number of loaves every day, and fortified themselves against the French.

Entrance is by means of the Porte des Champeaux, beneath the twin pencil-shaped turrets of the flamboyant Palais Neuf (1342–52), built by Clement VI, which extends south from the solid Palais Vieux (1334–42) of Benoit XII. In the new palace, the main courtyard, La Cour d'Honneur, is the grand central setting for the summer festival *(see p229)*. La Chambre du Pape in the Tour des Anges opposite the entrance has exquisite tiles, and there are fine 14th-century deer-hunting scenes painted by Matteo Giovanetti and others in the adjoining Chambre du Cerf. The larger rooms around the Palais Vieux include the 45-m (148-ft) banqueting hall, Le Grand Tinel, and La Salle du Consistoire, where pictures of all the popes are displayed. The chapel beside it has exquisite frescoes painted by Giovanetti between 1346 and 1348.

Bird tile in the Chambre du Pape

🏛 Cathédrale Notre-Dame-des-Doms

Pl du Palais. **Tel** 04 90 86 81 01.
Closed to the public. Call for update.
W cathedrale-avignon.fr

This building beside the Palais des Papes was begun in the 12th century. Since then it has been damaged and rebuilt several times. A gilded Madonna was added to the tower in the 19th century, and the original 6th-century altar is now in the Chapelle St-Roch, where two popes are buried.

🏛 Musée du Petit Palais

Pl du Palais. **Tel** 04 90 86 44 58.
Open Wed–Mon. **Closed** 1 Jan, 1 May, 1 Nov, 25 Dec. 🅿️ 🎫 📷
W petit-palais.org

Set around an arcaded court-yard, the "little palace", built in 1318, was modified in 1474 to suit Michelangelo's patron, Cardinal Rovere, later Pope Julius II. It became a museum in 1958, and houses Avignon's medieval collection, which includes works by Simone Martini and Botticelli, as well as works from the Avignon School, and many French and Italian religious paintings.

🏛 Musée Lapidaire

27 rue de la République. **Tel** 04 90 85 75 38. **Open** Tue–Sun. **Closed** 1 Jan, 1 May, 25 Dec. 🅿️ **W** musee-lapidaire.org

Once a 17th-century Baroque Jesuit college, the museum has Celtic-Ligurian, Egyptian, Gallic and Roman artifacts, including a 2nd-century Tarasque monster *(see p144)*.

🏛 Musée Calvet

65 rue Joseph Vernet. **Tel** 04 90 86 33 84. **Open** Wed–Mon. **Closed** 1 Jan, 1 May, 25 Dec. 🅿️ ♿ restricted.
W musee-calvet-avignon.com

This evocative museum was visited by the French writer Stendhal, who left his inscription behind. Renovated in 2003 to permit the display of many of the treasures previously stored in their vaults, the highlight is the 19th–20th-century collection, with works by Soutine, Manet, Dufy, Gleizes and Marie Laurencin.

🏛 Musée Angladon

5 rue Laboureur. **Tel** 04 90 82 29 03.
Open pm only Wed–Sun; also Tue in high season. 🅿️ 🎫 **W** angladon.com

This museum cleverly combines modern technology with the intimacy of a private home for displaying this outstanding private collection of 18th–20th-century works of art.

🏛 Collection Lambert

Musée d'Art Contemporain,
5 rue Violette. **Tel** 04 90 16 56 20.
Open Sep–Jun: Tue–Sun; Jul-Aug: daily. **Closed** 1 May. 🅿️ 🎫 ♿ 📷
🎨 **W** collectionlambert.com

Opened in 2000, the Collection Lambert is located in an 18th-century mansion, next to the School of Art. The museum houses an outstanding collection of contemporary art on loan for 20 years from gallery-owner Yvon Lambert. Paintings date from the 1960s, and represents all the major art movements since then.

⑬ Gordes

Road map C3. 🗻 2,000. 🛈 Pl de Château (04 90 72 02 75). 🚌 Tue. **W** gordes-village.com

Expensive restaurants and hotels provide a clue to the popularity of this hilltop village, which spills down in terraces from a Renaissance château and the church of St-Firmin. Its impressive position is the main attraction, although its vaulted, arcaded medieval lanes are also alluring. The village has been popular with artists since the academic Cubist painter André Lhote began visiting in 1938.

The **Château de Gordes** was built in the 16th century on the site of a 12th-century fortress. One of the château's best features is an ornate 16th-century fireplace in the great hall on the first floor, decorated with shells, flowers and pilasters. In the entrance there is an attractive Renaissance door. The building was rented and restored by the Hungarian-born Op Art painter Victor Vasarely (1908–97), and once housed a museum of his abstract works. The château

now hosts temporary exhibitions during the summer. The 17th-century Caves du Palais St-Firmin have an impressive old stone olive press. Just outside Gordes is the **Village des Bories** *(see box)*, now a museum of rural life.

🏠 Château de Gordes
Pl du Chateau. **Tel** 04 90 72 98 64.
Open daily. **Closed** in the winter. 📷

🏠 Village des Bories
Rte de Cavaillon. **Tel** 04 90 72 03 48.
Open daily. **Closed** 1 Jan, 25 Dec. 📷

Bories

The ancient dwellings known as *bories* were domed dry-stone buildings made from *lauzes* (limestone slabs), with walls up to 1.5 m (4 ft) thick. They dated from 2,000 BC and were regularly rebuilt, using ancient methods, until the last century when they were abandoned. Around 3,000 bories are still standing, many in fields where they were used for shelter or storing implements. Twenty have been restored in the Village des Bories, outside Gordes.

⑭ Roussillon

Road map C3. 🗻 1,350. 🛈 Pl de la Poste (04 90 05 60 25). 🚌 Thu. **W** otroussillon.pagesperso-orange.fr

The deep ochres used in the construction of this hilltop community are stunning. No other village looks so warm and rich, so harmonious and inviting. Its hues come from at least 17 shades of ochre discovered in and around the village, notably in the dramatic former quarries along the Sentier des Ochres. The entrance to the quarries is to the east of the village, a 1-hour and 30-minute trip from the information office. The Conservatoire des Ocres et de la Couleur in the old factory (*open daily in summer*), is worth visiting. It displays a huge collection of natural pigments, and runs day courses on the subject.

A superb panorama to the north can be seen from the Castrum, the viewing table beside the church, above the tables with umbrellas in the main square.

Before its housing boom, Roussillon was a typical Provençal backwater. In the 1950s, American sociologist Laurence Wylie spent a year in Roussillon with his family and wrote a book about village life, *Un Village du Vaucluse*. He concluded that Roussillon was a "hard-working, productive community" for all its feuds and tensions. Playwright Samuel Beckett lived here during WWII, but his impression was much less generous.

The hilltop village of Gordes, spilling down in terraces

The 1st-century Roman triumphal arch behind Cavaillon

⑮ Cavaillon

Road map B3. ⛰ 26,000. 🚃 🚌
ℹ️ Pl François Tourel (04 90 71 32 01).
🗓 Mon. 🌐 cavaillon-luberon.com

Perhaps the best place to get your bearings is the viewing table outside the **Chapelle St-Jacques** at the top of the town, which renders the Luberon range in perspective against Mont Ventoux and the Alpilles chain. In closer proximity are the acres of fruit and vegetable plots, for Cavaillon is France's largest market garden, synonymous especially with melons. Its local market competes with the one in Apt for renown as the most important in Vaucluse.

Colline St-Jacques was the site of the pre-Roman settlement that, under Rome, was moved down from its heights and prospered. There is a 1st-century Roman arch in place Duclos nearby. Roman finds have been collected in the **Musée Archéologique de l'Hotel Dieu** in the Grand Rue, which leads north from the church, a former cathedral dedicated to its 6th-century bishop, Saint Véran. The synagogue in rue Hébraïque dates from 1772, although there has been one on this site ever since the 14th century. A small museum, the **Musée Jouves et Juif Comtadin**, commemorates its history.

🏛 **Musée Archéologique de l'Hotel Dieu**
Hôtel Dieu, Porte d'Avignon. **Tel** 04 90 71 26 86. **Open** May–Sep: Wed–Mon. ♿

🏛 **Musée Jouves et Juif Comtadin (et de la Synagogue)**
Rue Hébraïque. **Tel** 04 90 71 21 06.
Open Oct–Apr: Mon, Wed–Sat; Apr–Sep: Wed–Mon. **Closed** 1 Jan, 1 May, 25 Dec. ♿

⑯ A Tour of the Petit Luberon

The Parc Naturel Régional covers 1,200 sq km (463 sq miles) of a limestone mountain range running east from Cavaillon towards Manosque in the Alpes-de-Haute-Provence. It embraces about 50 communities and a past peppered with such infamous figures as the Baron of Oppède and the Marquis de Sade. An unspoiled area, it is ideal for walking. Its two main centres are Apt and Lourmarin. The D943 in the Lourmarin Coomb valley divides the park: the Grand Luberon (see p176) is to the east; and to the west is the Petit Luberon, a land of limestone cliffs, hidden corries and cedar woods, with most towns and villages to the north side of the range.

① **Oppède-le-Vieux**
The dominating ruined castle belonged to Jean Maynier, Baron of Oppède, whose bloody crusade against the Luberon Vaudois in 1545 destroyed 11 villages.

Cedar Forest Botanical Trail, Bonnieux

0 kilometres 2
0 miles 2

Key
▬ Tour route
═ Other roads

Luberon Wildlife

The Parc Naturel Régional is rich in flora and fauna. The central massif is wild and exposed on the north side, sheltered and more cultivated in the south. A wide range of habitats exist in a landscape of white chalk and red ochre cliffs, cedar forests, moorlands and river-hewn gorges. Information is available from La Maison du Parc in Apt (see p176) which publishes suggested walks and tours.

Monkey orchid (Orcis simia) is found on the sunny, chalky grasslands.

The rugged peaks of the Petit Luberon

Tips for Drivers

Tour length: 40 km (25 miles).
Stopping-off points: Ménerbes
has several cafés, Bonnieux is
good for lunch and the Cedar
Forest has attractive picnic spots.
Lourmarin, where Albert Camus
lived and was buried, is handy
for the Petit and Grand Luberon.
All these villages are small, and
quickly fill with cars, so you may
have to walk some distance, and
even climb to castle heights.
W parcduluberon.fr

② **Ménerbes**
At the foot of this stronghold of
16th-century Calvinists is the Musée
du Tire-Bouchon, a fascinating
collection of corkscrews, dating
from the 17th century.

③ **Lacoste**
Little remains of the Marquis
de Sade's château. Arrested for
corrupt practices in 1778, he
spent 12 years in prison writing
up his experiences.

④ **Bonnieux**
The Musée de la Boulangerie gives
a history of bread making. From here
the two-hour Cedar Forest
Botanical Trail is a
pleasant, scenic walk.

• **Abbaye St-Hilaire**

Montagne du Luberon

⑤ **Lourmarin**
The Countess of Agoult, whose family
owned the village château, bore the
composer Franz Liszt (1811–86) three
children: one married Richard Wagner.

↓ *Aix-en-Provence*

Wild boar (*Sus scrofa*, known as
sanglier in French) is a hunter's
prize and a chef's delight.

Eagle owl (*Bubo bubo*, known
as *dugas* in Provençal) is judged
Europe's largest owl.

Beaver (*Castor fiber*, known as
Castor in French) builds dams
on the Calavon and Durance.

For additional map symbols *see back flap*

Grand Luberon

This spectacular range of mountains to the east of the Lourmarin Coomb rises as high as 1,125 m (3,690 ft) at Mourre Nègre. The fine view at the summit must be appreciated on foot, and takes several hours from where you leave the car at Auribeau. The area is outstandingly beautiful and ideal to escape from the crowds. The panorama from the top takes in Digne, the Lure mountain and Durance valley, the Apt basin, l'Etang de Berre and Mont Ventoux.

⓱ Apt

Road map C3. ⚒ 12,325. 🚌
🚉 Avignon. ℹ 20 av Philippe de Girard (04 90 74 03 18). 🛒 Tue & Sat.
🌐 **luberon-apt.fr**

Apt is the northern entry to the Parc Naturel Régional du Luberon (*see pp174–5*). The **Maison du Parc**, a restored 17th-century mansion, provides information on the area, with details of walks, *gîtes d'étapes* and flora and fauna.

The busy old town of Apt has a square for playing *boules*, fountains and plane trees. Surrounded by cherry orchards, it claims to be the world capital of crystallized fruit. The **Musée de l'Aventure Industrielle** explains how the production of crystallized fruits and earthenware pottery combined with the extraction of ochre to bring prosperity to Apt in the 18th and 19th centuries. The town is also famous for truffles and lavender essence. The Saturday market offers Provençal delicacies and entertainment, including jazz,

barrel organ music and stand-up comedy. Excursions can be made to the *Colorado de Rustrel*, the best ochre quarry site by the River Dôa, to the northeast.

The medieval **Cathédrale Ste-Anne** lies at the heart of Apt's old town. Legend has it that the veil of St Anne was brought back from Palestine and hidden in the cathedral by Auspice, who is thought to have been Apt's first bishop. Each July her festival is celebrated with a procession. The Royal Chapel commemorates Anne of Austria. She paid a pilgrimage to Apt to pray for fertility and contributed the funds to finish the chapel, which was finally completed around 1669–70. The treasury inside the sacristy contains the saint's shroud and an 11th-century Arabic standard

14th-century priest's embroidery

from the First Crusade (1096–9). In the apse is a 15th–16th-century window that depicts the tree of Jesse. Nearby is the 17th-century Hôtel d'Albertas.

The items on display in the **Musée d'Histoire et d'Archéologie** consist of prehistoric flints, stone implements, Gallo-Roman carvings, jewellery and mosaics from that period. Just a few miles from Apt, **L'Observatoire Sirene** has an idyllic location and state-of-the-art technology, ideal for star-gazing.

🏛 **Maison du Parc**
60 pl Jean-Jaurès. **Tel** 04 90 04 42 00.
Open Mon–Fri (& Sat May–Sep).
🌐 **parcduluberon.fr**

⛪ **Cathédrale Ste-Anne**
Rue Ste-Anne. **Tel** 04 90 04 85 44.
Closed Sat. 🌐 **apt-cathedrale.com**

🏛 **Musée de l'Aventure Industrielle**
Pl du Postel. **Tel** 04 90 74 95 30.
Open Oct–May: Tue-Sat; Jun–Sep: Mon–Sat. **Closed** Jan, public hols. 📷 ♿

🏛 **Musée d'Histoire et d'Archéologie**
27 rue de l'Amphithéâtre. **Tel** 04 90 74 95 30. **Open** by appointment for groups only. 📷

🏛 **L'Observatoire Sirene**
D34 Lagarde d'Apt. **Tel** 04 90 75 04 17.
Open daily by appt. **Closed** public hols. 📷 ♿ 🌐 **obs-sirene.com**

Jam label illustrating traditional produce of Apt

⓲ Cadenet

Road map C3. 🏔 4,250. 🚌 Avignon.
🚍 *i* 11 pl du Tambour d'Arcole (04
90 68 38 21). 🛒 Main square: Mon
& Sat (May–Oct behind the
church). **W** ot-cadenet.com

Tucked underneath the
hills in the Durance
valley, Cadenet has 11th-
century castle ruins and
a 14th-century church
with a square bell tower.
Its font is made from a
Roman sarcophagus. In
the main square, which is
used for Cadenet's bi-weekly
market, is a statue of the
town's heroic drummer
boy, André Estienne,
who beat such a
raucous tattoo in the
battle for Arcole Bridge in 1796
that the enemy thought they
could hear gunfire, and retreated.

Drummer boy in Cadenet
town square

⓳ Ansouis

Road map C3. 🏔 1,200. *i* Pl du
Château (04 90 07 50 29). 🛒 Sun.
W luberoncotesud.com

One of the most remarkable
things about the Renaissance
Château d'Ansouis is that it was
owned by the Sabran family from
1160 until 2008, when it was sold
to a new owner. The Sabrans have
a proven pedigree: in the 13th
century, Gersende de Sabran
and Raymond Bérenger IV's four
daughters became queens of
France, England, Romania and
Naples respectively. In 1298, Elzéar
de Sabran married Delphine de
Puy, a descendant of the Viscount

Duchess's bedroom in the Château d'Ansouis

of Marseille. But she had resolved
to become a nun, so agreed to the
marriage, but not to its consumma-
tion. Both were canonized
in 1369. The castle's original keep and two
of its four towers
are still visible. Its
gardens include the
Renaissance Garden
of Eden, built on the
former cemetery.
Rousset-Riviere family,
the new owners, has
restored the castle and
expanded its collection.
The **Musée Extraordinaire
de Georges Mazoyer**,
located south of
the village, displays
the artist's work,
Provençal furniture
and a recreated underwater
cave, all in 15th-century cellars.

🏠 **Château d'Ansouis**
Rue du Cartel. **Tel** 04 90 77 23 36.
Open Apr–Oct: Thu–Mon for guided
tours. **Closed** Nov–Mar. 🅿
W chateauansouis.com

🏛 **Musée Extraordinaire de
Georges Mazoyer**
Rue du Vieux Moulin. **Tel** 04 90 09
82 64. **Open** daily pm only. 🅿 🎫

⓴ Pertuis

Road map C3. 🏔 19,500. 🚉 🚌
i Le Donjon, pl Mirabeau (04 90
79 15 56). 🛒 Wed, Fri, Sat.
W tourismepertuis.fr

Once the capital of the Pays
d'Aigues, present-day Pertuis
is a quiet town, whose rich and
fertile surrounding area was

gradually taken over by Aix-en-
Provence. Pertuis was the
birthplace of the philandering
Count of Mirabeau's father, and
the 13th-century clock tower is
located in place Mirabeau.

The **Eglise St-Nicolas**, re-built
in Gothic style in the 16th
century, has a 16th-century
triptych and two 17th-century
marble statues. To the south-
west is the battlemented
14th-century **Tour St-Jacques**.

Triumphal arch entrance to La Tour d'Aigues'
Renaissance château

㉑ La Tour d'Aigues

Road map C3. 🏔 4,290. 🚌 to
Pertuis. *i* Château de la Tour
d'Aigues (04 90 07 50 29). 🛒 Tue.
W luberoncotesud.com

Nestling beside the grand
limestone mountain ranges
of Luberon, and surrounded
by scenic vineyards and
orchards, this beautiful
town takes its name from
a historic 10th-century tower.
The 16th-century castle com-
pletes the triumvirate of
Renaissance châteaux in
the Luberon (the others
are Lourmarin and Ansouis).
Built on the foundations of a
medieval castle by Baron de
Central, its massive portal is
based on the splendid Roman
arch at Orange *(see p165)*.
The castle was damaged
in the French Revolution
(1789–94), but has been
partially restored.

🏠 **Château de la Tour d'Aigues**
BP 48. **Tel** 04 90 07 50 29.
Courtyard: **Open** daily. 🅿
🎫 private tours only (06 71 10 48 28.

ALPES-DE-HAUTE-PROVENCE

In this, the most undiscovered region of Provence, the air is clearer than anywhere else in France, which is why it was the chosen site for France's most important observatory. But the terrain and the weather conditions can be severe. Inaccessibility to areas has restricted development and the traditional, rural way of life is still followed.

Irrigation has helped to improve some corners of this mountainous land. The Valensole plain is now the most important lavender producing area of France. Peaches, apples and pears have been planted in orchards only recently irrigated by the Durance, the region's main river, which has been tamed by dams and a hydro-electric power scheme. These advances have created employment and helped bring prosperity to the region. Another modern development is the Cadarache nuclear research centre, situated just outside Manosque. The town's population has grown rapidly to 20,300 inhabitants, overtaking the region's capital, Digne-les-Bains. Famous for its lavender and healthy living, Digne-les-

Bains is a handsome spa town that has attracted visitors for more than a century and now hopes to enhance its appeal through its devotion to sculpture, which fills the streets.

The region's history and architecture have also been greatly influenced by the terrain and climate. Strategically positioned citadels crown mountain towns such as Sisteron, which was won over by Napoleon in 1815, and the frontier town of Entrevaux. The design of towns and buildings has remained practical, mindful of the harsh winter and strong Mistral winds. Undoubtedly, the beauty of the region is revealed in the high lakes and mountains, the glacial valleys and the colourful fields of Alpine flowers.

Bundles of cut lavender drying in fields near the Gorges du Verdon

◄ Walker at the bottom of the cliff enclosing the Chambre du Roi, one of vast *grés d'Annot* sandstone outcrops in Annot

Exploring Alpes-de-Haute-Provence

This remote and rugged area in the north of Provence covers 6,944 sq km (2,697 sq miles) of mountainous landscape. Its main artery is the Durance river which is dotted with dams, gorges and lakes – a haven for mountaineers and canoeists. One tributary is the Verdon, which runs through the stunning Gorges du Verdon, Europe's answer to the Grand Canyon. The scenery becomes wilder and more rugged in the northeast, with Mont Pelat at the heart of the Parc National du Mercantour. Further south lie the plains of Valensole, which colour the landscape in July when the abundant lavender blossoms.

Fields of lavender on the Valensole plains

Sights at a Glance

1. Sisteron
2. Seyne-les-Alpes
3. Barcelonnette
4. Mont Pelat
5. Colmars
6. Digne-les-Bains
7. Les Pénitents des Mées
8. Lurs
9. Forcalquier
10. Manosque
11. Gréoux-les-Bains
12. Valensole
13. Riez
15. Moustiers-Ste-Marie
16. Castellane
17. St-André-les-Alpes
18. Annot
19. Entrevaux

Tour

14. *Gorges du Verdon pp188–9*

Key

- ═══ Motorway
- ── Major road
- ┄┄ Minor road
- ── Scenic route
- ─── Minor railway
- ▬▬ International border
- ▪▪ Regional border
- △ Summit

A quiet Provençal-style bar in the mountain town of Castellane, situated in the picturesque old quarter

For additional map symbols *see back flap*

Getting Around

The Durance river provides the point of entry into the region. The A51 autoroute from Aix-en-Provence follows the river to Sisteron and on to La Saulce, just short of Gap. National roads continue to follow the Durance, to Lac de Serre-Ponçon in the north, then east along the Ubaye to Barcelonnette. The region's capital, Digne-les-Bains, is well connected by national roads, but otherwise there are only minor roads. The region's railway line also follows the Durance, connecting Sisteron and Manosque with Aix.

The dramatic Rocher de la Baume, just outside the town of Sisteron

❶ Sisteron

Road map D2.  7,664. 🚊 🚌
ℹ️ Hôtel de Ville, 1 pl de la République
(04 92 61 36 50). 🔄 Wed & Sat.
W sisteron-tourisme.fr

Approaching Sisteron from the
north or south, it is easy to see
its strategic importance. The
town calls itself the "gateway to
Provence", sitting in a narrow
valley on the left bank of the
Durance river. It is a lively
town, protected by the most
impressive fortifications in
Provence. However, it has
suffered for its ideal military
position, most recently in heavy
Allied bombardment in 1944.

The **citadelle**, originally built
in the 12th century, dominates
the town and gives superb
views down over the Durance.
These defences, though incom-
plete, are a solid assembly of
keep, dungeon, chapel, towers
and ramparts, and offer a fine
setting for the Nuits de la
Citadelle, the summer festival
of music, theatre and dance.
The cathedral in the main
square, **Notre-Dame et
St-Thyrse**, is an example of the

A traditional Provençal farmhouse just outside the village of Seyne

Provençal Romanesque school,
dating from 1160. At its east
end, the 17th-century Chapelle
des Visitandines houses the
Musée Terre et Temps. In the
Old Town, small boutiques, cafés
and bars line the narrow alley-
ways called *andrônes*.

Rocher de la Baume on the
opposite bank is a popular
practice spot for mountaineers.

🏛 La Citadelle
Pl de la Citadelle, 04200 Sisteron.
Tel 04 92 61 27 57. **Open** Apr–11 Nov:
daily. 🔄 **W** citadelledesisteron.fr

Sisteron citadel, strategically positioned high above the Durance valley

❷ Seyne-les-Alpes

Road map D2.  1,460. 🚌 ℹ️ Place
d'Armes (04 92 35 11 00). 🔄 Tue & Fri.
W seynelesalpes.com

The small mountain village of
Seyne dominates the Vallée de la
Blanche, sitting 1,260 m (4,134 ft)
above sea level. Horses and
mules graze in the nearby fields,
and there is a celebrated annual
horse and mule fair in August.
Beside the main road is **Notre-
Dame de Nazareth**, a 13th-
century Romanesque church
with Gothic portals, sundial and
large rose window. The path by
the church leads up to the
citadelle, built by Vauban in
1693, which encloses the still-
standing 12th-century
watchtower. The town is also
a centre for winter sports, with
facilities nearby at St-Jean, Le
Grand Puy and Chabanon.

❸ Barcelonnette

Road map E2.  2,860. 🚌
ℹ️ Pl Frédéric Mistral (04 92 81
04 71). 🔄 Wed & Sat am only.
W barcelonnette.com

In the remote Ubaye Valley,
surrounded by a demi-halo of
snowy peaks, lies Provence's
northernmost town. It is a flat,
open town of cobbled streets,
smart cafés and restaurants
and quaint gift shops, selling specialities such as raspberry and
juniper liqueurs. The town was
named in 1231 by its founder
Raymond-Bérenger V, Count of
Barcelona and Provence, whose
great-grandfather of the same
name married into the House of

Napoleon in Provence

In his bid to regain power after his exile on Elba, Napoleon knew his only chance of success was to win over Sisteron. On 1 March, 1815, he secretly sailed from the island of Elba, landing at Golfe-Juan with 1,026 soldiers.

He hastily started his journey to Paris via Grenoble, making his first stop at Grasse, where the people shut their doors against him. Abandoning carriages, cannon and horses, Napoleon and his troops scrambled along mule-tracks and across difficult terrain, surmounting summits of more than 3,000 ft (1,000 m). At Digne, he lunched at the Hôtel du Petit Paris before spending the night at Malijai Château where he waited for news of the royalist stronghold of Sisteron. He was in luck. The arsenal was empty and he entered the town on 5 March – a plaque on rue du Jeu-de-Paume honours the event. The people were, at last, beginning to warm to him.

The dramatic *Napoleon Crossing the Alps*, painted by Jacques Louis David in 1800

One of the distinctive residential villas in Barcelonnette

Provence in 1112. The town's Alpine setting gives it a Swiss flavour; it also has Mexican spice. The Arnaud brothers, whose business in Barcelonnette was failing, emigrated to Mexico and made their fortune. Others followed, and on their return in the early 20th century, they built grand villas which encircle the town.

Housed in one of the villas is the **Musée de la Vallée**, where the Mexican connection is explained through illustrations and costumes. There are four other branches of this museum in the Ubaye valley, at St-Paul, Jauziers, Pontis and Le Lauzet.

In summer there is an information point here for the Parc National du Mercantour *(see p101)*. The park stretches along the Italian border and straddles the Alpes Maritimes region in the south. It is a haven for birds, wildlife and fauna, with two major archaeological sites.

Musée de la Vallée
10 ave de la Libération. **Tel** 04 92 81 27 15. **Open** Wed–Sat pm (Jul & Aug: daily). **Closed** mid-Nov–mid-Dec. in summer.

❹ Mont Pelat

Thorame-Verdon. Colmars, Allos. Pl de la Coopérative, Allos (04 92 83 02 81). **valdallos.com**

This is the loftiest peak in the Provençal Alps, rising to a height of 3,050 m (10,017 ft) and all around are mountains and breathtaking passes, some of them closed by snow until June. Among them are the Col de Cayolle (2,327 m/7,717 ft) on the D2202 to the east, and the hair-raising Col d'Allos (2,250 m/ 7,380 ft) on the D908 to the west. South of Mont Pelat, in the heart of the Parc National du Mercantour, is the beautiful 50-ha (124-acre) Lac d'Allos. It is the largest natural lake in Europe at this altitude. The setting is idyllic, ringed by snowy mountains, its crystal-clear waters swimming with trout and char. Another record-breaker is Cime de la Bonette, on the D64 northeast of Mont Pelat, at 2,862 m (9,390 ft) the highest pass in Europe. It has what is perhaps the most magnificent view in all this abundant mountain scenery.

Cime de la Bonette, the highest mountain pass in Europe

❺ Colmars

Road map E2. 🚠 400. 🚌
ℹ️ Ancienne Auberge Fleurie (04 92 83 41 92). 🏛️ Tue & Fri (Jun–Sep).
w colmars-les-alpes.fr

Colmars is an unusually complete fortified town, nestling between two 17th-century forts. You can walk along the 12-m (40-ft) ramparts, which look across oak-planked roofs. The town is named after the hill on which it is built, *collis Martis*, where the Romans built a temple to the god Mars. Vauban, the military engineer, designed its lasting look. On the north side, an alley leads to the 17th-century **Fort de Savoie**, a fine example of military architecture. From the Porte de France a path leads to the Fort de France.

Situated among wooded hills Colmars is popular in summer, when time is spent relaxing on wooden balconies (*soleillades lit*, sun-traps), or strolling along alpine paths, soaking up the beautiful views. Signposts lead from the town to the Cascade de la Lance, a waterfall half-an-hour's walk away.

🏛️ Fort de Savoie

04370 Colmars. **Tel** 04 92 83 41 92. **Open** Jul–Aug: daily pm; Sep–Jun: by appt only. 🚫 🎟️ obligatory.

❻ Digne-les-Bains

Road map D2. 🚠 17,700. 🚌 🚌
ℹ️ Pl du Tampinet (04 92 36 62 62). 🏛️ Wed & Sat (Blvd Gassendi).
w ot-dignelesbains.fr

The capital of the region has been a spa town since Roman times, primed by seven hot springs. It still attracts those seeking various cures, who visit the Thermes Digne-les-Bains, a short drive southeast of the town. Health seems to radiate from Digne's airy streets, particularly from the boulevard Gassendi, named after the local mathematician and astronomer Pierre Gassendi (1592–1655).

Street sculpture in Digne

The fortified town of Colmars, flanked by two compact forts

This is where the town's four-day lavender carnival rolls out in August (*see p229*), for Digne styles itself the *"capitale de la Lavande"*. In recent years, the town has promoted itself as an important centre for modern sculpture, which liberally furnishes the town.

The **Musée Gassendi** is found in the old town hospice and houses 16th–19th-century French, Italian and Dutch paintings, a collection of contemporary art and 19th-century scientific instruments. Among portraits of Digne's famous is Alexandra David-Néel, one of Europe's most intrepid travellers, who died in 1969 aged 101. Her house, *Samten-Dzong* (fortress of meditation) is now the **Maison Alexandra David-Néel** and includes a Tibetan centre and a museum. At the north end of boulevard Gassendi is the 19th-century **Grande Fontaine** and just beyond lies the oldest part of Digne-les-Bains. The grand cathedral of **Notre-Dame-du-Bourg**, built between 1200–1330, is the largest Romanesque church in Haute Provence. It has its own archaeological crypt with relics dating back to the Roman era.

The **Jardin des Cordeliers**, an enchanting walled garden in a converted convent, houses a large collection of medicinal plants and a sensory garden.

🏛️ Musée Gassendi

64 blvd Gassendi. **Tel** 04 92 31 45 29. **Open** Wed–Mon. **Closed** public hols, 25 Dec–2 Jan. 🚫 ♿ 📷 🔊
w musee-gassendi.org

🏛️ Maison Alexandra David-Néel

27 ave Maréchal Juin. **Tel** 04 92 31 32 38. **Open** daily by guided tour only. 🕐 3 per day (Oct–Jun only). 📷
w alexandra-david-neel.org

🌿 Jardin des Cordeliers

Couvent des Cordeliers, Ave Paul Martin. **Tel** 04 92 31 59 59. **Open** Mar–Nov: Mon–Fri. **Closed** public hols. ♿ 🎟️

❼ Les Pénitents des Mées

Road map D3. ✈ Marseille.
🚉 St-Auban. 🚌 Les Mées. ℹ 21 blvd
de la République (04 92 34 36 38) pms.

One of the most spectacular geological features in the region is Les Pénitents des Mées, a serried rank of columnar rocks more than 100 m (300 ft) high and over a mile (2 km) long. The strange rock formation is said to be a cowled procession of banished monks. In local mythology, monks from the mountain of Lure took a fancy to some Moorish beauties, captured by a lord during the time of the Saracen invasion in the 6th century. Saint Donat, a hermit who inhabited a nearby cave, punished their effrontery by turning them into stone.

The small village of Les Mées is tucked away at the north end. Walk up to the chapel of St-Roch for a view of the rocks' strange formation of millions of pebbles and stones.

❽ Lurs

Road map D3. 🚶 390. 🚌 La
Brillanne. ℹ Jul–Aug: Seminaire,
04700 Lurs (04 92 79 10 02); Sep–Jun:
Mairie (04 92 79 95 24).

The Bishops of Sisteron and the Princes of Lurs were given ownership of the fortified town of Lurs in the 9th century, under the command of Charlemagne. In the early 20th century the small town was virtually abandoned, and was only repopulated after World War II, mainly by printers and graphic artists, who keep their trade in the forefront of events with an annual competition.

The narrow streets of the old town, entered through the Porte d'Horloge, are held in by the medieval ramparts. North of the restored Château of the Bishop-Princes is the beginning of the 300-m (900-ft) **Promenade des Evêques** (Bishops' walk), lined with 15 oratories leading to the chapel of Notre-Dame-de-Vie and stupendous views over the sea of poppy fields and olive groves of the Durance valley.

Head north out of Lurs on the N96, to the 12th-century **Prieuré de Ganagobie**. The church has beautifully restored red-, black- and white- tiled mosaics, inspired by oriental and Byzantine design and imagery. Offices are held several times a day by the monks – visitors may attend.

🏠 **Prieuré de Ganagobie**
N96, 04310. **Tel** 04 92 68 00 04.
Open Tue–Sat pms, & Sun. 📷

The curiously-shaped Pénitents des Mées, dominating the area

Floor mosaic of the church of the 12th-century Prieuré de Ganagobie

Le Train des Pignes

An enjoyable day out is to be found on the Chemin de Fer de Provence, a short railway line that runs from Digne-les-Bains to Nice. It is the remaining part of a network that was designed to link the Côte d'Azur with the Alps, built between 1891 and 1911. Today the Train des Pignes, a diesel train, usually with two carriages, runs four times a day throughout the year. It is an active and popular service, used by locals going about their daily business as much as by tourists. It rattles along the single track at a fair pace, rolling by the white waters of the Asse de Moriez and thundering over 16 viaducts, 15 bridges and through 25 tunnels.

The train journey is a great way of seeing the countryside, although the ride can be bumpy at times. The most scenic parts are in uninhabited countryside, such as between St-André-les-Alps and Annot, where the *grès d'Annot* can be seen *(see p191)*. The journey takes about 3 hours each way and can be broken en route. Entrevaux *(see p191)* is a good place to stop. For tickets, call 04 92 03 80 80 (from Nice), 04 92 31 01 58 (from Digne-les-Bains) or visit www.train provence.com

Scenic view of Forcalquier, the former capital of Alpes-de-Haute-Provence

Durance. The centre has 13th- and 14th-century gates, Porte Soubeyran and Porte Saunerie. The perfume shop in rue Grande was once the atelier of writer Jean Giono's mother and the second floor belonged to his father *(see p32)*. The **Centre Jean Giono** tells the story of his life. The town's adoptive son is the painter Jean Carzou, who decorated the interior of the **Couvent de la Présentation** with apocalyptic allegories of modern life.

❾ Forcalquier

Road map C3. 4,875. 13 pl du Bourguet (04 92 75 10 02). Mon, Thu. forcalquier.com

Crowned by a ruined castle and domed chapel of the 19th-century Notre-Dame-de-Provence, this town – once an independent state and the capital of the region – is now a shadow of its former self. Although the weekly market is a lively affair drawing local artists and artisans.

There are some fine façades in the old town, but only one remaining gate, the Porte des Cordeliers. The Couvent des Cordeliers (closed to visitors) nearby dates from 1236, and is where the local lords have been entombed.

The **Musée Départemental Ethnologique** in nearby Mane preserves the history of the people and culture of Haute-Provence. The **Observatoire de Haute Provence** to the south of the town was sited here after

a study in the 1930s to find the town with the cleanest air. The Centre d'Astronomie nearby is a must for star-gazers.

ᨧ Musée Départemental Ethnologique

N100, Mane. **Tel** 04 92 75 70 50. **Open** daily (Nov: Sun only). **Closed** Jan, 24, 25 & 31 Dec. for groups.

ᨧ Observatoire de Haute Provence

St-Michel l'Observatoire. **Tel** 04 92 70 64 00. **Open** Easter–1 Nov: Wed pm. only. obs-hp.fr

❿ Manosque

Road map C3. 22,825. Pl du Docteur Joubert (04 92 72 16 00). Sat. manosque-tourisme.com

France's national nuclear research centre, Cadarache, has brought prosperity to Manosque, a town which has sprawled beyond its original hill site above the

ᨧ Centre Jean Giono

3 blvd E Bourges. **Tel** 04 92 70 54 54. **Open** Tue–Sat (Oct–Mar: pm only). **Closed** public hols, 25 Dec–2 Jan. centrejeangiono.com

ᨧ Couvent de la Présentation

9 blvd Elémir Bourges. **Tel** 04 92 87 40 49. **Open** Apr–Oct: 10am–12:30pm & 2–6pm Tue–Sat; Nov–Mar: 2–6pm Wed–Sat. **Closed** Sun, public hols, 23 Dec–2 Jan.

⓫ Gréoux-les-Bains

Road map D3. 2,640. 7 pl Hôtel de Ville (04 92 78 01 08). Tue & Thu. greouxlesbains.com

The thermal waters of this spa town have been enjoyed since antiquity, when baths were built by the Romans in the 1st century AD. Gréoux flourished in the 19th century, and the waters can still be enjoyed at the Etablissement Thermal, on the east side of the village, on Avenue du Verdon, where bubbling, sulphurous water arrives at the rate of 100,000 litres (22,000 gallons) an hour.

Lavender and Lavendin

The famous flower of Provence colours the Plateau de Valensole every July. Lavender began to be cultivated in the region in the 19th century and provides the world with around 80 per cent of its needs. Harvesting continues until September and is mostly mechanized although, in some areas, it is still collected in cloth sacks slung over the back. After two or three days' drying it is sent to a distillery.

These days the cultivation of a hybrid called lavendin has overtaken traditional lavender. Lavender is now used mainly for perfumes and cosmetics, lavendin for soaps.

Harvesting the abundant lavender in Haute Provence

The sweeping fields of the Plateau de Valensole, one of the largest lavender-growing areas of Provence

A restored castle ruin of the Templars is on a high spot and an open-air theatre is in the grounds. **Le Musée des Miniatures, poupées et jouets du Monde** is a museum with 148 miniatures from 1832 to the present, including dolls, costumes and toy trains.

 **Le Musée des Miniatures, poupées et jouets du Monde**
16 ave des Alpes. **Tel** 06 84 62 71 23. **Open** Apr–Aug: Mon–Fri pm (daily for groups by appt). **Closed** public hols. 🅿 ♿ 📷 for groups.

Corinthian columns front the Gallo-Roman baths in Gréoux-les-Bains

🄸 Valensole

Road map D3. 🄰 3,330. 🄸 Pl des Héros de la Résistance (04 92 74 90 02). 🄰 Sat. 🅆 valensole.fr

This is the centre of France's most important lavender-growing area. It sits on the edge of the Valensole plains with a sturdy-towered Gothic church at its height. Admiral Villeneuve, the unsuccessful adversary of Admiral Nelson at the Battle of Trafalgar,

was born here in 1763. Signs for locally made lavender honey are everywhere and just outside the town is the **Musée Vivant de l'Abeille**. This is an interactive museum explaining the intriguing life of the honey bee, with informative demonstrations, photographs and videos. In the summer, you can visit the beehives and see the beekeepers at work.

🄸 **Musée Vivant de l'Abeille**
Rte de Manosque. **Tel** 04 92 74 85 28. **Open** Tue–Sat. **Closed** public hols. ♿ 📷

🄳 Riez

Road map D3. 🄰 1,850. 🚌 🄸 Pl de la Mairie (04 92 77 99 09). 🄰 Wed & Sat. 🅆 ville-riez.fr

At the edge of the sweeping Valensole plateau is this unspoiled village, filled with small shops selling ceramics and traditional *santons*, honey and lavender. Its grander past is reflected in the Renaissance façades of the houses and mansions in the old town. This is entered through the late-13th-century Porte Aiguyère, which leads on to the peaceful, tree-lined Grand Rue, with fine examples of Renaissance architecture at numbers 27 and 29.

The most unusual site is the remains of the 1st-century AD Roman temple dedicated to Apollo. It stands out of time and place, in the middle of a field by the river Colostre; this

was the original site of the town where the Roman colony, *Reia Apollinaris*, lived. On the other side of the river is a rare example of Merovingian architecture, a small baptistry dating from the 5th century.

The village has a number of fountains: Fontaine Benoîte, opposite Porte Sanson, dates to 1819, although a fountain has existed on this spot since the 15th century; the 17th-century Fontaine de Blanchon is fed by an underground spring – its use was reserved for washing the clothes of the infirm in the days before antibiotics and vaccines; and the soft waters of the spring-fed Fontaine de Saint-Maxime were believed to possess healing qualities for the eyes.

Ruins of the Roman temple in Riez, built in 1st century AD

⑭ Tour of the Gorges du Verdon

The breathtaking chasm of the Gorges du Verdon is one of the most spectacular natural phenomena in France. The Verdon river, a tributary of the Durance, cuts into the rock up to 700 m (2,300 ft) deep. A tour of the gorges takes at least a day and this circular route encompasses its most striking features. At its east and west points are the historic towns of Castellane, the natural entry point to the gorges, and Moustiers-Ste-Marie. Parts of the tour are particularly mountainous, so drivers must be aware of hairpin bends and narrow roads with sheer drops. Weather conditions can also be hazardous and roads can be icy until late spring.

Hikers in one of the deep gorges

⑤ **La Palud-sur-Verdon**
Organized walking excursions start at the village of La Palud, the so-called capital of the Gorges.

④ **Moustiers-Ste-Marie**
Set on craggy heights, the town is famed for its faïence (p190).

Flowered-façade in Moustiers

Key

━━ Tour route

══ Other roads

☼ Viewpoint

③ **Aiguines**
The beautifully restored 17th-century château crowns the small village, with fine views down to the Lac de Ste-Croix.

Tips for Drivers

Tour length: 113 km (72 miles).
Stopping-off points: La Palud-sur-Verdon has several cafés and Moustiers-Ste-Marie is a good place to stop for lunch. For an overnight stop, there are hotels and campsites in the town of Castellane. (See also pp250–51.)

The azure-blue waters of the enormous Lac de Ste-Croix

Outdoor Activities

The Verdon gorges have offered fantastic opportunities for the adventurous since Isadore Blanc (1875–1932) made the first complete exploration in 1905. Today's activities include hiking, climbing, canoeing and white-water rafting *(see pp230–1)*. Boating needs to be supervised as the river is not always navigable and the powerful water flow can change dramatically.

White-water rafting down the fast-flowing Verdon river

Gorge explorer
Isadore Blanc

⑥ Point Sublime

This is one of the best viewing points. Signposted walks lead down to the canyon floor, but a torch is required to walk through the long tunnels.

① Castellane

An ancient clock tower and gate remain in the Old Town of Castellane, a popular tourist centre *(p190)*.

View of Pont de Tusset

0 kilometres   2

0 miles   2

② Pont de l'Artuby

Park at either end of the 100-m (328-ft) bridge, which spans the Artuby river, and marvel at the superb views. It is also a favourite spot for bungee jumping.

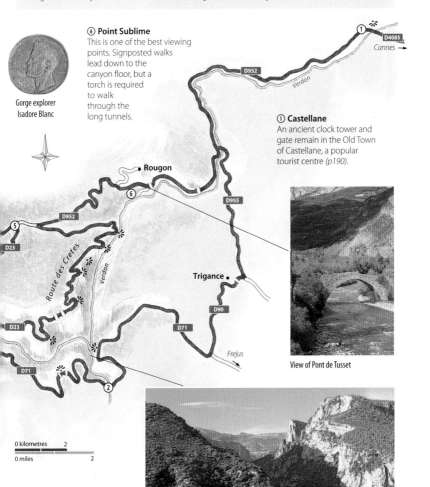

Stunning view across the meandering river Verdon

Cannes →

Rougon

Trigance

Frejus

Route des Cretes

Verdon

Verdon

D4085

D952

D955

D952

D23

D23

D71

D71

D90

⓯ Moustiers-Ste-Marie

Road map D3. 🚏 700. 🚌 *i* Pl de l'Eglise (04 92 74 67 84). 🔺 Fri am; craft market (Jul/Aug).
w moustiers.fr

The setting of the town of Moustiers is stunning, high on the edge of a ravine, beneath craggy rocks. Situated in the town centre is the parish church, with a three-storey Romanesque belfry. Above it, a path meanders up to the 12th-century chapel of Notre-Dame-de-Beauvoir. The view across Lac de Ste-Croix is magnificent.

A heavy iron chain, 227 m (745 ft) in length, is suspended above the ravine. Hanging from the centre is a five-pointed, golden star. Although it was renewed in 1957, it is said to date back to the 13th century, when the chevalier Blacas hoisted it up in thanks for his release from captivity during the Seventh Crusade of St Louis *(see p46)*.

Moustiers is a popular tourist town, the streets crowded in summer. This is due to its setting and its ceramics. The original Moustiers ware is housed in the **Musée de la Faïence**. Modern reproductions can be bought in the town. The new **Musée de la Préhistoire** in Quinson, 40 km (25 miles) south, is a must.

🏛 Musée de la Faïence
Le Village, Rue du Seigneur de la Clue, Moustiers-Ste-Marie. **Tel** 04 92 74 61 64. **Open** Mar–Oct: Wed–Mon (Jul, Aug: daily); Nov & Dec: Sat–Sun pm only. **Closed** Jan & Feb. 🔲 🔲

The narrow streets of Moustiers

Notre-Dame-du-Roc chapel, perched high above the town of Castellane

⓰ Castellane

Road map D3. 🚏 1,600. 🚌 *i* Rue Nationale (04 92 83 61 14). 🔺 Wed & Sat.
w castellane-verdontourisme.com

This is one of the main centres for the Gorges du Verdon, surrounded by campsites and caravans. Tourists squeeze into the town centre in summer and, in the evenings, fill the cafés after a day's hiking, climbing, canoeing and white-water rafting. It is a well-sited town, beneath an impressive 180-m (600-ft) slab of grey rock. On top of this, dominating the skyline, is the chapel of **Notre-Dame-du-Roc**, built in 1703. A strenuous, 30-minute walk from behind the parish church to the top is rewarded with superb views. Castellane was once a sturdy fortress and repelled invasion several times. The lifting of the siege by the Huguenots in 1586 is commemorated every year with firecrackers at the Fête des Pétardiers (last Sun in Jan).

The town's fortifications were completely rebuilt in the 14th century after most of the town, dating from Roman times, crumbled and slipped into the Verdon valley. Most social activity takes place in the main square, place Marcel-Sauvaire, which is lined with small hotels that have catered for generations of visitors.

All that remains of the ramparts is the Tour Pentagonal and a small section of the old wall, which lie just beyond the 12th-century St-Victor church, on the way up to the chapel.

Moustiers Ware

The most important period of Moustiers faïence was from its inception in 1679 until the late 18th century, when a dozen factories were producing this highly glazed ware. Decline followed and production came to a standstill in 1874, until it was revived in 1925 by Marcel Provence. He chose to follow traditional methods, and output continues.

The distinctive glaze of Moustiers faïence was first established in the late 17th century by Antoine Clérissy, a local potter who was given the secret of faïence by an Italian monk. The first pieces to be fired had a luminous blue glaze and were decorated with figurative scenes, often copied from engravings of hunting or mythological subjects. In 1738, Spanish glazes were introduced and brightly coloured floral and fauna designs were used.

A number of potters continue the tradition, with varying degrees of quality, and can be seen at work in their *ateliers*.

A tureen in Moustiers' highly glazed faïence ware

⓱ St-André-les-Alpes

Road map D3. 🗠 920. 🚌 🚊 🚉 Place Marcel Pastorelli (04 92 89 02 39). 🚩 Wed & Sat. 🆆 **ot-st-andre-les-alpes.fr**

Lying at the north end of the Lac de Castillon, where the river Isolde meets the river Verdon, is St-André. It is a popular summer holiday and leisure centre, scattered around the sandy flats on the lakeside. The lake is man-made, formed by damming the river by the 90-m (295-ft) Barrage de Castillon and is a haven for rafting, canoeing and kayaking as well as swimming and fishing.

Inland, lavender fields and orchards make for picturesque walks and hang-gliding is so popular here that one of the local producers advertises its wine as "the wine of eagles".

⓲ Annot

Road map E3. 🗠 1,120. 🚊 🚉 Place du Germe (04 92 83 23 03). 🚩 Tue. 🆆 **annot-tourisme.com**

The town of Annot, on the Train des Pignes railway line (see p185), has a distinct Alpine feel. Annot lies in the Vaïre valley, crisscrossed by icy waters streaming down from the mountains. The surrounding scenery however, is a more unfamiliar pattern of jagged rocks and deep caves.

Vast sandstone boulders, known as the *grès d'Annot,* are strewn around the town, and local builders have constructed

The steep path of zigzag ramps leading to the citadel of Entrevaux

houses against these haphazard rocks, using their sheer faces as outside walls. The *vieille ville* lies behind the main road, where there is a Romanesque church. The tall buildings that line the narrow streets have retained some of their original 15th- to 18th-century carved stone lintels.

Most Sundays (May–Oct) in summer, a 1909 *belle époque* steam train chugs its way from Puget-Théniers to Annot, a pleasant way for visitors to enjoy the unspoiled countryside.

⓳ Entrevaux

Road map E3. 🗠 950. 🚊 🚌 🚉 Porte Royale du Pont Levis (04 93 05 46 73). 🆆 **entrevaux.info**

It is clear why Entrevaux is called a "fairy-tale town", as you cross the drawbridge and enter through the Porte Royale. The dramatic entrance is flanked by twin towers and from here you enter the Ville Forte.

Fortified in 1690 by the military engineer Vauban (1633–1707), Entrevaux became one of the strongest military sites on the Franco-Savoy border. Even the 17th-century cathedral was skilfully incorporated into the turreted ramparts.

Unlike most military strongholds, the citadel was not built on top of a hill, but strategically placed on a rocky outcrop. It was last used during World War I as a prison for German officers. A steep, zigzag track leads to the citadel, 156 m (511 ft) above the village. The 20-minute climb to the top, past basking lizards, should not be made in the midday heat.

Houses in the town of Annot built against huge sandstone rocks

TRAVELLERS' NEEDS

WHERE TO STAY

The diversity of Provence is reflected in the wide range of hotels it has to offer. Accommodation varies from luxurious palaces like the InterContinental Carlton in Cannes to simple country inns where a warm welcome, peaceful setting and often excellent cuisine are more customary than mod cons. Self-catering holidays are a popular and inexpensive option and on pages 196–7 information is given on renting a rural home or *gîte*, and on camping, as well as how to find B&Bs and youth hostels in the area.

Where to Look

There is no shortage of hotels in Provence and the Côte d'Azur. Ever since the crusades of the Middle Ages, the region has been hosting travellers in a variety of hotels across all price levels. Some of the best value coastal accommodation, especially for families, is found along the shores of the Var between Toulon and St-Tropez. The glamour and glitz come further east – the coast from Fréjus to Menton is predictably extravagant, but you can find accommodation to suit all budgets, from the exclusive Hotel du Cap-Eden-Roc, popular with film stars on Cap d'Antibes, to the 15th-century inn of the Hôtel des Arcades in Biot.

Inland, the major towns of Provence offer a good variety of hotels, from the luxurious mansions of Aix-en-Provence, Avignon and Arles to the more simple hostelries of the Luberon and the Var. Boutique hotels and deluxe *chambres d'hôtes* (B&Bs) have become very fashionable, making the picturesque fantasy of a converted farmhouse or medieval priory set in lavender fields a reality.

Palm trees shading the garden pool, Pastis Hotel St-Tropez *(see p199)*

Travellers seeking tranquillity can travel north to the wilds of Haute Provence where several historic châteaux, *auberges* (country inns) and *relais de poste* (post-houses) provide excellent accommodation and regional cuisine in rustic surroundings.

Those looking for a country idyll should head to the hills and valleys of the Central Var, the Luberon National Park or the foothills of Mont Ventoux. For an exciting, cosmopolitan base, Marseille is a great choice, with excellent hotels and restaurants on offer.

Hotel Types

Hotels in Provence can be divided into several categories. The region's famous luxury establishments include some of the most spectacular hotels in France. Many of these are located near the Mediterranean Sea, or in beautiful inland or hilltop settings. They come with a wide array of sports and spa facilities, private beaches, and usually a gastronomic restaurant.

Known for its art, Provence and the French Riviera also have some of the country's most chic and contemporary boutique hotels and B&Bs, many featuring minimalist or exotic interiors by hip designers. These tend to be located in the cities and resorts, and come equipped with all the modern conveniences, from iPod docks to rain showers. Many of them have spas or beauty and wellness centres.

Provence and the Cote d'Azur also boasts beautiful historic hotels and charming B&Bs. Located in castles, farmhouses, convents, medieval inns or mills, these establishments offer guests a chance to immerse themselves in the region's rich past. Rooms here are generally

Stylish guest room at the luxurious InterContinental Carlton, Cannes *(see p198)*

furnished with antiques, and many are set in century-old parks and gardens.

For those travelling with children, family hotels are the ideal option. While the romantic boutique hotels or upmarket B&Bs with antique furnishings may refuse guests under a certain age, most of the family hotels are quite welcoming, and may offer interconnecting rooms. Numerous country hotels now have annexes with bungalow apartments specifically designed for families. These may be only a few steps away from the swimming pool.

Classic hotels are generally purpose-built hotels and inns, many of which are still family-run. These establishments are found in virtually every village and the atmosphere is often extremely informal. The hotel is likely to be the focal point of the village, with the dining room and bar open to non-residents. The annual *Logis de France Fédération* guide, available from the **French Government Tourist Office** lists these one- and two-star restaurants-with-rooms *(auberges)*, often specializing in regional cuisine. Many are basic roadside inns, with a few listed in the main towns and cities, but off the beaten track you can find charming farmhouses and inexpensive seaside hotels.

The classic category also includes some chain hotels. For those searching for inexpensive accommodation on the outskirts of towns, the **Campanile** and **Ibis** chains offer modern and comfortable rooms. They are a reliable option and can be booked directly online or over the phone by credit card.

Other modern chains are geared to the business traveller and are found in most major towns. **Sofitel**, **Novotel** and **Mercure** all have hotels in Aix, Nice, Marseille and Avignon.

Hotel Prices

In many hotels, the price of each room depends on the view, size, decor or plumbing. Single occupancy rates are usually the same as two sharing – prices are

La Bastide de Voulonne, Cabrières d'Avignon-Gordes *(p201)*

normally per room, not per person. Tax and service are included in the price, with the exception of *pension* (full board) and *demi-pension* (half board), and rates posted are exclusive of breakfast. In more remote areas, half board may be obligatory and is often necessary in places where the hotel has the only restaurant. For stays of just one night, many hotels offer a fixed-price, good value pack-age including the room, dinner and breakfast *(soirée étape)*. In high season, popular coastal hotels may give preference to visitors who want half board.

Prices drop considerably in Provence in low season (Oct–Mar). Many hotels close for five months of the year, reopening for Easter. During festivals *(see pp36–9 and pp228–9)*, prices can rival high-season tariffs. In low season, discount packages are common along the coast. It is worth checking the Internet and the hotel website, as many of the biggest and most famous hotels offer fabulous deals during this period – even the palaces of the Riviera need to fill their rooms in winter.

Hotel Gradings

French hotels are classified by the tourist authorities into five categories: one to five stars. A few very basic places are unclassified. These ratings give you an indication of the level of facilities you can expect but offer little idea of cleanliness,

ambience or friendliness of the owners. Some of the most charming hotels are blessed with few stars, while the higher ratings sometimes turn out to be impersonal business hotels.

Bed and Breakfast

As old-fashioned family hotels in Provence have been closed down by EU regulations, *chambres d'hôtes* (B&Bs) have risen to take their place. They come in all shapes and sizes, including some very stylish ones as pricey as four-star hotels. Many provide *table d'hôte* dinners on request. They are listed separately in tourist office brochures, and many are inspected and registered by the **Gîtes de France** organization.

Stays on working farms are also an excellent option for families. Listings and useful information pertaining to these can be found on the **Accueil en Provence Paysanne** and **Bienvenue à la Ferme** websites.

Impressive staircase and glass lift at the exclusive Hotel du Cap-Eden-Roc *(see p198)*

Antique-furnished guest room at the romantic Jardins Secrets, Nîmes *(see p200)*

Facilities and Meals

Facilities will vary greatly depending on the location and rating of each hotel. In more remote areas, most hotels have adjoining restaurants and nearly all feature a breakfast room or terrace. Many three-star hotels have swimming pools, which can be a godsend in the summer. Parking is readily available at country hotels. Some city hotels have underground or guarded parking – in larger cities like Marseille and Nice this is becoming a necessity as car crime is a serious problem.

Many Provençal hotels are converted buildings and, while this adds a definite charm, it can mean eccentric plumbing and disturbing creaks and bumps in the night. Some hotels are near a main road or a town square – choosing a room at the back is usually all that is required for a peaceful night. Most hotels and *chambres d'hôtes* now offer free Wi-Fi, at least in the public areas, if not in the rooms.

Traditional French breakfasts are common in Provence and in summer are often enjoyed outside. Evening meals are served daily until about 9pm. Dining rooms are often closed on Sunday – check before you arrive. Check-out time is usually late morning; if you stay any longer you will have to pay for an extra day.

Booking

In high season, it is imperative to book well in advance, especially for any popular coastal hotel. During peak season (Jun–Sep), proprietors may ask for a deposit. Outside peak season you may be able to turn up on the day, but it is always wise to phone ahead to make sure the establishment is open. Check hotel websites, many of which allow you to book online and offer some good deals for Internet bookings.

Self-Catering

Provence is a popular self-catering destination, and many companies specialize in renting anything from rural farm cottages to beach apartments. One of the best organizations is **Gîtes de France**, with its headquarters in Paris, which provides detailed lists of accommodation to rent by the week in each *départment*.

The *gîte* owners are obliged to live nearby and are always welcoming, but rarely speak much English. Do not expect luxury from your *gîte* (holiday cottage) as facilities are basic, but it is a great way to get a better insight into real Provençal life. The websites of **Clévacances**, **AirBNB**, **Homelidays** and **Owners Direct** list affordable *gîte* and apartment rentals.

Hostels

For the independent traveller, this is the cheapest, and often the most convivial accommodation option. There are nine youth hostels in Provence, all of which are under the umbrella of **Hostelling International**. A membership card from your national **Youth Hostel Association** is required, or an *Ajiste* card, which you can obtain from French hostels. In each university town, the **Centre Régional Information Jeunesse (CRIJ)** can provide a great deal of information about student life and a list of inexpensive accommodation options.

Camping

A popular pastime in Provence, camping remains an inexpensive and atmospheric way of seeing the area. Facilities range from a basic one-star farm or vineyard site to the camping metropolises of the Riviera, complete with water fun parks and satellite TV. **Eurocamp** specializes in family holidays. Luxury tents are pre-assembled

Camping in Provence, a popular accommodation alternative

at the campsite of your choice, and everything is ready on arrival. Organized children's entertainment and baby-sitting are available on site. Some campsites will not accept visitors unless they have a special *camping carnet*, available from clubs such as the **Fédération Française de Camping et de Caravaning**.

Disabled Travellers

Due to the venerable design of most Provençal hotels, few are able to offer unrestricted wheel-chair access. Larger hotels have lifts, and hotel staff will go out of their way to aid disabled guests. Most resort hotels and many B&Bs have at least one or two accessible rooms. The **Association des Paralysés de France (APF)** has useful information on their website.

Other useful sources of information are **Mobility International** and **Tourism for All**, who publish a guide to France listing specialized tour operators for disabled travellers.

Recommended Hotels

The hotels and B&Bs listed in this guide have been carefully chosen and are among the best in Provence in their categories: Boutique, Classic, Family, Luxury and Historic. The establishments have been chosen from all over Provence for the quality of accommodation they offer and in some cases, for offering good value for money. The hotel listings on pages 198–201 are arranged by *département* and town according to price.

Among the listings, hotels and B&Bs have been designated as "DK Choice" for one or more of their outstanding features. This could be for the beauty of the location or the views, for the exceptional facilities on offer or the historic charm of the places, or any other feature that sets them apart from the rest of the entries here.

Olive groves surround the pool at serene La Bonne Etape, Château-Arnoux *(see p201)*

DIRECTORY

Hotel Types

Campanile
📷 campanile.com

French Government Tourist Office
UK: Lincoln House, 300 High Holborn, London WC1V 7JH.
Tel (09068) 244 123.
📷 uk.rendezvous enfrance.com
US: 29th Floor, 825 Third Ave, New York, NY 10022.
Tel (212) 838 7800.
📷 us.rendezvous enfrance.com

Ibis, Novotel, Sofitel, Mercure
Tel (087) 1663 0624 (UK).
Tel 08 25 88 00 00 (France).
📷 accorhotels.com

Bed and Breakfast

Accueil en Provence Paysanne
📷 accueil-paysan-paca.com

Bienvenue à la Ferme
📷 bienvenue-a-la-ferme.com

Self-Catering

AirBNB
📷 airbnb.fr

Clévacances
📷 clevacances.com

Gîtes de France
59 rue St Lazare, 75009 Paris.
Tel 01 49 70 75 75.
📷 gites-de-france.com

Homelidays
📷 homelidays.com

Owners Direct
📷 ownersdirect.co.uk

Hostels

American Youth Hostel Association
Tel (240) 650 2100 (US).
📷 hiusa.org

CRIJ Provence Alpes
96 la Canebière, 13001 Marseille.
Tel 04 91 24 33 50.
📷 crijpa.fr

CRIJ Cote D'Azur
19 rue Gioffredo, 06000 Nice.
Tel 04 93 80 93 93.
📷 ijca.fr

Hostelling International
UK **Tel** (01707) 324170.
📷 hihostels.com

Camping

Eurocamp UK
UK. **Tel** (08444) 060 402.
📷 eurocamp.co.uk

Fédération Française de Camping et de Caravaning
78 rue de Rivoli, 75004 Paris.
Tel 01 42 72 84 08.
📷 ffcc.fr

Disabled Travellers

APF
9 blvd Auguste Blanqui, 75013 Paris.
Tel 01 53 62 84 00.
📷 apf.asso.fr

Mobility International USA
132 E Broadway, Eugene, Oregon 97401.
Tel (541) 343 1284.
📷 miusa.org

Tourism for All
7A Pixel Mill, 44 Appleby Road, Kendall, Cumbria LA9 6ES.
Tel (0845) 124 9971.
📷 tourismforall.org.uk

Where to Stay

The Riviera and the Alpes Maritimes

ANTIBES: Mas Djoliba €€
Family   Map E3
29 av Provence, 06600
Tel *04 93 34 02 48*
W hotel-djoliba.com
Charming, old-fashioned farmhouse with palm trees around its pool and terrace.

BEAULIEU-SUR-MER: La Réserve de Beaulieu €€€
Luxury   Map F3
5 blvd du Maréchal Leclerc, 06310
Tel *04 93 01 00 01*
W reservebeaulieu.com
Elegant hotel with a magnificent seaside pool and spa. Michelin-starred restaurant.

BIOT: Hôtel des Arcades €
Historic   Map E3
14/16 pl des Arcades, 06410
Tel *04 93 65 01 04*
W hotel-restaurant-les-arcades.com
Small but comfortable rooms in a 15th-century inn with a quiet, homely atmosphere.

CANNES: L'Hotel Carolina €
Classic   Map E4
35 rue Hoche, 06400
Tel *01 57 32 35 66*
A good budget option offering bright, airy rooms. Free Wi-Fi.

CANNES: InterContinental Carlton €€€
Luxury   Map E4
58 la Croisette, 06400
Tel *04 93 06 40 06*
W intercontinental-carlton-cannes.com
Glamorous Art Deco landmark with breathtaking suites and a fabulous private beach.

CAP D'ANTIBES: La Gardiole et La Garoupe €
Family   Map E3
60–74 chemin de la Garoupe, 06160
Tel *04 92 93 33 33*
W hotel-lagaroupe-gardiole.com
Quiet, simple rooms in a 1920s building surrounded by trees. Friendly, helpful staff.

CAP D'ANTIBES: Hotel du Cap-Eden-Roc €€€
Luxury   Map E3
Blvd Kennedy, 06601
Tel *04 93 61 39 01*
W hotel-du-cap-eden-roc.com
A Riviera hideaway for the rich and famous; features luxury suites, apartments and seaside cabanas.

EZE: Hermitage du Col d'Eze €
Classic   Map F3
1951 av des Diables Bleus, 06360
Tel *04 93 41 00 68*
W ezehermitage.com
A good budget option with fine mountain views. Free Wi-Fi.

EZE: La Chèvre d'Or €€€
Luxury   Map F3
Rue du Barri, 06360
Tel *04 92 10 66 66*
W chevredor.com
A plush hotel with romantic, individually decorated rooms.

JUAN-LES-PINS: Hotel des Mimosas €
Classic   Map E4
Rue Pauline, 06160
Tel *04 93 61 04 16*
W hotelmimosas.com
Gracious century-old hotel with cool and comfortable rooms.

MENTON: Hotel Napoléon €€
Classic   Map F3
29 porte de France, 06500
Tel *04 93 35 89 50*
W napoleon-menton.com
Bright, modern rooms overlooking the sea and mountains.

MONACO: Hôtel Hermitage €€€
Luxury   Map F3
Square Beaumarchais, 98000
Tel *00 377 98 06 40 00*
W hotelhermitagemontecarlo.com
Opulent *belle époque* landmark with a spectacular, glass-domed Winter Garden foyer.

MONACO: Novotel Monte Carlo €€€
Family   Map F3
16 blvd Princesse Charlotte, 98000
Tel *00 377 99 99 83 00*
W novotel.com
Stylish hotel equipped with all modern facilities. Good location.

NICE: Hotel Windsor €
Boutique   Map F3
11 rue Dalpozzo, 06000
Tel *04 93 88 59 35*
W hotelwindsornice.com
Hotel Windsor offers a vibrant and artistic ambience. Relax in the pool in the exotic garden.

NICE: Le Négresco €€€
Luxury   Map F3
37 promenade des Anglais, 06000
Tel *04 93 16 64 00*
W hotel-negresco-nice.com
Popular vintage hotel decorated with superb works of art.

ST-JEAN-CAP-FERRAT: Hotel Brise Marine €
Family   Map F3
58 Jean Mermoz, 06230
Tel *04 93 76 04 36*
W hotel-brisemarine.com
Family-run hotel offering good views of the harbour. Welcoming staff.

DK Choice

ST-JEAN-CAP-FERRAT: Royal Riviera €€€
Luxury   Map F3
3 av Jean Monnet, 06230
Tel *04 93 76 31 00*
W royal-riviera.com
Built in 1904 at a superb location overlooking "Billionaire's Bay", Royal Riviera features luminous and elegantly decorated rooms. This ultra-stylish hotel has warm, friendly staff and offers an impeccable service.

Elegantly laid out breakfast table in a "sea-view" room at Le Négresco, Nice

ST-PAUL DE VENCE: Hostellerie des Remparts €
Historic   Map E3
72 rue Grande, 06570
Tel *04 93 24 10 47*
W hostellerielesremparts.com
Charming hotel in a medieval setting. Furnished with antiques, but offers all modern comforts.

ST-PAUL DE VENCE: Le Saint Paul €€€
Luxury   Map E3
86 rue Grande, 06570
Tel *04 93 32 65 25*
W lesaintpaul.com
Peaceful and artistic place with lavishly furnished rooms. Exquisite walled-in restaurant terrace.

VENCE: Hotel Villa Roseraie €
Boutique   Map E3
128 av Henri Giraud, 06140
Tel *04 93 58 02 20*
W villaroseraie.com
Belle époque town house with a colourful, rustic chic decor and delightful pool and garden.

VILLEFRANCHE-SUR-MER: Hôtel Versailles €€
Family   Map F3
7 av Princesse Grace, 06230
Tel *04 93 76 52 52*
W hotelversailles.com
Sleek, modern hotel with magnificent views and a fine Mediterranean restaurant.

The Var and the Iles d'Hyères

BORMES-LES-MIMOSAS: Domaine du Mirage €€
Family   Map D4
38 rue de la Vue des Iles, 83230
Tel *04 94 05 32 60*
W domainedumirage.com
Victorian-style hotel with some family rooms. Attentive staff.

COLLOBRIÈRES: Hôtel des Maures €
Classic   Map D4
19 blvd Lazare-Carnot, 83610
Tel *04 94 48 07 10*
W hoteldesmaures.fr
Family-run hotel offering pleasant, budget-friendly rooms. Superb traditional restaurant.

FAYENCE: Moulin de la Camandoule €€
Historic   Map E3
159 chemin de Notre Dame des Cyprès, 83440
Tel *04 94 76 00 84*
W camandoule.com
Provençal-style rooms in a converted 15th-century olive mill. Excellent on-site restaurant.

FOX-AMPHOUX: Auberge du Vieux Fox €
Historic   Map D3
Pl de l'Eglise, 83670
Tel *04 94 80 71 69*
Small and cosy rooms in an evocative medieval inn.

FRÉJUS: Hôtel L'Arena €€
Classic   Map E4
139–145 rue Gén de Gaulle, 83600
Tel *04 94 17 09 40*
W hotel-frejus-arena.com
Elegant hotel with a warm Mediterranean decor and exotic landscaped garden.

GRIMAUD: Les Aurochs €
Classic   Map E4
Quartier Embaude, 83310
Tel *04 94 81 31 90*
W lesaurochs.com
Housed in a converted sheep farm near the Grimaud castle. Choose between tranquil cottages and rooms with private terraces.

ÎLE DE PORQUEROLLES: Hôtel Résidence Les Medes €€
Family   Map D5
Rue de la Douane, 83400
Tel *04 94 12 41 24*
W hotel-les-medes.fr
Close to Courtade beach. Smartly furnished rooms and apartments.

ÎLE DE PORT-CROS: Le Manoir €€€
Historic   Map D5
Île de Port-Cros, 83400
Tel *04 94 05 90 52*
W hotel-lemanoirportcros.com
Simple and romantic century-old mansion offering a warm welcome and delicious food.

LA CADIERE D'AZUR: Hostellerie Bérard & Spa €€
Historic   Map C4
6 rue Gabriel-Péri, 83740
Tel *04 94 90 11 43*
W hotel-berard.com
Converted 11th-century convent with bright, spacious rooms.

LA CELLE: L'Hostellerie de l'Abbaye de la Celle €€€
Luxury   Map D4
10 pl du Général de Gaulle, 83170
Tel *04 84 49 05 24*
W abbaye-celle.com
Sublimely relaxing 12th-century abbey hotel with stunning rooms and a fabulous restaurant.

PORT-GRIMAUD: Hôtel le Suffren €€
Family   Map E4
16 pl du Marché, 83310
Tel *04 94 55 15 05*
W hotel-suffren.com
Pleasant waterfront hotel with bright, airy rooms.

Cosy and well-furnished room at the Pastis Hotel, St-Tropez

SEILLANS-VAR: Hôtel des Deux Rocs €
Historic   Map E3
1 pl Font d'Amont, 83440
Tel *04 94 76 87 32*
W hoteldeuxrocs.com
This lovely 18th-century mansion is good for families. Fantastic Mediterranean restaurant.

ST-TROPEZ: Lou Cagnard €€
Classic   Map E4
18 av Paul Roussel, 83990
Tel *04 94 97 04 24*
W hotel-lou-cagnard.com
Charming old town house with pretty rooms and a lush garden.

ST-TROPEZ: Château de la Messardière €€€
Luxury   Map E4
Route de Tahiti, 83990
Tel *04 94 56 76 00*
W messardiere.com
This sumptuous hotel in elegant grounds features a spa, pool and gourmet restaurants.

DK Choice

ST-TROPEZ: Pastis Hotel St-Tropez €€€
Boutique   Map E4
75 av du Général Leclerc, 83990
Tel *04 98 12 56 50*
W pastis-st-tropez.com
An intimate hideaway furnished with an eclectic mix of modern and antique art. The private garden with centuries-old palm trees and a pool is the perfect spot for breakfast or a nightcap.

TOULON: Ibis Styles Toulon Centre Congrès €
Family   Map D4
Pl Besagne, 83000
Tel *04 98 00 81 00*
W accorhotels.com
Chain hotel decorated in bright colours. Babysitting available.

For more information on types of hotels *see pages 194–5*

TOURTOUR: L'Auberge St-Pierre €
Family Map D3
Route d'Ampus, 83690
Tel 04 94 50 00 50
W aubergesaintpierre.com
Rural tranquility in a 16th-century farmhouse with stunning views.

Bouches-du-Rhône and Nîmes

AIX-EN-PROVENCE: Hôtel Saint Christophe €
Family Map C4
2 av Victor-Hugo, 13100
Tel 04 42 26 01 24
W hotel-saintchristophe.com
Superb, well-equipped hotel with Art Deco flair, and a bustling old-fashioned brasserie.

AIX-EN-PROVENCE: Hôtel Cézanne €€
Boutique Map C4
40 av Victor Hugo, 13100
Tel 04 42 91 11 11
W hotelaix.com
Classy place with a colourful, arty decor. Excellent breakfast buffet.

ARLES: Hôtel de l'Amphithéâtre €
Family Map B3
5–7 rue Diderot, 13200
Tel 04 90 96 10 30
W hotelamphitheatre.fr
Characterful hotel with charming Provençal decor and friendly staff.

ARLES: Hôtel Calendal €€
Classic Map B3
5 rue Porte de Laure, 13200
Tel 04 90 96 11 89
W lecalendal.com
Hotel Calendal offers bright, sunny rooms and a fabulous spa.

DK Choice

ARLES: L'Hôtel Particulier €€€
Historic Map B3
4 rue de la Monnaie, 13200
Tel 04 90 52 51 40
W hotel-particulier.com
A beautiful mansion with an aristocratic feel, featuring a walled garden, a swimming pool and an exquisite spa and hammam. The guest rooms are elegantly decorated with antiques. Impeccable service.

CASSIS: Le Clos des Arômes €
Classic Map C4
10 rue Abbé Paul Mouton, 13260
Tel 04 42 01 71 84
W leclosdesaromes.fr
Peaceful and attractive Provençal hotel with a lovely garden.

The colourful interior of Hôtel Cézanne, Aix-en-Provence

FONTVIEILLE: Villa Régalido €€
Boutique Map B3
118 av Frédéric Mistral, 13990
Tel 04 90 54 60 22
W laregalido.com
Housed in a converted olive oil mill; offers luxurious rooms.

LES BAUX-DE-PROVENCE: L'Hostellerie de la Reine Jeanne €
Classic Map B3
Grande Rue, 13520
Tel 04 90 54 32 06
W la-reinejeanne.com
Simple but attractive rooms with panoramic views over Les Baux.

LES BAUX-DE-PROVENCE: La Cabro D'Or €€€
Luxury Map B3
Chemin Departmental 27 Carita, 13520
Tel 04 90 54 33 21
W lacabrodor.com
Beautiful country house set in an idyllic location. Superb restaurant.

MARSEILLE: Hôtel Saint-Ferreol €
Classic Map C4
19 rue Pisançon, 13000
Tel 04 91 33 12 21
W hotel-stferreol.com
Modern hotel with small but thoughtfully designed rooms.

MARSEILLE: Hotel La Résidence du Vieux Port €€
Boutique Map C4
18 quai du Port, 13002
Tel 04 91 91 91 22
W hotel-residence-marseille.com
Stylish waterfront hotel with a vibrant 1950s decor. Free Wi-Fi.

MARSEILLE: Sofitel Marseille Vieux Port €€€
Classic Map C4
36 blvd Charles Livon, 13007
Tel 04 91 15 59 00
W sofitel.com
Luxury hotel with minimalist style and splendid views of Vieux Port.

NÎMES: Hôtel des Tuileries €
Classic Map A3
22 rue Roussy, 30000
Tel 04 66 21 31 15
W hoteldestuileries.com
Excellent centrally located budget hotel with charming owners.

NÎMES: Jardins Secrets €€
Boutique Map A3
3 rue Gaston Maruejols, 30000
Tel 04 66 84 82 64
W jardinssecrets.net
Stylish, romantic hotel furnished with antiques. Superb breakfast spread. Garden oasis with a pool.

SAINTES-MARIES-DE-LA-MER: Hotel de Cacharel €€
Historic Map A4
Route de Cacharel, 13460
Tel 04 90 97 95 44
W hotel-cacharel.com
Popular ranch-hotel with excellent horse-riding facilities.

SAINTES-MARIES-DE-LA-MER: Mas de la Fouque €€€
Boutique Map A4
Route du Petit Rhône, Departmental 38, 13460
Tel 04 90 97 81 02
W masdelafouque.com
Luxurious hotel and spa with great views of Camargue Nature Park.

SALON-DE-PROVENCE: Abbaye de Sainte-Croix €€
Historic Map B3
Route de Val de Cuech, 13300
Tel 04 90 56 24 55
W abbayedesaintecroix.com
Rustic style former monks' cells in a 12th-century abbey, with fine views from the pool terrace.

ST-RÉMY-DE-PROVENCE: Hôtel L'Amandiere €
Classic Map B3
Av Théodore-Aubanel, 13210
Tel 04 90 92 41 00
W hotel-amandiere.com
Peaceful retreat with a rustic feel. Beautiful gardens.

ST-REMY-DE-PROVENCE: Le Mas des Carassins €€
Family Map B3
1 chemin Gaulois, 13210
Tel 04 90 92 15 48
W masdescarassins.com
Stylish rooms in a traditional farmhouse. Well-tended garden.

VILLENEUVE-LÈS-AVIGNON: La Magnaneraie €€
Historic Map B3
37 rue Camp de Bataille, 30400
Tel 04 90 25 11 11
W magnaneraie.najeti.fr
Refined hotel with lovely gardens and a frescoed restaurant in a 15th-century silkworm nursery.

Vaucluse

AVIGNON: Bristol Hotel €€
Classic **Map** B3
44 cours Jean Jaurès, 84000
Tel *04 90 16 48 48*
w bristol-avignon.com
Pleasant hotel at a convenient location in the city centre. Family rooms and garage available.

AVIGNON: Hotel d'Europe €€
Historic **Map** B3
12 pl Crillon, 84000
Tel *04 90 14 76 76*
w heurope.com
A sumptuous 16th-century hotel elegantly decorated with period furniture. Beautiful fountain in the garden.

AVIGNON: La Mirande €€€
Luxury **Map** B3
4 pl de l'Amirande, 84000
Tel *04 90 14 20 20*
w la-mirande.fr
Splendid cardinal's mansion immaculately renovated in 18th-century style. Situated near the Palais de Papes.

DK Choice

CABRIÈRES D'AVIGNON-GORDES: La Bastide de Voulonne €€
Family **Map** B3
Cabrières d'Avignon, Route des Beaumettes, Dept 148, 84220
Tel *04 90 76 77 55*
w bastide-voulonne.com
Set in a traditional 18th-century farm and surrounded by acres of beautiful grounds, La Bastide de Voulonne is the ideal spot for a family break. The heated pool and terrace offer fantastic views over the Luberon. The guesthouse has three family suites and the friendly owner offers superb *table d'hôte* meals. Choose from a variety of exciting theme-based stays.

GORDES: Le Mas des Romarins €€
Historic **Map** C3
Route de Sénanque, 84220
Tel *04 90 72 12 13*
w masromarins.com
Charming 18th-century country house with traditional Provençal features such as stone fireplaces.

LOURMARIN: Villa Saint Louis €
Historic **Map** C3
35 rue Henri Savournin, 84160
Tel *04 90 68 39 18*
w villasaintlouis.com
Handsome B&B in an 18th-century villa furnished with antiques.

PERNES-LES-FONTAINES: Mas de la Bonoty €
Historic **Map** B3
355 chemin de la Bonoty, 84210
Tel *04 90 61 61 09*
w bonoty.com
Renovated 17th-century farmhouse surrounded by fragrant lavender fields and olive groves.

SEGURET: Domaine de Cabasse €€
Classic **Map** B2
Route de Sablet, 84110
Tel *04 90 46 91 12*
w cabasse.fr
Comfortable rooms in a working vineyard with wine tastings for guests. Excellent restaurant.

VAISON-LA-ROMAINE: Le Mas d'Hélène €
Classic **Map** B2
Quartier Chante Coucou, 84110
Tel *04 90 36 39 91*
w lemasdhelene.com
Provençal style rooms with all modern comforts.

VAISON-LA-ROMAINE: Les Tilleuls d'Elisée €
Historic **Map** B2
Chemin du Bon Ange, 1 av Jules Mazen, 84110
Tel *04 90 35 63 04*
w vaisonchambres.info
Charming B&B in a traditional farmhouse. Helpful owners.

Alpes-de-Haute-Provence

CASTELLANE: Nouvel Hôtel du Commerce €
Family **Map** D3
Pl Marcel Sauvaire, 04120
Tel *04 92 83 61 00*
w hotel-du-commerce-verdon.com
Excellent hotel with clean, pretty rooms and fine garden-restaurant. The owners are warm and friendly.

DK Choice

CHÂTEAU-ARNOUX: La Bonne Etape €€
Classic **Map** D2
Chemin du Lac, 04160
Tel *04 92 64 00 09*
w bonneetape.com
This 18th-century post house, owned by master chef Jany Gleize, makes a serene retreat. Rooms are stunningly decorated with antiques and there is a charming heated pool in the olive groves. Explore the vast organic gardens that provide the produce served in the two excellent restaurants.

FORCALQUIER: Charembeau €
Historic **Map** C3
Route de Niozelles, 04300
Tel *04 92 70 91 70*
w charembeau.com
Relax and de-stress in an 18th-century farmhouse amid rolling hills. Delicious breakfasts.

MOUSTIERS-STE-MARIE: La Bonne Auberge €
Classic **Map** D3
Rue Principale "Le Village", 04360
Tel *04 92 74 66 18*
w bonne-auberge-moustiers.com
Bright, cheerful rooms in this fine budget hotel close to the breathtaking Gorges du Verdon.

MOUSTIERS-STE-MARIE: La Bastide de Moustiers €€€
Boutique **Map** D3
Chemin de Quinson, 04360
Tel *04 92 70 47 47*
w bastide-moustiers.com
Rustic chic in a 17th-century inn with attractive gardens and splendid mountain views. Superb Alain Ducasse restaurant.

REILLANNE: Auberge de Reillanne €
Historic **Map** C3
D214 Le Pigonnier, 04110
Tel *04 92 76 45 95*
w auberge-de-reillanne.com
Set in beautiful gardens, this serene country house offers spacious, well-furnished rooms.

Outdoor swimming pool surrounded by trees at Domaine de Cabasse, Seguret

For more information on types of hotels *see pages 194–5*

WHERE TO EAT AND DRINK

One of the joys of this sunny region is the abundance of fresh, enticing food on offer. The coast of Provence is famous for its sea-food restaurants – the best are in the coastal towns of Marseille and Nice, though generally they do not come cheap. For traditional Provençal fare, head inland to the villages of the Var and northern Vaucluse. In the valleys of Haute Provence, the cuisine is simpler, but still delicious, often featuring local game and produce, and the much-loved truffle. Life in the south revolves around mealtimes and villages and towns come to a standstill during the midday meal and at dinner. Lunch is served from noon until 2pm with dinner from 7:30pm until about 10pm, while cafés and bars in towns tend to stay open later, especially in high season (see pp218–19).

Types of Restaurant

The restaurants on pages 208–17 have been selected for their excellent food, decor and ambience. Within each area, entries are listed alphabetically within each price category, from the least to the most expensive. At the expensive end are the gastronomic palaces, where famous chefs showcase French *haute cuisine*. These are usually honoured with one or more Michelin stars. In some restaurants, chefs creatively combine fresh local ingredients. Provençal restaurants specialize in the region's traditional recipes. At classic restaurants you'll find French favourites such as steak and *moules-frites*, or *escargots* and *tournedos Rossini* at more upmarket places. Bistros and brasseries – pub-restaurants serving beer and alcoholic drinks are less formal, and often stay open throughout the day and night. You will also find many places serving foreign cuisine, especially Italian restaurants and pizzerias.

How Much to Pay

Prices in Provence, notably along the fashionable Côte d'Azur, are relatively high. Most restaurants offer fixed-price menus that are better value than à la carte. Lunch is always a good deal – you can enjoy a large repast with wine for around €15–20. Inland, you can dine well for under €40 a head, while on the coast, a good restaurant will generally charge more in the evening. In the deluxe dining rooms of the Côte d'Azur, expect to spend at least €70 a head, although the food will usually be outstanding.

Restaurants are obliged by law to post menu prices outside. These generally include service, but a tip is often expected for good service – up to five per cent of the bill. Tips are usually given in cash. The most widely accepted credit cards are Visa and MasterCard. American Express and Diners Club are also accepted in some restaurants.

Making Reservations

No matter where you are dining, it is always advisable to book, especially for dinner. Most up-market restaurants only have one sitting and are often packed, particularly during high season.

Dining al fresco at Les Deux Garçons brasserie in Aix (see p219)

Reading the Menu

Menus usually comprise three or four courses, with cheese eaten before the dessert, while some country restaurants serve six-course extravaganzas, which can take several hours to eat. These days even fixed-price menus tend to offer several choices of *entrée* (starter), main course and dessert. Gastronomic restaurants may serve numerous small, immaculate courses, on a choice of *dégustation* (tasting) menus.

The *entrée* usually includes salads, pâté, Provençal soups and often shellfish. Main dishes are predominantly a choice of lamb, chicken or fish – game is widely available in season.

Coffee is always served after, not with, dessert – you will need to specify how you like your coffee.

Choice of Wine

Wine is so much a part of everyday life in Provence that you will find a good range at even the smallest establishments (see pp206–7). The price may be

L'Olivier, Île de Porquerolles (see p211)

Ferdinand Léger's tiled mural still graces the terrace at La Colombe d'Or, St-Paul de Vence *(see pp210–11)*

off-putting as all restaurants put a large mark-up on wine (up to 300 per cent). Most wine is locally produced and usually served in carafes. If in doubt, choosing the house wine (*la réserve* or *vin de la maison*) is a safe bet. Ordering a *demi* (50 cl) or *quart* (25 cl) is an inexpensive way of sampling the wine before ordering more. French law divides the country's wines into four classes, in ascending order of quality: Vin de Table, Vin de Pays, Vin Délimité de Qualité Supérieure (VDQS) and Appellation d'Origine Contrôlée (AOC).

Vegetarian Food

Uniquely vegetarian restaurants are hard to find, as this concept largely has yet to filter down to the carnivorous south, although *bio* (organic) restaurants are increasingly springing up. Most establishments will offer salads, omelettes or soup, or dishes from the *entrée* menu. Pasta and pizza are popular vegetarian standbys.

Children

Meals in Provence are very much a family affair and children are welcome in most places. However, special facilities like high chairs or baby seats are rarely provided. Many establishments have a children's menu and most will be happy to provide smaller dishes at reduced rates.

Service

As eating is a leisurely pastime in France, service can be slow. In small restaurants do not expect rapid attention: there may be only one waiter and dishes are cooked to order.

Wheelchair Access

Wheelchair access to many restaurants is restricted. In summer, this will be less of a problem at establishments with outside terraces. Even so, when booking ahead, ask for a conveniently situated table.

Smoking

Smoking is banned in all public places in France, with restaurant and bar owners facing heavy fines if they do not adhere to

Château Eza in the *village perché* of Eze *(see p209)*

the rules. Outdoors, there may be a special section of the terrace set aside for smokers.

Picnics

Picnicking is the best way to enjoy the wonderful fresh produce, bread, cheeses and *charcuterie* from Provence's enticing markets and shops. Picnic areas along major roads are well marked and furnished with tables and chairs; those along country lanes are better still.

Recommended Restaurants

The restaurants recommended on pages 208–17 include some of the best in Provence. They have been chosen for their reliably good food and service, with the aim of presenting a wide range of cuisine and price ranges in the region's most visited cities, towns, villages and countryside. Many rural restaurants are attached to hotels but serve a predominantly non-residential clientele. These often offer good value for money and are mostly the focus of local social activity.

Among the listings are entries marked as "DK Choice". These are restaurants that have been selected for one or more exceptional features, whether it is the superb quality of the cuisine, the fine atmosphere, a beautiful setting or spectacular views.

The Flavours of Provence

The cooking of Provence is known as *cuisine du soleil* ("the cuisine of the sun") with good reason. Famous for its abundance of glorious, sun-ripe fruit and vegetables, it is also healthy with plenty of fresh fish and seafood and fine-quality, lean meat from mountain pastures. Cheeses tend to be made with goats' milk. Good produce is enhanced by key ingredients: olive oil, garlic and aromatic herbs. Local markets are a colourful feast of seasonal produce: tomatoes, aubergines (eggplants), peppers and courgettes (zucchini), and freshly picked cherries, melons, lemons and figs. Most of all, though, Provence is the land of olives and of rich green olive oil.

Olives and olive oil

Scented, sun-ripened Cavaillon melons in a Provençal market

Vegetables

In Provençal cooking, vegetables play a leading role. They may be served raw as crudités with *aioli* (garlic mayonnaise) or *tapenade* (puréed anchovies, olives and capers). Tomatoes and courgettes (zucchini) are often stuffed in the Niçois style, with minced meat, rice and herbs. Small violet artichokes come with a sauce of lemon and butter, or sautéed with bacon. A favourite soup is the robust *soupe au pistou*, beans and vegetables laced with a sauce of basil, pine nuts and garlic. *Ratatouille* is a fragrant stew of vegetables cooked with olive oil, garlic and herbs. Popular salads include *salade niçoise* and *mesclun*, a regional mixture of leaves, including rocket, lamb's lettuce, dandelion leaves and chervil.

Mediterranean Fish

The fish of the Mediterranean is highly prized, culminating in the famous *bouillabaisse*. A wide range of fish is caught, including rockfish, *rascasse* (scorpion fish), red mullet, sea bream, John Dory, monkfish and squid. Around Nice, the main catch is sardines and anchovies. Most are best enjoyed simply grilled with herbs, like the classic *loup* (sea

Lobster — Mussels — Prawns (shrimp) — Sea bass — Monkfish — Squid — Clams
Selection of Mediterranean seafood available in Provence

Provençal Dishes and Specialities

Provence has produced several renowned dishes, of which *bouillabaisse* is the most famous. The ingredients of this fish stew vary from place to place, though Marseille claims the original recipe. A variety of local seafood (always including *rascasse*, or scorpion fish) is cooked in stock with tomatoes and saffron. The fish liquor is traditionally served first, with croûtons spread with *rouille*, a spicy mayonnaise, and the fish served afterwards. Once a fishermen's supper, it is now a luxury item you may need to order 24 hours in advance. A simpler version is *bourride*, a garlicky fish soup. Rich red wine stews, known as *daubes*, are another speciality, usually made with beef, but sometimes tuna or calamari. Other classics include *ratatouille* and *salade niçoise*.

Fresh figs

Bouillabaisse Fish often found in this Provençal classic includes monkfish, snapper and conger eel.

Dried spices and herbs on sale at the market in Nice

bass) with fennel. Seafood includes mussels *(moules)*, tiny crabs, giant prawns *(gambas)* and sea urchins *(oursins)*. Look out for trout from the Alpine streams north of Nice and freshwater eels in the Camargue. Popular fish dishes include *soupe de poissons* (fish soup), octopus cooked Provençal style with white wine, tomatoes and herbs, and the famous *brandade de morue*, a speciality of Nîmes, a purée of salt cod, cream, potatoes and olive oil.

Meat and Game

Lamb is one of the popular meats, especially that of Sisteron, where it is grazed on high mountain pastures, resulting in delicately herb-flavoured flesh. Beef is most often served as a *daube*, named after the pot-bellied terracotta dish *(daubière)* in which it is gently cooked for hours. Another speciality is *boeuf gardien*, the bull's-meat stew of the Camargue, served with nutty local red rice. Game from the mountains and woods includes wild rabbit, hare and wild boar. Regional *charcuterie* features *caillettes* (cakes of chopped pork and

Display of the famous and delicious *saussicons d'Arles*

liver with spinach and juniper berries) and the *saucisson* of Arles, once made from donkey but now usually pork.

Fruit and Honey

Elaborate desserts are rare, since there is so much sweet ripe fruit for the picking. Cavaillon melons are among the best in France, and the famous lemons of Menton are celebrated in an annual festival. Candied fruit has been produced in Apt since the Middle Ages. Local honeys are scented with chestnut, lavender or rosemary.

ON THE MENU

Beignets des fleurs de courgette Courgette (zucchini) flower fritters.

Fougasse Flat olive oil bread often studded with olives.

Ratatouille Stew of aubergine (eggplant), tomatoes, courgettes (zucchini) and peppers.

Salade Niçoise Lettuce with hard-boiled egg, olives, green beans, tomatoes and anchovies.

Socca Chickpea (garbanzo) pancakes, a speciality of Nice.

Tarte Tropezienne, St-Tropez's indulgent sponge cake stuffed with *crème patissière.*

Tourte des blettes Pie of chard, raisins and pine kernels.

Artichauts à la barigoule Small violet artichokes are stuffed with bacon and vegetables, cooked in wine.

Loup au fenouil A sea bass is stuffed with fennel twigs and baked with white wine or grilled over more twigs.

Boeuf en daube Beef is marinated in red wine, onions and garlic, then stewed with orange peel and tomato.

What to Drink in Provence

The region covered by this book could not encompass a more varied and enticing range of wines. To the north, the stony, heat-baked soil of the southern Rhône nurtures intense, spicy red wines, the best of which is Châteauneuf-du-Pape. In the south, the Mediterranean coast produces a range of lighter, fresh and fruity whites and rosés, as well as some delicious red wines. Especially good are the dry white wines of seaside Cassis and reds or rosés from the tiny fine wine pocket of Bandol. In the past, some Provençal wines had a reputation for not "travelling" well, but the introduction of modern wine-making techniques and more suitable grape varieties are fast improving quality. Here, we suggest a selection of wines to look out for on local menus.

Two bottle styles distinctive of the region's wines

White Wines

Grenache blanc grapes are often blended with other grape varieties to give a rich, bright flavour and crisp acidity to Provençal white wine. Those listed below are perfect with the region's delicious seafood.

Recommended Whites

Clos Ste-Magdeleine
Cassis

Château Val Joanis
Côtes du Luberon

Domaine St-André-de-Figuière
Côtes de Provence

Domaines Gavoty
Côtes de Provence

A fine white
Châteauneuf-du-Pape

White Côtes
du Rhône

Rosé Wines

Provençal rosé is no longer just a sweetish aperitif wine in a skittle-shaped bottle. Grape varieties like Syrah give a full flavour and more body. Tavel is a typical example – dry and weighty enough to accompany Provençal flavourings such as garlic and herbs. Bandol's *vin gris* is also highly regarded.

Recommended Rosés

Château Romassan
Bandol

Commanderie de Bargemone
Côtes de Provence

Commanderie de Peyrassol
Côtes de Provence

Domaine la Forcadière
Tavel

Domaines Gavoty
Côtes de Provence

Pale rosé *(gris)*
from Bandol

Wine Areas of Provence

Wine-producing areas are concentrated in the southwest of the region, where vineyards cluster on the rocky hillsides (côtes). Les Arcs is a good base for a Côtes de Provence wine tour (see pp112–13).

Terraced vineyards on the coast above Cassis

Red Wines

At its best, Châteauneuf-du-Pape produces heady, intense wines to accompany the most robust meat dishes. Bandol also makes superb, long-lived red wines. For a lighter alternative, choose a Provençal or Côtes du Rhône red. Wines from one of the named Rhône villages should be of superior quality – or seek out reds from reliable producers in, for example, Les Baux-de-Provence, or the Côtes du Luberon.

Fine red wine from Les Baux

A jewel in Côtes du Luberon's crown

A spicy Château-neuf-du-Pape

Recommended Reds

Château de Beaucastel
Châteauneuf-du-Pape

Château du Trignon
Sablet, Côtes du Rhône

Château Val Joanis
Côtes du Luberon

Château de Pibarnon
Bandol

Domaine des Alysses
Coteaux Varois

Domaine Font de Michelle
Châteauneuf-du-Pape

Domaine Tempier
Bandol

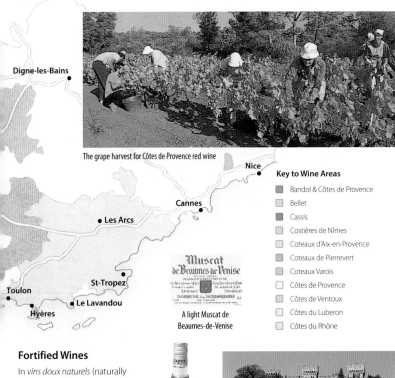

The grape harvest for Côtes de Provence red wine

Key to Wine Areas

Bandol & Côtes de Provence
Bellet
Cassis
Costières de Nîmes
Coteaux d'Aix-en-Provence
Coteaux de Pierrevert
Coteaux Varois
Côtes de Provence
Côtes de Ventoux
Côtes du Luberon
Côtes du Rhône

A light Muscat de Beaumes-de-Venise

Fortified Wines

In *vins doux naturels* (naturally sweet wines) fermentation is stopped before all the sugar has turned to alcohol, and the wine is then lightly fortified with spirit. Delicious as a chilled apéritif, with desserts or instead of a liqueur, most are based on the exotically scented Muscat grape and range from cloyingly sweet to lusciously fragrant. Others are based on the red Grenache grape.

Typical Muscat bottle shape

The stony, sun-reflecting soil of the Rhône valley

Where to Eat and Drink

The Riviera and the Alpes Maritimes

ANTIBES: Aubergine €
Provençal **Map** E3
7 rue Sade, 06600
Tel *04 93 34 55 93* **Closed** *Tue*
Lots of aubergines (eggplants), as the name implies, but also many other excellent Provençal dishes. Good home-made desserts.

ANTIBES: Chez Helen €
Bistro **Map** E3
35 rue des Revennes, 06600
Tel *04 92 93 88 52* **Closed** *Sun*
Everything in this organic and vegetarian restaurant – a rare sight in Provence – is made from local produce. Inventive main dishes and *salades composées*.

ANTIBES: Le Nacional €€
Contemporary **Map** E3
61 Pl Nacional, 06600
Tel *04 93 61 77 30* **Closed** *Sun, Mon lunch (Sep–Jun)*
Stylish place serving a wide choice of beef cuts such as Black Angus American and beef tartare cut. Impressive list of French wines.

ANTIBES: Le Vauban €€
Provençal **Map** E3
7 bis rue Thuret, 06600
Tel *04 93 34 33 05* **Closed** *Tue*
Excellent good-value cooking in this ordinary-looking restaurant. Try the roast partridge with truffles or the ox tail ravioli in *consommé*.

BAR-SUR-LOUP:
L'Ecole des Filles €€
Bistro **Map** E3
380 ave Amiral de Grasse, 06620
Tel *04 93 09 40 20* **Closed** *Mon, Thu lunch & Sun dinner*
Located in a former village girls' school; offers inventive cooking with an emphasis on seafood.

BEAULIEU-SUR-MER:
Le Petit Darkoum €
Moroccan **Map** F3
18 blvd General Leclerc, 06310
Tel *04 93 01 48 59* **Closed** *Mon & Tue*
Refined cuisine from Morocco's south with dishes such as kebabs, tagines and couscous royale served amidst a delightful decor.

BIOT: Les Terraillers €€€
Haute Cuisine **Map** E3
11 route chemin Neuf, 06410
Tel *04 93 65 01 59* **Closed** *Wed & Thu; mid-Oct–Nov*
Enjoy culinary delights such as lobster bisque, truffles and *foie gras* with excellent Provençal wines at this sumptuous restaurant.

BREIL-SUR-ROYA: Le Flavie €
Provençal **Map** F3
17 blvd Jean-Jaurès, 06540
Tel *04 93 54 65 74* **Closed** *Thu; Fri lunch; Nov–mid-Dec*
Cosy and cheerful café that serves delectable stews, roasts and grills, as well as fresh salads and desserts.

CAGNES-SUR-MER:
Fleur de Sel €€
Bistro **Map** E3
85 montée de la Bourgade, 06800
Tel *04 93 20 33 33* **Closed** *Apr–Sep: Wed; Oct–Mar: Wed or Thu*
Lofty Haut-de-Cagnes is the lovely setting for this restaurant serving exceptionally refined cooking. Great value set menus.

CAGNES-SUR-MER:
Château Le Cagnard €€€
Haute Cuisine **Map** E3
54 rue Sous Barri, 06800
Tel *04 93 20 73 21* **Closed** *Mid-Mar–Apr: Mon & Tue; Oct–mid-Mar: Sun–Wed*
Boasts a scrumptious menu with roast pigeon, langoustines and more. The terrace offers splendid views of the Mediterranean Sea.

> **Price Guide**
> Prices are based on a three-course meal for one with half a bottle of house wine, and include tax and service charges.
>
> € up to €40
> €€ €40 to €60
> €€€ over €60

CANNES: L'Assiette Provençale €
Provençal **Map** E4
9 quai Saint-Pierre, 06400
Tel *04 93 38 52 14* **Closed** *Mon*
Popular restaurant in the port with a good-value menu that includes oyster platters and dishes such as courgette (zucchini) blossoms, duck and snails.

CANNES: Angolo Italiano €€
Italian **Map** E4
18 rue du Commandant Andre, 06400
Tel *04 93 39 82 57* **Closed** *Mon*
Near the Croisette. Neapolitan-run place with Italian *charcuterie* and cheeses, a range of pasta dishes, grilled meats and seafood on the menu.

CANNES: Le Pastis €€
Bistro **Map** E4
28 rue du Commandant André, 06400
Tel *04 92 98 95 40*
Good for both casual lunches and dinners. Pastas, salads, sandwiches and omelettes are served over a counter or in booths like an American diner.

CANNES: La Cave €€€
Provençal **Map** E4
9 blvd de la République, 06400
Tel *04 93 99 79 87* **Closed** *Mon lunch, Sat lunch & Sun*
A favourite with both locals and visitors for its upmarket versions of Provençal dishes such as *aïoli aux legumes*, stuffed vegetables and sardines. Excellent wine list.

CANNES: La Palme d'Or €€€
Haute Cuisine **Map** E4
73 la Croisette, 06400
Tel *04 92 98 74 14* **Closed** *Sun–Tue; Jan & Feb*
Exquisitely fashionable restaurant of the famous Hôtel Martinez. A favourite with celebrities. Boasts two Michelin stars. Superb food and an exquisite wine list.

CANNES: Plage L'Ondine €€€
Seafood **Map** E4
64 la Croisette, 06400
Tel *04 93 94 23 15* **Closed** *Wed (off season); mid-Nov–mid-Dec*
Right on the beach, Plage L'Ondine offers the perfect setting to enjoy specialities such as grilled fish and lobster at outdoor tables. Excellent wine list.

Tables on the charming terrace of Les Terraillers, Biot

Fine cured meats displayed in the *salumeria* at La Trattoria, Monaco

COURMES: Auberge de Courmes €
Provençal **Map** E3
3 rue des Platanes, 06620
Tel *04 93 77 64 70* **Closed** *Mon*
This gracious village inn overlooking the Gorges du Loup offers succulent meat dishes and home-made *clafoutis* for dessert.

EZE: La Gascogne Café €
Bistro **Map** F3
151 ave de Verdun, 06360
Tel *04 93 41 18 50*
Friendly restaurant in the Hôtel du Golf offering innovative dishes with an Italian-Provençal twist.

EZE: Château Eza €€€
Haute Cuisine **Map** F3
Rue de la Pise, 06360
Tel *04 93 41 12 24* **Closed** *Mon & Tue (Jan–Mar)*
Delicate and imaginative dishes, garnished with flowers, are served in this Michelin-starred restaurant with splendid Riviera views.

GRASSE: La Bastide St Antoine €€€
Haute Cuisine **Map** E3
48 ave Henri-Dunant, 06130
Tel *04 93 70 94 94*
Enjoy a feast of unique colours and aromas worthy of the perfume capital in an attractive, flower-filled courtyard.

JUAN-LES-PINS: Ti Toques €
Bistro **Map** E4
9 ave Louis Gallet, 06160
Tel *04 92 90 25 12* **Closed** *Mon, Sun*
Hidden on a back street, Ti Toques serves delicious meat dishes with plenty of options for vegetarians. Great range of Belgian beers.

LA TURBIE: Café de la Fontaine €
Brasserie **Map** F3
4 ave Général de Gaulle, 06320
Tel *04 93 28 52 79*
The bistro at the Hostellerie Jérôme offers the exceptional cooking of chef Bruno Cirino for bargain prices. The menu features traditional Provençal dishes.

LA TURBIE: Hostellerie Jérôme €€€
Haute Cuisine **Map** F3
20 rue Comte de Cessole, 06320
Tel *04 92 41 51 51* **Closed** *Mon & Tue (Sep–Jun); Dec–Mar*
Renowned chef Bruno Cirino presides over this Michelin-starred establishment. The daily menu depends on what is available in the local markets.

MANDELIEU-LA-NAPOULE: Côté Place €
Provençal **Map** E4
21 pl de la Fontaine, 06210
Tel *04 93 47 59 27* **Closed** *Sun*
Unpretentious and popular, Côté Place serves dishes from around the Mediterranean: Moroccan tagines, Spanish seafood and Italian *saltimbocca*. All satisfying and fabulously done.

MANDELIEU-LA-NAPOULE: La Brocherie €€
Seafood **Map** E4
11 ave Henri Clews, 06210
Tel *04 93 49 80 73*
A memorable menu with five seafood starters and all the fish you need: oysters, shellfish platters and mixed grills. Situated right on the quay.

MENTON: Coté Sud €
Italian **Map** F3
15 quai Bonaparte, 06500
Tel *04 93 84 03 69*
Elegant restaurant with a stylish white decor and exquisitely presented dishes. Serves delicious pizzas, seafood and pasta dishes. Warm, friendly welcome.

MENTON: Le Martina €€
Italian **Map** F3
11 pl du Cap, 06500
Tel *04 93 57 80 22* **Closed** *Wed; Jan*
Le Martina offers a wide choice of antipasti, risotto and pasta dishes, as well as excellent seafood. Good children's menu.

DK Choice

MENTON: Le Mirazur €€€
Haute Cuisine **Map** F3
30 ave Aristide Briand, 06500
Tel *04 92 41 86 86*
Closed *Mon & Tue; Nov–mid-Feb*
A visual and culinary delight, Le Mirazur offers some of the most aesthetically flamboyant dishes ever seen. Chef Mauro prepares colourful combinations of meat and seafood made with herbs and vegetables freshly picked from the restaurant's garden. Savour the meals with superb wine and magnificent views of Menton and the sea.

MONACO: Maya Bay €€
Asian **Map** F3
24 ave Princesse Grace, 98000
Tel *00 377 97 70 74 67* **Closed** *Sun & Mon*
Thai cooking with a French touch at this stylish eatery. Plenty of *nems* and dumplings. A separate Japanese restaurant serves *teppan-yaki* and sushi.

MONACO: La Trattoria €€€
Italian **Map** F3
Sporting Monte Carlo, ave Princesse Grace, Monte-Carlo, 98000
Tel *00 377 98 06 71 71* **Closed** *Oct–mid-May*
Choose from a selection of Italian favourites, including elaborate antipasti, mini pizzas and prosciutto. Spectacular sea views.

MONACO: Le Louis XV €€€
Haute Cuisine **Map** F3
Hôtel de Paris, pl du Casino, Monte-Carlo, 98000
Tel *00 377 98 06 88 64* **Closed** *Tue & Wed; Dec, mid-Feb–Mar*
Capital of Alain Ducasse's culinary empire for more than 25 years, this splendid restaurant in the Hôtel de Paris serves haute cuisine.

MOUGINS: Resto des Arts €
Provençal **Map** E3
Rue du Maréchal-Foch, 06250
Tel *04 93 75 60 03* **Closed** *Sun & Mon (off season)*
Trendy and artistic place that serves simple, good cooking. Best for grilled meats and stews.

MOUGINS: La Place de Mougins €€€
Haute Cuisine **Map** E3
Pl du Commandant Lamy, 06250
Tel *04 93 90 15 78* **Closed** *Mon & Tue*
Stylish restaurant on the village square offering ultra-refined cuisine with unusual combinations of ingredients. Good-value lunch menus.

Splendid dining room at Le Louis XV in the Hôtel de Paris, Monaco

NICE: Chez Palmyre   €
Provençal   Map F3
5 rue Droite, 06300
Tel *04 93 85 72 32*   **Closed** *Sun*
An institution since the 1920s.
There are only six tables in a tiny
retro dining room that serves real
Niçois home cooking. Always
packed so be sure to book ahead.

NICE: L'Acchiardo   €
Provençal   Map F3
38 rue Droite, 06300
Tel *04 93 85 51 16*   **Closed** *Sat &
Sun; Aug*
Set in the heart of Nice's Old
Town. Delicious food in a great
atmosphere and Provençal wine
directly from the barrel.

NICE: Les Amoureux   €
Italian   Map F3
46 blvd Stalingrad, 06300
Tel *04 93 07 59 73* **Closed** *Sun & Mon*
This pizzeria boasts the best
Neapolitan pizza on the Riviera,
with the perfect crust. The menu
also offers other Italian specialities.
Reservations recommended.

NICE: Au Moulin Enchanté €€
Bistro   Map F3
1 rue Barbéris, 06300
Tel *04 93 55 33 14* **Closed** *Sun & Mon*
A local haunt outside the tourist
zone. Delicious fare with a wide
choice of meat and fish mains.
Good value lunch menu.

NICE: La Merenda   €€
Provençal   Map F3
4 rue Raoul Bosio, 06300
Closed *Sat & Sun*
Michelin star chef Dominique Le
Stanc prepares authentic regional
classics. The place doesn't have
any telephone. Friendly service.

NICE: Le Bistrot d'Antoine €€
Bistro   Map F3
27 rue de la Préfecture, 06300
Tel *04 93 85 29 57* **Closed** *Sun & Mon*
An ancient favourite in the Vieille
Ville, revived by a young couple.
Perfect traditional cooking.

NICE: Le Chantecler   €€€
Haute Cuisine   Map F3
37 promenade des Anglais, 06000
Tel *04 93 16 64 00*   **Closed** *Sun &
Mon; Jan*
Located in the Hotel Négresco.
Opulent 19th-century dining
room; offers a menu lavishly
punctuated with truffles and
caviar. Famous wine cellar.

NICE: Luc Salsedo   €€€
Haute Cuisine   Map F3
14 rue Maccarani, 06000
Tel *04 93 82 24 12*   **Closed** *Wed*
Chef Luc Salsedo takes classics
such as lamb and *ratatouille* and
makes them his own. Good
vegetarian choices.

PEILLON: L'Authentique   €€€
Provençal   Map F3
2 pl Auguste Arnulf, 06440
Tel *04 93 79 91 17*   **Closed** *Wed*
Elegant Niçois cooking served on
a shaded terrace with fine views.
Locally sourced ingredients and
many vegetarian options.

ROQUEBRUNE-CAP-MARTIN:
Au Grand Inquisiteur   €
Classic French   Map F3
15 & 18 rue du Château, 06190
Tel *04 93 35 05 37*   **Closed** *Mon*
An intimate, family-run place
at the heart of the village. The
menu features traditional dishes
made with quail, *escargots*
and venison.

SOSPEL: Bel Aqua   €
Provençal   Map F3
7 ave de Verdun, 06380
Tel *04 93 04 00 09*   **Closed** *Tue &
Wed; mid-Nov–mid-Mar*
Bel Aqua offers sophisticated
mountain cooking with an Italian
touch. Lovely desserts.

STE-AGNÈS: Le Righi   €
Provençal   Map F3
1 pl du Fort, 06500
Tel *04 92 10 90 88*   **Closed** *Wed*
Enjoy good solid home cooking
and amazing views at Le Righi. Try
the ravioli, gnocchi, stewed boar
and lamb cooked in hay.

ST-JEAN-CAP-FERRAT:
Le Pirate   €€
Seafood   Map F3
Nouveau Port, 06230
Tel *04 93 76 12 97*   **Closed** *Nov–
Mar dinner*
Perfect setting on the picturesque
port and an appetizing menu.
Choose from a variety of grilled
fish and seafood risottos.

ST-MARTIN-VESUBIE:
L'Ô à la Bouche   €
Classic French   Map F2
Le Boréon, 06450
Tel *04 93 02 98 42* **Closed** *mid-Nov–
mid-Dec*
Quality cooking in the mountains
with a chance to catch your own
trout. Also a brasserie offering
burgers, fondues and raclette.

ST-PAUL DE VENCE:
La Colombe d'Or   €€
Provençal   Map E3
Pl du Général de Gaulle, 06570
Tel *04 93 32 80 02* **Closed** *Nov–Dec*
Legendary artists' retreat packed
with original pieces of art. Simple

Luxurious Regency-style decor at Le Chantecler in Le Négresco, Nice

Fresh vegetables from the chef's garden at Hostellerie Berard, La Cadière-d'Azur

but excellent Provençal cooking that still attracts the rich and famous. Superb wine list.

THÉOULE-SUR-MER: Jilali B €€
Seafood   **Map** E4
16 rue Trayas, 06590
Tel 04 93 75 19 03   **Closed** Mon–Wed lunch; mid-Nov–Jan
Innovative seafood dishes with a touch of the exotic – spices, saffron and coconut. Splurge on the excellent bouillabaisse. Terrace with splendid sea views.

TOUET-SUR-VAR: Chez Paul €
Classic French   **Map** E3
4260 ave Général de Gaulle, 06710
Tel 04 93 05 71 03   **Closed** Wed; Sun–Tue dinner
A simple village inn offering tasty home-made fare: steaks, rabbit and game dishes. Pizzas and a good kids' menu too.

VALBONNE: Lou Cigalon €€€
Haute Cuisine   **Map** E3
6 blvd Carnot, 06560
Tel 04 93 12 01 61   **Closed** Sun, Mon & Thu
An elegant emerging restaurant, north of Cannes, with a hearty menu based around game dishes, duck and wild mushrooms.

VENCE: La Litote €
Bistro   **Map** E3
5 rue de l'Evêché, 06140
Tel 04 93 24 27 82   **Closed** Mon
Relaxing and full of charm with tables under shaded lime trees, La Litote offers the perfect setting to enjoy inventive cooking from a rising young chef.

VILLEFRANCHE-SUR-MER: La Mère Germaine €€
Seafood   **Map** F3
9 quai Courbet, 06230
Tel 04 93 01 71 39   **Closed** mid-Nov–Christmas
A favourite on the port since 1938. The cuisine at La Mère Germaine revolves around dishes made from fish and shellfish. They take their bouillabaisse seriously.

VILLEFRANCHE-SUR-MER: L'Oursin Bleu €€
Seafood   **Map** F3
11 quai de l'amiral Courbet, 06230
Tel 04 93 01 90 12   **Closed** Jan
Combines traditional seafood recipes with new interpretations to create stylish dishes, rich in colour. There's a big aquarium in the foyer to enjoy while waiting.

The Var and the Iles d'Hyères

COGOLIN: Grain de Sel €€
Bistro   **Map** E4
6 rue du 11 Novembre, 83310
Tel 04 94 54 46 86   **Closed** Sun & Mon; late Nov–early Dec
Bright and cheerful bistro with an open kitchen. Deceptively simple Provençal dishes are packed with flavour. Outside tables in summer.

COLLOBRIÈRES: La Petite Fontaine €
Provençal   **Map** D4
1 pl de la République, 83610
Tel 04 94 48 00 12   **Closed** Mon; Feb, two weeks in Sep
Provençal home cooking with large portions and wonderful flavours. Try the chicken and garlic fricassee. Superb wines.

DK Choice

FAYENCE: L'Escourtin €€
Provençal   **Map** E3
159 Chemin de Notre Dame des Cyprès, 83440
Tel 04 94 76 00 84
Closed Wed, Thu lunch
Set in an idyllic location within an ancient olive mill, L'Escourtin is part of the Hôtel Moulin de la Camandoule. The interiors are furnished with antiques and flowers. Authentic cuisine with game dishes, foie gras and fish in subtle sauces flavoured with fresh herbs and produce from the delightful garden.

FAYENCE: Le Castellaras €€
Provençal   **Map** E3
461 chemin de Peymeyan, 83440
Tel 04 94 76 13 80   **Closed** Mon & Tue; Jan–mid-Feb
A beautiful farmhouse where the chef combines lamb, veal and crayfish with local produce to create wonderful dishes. A flowery terrace with spectacular views. Côtes de Provence wines.

FRÉJUS: Faubourg de Saigon €
Vietnamese   **Map** E4
126 rue St-François de Paule, 83600
Tel 04 94 53 65 80   **Closed** Sun & Mon
Enjoy hearty portions of authentic, spicy Vietnamese dishes at this small, unassuming restaurant. Try spring rolls, the house speciality.

HYÈRES: Grand Baie €
Seafood   **Map** D4
5 pl du Belvédère, Giens, 83400
Tel 04 94 58 28 16
A terrace with a wonderful view over the bay and simple, first-rate seafood. All-you-can-eat shellfish buffet some nights.

HYÈRES: Le Désiré €
Brasserie   **Map** D4
13 rue Crivelli, 83400
Tel 04 94 20 27 38   **Closed** Wed
An unassuming place, Le Désiré serves high quality cooking in a peaceful atmosphere. Feast on the fabulous desserts here.

ÎLE DE PORQUEROLLES: L'Olivier €€€
Seafood   **Map** D5
Île de Porquerolles Ouest, 83400
Tel 04 94 58 34 83   **Closed** Mon (except Jul & Aug); Oct–Apr
Located in the Hotel Le Mas du Langoustier, an island retreat, L'Olivier offers a unique culinary experience. The menu features mostly seafood, including lobster, langoustines and shellfish.

LA CADIÈRE D'AZUR: Hostellerie Bérard €€€
Classic French   **Map** C4
6 rue Gabriel-Péri, 83740
Tel 04 94 90 11 43   **Closed** Mon & Tue
Michelin-starred restaurant using produce from the chef's garden. French haute cuisine, cooked with sincerity. Also an informal bistro with an excellent seasonal menu.

LE LAVANDOU: La Farigoulette €
Seafood   **Map** D4
1 ave du Capitaine Thorel, La Fossette 83980
Tel 04 94 71 06 85
La Farigoulette offers inventive and colourful dishes. Especially good for seafood: bouillabaisse, grilled fish and lobster pasta.

For more information on types of restaurants see page 202

Stylish dining terrace overlooking the Mediterranean at La Vague d'Or

ST-RAPHAËL: L'Etoile €
Provençal **Map** E4
2170 route de la Corniche, 83700
Tel *04 94 83 10 44* **Closed** *Wed; mid-Nov–mid-Feb*
Welcoming, laid-back place with the perfect setting on the little Port de Boulouris. Good risottos and Provençal seafood.

ST-RAPHAËL: Le Bouchon
Provençal €€
Contemporary **Map** E4
45 rue de la République, 83700
Tel *04 94 53 89 18* **Closed** *Sun & Mon*
Charming restaurant with tables under plane trees. A good place for *aïoli façon pastorel* (an assortment of seafood and vegetables with garlic mayonnaise).

ST-TROPEZ: Le Sporting €
Bistro **Map** E4
42 pl des Lices, 83990
Tel *04 94 97 00 65*
Escape the excess of St-Tropez without leaving town in this local's refuge that serves good main dishes, as well as burgers, salads and omelettes.

ST-TROPEZ: Le Bistrot St-Tropez €€
Bistro **Map** E4
3 pl des Lices, 83990
Tel *04 94 97 11 33*
Trendy brasserie with low lighting and elegant interiors. The eclectic menu has something for everyone – grilled fish, steak tartare, sushi and spring rolls.

ST-TROPEZ: Au Caprice des Deux €€€
Provençal **Map** E4
40 rue du Portail Neuf, 83990
Tel *04 94 97 76 78* **Closed** *Tue (except Jul & Aug); Sun–Wed winter; Nov–mid-Feb*
Cheerful ambience with candles and mirrors in an old Provençal house. Refined cuisine with dishes such as *foie gras* terrine with onion jam. Do not miss the piña colada sorbet.

ST-TROPEZ: La Vague d'Or €€€
Haute Cuisine **Map** E4
Plage de la Bouillabaisse, 83990
Tel *04 94 55 91 00* **Closed** *early Oct–late April*
Luxurious Michelin-starred restaurant in Hotel Résidence de la Pinède. Chef Arnaud Donckele creates elegant dishes using exotic ingredients such as cedar, salicornia and chestnut honey.

TOULON: La Lampa €
Brasserie **Map** D4
117 quai de la Sinse, 83000
Tel *04 94 03 06 09*
Set on the quay with outside tables offering fine views. Good for a light lunch of salads and *moules-frites*, as well as something more ambitious such as grilled fish and meat dishes.

TOULON: La Promesse €€
Bistro **Map** D4
250 rue Jean Jaurès, 83000
Tel *04 94 98 79 39* **Closed** *Sun & Mon; three weeks in Jan*
Unpretentious dining room and real, award-winning *cuisine d'auteur* with influences from Italy and beyond. Popular with locals so book well in advance.

Bouches-du-Rhône and Nîmes

AIGUES-MORTES: Le Dit-Vin €
Bistro **Map** A4
6 rue du 4 Septembre, 30220
Tel *04 66 53 52 76*
Chic restaurant and tapas bar, and a wine cellar visible through the floor. Don't miss the delicious *bouillabaisse*. Pretty garden setting and attentive staff.

Tranquil park setting at Le Mas d'Entremont, Aix-en-Provence

AIGUES-MORTES: Le Millesime €€
Contemporary **Map** A4
38 rue de la République, 30220
Tel *04 66 53 74 60* **Closed** *Mon & Tue*
Dishes, including tapas, are prepared using ingredients sourced locally. Champagne and wine tasting at weekends.

AIX-EN-PROVENCE: Brasserie Leopold €
Brasserie **Map** C4
2 ave Victor-Hugo, 13100
Tel *04 42 26 01 24*
This Art Deco classic is great for a full-scale meal, snack or just a drink. The menu features regional cuisine and traditional brasserie fare including *sauerkraut*.

AIX-EN-PROVENCE: Le Comté d'Aix €
Classic French **Map** C4
17 rue Couronne, 13010
Tel *04 42 26 79 26* **Closed** *Sun*
A rare bargain in pricey Aix-en-Provence, Le Comté offers simple but well-prepared dishes, including many local specialities.

AIX-EN-PROVENCE: Le Formal €€
Gastronomic **Map** C4
32 rue Espariat, 13100
Tel *04 42 27 08 31* **Closed** *Sun & Mon; late Aug–early Sep*
Refined culinary works of art, featuring plenty of truffles, served in a contemporary designed vaulted cellar. Good value lunch menus.

AIX-EN-PROVENCE: Le Mas d'Entremont €€
Provençal **Map** C4
315 route d'Avignon, 13090
Tel *04 42 17 42 42* **Closed** *Nov–mid-Mar*
Enjoy fine dishes such as roasted wild prawns with citrus fruits and fillet of Montbéliard beef at this hotel-restaurant in the middle of a park. Excellent Provençal wines.

ARLES: La Grignotte €
Provençal **Map** B3
6 rue Favorin, 13200
Tel *04 90 93 10 43* **Closed** *Sun*
Cheerful and unpretentious place. Try the fish soup and beef stew with Camargue rice and a carafe of house wine.

ARLES: La Gueule du Loup €
Provençal **Map** B3
39 rue des Arènes, 13200
Tel *04 90 96 96 69* **Closed** *Sun, Mon lunch; mid-Jan–mid-Feb*
Charming restaurant with a handful of tables in a former family home. Serves exquisite Provençal fare. Superb desserts.

ARLES: Chez Bob €€€
Provençal **Map** B3
Route du Sambuc, Villeneuve
Gageron 13200
Tel *04 90 97 00 29* **Closed** *Mon & Tue*
Relish regional specialities while
sitting in the eclectically decorated
dining room or the pleasant
terrace. Reserve at least a week
in advance.

ARLES: L'Atelier de Jean-Luc
Rabanel €€€
Gastronomic **Map** B3
7 rue des Carmes, 13200
Tel *04 90 91 07 69* **Closed** *Mon & Tue*
Michelin star chef Jean-Luc
Rabanel creates exquisite artistic
masterpieces based on organic
produce from his garden. Book
well in advance.

ARLES: La Chassagnette €€€
Organic **Map** B3
Le Sambuc, 13200
Tel *04 90 97 26 96* **Closed** *Tue, Wed;*
Feb, Nov & Christmas week
Chef Armand Arnal runs France's
most famous organic restaurant
surrounded by lush gardens near
the Camargue. Special vegetarian
menu featuring truffles.

ARLES: Lou Marques €€€
Gastronomic **Map** B3
9 blvd Lices, 13200
Tel *04 90 52 52 52*
Elegant restaurant located in the
characterful Hôtel Jules César,
with a garden terrace and classic
Provençal dishes. Excellent value
lunch menus.

CASSIS: Le Grand Bleu €€
Seafood **Map** C4
12 quai les Baux, 13260
Tel *04 42 01 23 23* **Closed** *Wed*
Informal portside restaurant
specializing in simply prepared
fresh seafood at affordable prices.
The service is warm and friendly.

CASSIS: La Villa Madie €€€
Gastronomic **Map** C4
Ave Revestel, Anse de Corton, 13260
Tel *04 96 18 00 00* **Closed** *Mon &*
Tue; Jan–mid-Feb
Enjoy idyllic views over the
Mediterranean along with
spectacular seafood at this
Michelin-starred restaurant.
Alternatively, try its less expensive
La Petite Cuisine bistro.

LES BAUX-DE-PROVENCE: Le
Café des Baux €
Provençal **Map** B3
Rue du Trencat, 13520
Tel *04 90 54 52 69* **Closed** *Nov–Mar*
Hip restaurant run by award-
winning pastry chef Pierre Walter.
The savoury dishes are a culinary
delight as well.

A view of the excellent wine cellar at Le Julien, Marseille

LES BAUX-DE-PROVENCE:
L'Oustau de Baumanière €€€
Gastronomic **Map** B3
Chemin Départementale 27, Le Val
d'Enfer, 13520
Tel *04 90 54 33 07* **Closed** *Jan–Mar*
Popular with celebrities, this
superb restaurant in a gorgeous
setting boasts two Michelin stars
and a private heliport. Inventive
cuisine using exquisite ingredients.

MARSEILLE: Beach Café €
Classic French **Map** C4
214 quai du Port, 13002
Tel *04 91 91 55 40* **Closed** *Mon; two*
weeks at Christmas
Informal outdoor terrace and a
menu comprising tasty salads,
meats, fish, snacks and lots of ice
cream choices. Perfect for kids.

MARSEILLE: Le Boucher €
Steakhouse **Map** C4
10 rue de Village, 13006
Tel *04 91 48 79 65* **Closed** *Sun &*
Mon; Aug, Easter
Secret restaurant for meat lovers
hidden behind the façade of a
butcher shop. Traditional recipes
and succulent *entrecôtes* for two.
Delicious home-made fries.

MARSEILLE: Toinou €
Seafood **Map** C4
3 cours Saint-Louis, 13001
Tel *04 91 33 14 94*
The place for seafood platters;
features the freshest of oysters,
mussels and prawns served with
crusty bread and white wine.

MARSEILLE: La Table du Fort €€
Bistro **Map** C4
8 rue Fort Notre Dame, 13007
Tel *04 91 33 97 65* **Closed** *Sat lunch,*
Sun–Mon lunch; Jul
Charming restaurant run by a
young couple. Serves beautifully
prepared seafood, poultry and
meat dishes, plus scrumptious
desserts. Reservations essential.

MARSEILLE: Le Julien €€
Classic French **Map** C4
114 rue Paradis, 13006
Tel *04 91 37 06 22* **Closed** *Sat lunch,*
Sun, Mon dinner
Friendly place specializing in
French classics such as veal sweet-
breads with morels and *baba au*
rhum. Wide-ranging menu.

MARSEILLE: Vinonéo €€
Classic French **Map** C4
6 pl Daviel, 13002
Tel *04 91 90 40 26* **Closed** *Sun;*
Mon–Wed dinner
Cool, contemporary cuisine by a
winemaker. Features hot dishes,
cold meats and cheese platters.
Great wine pairings by the glass.

DK Choice

MARSEILLE: L'Epuisette €€€
Seafood **Map** C4
158 rue du Vallon des Auffes, 13007
Tel *04 91 52 17 82* **Closed** *Sun &*
Mon; one week in Mar
A glass dining room overlooking
the turquoise sea is L'Epuisette's
unbeatable setting. This elegant
restaurant has been in business
for decades and from the calm
and relaxing atmosphere to the
charming staff, everything is
perfect. The cuisine includes
heavenly *bouillabaisse*, lobster
tagine and other seafood
delicacies. Extensive wine list
and gorgeous desserts.

MARSEILLE: Le Petit Nice –
Passédat €€€
Seafood **Map** C4
Anse de Maldormé, Corniche du
Président J F Kennedy, 13007
Tel *04 91 59 25 92* **Closed** *Sun & Mon*
This hotel-restaurant boasts three
Michelin stars. Relish chef Gerard
Passédat's sublime *bouillabaisse*,
seafood and wonderful desserts.
Splendid Mediterranean views.

MARTIGUES: Le Cabanon de Maguy €
Provençal **Map** B4
2 quai des Anglais,13500
Tel 04 42 49 32 51 **Closed** Sun & Mon; three weeks in Jan
Feast on delicious duck breast in honey and rosemary, aubergine caviar and fish soup in a relaxed atmosphere. Delightful terrace.

MAUSSANE-LES-ALPILLES: La Fleur de Thym €
Provençal **Map** B3
15 ave de la Vallée des Baux, 13520
Tel 04 90 54 54 00 **Closed** Sat lunch, Sun dinner (Sep–Jun), Mon; Dec
One of the best bargains around Les Baux. Limited but excellent menu. Charming atmosphere and friendly service.

MAUSSANE-LES-ALPILLES: La Place €€
Bistro **Map** B3
65 ave de la Vallée des Baux, 13520
Tel 04 90 54 23 31 **Closed** Tue, also Wed (Oct–mid-Apr); Jan
A change in chef has brought back the glitz and glamour to this bistro run by Les Baux's Baumanière empire. Often packed; reserve in advance.

NÎMES: Au Flan Coco €
Classic French **Map** A3
21 rue du Grand Couvent, 30900
Tel 04 66 21 84 81 **Closed** Sun & Mon
Set in a medieval convent; offers huge salads, classic mains and tasty pat' à coco (potato pie). The takeaway menu is ideal for picnics.

NÎMES: Le Vintage €
Bistro **Map** A3
7 rue de Bernis, 30000
Tel 04 66 21 04 45 **Closed** Sun, Mon (except Jul & Aug)
Cosy restaurant and wine bar with a menu that features foie gras, duck and steaks. Shaded outdoor tables.

NÎMES: Au Plaisirs des Halles €€
Provençal **Map** A3
4 rue Littré, 30000
Tel 04 66 36 01 02 **Closed** Sun & Mon
Sleek, contemporary ambience to match the cuisine. Try the shrimp and scallop tempura or the local speciality, brandade. Exceptional regional wine list.

NÎMES: Alexandre €€€
Gastronomic **Map** A3
2 rue Xavier Tronc, Garons, 30128
Tel 04 66 70 08 99 **Closed** Sep–Jun: Sun dinner, Mon & Tue; Jul–Aug: Sun & Mon; mid-Feb–mid-Mar; 2 weeks in summer.
An unforgettable dining experience in a lovely garden setting. Sublime food and enchanting desserts from the Michelin-star chef Michel Kayser.

Shaded outdoor terrace overlooking the garden at Alexandre, Nîmes

NÎMES: Vincent Croizard €€€
Gastronomic **Map** A3
17 rue des Chassaintes, 30900
Tel 04 66 67 04 99 **Closed** Sun dinner–Tue lunch; Sun & Mon (jul–Sep)
Ring a doorbell to enter this chic restaurant hidden on a narrow street. Chef Vincent Croizard prepares an exquisite parade of little dishes. Vegetarian menu available.

SAINTES-MARIES-DE-LA-MER: El Campo €
Spanish **Map** A4
13 rue Victor Hugo, 13460
Tel 04 90 97 84 11 **Closed** Wed, except in Jul and Aug
Lively restaurant with a great service. Paella is a speciality, but there are plenty of other options. Live Flamenco and Gipsy Kings-style guitar music in the evenings.

SAINTES-MARIES-DE-LA-MER: L'Estelle en Camargue €€€
Gastronomic **Map** A4
D38 route du Petit-Rhône, 13460
Tel 04 90 97 89 01 **Closed** Mon (except Jul & Aug); mid-Nov–Mar
Sit out in a Mediterranean garden and enjoy a feast of seasonal delicacies. The menu also includes a wide variety of seafood and creamy desserts.

SALON-DE-PROVENCE: La Salle à Manger €
Provençale **Map** B3
6 rue du Marechal-Joffre, 13300
Tel 04 90 56 28 01 **Closed** Sun & Mon
Rococo dining room with a patio for summer months. Famous for delectable desserts, with over 40 varieties to choose from.

ST-RÉMY-DE-PROVENCE: La Cantina €
Italian **Map** B3
18 blvd Victor Hugo, 13210
Tel 04 90 92 40 02 **Closed** Mon & Tue; mid-Feb–mid-Mar, mid-Nov–early Dec
Informal and relaxed trattoria specializing in thin crust pizzas and pasta dishes. Good selection of Italian wines. Perfect for kids.

ST-RÉMY-DE-PROVENCE: La Medina €
Moroccan **Map** B3
34 blvd Mirabeau, 13210
Tel 06 63 00 14 28 **Closed** Wed
A nice change of pace, this quiet restaurant offers excellent tagines, couscous and a variety of French dishes. Pleasant summer terrace.

ST-RÉMY-DE-PROVENCE: Comptoir 36 €€
Bistro **Map** B3
36 ave Marechal Juin, 13210
Tel 04 90 94 41 12 **Closed** Sun
Young chefs Lisa and Rudy prepare delectable food from fresh, locally sourced produce at this modern bistro and wine bar. Regular live music.

VERS-PONT-DU-GARD: La Petite Gare €€
Classic French **Map** A3
435 route d'Uzès, 30210
Tel 04 66 03 40 67 **Closed** Sun & Mon
Contemporary versions of tasty classics served in an old train station or outside under century-old plane trees. Good value lunch menus.

The graceful façade of La Petite Gare, Vers-Pont-du-Gard

The elegant restaurant in the Bastide de Capelongue hotel, Bonnieux

VERS-PONT-DU-GARD:
Les Terrasses €€
Provençal **Map** A3
La Begude, 400 route du Pont-du-Gard, 30210
Tel *04 66 63 91 37* **Closed** *Nov–Easter*
Enjoy delicious, locally sourced food against the backdrop of the aqueduct – a spectacle by night when the bridge is illuminated.

VILLENEUVE-LÈS-AVIGNON: La
Guinguette du Vieux Moulin €
Seafood **Map** B3
5 rue du Vieux Moulin, 30400
Tel *04 90 94 50 72* **Closed** *Sun–Wed dinner; Oct–Mar*
Lively and atmospheric riverside restaurant specializing in grilled sardines and other fish dishes. Hosts frequent events and music. Also has a summer pontoon.

VILLENEUVE-LÈS-AVIGNON:
Le Prieuré €€€
Gastronomic **Map** B3
7 pl du Chapître, 30400
Tel *04 90 15 90 15* **Closed** *Mon; Nov–Mar*
This gorgeous hotel-restaurant is set in a 14th-century priest's residence and offers sophisticated seasonal cuisine.

Vaucluse

AVIGNON: L'Epice and Love €
Provençal **Map** B3
30 rue des Lices, 84000
Tel *04 90 82 45 96* **Closed** *Sun*
Wonderfully romantic restaurant, run with *joie de vivre* by a superb chef who bases her meals on the market ingredients available. Reservations recommended.

AVIGNON: Why Not €
Bistro **Map** B3
25 rue Carnot, 84000
Tel *04 90 82 69 24* **Closed** *Mon–Wed lunch*
Trendy, informal restaurant with a 1980s theme run by a young couple. Offers simple but sophisticated dishes. The menu changes monthly.

AVIGNON: La Fourchette €€
Provençal **Map** B3
17 rue Racine, 84000
Tel *04 90 85 20 93* **Closed** *Sat & Sun*
Quirky, much-loved bistro with its own take on the regional classics, with lots of seafood and excellent cheeses. Booking essential.

AVIGNON: L'Hermitage €€
Provençal **Map** B3
7 rue Figuière, 84000
Tel *04 90 86 21 36* **Closed** *Sun lunch*
Beautiful setting in a courtyard. Try tasty goat's cheese parcels, steak tartare, salmon and duck. A cool refuge in summer.

AVIGNON: Christian Etienne €€€
Provençal **Map** B3
10 rue Mons, 84000
Tel *04 90 86 16 50* **Closed** *Sun & Mon*
Masterchef Christian Etienne offers superb seasonal menus in a 14th-century dining room. Good value set lunch menu.

AVIGNON: La Mirande €€€
Gastronomic **Map** B3
4 pl de la Mirande, 84000
Tel *04 90 14 20 20* **Closed** *Tue & Wed; mid-Jan–mid-Feb*
Dine indoors in an aristocratic setting or outside on the shaded terrace. Dazzling menu by a top chef and friendly service.

AVIGNON: La Vieille Fontaine €€€
Haute Cuisine **Map** B3
12 pl Crillon, 84000
Tel *04 90 14 76 76* **Closed** *Sun & Mon; mid-Feb–mid-Mar*
Beautifully appointed restaurant in the Hotel d'Europe. Savour chef Bruno d'Angelis's Michelin-starred creative cuisine. Excellent wines.

BONNIEUX: Un p'tit Coin de
Cuisine €
Bistro **Map** C3
Pl Gambetta, 84480
Tel *09 81 64 85 81* **Closed** *Mon, Sun lunch*
Smart bistro with a short but delicious menu. Extensive list of Côte du Rhône wines.

BONNIEUX: Edouard Loubet €€€
Haute Cuisine **Map** C3
Les Claparèdes, chemin des Cabanes, 84480
Tel *04 90 75 89 78* **Closed** *Wed; winter (except holiday period)*
Housed in the stunning Bastide de Capelongue hotel. The chef prepares delicious locally sourced dishes.

CADENET: Auberge La Fenière €€€
Haute Cuisine **Map** C3
D943 Route de Lourmarin, 84160
Tel *04 90 68 11 79* **Closed** *Mon & Tue; Jan*
Lovely inn with superb seafood and vegetable creations from one of Provence's top chefs. Reine Sammut. Holds regular concerts.

CARPENTRAS: Chez Serge €€
Bistro **Map** B3
90 rue Cottier, 84200
Tel *04 90 63 21 24*
Trendy decor and a creative menu featuring fresh fish and wild mushrooms. Extensive wine list.

For more information on types of restaurants *see page 202*

CAVAILLON: Restaurant
Prévot €€€
Provençal **Map** B3
353 av du Verdun, 84300
Tel *04 90 71 32 43* **Closed** *Sun & Mon; mid-Feb–mid-Mar*
A stylish culinary treat by Chef Jean Jacques Prévot. Fabulous ingredient-based seasonal menus – asparagus (spring); melons (summer); mushrooms (autumn) and black truffles (winter).

CHÂTEAUNEUF-DU-PAPE:
La Mère Germaine €€
Provençal **Map** B3
3 rue Commandant Lemaitre, 84230
Tel *04 90 22 78 34* **Closed** *Wed; (Oct–mid-Mar)*
Surrounded by vineyard views, this restaurant features classic Provençal dishes and outstanding regional wines. Good value lunch.

CHÂTEAUNEUF-DU-PAPE:
La Sommellerie €€
Bistro **Map** B3
2268 route de Roquemaure, 84230
Tel *04 90 83 50 00* **Closed** *Mon from Oct–Mar, Sat lunch, Sun dinner*
Located in a 17th-century sheep-fold, offers exceptional dinners focusing on regional Côtes du Rhône wines. A superlative five-course, all-lobster menu for €65.

GIGONDAS: Les Florets €
Bistro **Map** B2
Route des Dentelles, Chemin des Florets, 84190
Tel *04 90 65 85 01* **Closed** *Wed*
Les Florets offers artful dishes well complimented by local wines. Diners enjoy enchanting views of the Dentelles de Montmirail from its terrace.

GORDES: La Ferme de la
Huppe €€
Provençal **Map** C3
RD 156, Les Pourquiers, 84220
Tel *04 90 72 12 25* **Closed** *Sun; Nov–Mar*
Charming owners and enchanting garden on an 18th-century farm. Limited but delicious menu of Provençal treats.

Delectable, creatively presented dishes at Le Mesclun, Seguret

Delightful courtyard at 18th-century La Ferme de la Huppe, Gordes

L'ISLE-SUR LE SORGUE: Le
Vivier €€
Provençal **Map** B3
800 cours Fernande Peyre, 84800
Tel *04 90 38 52 80* **Closed** *Mon; Fri & Sat lunch; Sun dinner*
Superb fresh food on a magical riverside terrace. Try the pigeon pie with porcini mushrooms.

MENERBES: Café Veranda €
Bistro **Map** C3
Av Marcellin-Poncet, 84560
Tel *04 90 72 33 33* **Closed** *Mon lunch; Sun & Tue dinner*
A welcoming dining room and terrace with views over the hills. Creative European cooking.

OPPÈDE: Restaurant Celinà €
Italian **Map** C3
1367 Route des Petitons-Hinguets, 84580
Tel *04 32 52 17 85* **Closed** *May–Aug: Mon; Sep–Apr: Mon–Thu*
Charming 19th-century bastide setting and cuisine with an Italian flair. Book for a delightful brunch.

PERNES-LES-FONTAINES:
Coté Jardin €
Classic French **Map** B3
221 quai de Verdun, 84210
Tel *04 90 60 08 93* **Closed** *Oct–mid-Apr*
Enjoy generous salads and grilled meats while sitting in a pretty garden. Superb home-made ice creams.

SEGURET: Le Mesclun €€
Bistro **Map** B2
Rue des Poternes, 84110
Tel *04 90 46 93 43* **Closed** *Wed; Sun & Tue dinner (Sep–Jun)*
Charming terrace with lovely views of the Rhône valley and sophisticated fare that draws on Asian, Caribbean and Mexican cuisines. Good children's menu.

SERIGNAN-DU-COMTAT: Le Pré
du Moulin €€€
Provençal **Map** B2
Cours Joël Esteve/ Route de Sainte-Cécile les Vignes, 84830
Tel *04 90 70 14 55* **Closed** *Mon, Sun dinner (Sep–Jun)*
Dine under giant plane trees on refined delicacies such as lobster ravioli with chicory and dill in this stylish hotel-restaurant. Vintage Rhône valley and Gigondas wines.

VAISON-LA-ROMAINE: Moulin
à Huile €€€
Provençal **Map** B2
1 quai du Maréchal Foch, 84110
Tel *04 90 36 20 67* **Closed** *Sun & Mon; winter (till mid-Apr)*
Housed in a 12th-century oil mill, this Michelin-starred restaurant offers excellent Provençal cuisine Try the delicious lobster menu. Alfresco dining on terrace-balcony.

Alpes-de-Haute-Provence

CASTELLANE: Auberge du
Teillon €€
Bistro **Map** D3
Route Napoléon le Garde, 04120
Tel *04 92 83 60 88* **Closed** *Mon, Sun dinner; Nov–Mar*
Pleasant country inn famed for its hand-smoked Norwegian salmon, *foie gras*, scallop and morel risotto, millefeuille and local cheeses.

L'Olivier restaurant, Digne-les-Bains

CHÂTEAU-ARNOUX: La Bonne Etape €€€
Haute Cuisine **Map** D2
Chemin du Lac, 04160
Tel *04 92 64 00 09* **Closed** *Mon & Tue; Jan–mid-Feb, late Nov*
Elegant inn specializing in dishes with a personal touch using fresh local produce, especially lamb and seafood. Superb wine list.

DIGNE-LES-BAINS: L'Olivier €
Bistro **Map** D2
1 rue des Monges, 04000
Tel *04 92 31 47 41* **Closed** *Mon & Tue*
Delightful family-run restaurant with tasty seafood and meat main courses in a pretty alfresco setting.

DIGNE-LES-BAINS: Villa Gaïa €
Provençal **Map** D2
24 route de Nice, 04000
Tel *04 92 31 21 60* **Closed** *Nov–mid-Apr*
Simple and delicious seasonal fare with fresh vegetables from the garden – sautéed coriander and lemon lamb. By reservation only.

FORCALQUIER: Aux 2 Anges €
Bistro **Map** C3
3 pl Saint-Michel, 04300
Tel *04 92 75 04 36* **Closed** *Feb*
Friendly, unpretentious and intimate, with outdoor tables and delectable Provençal dishes. Excellent, good-value set menu.

FORCALQUIER: Le 9 €
Bistro **Map** C3
9 av Jean Giono, 04300
Tel *04 92 75 03 29*
Closed *Tue, Wed (in winter); Jan & Feb*
Simple, fresh dishes combine here with lovely views from the garden and terrace. Do not miss the venison sautéed with cranberries.

DK Choice

MOUSTIERS-STE-MARIE: La Treille Muscate €
Provençal **Map** D3
Pl de l'Eglise, 04360
Tel *04 92 74 64 31* **Closed** *Wed, Thu (in winter)*
Set under the crags, with a shaded terrace near a waterfall, this warm and welcoming restaurant is the perfect setting for some exceptional Provençal cuisine. The menu includes specialities such as rabbit confit in rosemary and an utterly mouthwatering penne with mushrooms and *foie gras*. Reservations recommended.

MOUSTIERS-STE-MARIE: Ferme Ste Cécile €€
Bistro **Map** D3
Rte des Gorges du Verdon
Tel *04 92 74 64 18* **Closed** *Mon, Sun dinner; Nov–Mar*
Bucolic setting and excellent value on tasty dishes using spelt, partridge, veal and seafood. Good wines. Shaded summer terrace. Book ahead.

MOUSTIERS-STE-MARIE: La Bastide de Moustiers €€€
Provençal **Map** D3
Chemin de Quinson, 04360
Tel *04 92 70 47 47* **Closed** *Tue & Wed; Jan–Feb*
Superb, fresh cuisine. The menu here changes daily, based on the herbs and ingredients plucked that day in the Bastide's fine vegetable garden and orchards. Book "Le salon de Amoureux" for a romantic dinner.

ROUGON: Le Mur D'Abeilles €
Crêperie **Map** D3
D955 – La route du Grand Canyon, 04120
Tel *04 92 83 76 33* **Closed** *Nov–Mar*
Great stop for lunch while visiting the Grand Canyon. Spectacular views, delightful picnic tables and delicious, generous-sized savoury and sweet crêpes.

STE-CROIX DU VERDON: Le Comptoir €
Classic **Map** D3
Le Village, 04500
Tel *04 92 73 74 62* **Closed** *Nov–Easter*
Beautiful terrace overlooking the lake. Serves huge salads, grilled fish and meats, and *moules-frites*. Perfect for lunch. Good children's menu.

VALENSOLE: Hostellerie de la Fuste €€€
Provençal **Map** D3
Route d'Oraison, Valensole, 04210
Tel *04 92 72 05 95* **Closed** *Mon, Sun dinner*
Elegant country inn featuring dishes prepared from home-grown vegetables, seafood and succulent meats on a terrace shaded by plane trees.

The magnificent dining room of La Bonne Etape, Château-Arnoux

For more information on types of restaurants *see page 202*

Cafés, Bars and Casual Eating

In rural areas the world over the local bar is the centre of village life, and nowhere is this more true than in Provence. Everywhere you go you will find lively watering holes, often with outside terraces or gardens. Most bars and cafés double as lunchtime restaurants, serving straightforward daily specials at reasonable prices. Snacks are not really a part of French life but nearly all bars will make you a traditional *baguette* sandwich or a *croque monsieur* (toasted ham and cheese sandwich). Drinking is a subject close to Provençal hearts – *pastis*, the aniseed spirit synonymous with Marseille, is the region's lifeblood. In many country towns, you will see the locals sitting outside sipping *pastis* from the early morning onwards, along with strong black coffee. Lunchtime tipples include ice-cold rosé, which makes the perfect accompaniment to a sun-filled day.

Cafés

There is little distinction between cafés and bars in Provence and most serve alcohol all day. In the country, village cafés will often close around 8pm. In larger towns, many places stay open much later – popular Marseillais and Niçois bars close when the last person leaves. Many stay open all night, serving breakfast to the diehards as dawn breaks. A lot of cafés are also *tabacs* (tobacconists) selling cigarettes, tobacco, sweets and stamps.

While most Provençal cafés are simple places, where decor is restricted to the local fire brigade calendar and fashion to a hunting jacket and boots, there are several stylish exceptions. No visit to Aix is complete without an hour or two spent sipping coffee on the cours Mirabeau, one of the places in Provence to see and be seen. On the Côte d'Azur, chic cafés abound. In Cannes, **Restaurant Carlton** is the place to spot film stars during the festival. In Nice, the cafés on the cours Saleya are the hub of day- and nightlife, while Monaco boasts the crème de la crème, **La Brasserie du Café de Paris**.

What to Eat

Most Provençal cafés serve breakfast although, in village establishments, this will just be a couple of slices of *baguette* and coffee. More elaborate affairs are served in towns, with fresh orange juice, warm croissants and jam. Café lunches usually include a *plat du jour* (dish of the day) and a dessert, along with a quarter litre of wine. These can be great bargains, costing little more than €12. For more basic lunches, sandwiches, omelettes and salads can be ordered. Evening meals are usually the reserve of restaurants, although in rural areas, the local bar will also serve dinner, normally a variant on the lunchtime menu.

What to Drink

Since Roman days, when the legionnaires introduced wine to the region, drinking has been a favoured pastime in Provence. Cold beer seems to surpass the fruit of the vine in the hearts of most farmers, as village bars are filled with locals downing *pressions* (half-pint glasses of beer). More potent tipples include *pastis*, a 90 per cent proof nectar flavoured with aniseed, vanilla and cinnamon, and *marc*, a brandy distilled from any available fruits. Soft drinks such as *un diabolo* (fruit syrup mixed with lemonade) and *orange pressée* (freshly squeezed orange juice) are also popular. As in most Mediterranean lands, coffee is a way of life – *un café* is a cup of strong and black espresso. If you want

white coffee, ask for *un café crème*. For filter or instant coffee order *un café filtre* or *un café américain*. Tea is served black unless you ask for milk or lemon. Herbal teas are also available, known as *tisanes* or *infusions*.

Bars

In most towns you will find a handful of bars that only serve beer and miscellaneous alcohol, rather than the more diverse range offered by cafés. These bars are lively in true Mediterranean style. Student centres such as Nice, Marseille and Aix contain British-style pubs, offering a large selection of European bottled and draught beer. Some have live bands, such as **Wayne's Bar** and **De Klomp** in Nice.

More upmarket bars are found in the plush hotels of the Côte d'Azur. Here, in *belle époque* splendour, you can sip champagne listening to jazz piano, string quartets or opera singers. Among the most impressive are the bars of the Carlton and Martinez hotels in Cannes, Le Négresco in Nice, **Le Bar** at the Grand Hôtel in St-Jean-Cap-Ferrat and the Hermitage in Monte-Carlo (*see Where to Stay, pp194–201*).

Picnic and Take-Away Food

You are never far from food in Provence. The traditional street food of Provence is the *pan bagnat*, a thick bun filled with crisp salade Niçoise and doused in olive oil. Pizza is a local favourite, and every small town has its pizza van, where your choice is cooked to order. A particularly Provençal form of pizza is *pissaladière*, an onion pizza coated with anchovies and olives. In Nice, the number one snack is *socca*, thick crêpes made from chickpea flour (*see pp204–5*).

The French love picnics, and the *Provençaux* are no exception. French alfresco eating is often complex – families set out tables, chairs, barbecues and portable fridges.

To service this penchant for portable dining, Provençal villages have specialist shops offering ready-to-eat food. *Boulangeries* and *pâtisseries* serve everything from fresh croissants to quiches and a dazzling array of cakes and tarts. Nearly all *boulangeries* provide delicious, freshly made baguette sandwiches.

In the main towns, specialist butchers called *traîteurs* provide ready-made dishes, such as salads, cold meats and roast chicken, sold in cartons according to weight. **Au Flan Coco** in Nîmes and **Bataille** in Marseille are fine examples. Most supermarkets also have similar delicatessen counters. *Charcuteries* specialize in pork dishes, particularly pâtés and sausages. For traditional spicy sausages much prized in the Camargue, head to the **Maison Genin** in Arles.

The best place to buy picnic food is the local market. Every town in Provence has its market, some daily, like Aix-en-Provence, some just once or twice a week. No Provençal picnic is complete without French bread – the *baguette* is the mainstay of the country and Provence is no exception. The only difference is that the region boasts numerous local breads, incorporating traditional ingredients. *Pain aux olives* is found almost everywhere, often in the form of *fougasse*, a flat, lattice-like loaf. Alternatively, this may contain anchovies *(pain aux anchois)*, or spinach *(pain aux épinards)* and there is a sweet version flavoured with almonds. Wholemeal or brown bread is an anathema to the traditional Provençaux, although many bakeries now produce it – ask for *pain aux*

céréales. The nearest to healthy bread is *pain de campagne*, a sturdier baguette made with unrefined white flour. One of the finest *boulangeries* in the region is **Le Four à Bois**, in the old quarter of Nice, where the same recipes have been used for generations.

Boulangeries are found in every village and usually have a good selection of *pâtisseries*, cakes and tarts. Provençal ingredients are combined to make these delights, such as honey, almonds and fruit – try those at **Béchard** in Aix-en-Provence. For those with an even sweeter tooth, these same ingredients are used in the handmade chocolates and candied fruit. *Calissons* (an almond-paste sweet) and *suce-miel* (honey-based candy) are very popular. Two of the best shops are **Puyricard** in Aix and **Auer** in Nice.

DIRECTORY

Cafés

AIX-EN-PROVENCE

Brasserie Les Deux Garçons
53 cours Mirabeau.
Tel 04 42 26 00 51.

CANNES

Restaurant Carlton
58 la Croisette.
Tel 04 93 06 40 06.

EZE

Château Eza
Rue de la Pise.
Tel 04 93 41 12 24.

MONACO

La Brasserie du Café de Paris
Le Casino, place du Casino.
Tel 00 377 98 06 76 23.

NICE

Le Grand Café de Turin
5 place Garibaldi.
Tel 04 93 62 29 52.

NÎMES

Le Café Olive
22 blvd Victor Hugo.
Tel 04 66 67 89 10.

ST-PAUL DE VENCE

Café de la Place
1 place du Général de Gaulle.
Tel 04 93 32 80 03.

ST-TROPEZ

Brasserie des Arts
5 place des Lices.
Tel 04 94 40 27 37.

Le Café de Paris
Le Port, 15 quai de Suffren.
Tel 04 94 97 00 56.

Senequier
Quai Jean Jaurès.
Tel 04 94 97 20 20.

Bars and Pubs

AVIGNON

Pub Z
58 rue de la Bonneterie.
Tel 04 90 85 42 84.

CANNES

3.14
5 rue François Einesy.
Tel 04 92 99 72 09.

JUAN-LES-PINS

Pam-Pam
137 blvd Wilson.
Tel 04 93 61 11 05.

MARSEILLE

Le Bar de la Marine
15 quai de Rive Neuve.
Tel 04 91 54 95 42.

La Part des Anges
33 rue Sainte.
Tel 04 91 33 55 70.

MONACO

Flashman's
7 ave Princesse Alice. **Tel** 00 377 93 30 09 03.

NICE

De Klomp
6 rue Mascoinat.
Tel 09 82 34 14 21.

Les Trois Diables
2 cours Saleya.
Tel 06 34 08 76 11.

Wayne's Bar
15 rue de la Préfecture.
Tel 04 93 13 46 99.

NÎMES

La Grande Bourse
2 blvd des Arenes.
Tel 04 66 67 68 69.

ST-JEAN-CAP-FERRAT

Le Bar
Grand Hôtel de Cap–Ferrat, 71 blvd du Général de Gaulle.
Tel 04 93 76 50 50.

VILLEFRANCHE-SUR-MER

Le Cosmo Bar
11 pl Amélie Pollonais.
Tel 04 93 01 84 05.

Picnic and Take-Away Food

AIX-EN-PROVENCE

Béchard
12 cours Mirabeau.

Puyricard
7–9 rue Rifle-rafle.

ARLES

Maison Genin
11 rue des Porcelets.

MARSEILLE

Bataille
18 rue Fontange.

Le Four des Navettes
136 rue Sainte.

NICE

Auer
7 rue St-François- de-Paule.

Le Four à Bois
35 rue Droite.

NÎMES

Au Flan Coco
21 rue du Grand Couvent.

SHOPS AND MARKETS

Shopping in Provence is one of life's great delights. Even the tiniest village may be home to a potter or painter, or you may arrive on market day to find regional produce – artichokes, asparagus, wild mushrooms – still fresh with the dew from the surrounding fields. Larger towns are packed with individual boutiques selling anything from dried flowers to chic baby clothes, and the fashion-conscious will always be able to find an avenue or two of famous names in which to window-shop. If the idea of cramming fresh foodstuffs into your luggage to take back home proves too daunting, Provence has perfected the fine art of packaging its produce, with the bottles, jars and boxes often works of art in themselves. This section provides guidelines on opening hours and the range of goods with a Provençal flavour to be found in the many stores and markets.

A butcher and a store selling household goods in a village in Provence

Opening Hours

Food shops open at around 8am and close at noon for lunch, a break that may last for up to three hours. After lunch, most shops stay open until 7pm, sometimes even later in big towns. Bakers often stay open until 1pm or later, serving tasty lunchtime snacks. Most supermarkets and hypermarkets stay open throughout lunchtimes.

Non-food shops are open 9am–7pm Mon–Sat, but most will close for lunch. Many are closed on Monday mornings.

Food shops and newsagents open on Sunday mornings but almost every shop is closed on Sunday afternoon. Small shops may close for one day a week out of high season.

Larger Shops

Hypermarkets (hypermarchés or grandes surfaces) can be found on the outskirts of every sizeable town: look out for the signs indicating the Centre Commercial. Among the largest are Casino, Auchan, E.LeClerc and Carrefour. Discount petrol is usually sold: you may have to pay in cash.

Supermarkets selling clothes and sundries (supermarchés), such as Monoprix and Champion, are usually found in town centres. Most of the upscale department stores (grands magasins), such as Galeries Lafayette and Printemps are located in cities.

Specialist Shops

One of the great pleasures of shopping in Provence is that specialist food shops still flourish despite the presence of large supermarkets. The bread shop (boulangerie) is usually combined with the pâtisserie selling cakes and pastries. The cheesemonger (fromagerie) may also be combined with a shop selling other dairy produce (laiterie), but the boucherie (butcher) and the charcuterie (delicatessen) tend to be separate shops. A traiteur sells prepared foods. For dry goods and general groceries, you will need to go to an épicerie.

Cleaning products and household goods are sold at a droguerie and hardware at a quincaillerie. Booksellers (librairies) in the main towns sometimes sell English books.

Markets

This guide gives the market days for every town featured. To find out where the market is, ask a passer-by for le marché. Markets are morning affairs, when the produce is super-fresh – by noon the stall-holders will already be packing up and the best bargains will have sold out hours ago. By French law, price tags must state the origin of all produce: du pays means local.

Les marchés de Provence were immortalized in song by Gilbert Bécaud, and rightly so. In a country famed for its markets, these are among the best. Some are renowned – cours Saleya (see p88) in Nice and the food and flower markets of Aix (see p152), for example, should not be missed. Others take more searching out, such as the truffle markets of the Var. Try Aups (see p108) on a Thursday during truffle season, from November to February.

Enjoying a drink next to a flower shop in Luberon, Vaucluse

Bags of dried herbs on display in the market of St-Rémy-de-Provence

Regional Specialities

The sunshine of Provence is captured in its distinctive, vividly coloured fabrics, known as *indiennes*. Many shops sell them by the metre; others, such as **Mistral – Les Indiennes de Nîmes** and **Souleïado** also make them into soft furnishings, cowboy shirts and boxer shorts.

Throughout Provence, working olive mills churn out rich, pungent oil, which is also used to make the chunky blocks of soap, *savon de Marseille*. Tins and jars of olives, often scented with *herbes de Provence*, are widely available, as are bags of the herbs themselves. Bags of lavender, and honey from its pollen, are regional specialities; local flowers appear in other forms too, from dried arrangements to scented oils, or perfumes from Grasse (*see p71*).

Traditional sweets (*confiseries*) abound, using regional fruits and nuts: almond *calissons* from Aix, fruity *berlingots* from Carpentras and *fruits confits* from Apt are just a few.

Local Wines

Provence is not one of the great wine regions of the world, but its many vineyards (*see pp206–7*) produce a wide range of pleasant wines and you will see plenty of signs inviting you to a *dégustation* (tasting). You will usually be expected to buy at least one bottle. Wine co-operatives sell the wines of numerous smaller producers. Here you can buy wine in five- and ten-litre containers (*en vrac*). This wine is "duty free" but, with vineyards such as Châteauneuf-du-Pape and Beaumes-de-Venise, wise buyers will drink *en vrac* on holiday and pick up bargains in fine wine to bring home.

Marseille's anise-flavoured aperitif *pastis* is an evocative, if acquired, taste.

Arts and Crafts

Many of the crafts now flourishing in Provence are traditional ones that had almost died out 50 years ago. The potters of Vallauris owe the revival in their fortunes to Picasso (*see pp76–7*) but, more often, it is the interest of visitors that keeps a craft alive. From the little pottery *santons* of Marseille to the flutes and tambourines of Barjols, there is plenty of choice for gifts and mementos. Many towns have unique specialities. Biot (*see p78*) is famous for its bubbly glassware, Cogolin for pipes and carpets and Salernes for hexagonal terracotta tiles.

Works by local artists sold on the harbour at St-Tropez

DIRECTORY

Regional Specialities

AVIGNON

Souleïado
19 rue Joseph Vernet.
Tel 04 90 86 32 05.
One of several branches.

GRASSE

Huilerie Ste-Anne
138 route de Draguignan.
Tel 04 93 70 21 42.

Parfumerie Fragonard
20 blvd Fragonard.
Tel 04 92 42 34 34.
ⓦ fragonard.com

Parfumerie Galimard
73 route de Cannes.
Tel 04 93 09 20 00.
ⓦ galimard.com

NICE

Alziari
14 rue St-François-de-Paule.
Tel 04 93 62 94 03.
Olive press.

NÎMES

Mistral – Les Indiennes de Nîmes
2 blvd des Arènes.
Tel 04 66 21 69 57.

Arts and Crafts

COGOLIN

Fabrique de Pipes Courrieu
58–60 ave G Clemenceau.
Tel 04 94 54 63 82.

Manufacture des Tapis de Cogolin
Tel 04 94 55 70 65.

MARSEILLE

Ateliers Marcel Carbonel
47–49 rue Neuve Ste-Catherine.
Tel 04 91 13 61 36.
ⓦ santonsmarcelcarbonel.com
Workshop and museum.

VALLAURIS

Céramiques Dominique N B
Ave Maréchal Juin.
Tel 04 93 64 02 36.

English Language Bookshops

ANTIBES

Heidi's English Bookshop
24 rue Aubernon.
Tel 04 93 34 74 11.

AIX-EN-PROVENCE

Book in Bar
4 rue Joseph Cabassol.
Tel 04 42 26 60 07.

CANNES

Cannes English Bookshop
11 rue Bivouac Napoléon.
Tel 04 93 99 40 08.

MARSEILLE

Librairie Internationale Maurel
95 rue de Lodi.
Tel 04 91 42 63 44.

MONTPELLIER

Le Bookshop
6 rue de l'Université.
Tel 04 67 66 09 08.

What to Buy in Provence

Best buys to be found in Provence are those that reflect the character of the region – its geographical blessings of bountiful produce and its historic traditions of arts and crafts. While the chic boutiques of St-Tropez or Cannes may rival Paris in predicting the latest fashion trend, your souvenirs of Provence should be far more timeless. The evocative scents, colours and flavours they offer will help to keep your holiday memories alive throughout the darkest winter months, and longer – at least until your next visit.

Lavender, one of the perfumes of Provence

The Scents of Provence

Provençal lavender is used to perfume a wide range of goods, but most popular are pretty fabric sachets full of the dried flowers. Bath times can be heady with the scent of local flowers and herbs, captured in delightful bottles, and Marseille's famous olive oil soaps.

Olive oil savons de Marseille

Orange water from Vallauris

Linden-scented bubble bath

Dried lavender, packed in Provençal fabrics

Mallow-scented bubble bath

Glassware

Glassblowing is a modern Provençal craft. At Biot (see p78) you can watch glassblowers at work, as well as buy examples of their art to take home.

Pottery

Look for traditional tiles, cookware and storage jars made from *terre rouge*, formal china of Moustiers faïence (see p190) or artworks of *grès* clay.

Terracotta Santons

Provençal Christmas cribs are peopled with these gaily painted traditional figures. Most crafts shops offer a good choice of characters.

Olive Wood
As rich in colour and texture as its oil, the wood of the olive can be sculpted into works of art or turned into practical kitchenware.

Hunting Knives
The huntsmen's shops of Provence are an unexpected source for the perfect picnic or kitchen knife, safe yet razor sharp.

Provençal Fabrics
Using patterns and colours dating back centuries, these traditional prints are sold by the metre or made up into fashionable items.

The Flavours of Provence

No-one should leave Provence without at least a jar of olives or a bottle of olive oil, but consider also easy-to-pack tins, jars and boxes of preserved fruits, scented honey or savoury purées – prettily packaged, they make ideal gifts.

Almond sweetmeats, the speciality of Aix-en-Provence

Candied chestnuts or *marrons glacés*

Goats' cheese, wrapped in chestnut leaves

Tuna packed in olive oil

Basil flavoured olive oil

Virgin olive oil

Puréed salt cod or *brandade de morue*

Almond and orange conserve

Lavender honey and hazelnut *confit*

ENTERTAINMENT IN PROVENCE

Provence offers a wealth of cultural options to visitors. Barely a month goes by without some major festival *(see pp36–9 & pp228–9)*. Events take place all year round, with first-class dance, opera and jazz in Nice and Marseille, rock concerts in Toulon, theatre in Avignon and blockbuster art shows in Nice, Antibes, Monaco and Aix-en-Provence. Nightlife tends to be restricted to the fashionable coastal resorts, like Juan-les-Pins and St-Tropez, where clubs and bars often stay open all night. In winter, things are quieter, but the small bars and cafés of Marseille, Nîmes and Nice remain open and full of life. Provence's most common entertainment is free – locals spend much of their time enjoying the fresh air, walking and playing *pétanque*, or Provençal bowls.

Practical Information

Information about what's on in Provence is fairly localized, with tourist offices providing listings of various events. Most large towns publish a weekly paper that outlines the best of each week's events. Local papers can also provide details of important festivals and sporting events. *Le Provençal* serves western Provence, while *Nice Matin* and its derivatives cover the east of the region. You can purchase regional newspapers and magazines at newsagents and *tabacs*.

The large English-speaking community in Provence has its own radio station, Riviera Radio, which broadcasts from Monte-Carlo in English on 106.3 FM and 106.5 FM. English-language publications such as *The Riviera Times* and *The Riviera Reporter* include event listings and websites.

Buying Tickets

Depending on the event, most tickets can be bought on the door, but for blockbuster concerts, particularly during the summer months, it is best to reserve in advance. Tickets can be purchased at branches of the **FNAC** and **Carrefour** chains in major towns.

Theatre box offices are open from approximately 11am until 7pm seven days a week and will usually accept credit card bookings over the telephone.

As a last resort, if you haven't booked in advance, tickets to popular concerts can be bought from touts at the venue doors on the night. However, they will be much more expensive and possibly counterfeit.

Opera and Classical Music

Music is everywhere in Provence, from small village churches to the *belle époque* opera houses of Marseille, Toulon and Nice. The **Opéra de Nice** is one of the best in France, and the **Monte-Carlo Philharmonic Orchestra** features many illustrious conductors. Classical and jazz festivals are held throughout the summer in major cities.

Every year on 21 June, the Fête de la Musique is held throughout France. Amateur and professional musicians alike set up their stages in villages and towns and perform. Take in as many different "concerts" as you can to enjoy an impressive range of genres.

Classical cello

Rock and Jazz

These days Provence is a major venue on most world tours, with big stadium performances at Toulon's **Zenith-Omèga** or Marseille's soccer stadium, **Le Nouveau Stade-Vélodrome**. The **Nice Festival du Jazz** in the Cimiez arena *(see p88)* is one of the world's best. It was here that Miles Davis gave one of his last performances among the Roman walls and olive groves. Also popular is the **Jazz à Juan** festival in Juan-les-Pins, which has included Ray Charles and the jazz debut of classical violinist Nigel Kennedy.

Theatre

Going to the theatre in Provence can be as formal or as relaxed as you choose. A trip to a big theatre can involve dressing up, special *souper* (late dinner) reservations at a nearby restaurant and pricey champagne during the interval. On the other hand, a visit to a smaller theatre can be cheap and casual, with a real feeling of intimacy and immediacy.

Leonard Cohen performing at the Nice Festival du Jazz

Marseille is the centre of theatre in Provence and boasts one of France's top theatrical companies, the **Théâtre National de la Criée**. Various smaller companies stage innovative plays, many of which end up in Paris. Avignon is also famous for its **Théâtre des Carmes**, the main venue for the **Festival d'Avignon** (see p229). There is also a "fringe" festival, the **Avignon Public Off**, with its own directors and box office.

Spectator Sports

With its superb weather and glamorous reputation, the regions of Provence and the Côte d'Azur are ideal venues for some of France's top sporting events. The gruelling **Tour de France** passes through the area each July, while the Monte-Carlo and Nice tennis tournaments attract the best players. The **Grand Prix de Monaco** (see p36) is one of the highlights of the Formula 1 motor-racing season, and horse-racing enthusiasts can visit the **Hippodrome de la Côte d'Azur** track at Cagnes-sur-Mer between December and March.

Provence boasts two of the top soccer teams in France – **Olympique de Marseille** and **AS Monaco FC**, known as the millionaires' club. Rugby is also popular in Provence, with top-class clubs in Nice and Toulon.

Dance

Marseille's eclectic mixture of nationalities and styles has led

The Open Tennis Championships in Monte-Carlo

to highly original and powerful dance productions.

The National Ballet Company is based at the Ecole de Danse in Marseille. Companies such as the **Bernardines** sometimes take their productions to Paris, while **La Friche La Belle de Mai**, located in an old tobacco

View over the harbour in Monaco to the glittering casino

factory, is a popular venue for experimental performance and music.

The new **Centre Choré-graphique National** in Aix-en-Provence is an exciting addition to the Provençal dance scene.

Gambling

The French Riviera is famed for its opulent casinos. If you are 18 and over you can play in most resorts. Monaco has the coast's most popular casino – **Le Casino** – where you have to pay an entrance fee and show an ID card before you can start gambling. Other casinos worth visiting for architecture and atmosphere are Cannes' **Casino Croisette** and **Casino Ruhl** in Nice. Even if you are not a high-roller, there is always a dazzling array of slot machines.

nîmes feria 9

Bullfighting

The annual *ferias*, or bullfighting festivals, are always dramatic occasions. The traditional bullfight of Provence is the *course à la cocarde*, which starts with an *abrivado* when the bulls are chased through the town to the local arena. The bull enters the ring with a red *cocarde*, or rosette, tied to its horns, which the *razeteurs*, or matadors, try to snatch, providing riveting but goreless entertainment. At the end of the season, the bullfighter with the most rosettes receives fame and adulation, as well as cash.

Sometimes bullfights will end in death in the full-blooded Spanish-style *corrida*, but this is usually only in the main arenas in Nîmes and Arles (see p36), and it will always be advertised first. In one session there are usually six bullfights, of which two may be advertised as *mise à mort* (to the death).

Bullfighting poster for the 1992 Nîmes *feria* by Francis Bacon

Cinema

The small port of La Ciotat is where Louis Lumière shot the world's first motion picture, and Marcel Pagnol *(see p157)* laid the foundations for modern French cinema from his studios in Marseille. The French are very supportive of *la Septième Art*, as they refer to film, and there are plenty of local, independent cinemas. If your language skills won't stretch to watching a French film, look out for cinemas that show films in their *V.O. (Version Original)* – that is, screened in their original language. *V.F. (Version Française)* denotes a dubbed screening in French.

Popcorn or other snacks are available, but it tends to be the foreigners that snack their way through a movie. However, there are some French cinemas that have bars and restaurants attached, so that you may dissect the movie while enjoying a meal or a drink afterwards.

As the fame of Cannes *(see pp72–3)* reflects, film festivals are taken seriously by the French. Cannes itself is a maelstrom of media hype, old-school glamour and shiny new cash. It is an amazing experience if you can get tickets to any of the films or parties, but these are notoriously difficult to get as they are by invitation only.

Discotheques and Nightclubs

During the summer, the main towns of Provence boogie all night long. The music is far from trend-setting, usually following styles set the previous year in New York and London, but the dancers are chic and the prices high. A handful of clubs such as **Jimmy'Z** in Monaco and **Les Caves du Roy** in St-Tropez cater for the jet set, while **Kiss Club** in Juan-les-Pins and **Gotha Club** in Cannes serve a younger crowd. The dress code is usually smart, and trainers are almost always forbidden.

Children's Entertainment

Provence offers the traditional attractions of beach and sea, although small children may better appreciate them in smaller resorts. Alternatives include aqua parks like **Marineland** and **Aqualand**, zoos and aquariums. There are also numerous adventure parks for rock-climbing, cycling and zip-lining, such as the **Canyon Forest** at Villeneuve-Loubet and **Coudou Parc** at Six-Fours-les-Plages. Marseille has **Préau des Accoules**, the only children's museum in the region. In the bigger towns, museums and theatres may organize activities (ask at the tourist office). Smaller towns and villages will have playgrounds or a square where your offspring can play with other children while you relax in a café. For more action, there are plenty of sporting activities, such as biking, canoeing, tennis, horse-riding and fishing.

DIRECTORY

Buying Tickets

Carrefour
W spectacles.carrefour.fr
Marseille
Carrefour Tasso, 4 pl du
4 sept.
Nice
Carrefour Nice Notre-Dame,
17–19 ave des Embrois.
FNAC
Tel 08 25 02 00 20.
W fnac.com
Avignon
19 rue de la République.
Marseille
Centre Commercial Bourse,
12 cours Belsunce.
Nice
40–46 ave Jean Médecin.

Opera and Classical Music

AIX-EN-PROVENCE

Grand Théâtre de Provence
380 ave Max Juvénale.
Tel 04 42 91 69 70.
W iestheatres.net

MARSEILLE

Opéra Municipal
2 rue Molière.
Tel 04 91 55 21 12.
W opera.marseille.fr

MONACO

Monte-Carlo Philharmonic Orchestra
Auditorium Rainier III, Blvd
Loius II, BP 197
Tel 00 377 98 06 28 28.
W opmc.mc

NICE

Forum Nice Nord
10 blvd Comte de Falicon.
Tel 04 93 84 24 37.
W forumnicenord.com

Opéra de Nice
4–6 rue St-François-de-
Paule. Tel 04 92 17 40 00.
W opera-nice.org

Salle-Grapelli – CEDAC de Cimiez
49 ave de la Marne.
Tel 04 93 53 89 66.
W salle-grapelli-nice.org

TOULON – OLLIOULES

Châteauvallon
Tel 04 94 22 02 02.
W chateauvallon.com

Festival de Musique Classique
Tel 04 94 93 55 45.
W festivalmusique
toulon.com

Opéra de Toulon
Blvd de Strasbourg.
Tel 04 94 93 03 76.
W operadetoulon.fr

Rock and Jazz

AIX-EN-PROVENCE

HotBrass Club
1857 chemin d'Eguilles-
Célony. Tel 04 42 21 05 57.

Le Scat
11 rue de la Verrerie.
Tel 04 42 23 00 23.

JUAN-LES-PINS

Jazz à Juan
Office de Tourisme, 60
chemin des Sables, Antibes.
W jazzajuan.com

MARSEILLES

Espace Julien
39 cours Julien.
Tel 04 91 24 34 10.
W espace-julien.com

L'Intermédiaire
63 pl Jean-Jaurès.
Tel 06 34 17 71 99.

Le Nouveau Stade Vélodrome
3 blvd Michelet.
Tel 04 13 64 64 71.

Le Pelle-Mêle
8 pl aux Huiles.
Tel 04 91 54 85 26.

NICE

Festival du Jazz
Pl Massena, Theatre de
Verdure Tel 08 92 68 36 22.
W nicejazzfestival.fr

Theatre des Oiseaux
6 rue d'Abbaye.
Tel 04 93 80 21 93.

TOULON

Zenith-Oméga
Blvd Commandant Nicolas.
Tel 04 94 22 66 77.
W zenith-omega-
toulon.com

DIRECTORY

Theatre

AVIGNON

Avignon Public Off
Tel 04 90 85 13 08.

Festival d'Avignon
Espace St-Louis, 20 rue
Portail Boguier.
Tel 04 90 27 66 50.
W festival-avignon.com

Théâtre des Carmes
6 place des Carmes.
Tel 04 90 82 20 47.
W theatredescarmes.com

MARSEILLE

Théâtre du Merlan
Avenue Raimu. Tel 04 91
11 19 30. W merlan.org

**Théâtre National
de la Criée**
30 quai de Rive-Neuve.
Tel 04 91 54 70 54.
W theatre-lacriee.com

NICE

Théâtre de l'Alphabet
19 rue Delille.
Tel 06 60 89 10 04.
W theatrenice.fr

Théâtre de la Semeuse
2 montée Auguste Kerl.
Tel 04 93 92 85 08.

Spectator Sports

CAGNES-SUR-MER

**Hippodrome de la
Côte d'Azur**
Tel 04 92 02 44 44.
W hippodrome-
cotedazur.com

MARSEILLE

ASPTT Tennis
Tel 04 91 77 16 42.
W marseille.asptt.com

Olympique de Marseille
W om.net

MONACO

AS Monaco FC
W asmonaco.com

Grand Prix de Monaco
W acm.mc

NICE

**Ligue de la Côte
d'Azur Tennis**
Tel 04 97 25 76 80.

Tour de France
W letour.fr

Dance

AIX-EN-PROVENCE

**Centre Chorégraphique
National**
530 ave Mozart.
Tel 04 42 93 48 00.

MARSEILLE

Bernardines
17 blvd Garibaldi. Tel 04
91 24 30 40. W theatre-
bernardines.org

**La Friche la
Belle de Mai**
41 rue Robin.
Tel 04 95 04 95 95.
W lafriche.org

Gambling

CANNES

Casino Croisette
1 espace Lucien Barriere.
Tel 04 92 98 78 00.
W lucienbarriere.com

MONACO

Le Casino
Place du Casino.
Tel 00 377 98 06 21 21.
W casinomontecarlo.com

NICE

Casino Ruhl
1 promenade des Anglais.
Tel 04 97 03 12 22.

Bullfighting

ARLES

Arènes d'Arles
Rond-point des Arènes.
Tel 04 90 49 59 05.

NÎMES

Les Arènes
Blvd des Arènes.
Tel 08 91 70 03 70.
W arenes-arles.com

Cinema

AIX-EN-PROVENCE

Le Mazarin
6 rue Laroque.
Tel 08 92 68 72 70.

AVIGNON

Utopia Cinéma
4 rue des Escaliers Sainte
Anne. Tel 04 90 82 65 36.

CANNES

Cannes Film Festival
W festival-cannes.fr

MARSEILLE

Cinéma Le Chambord
283 ave du Prado.
Tel 04 91 25 70 06.

MONTE-CARLO

Le Sporting d'Hiver
Place du Casino.
Tel 00 377 98 06 17 17.

NICE

Cinémathèque
3 esplanade Kennedy.
Tel 04 92 04 06 66.

Mercury Cinéma
16 place Garibaldi.
Tel 04 93 55 37 81.

NÎMES

Le Sémaphore
25a rue Porte de France.
Tel 04 66 67 83 11.

Discotheques and Nightclubs

AIX-EN-PROVENCE

Le Mistral
3 rue Frédéric Mistral.
Tel 04 42 38 16 49.

AVIGNON

Les Ambassadeurs Club
27 rue Bancasse.
Tel 04 90 86 31 55.

CANNES

Gotha Club
Palm Beach Point Croisette,
Pl Franklin Roosevelt.
Tel 04 93 45 11 11.

Le Bâoli
Port Canto, La Croisette.
Tel 04 93 43 03 43.

HYÈRES

Dolce Vita
4030 rte des giens.
Tel 07 50 85 32 63.

Les Coulisses
R9 98, Quartier St Nicholas,
La Londe-les-Maures.
Tel 07 78 66 89 07.

JUAN-LES-PINS

Kiss Club
5 ave George Gallice.
Tel 06 30 71 46 18.

Le Village
Carrefour de la nouvelle
orleans. Tel 04 92 93 90 00.

MARSEILLE

The Trolleybus
24 quai de Rive-Neuve,
Vieux Port. Tel 04 9154 3045.

MONACO

Black Legend
Quai Albert 1er.
Tel 00 377 93 30 09 09.

Jimmy'Z
26 ave Princesse Grace.
Tel 00 377 98 06 36 36.
W fr.jimmyzmonte
carlo.com

NICE

High Club/Studio 47
45 promenade des Anglais.
Tel 07 81 88 42 04.

ST-RAPHAËL

La Réserve
Promenade René Coty.
Tel 06 27 13 88 99.

ST-TROPEZ

Les Caves du Roy
Palace de la Côte d'Azur,
Ave du marechal foch.
Tel 04 94 56 68 00.
W lescavesduroy.com

Papagayo
Résidence du Port.
Tel 04 94 97 95 96.

Children's Entertainment

Aqualand
RN 98, 83600 Fréjus.
Tel 04 94 51 82 51.
W aqualand.fr

Canyon Forest
Parc des Rives du Loup,
26 rte de Grasse Villeneuve-
Loubet. Tel 04 92 02 88 88.
W canyonforest.com

Coudou Parc
34 rue de la République,
Six-Fours-les-Plages.
Tel 06 63 77 02 06.
W coudouparc.com

Marineland
RN 7, 06600 Antibes.
Tel 04 93 33 55 77.
W marineland.fr

**Museum of
Oceanography and
Aquarium**
Ave St Martin, Monte-Carlo.
Tel 00 377 93 15 36 00.

**Park Zoologique de
Fréjus**
Le Capitou, Fréjus.
Tel 04 98 11 37 37.

**Préau des Accoules
(Children's Museum)**
29 montee des Accoules,
Marseille. Tel 04 91 91 52 06.

Festivals in Provence

Festivals in Provence are very much part of the way of life. They are not staged purely for the benefit of visitors and tourism, but more to continue the seasonal celebrations that are deeply rooted in tradition. Many *fêtes* are based on pagan rites while others are celebrations of historic occasions – only a few have been hijacked by fun-loving holiday-makers on the coast. Here is a selection of the best festivals from each of the *départements*.

One of the spectacular floats in the procession at the Nice Carnival

The Riviera and the Alpes Maritimes

The brilliant explosion of fireworks at the Carnaval de Nice above the Baie des Anges is one of the most popular images of Nice *(see pp84–9)*. It is the largest pre-Lent carnival in France, and crescendos on Shrove Tuesday with fireworks and the immolation of King Carnival, *Sa Majesté Carnaval.*

Carnival festivities, held in all Catholic countries, are based on the pagan celebrations of the death of winter and the birth of spring and life. It is a time of feasting (*mardi gras* means "fat Tuesday") before the fasting of Lent (*carne vale* is Latin for "farewell to meat").

Festivities begin three weeks before Mardi Gras, when the king is wheeled out into the streets. During the two weekends between then and his departure, the colourful, flower-decked floats of the procession parade along the 2-km (1-mile) route round Jardin Albert I, amid confetti battles, bands and mounted escorts.

Carnival characters in the streets of Nice

By the 19th century, the Nice Carnival had developed into little more than a chalk and flour battle. The floats did not appear until 1873, inspired by the local artist, Alexis Mossa, who also resurrected the figure of King Carnival. Since then, great effort and time has been put into making the costumes.

Meanwhile, the whole town is *en fête*, and parties and balls are held in hotels and public venues all night long. Visitors should book well in advance to secure accommodation.

The Var and the Iles d'Hyères

A number of festivals in the region feature the firing of muskets, reminiscent of ancient witch-scaring rites. Spectacular volleys are set off into the air in St-Tropez *(see pp122–6)* for the biannual *bravade*, commemorating two significant events.

The first one takes place on 16–18 May and is a religious procession devoted to the town's patron, Saint Torpès, He was a Roman soldier in the service of the emperor, Nero. In AD 68, Torpès converted to Christianity and was martyred by decapitation. His body was placed in a boat along with a hungry dog and a cockerel. Miraculously, the saint's body was untouched. The vessel was washed up onto the shores of southern France, on the spot where St-Tropez stands today.

The May *bravade* honours his arrival. Celebrations begin with the blessing of a lance by the town's priest in the Eglise de St-Tropez. From here, the saint's gilded wooden bust is taken and carried around the flag-decked town in a terrific flurry of musket volleys. The procession winds down to the beach, and the sea is blessed for safely conveying the saint.

The second *bravade* takes place on 15 June and is honoured with earth-shattering fusillades and military parades. It marks the anniversary of the day in 1637, when the local militia saw off a Spanish fleet, about 22 vessels strong, after an attempt to capture four ships of the Royal French fleet.

La bravade procession in St-Tropez, honouring the town's patron saint

Bouches-du-Rhône and Nîmes

Europe's largest Romany festival, the Pèlerinage des Gitans in Saintes-Maries-de-la-Mer *(see p142)*, is a simple yet very moving occasion. At the end of May, usually 24th–26th, Romanies from all over the continent gather to pay their respects to the patron saint of

Procession of the saints down to the sea in Saintes-Maries-de-la-Mer

gypsies, Saint Sarah, known as the Black Madonna. This takes place in the picturesque town of Saintes-Maries-de-la-Mer.

The pilgrimage is a colourful occasion, brightened by traditional Arlesian costumes and *gardian* cowboys. The object of their veneration is Saint Sarah, the Ethiopian servant. As legend has it, she arrived on the shores of the Camargue by boat. Also on board was Mary Magdalene, and the saints Mary Jacobe (sister of the Virgin Mary) and the elderly Mary Salome (mother of the apostles Saint James and Saint John). Sarah and the Marys decided to stay in the town and they built an oratory on which the fortified church of Notre-Dame-de-la-Mer was built. The saints started to preach the gospel and the town became known as the "Mecca of Provence".

Saint Sarah stands serene and excessively robed in the crypt. On the two nights and days of celebration in May, she is remembered with a Mass and all-night vigil. The next day, the statues of the saints are borne down to the sea where the Camargue cowboys take their horses, neck-deep, into the water and the Bishop of Arles blesses the sea.

After the statues have been returned to the church, the great folk festival begins, with rodeos, bull-running, horse racing, Arletan dancing and all manner of entertainment. The *gardians* return for a smaller celebration of Mary Salome in October, when there is a procession around the church.

Vaucluse

The Papal city of Avignon *(see pp170–2)* is a splendid setting for the foremost arts festival in Provence, the Festival d'Avignon. Theatre, music, dance and film are all covered in the month-long programme which runs from July to early August. More than a quarter of a million visitors travel to Avignon every year to attend the largest arts festival in France. It is advisable to reserve hotels and tickets in advance to avoid disappointment *(see pp226–7 for reservations)*.

Lavender from the festival in Digne

The festival was established in 1947 by the late Jean Vilar whose aim was to bring theatre to the masses. He devised a number of productions to be staged in the courtyard of the Papal Palace and his Théâtre

National Populair still performs every year. Other venues include the theatres and cinemas, where films are shown all day, the opera house and churches.

Since the 1960s, the fringe-style Avignon Public Off, brings some 520 events to over 100 venues including many specially set-up theatres. Amateur performers can be seen for free in the main square outside the opera, the place de l'Horloge.

Alpes-de-Haute-Provence

Provence's most particular flower has its festival, the Corso de la Lavande, in the mountain spa town of Digne-les-Bains *(see p184)*. The colourful event, which lasts for four days, takes place in August and celebrates the harvesting of the crop. There are jars and pots of honey and all kinds of lavender produce for sale in the town, and events centre on the main street, boulevard Gassendi.

The climax of the festival comes on the last day when the flower-decked floats, representing a variety of themes, parade through the streets, accompanied by music, dancing and cheering. Preceding the floats is a municipal truck spraying the roads with litres of lavender water leaving the whole town heady with the distinctive, sweet perfume.

Lively street performers at the summer Festival d'Avignon

SPECIALIST HOLIDAYS AND OUTDOOR ACTIVITIES

Everything is on offer from sun and sea bathing to skiing and extreme sports in this extraordinarily varied region of France. Watersports are extremely popular and sailing boats can be rented in most towns. For windsurfing, the experienced will want to head for Brutal Beach, just west of Toulon, although boards can be rented at most coastal resorts. Some of the best diving in the whole of the Mediterranean is around the Iles d'Hyères. There are also plenty of opportunities for canoeing and whitewater rafting in the Verdon and Gard inland. Opportunities for walking, cycling, mountain-biking and horse riding are endless. The Féderation Française de la Randonnée Pédestre publishes the widely available *Topo Guides*, which give descriptions of the tracks with details of overnight stops and transport.

Arts and Crafts

The **French Institute** is a good resource for courses in learning French combined with other activities. Students can under-take a French-speaking holiday by working part time on the restoration of historic sites with **Union Rempart** (Union pour la Réhabilitation et Entretien des Monuments et du Patrimoine Artistique).

You can also learn sculpting on a weekend course in a beautiful rural setting. Contact **Provence Verte** for details.

Several specialist tour oper-ators organize dedicated painting holidays. For infor-mation, contact the **Maison de la France** tourist board.

Cookery Courses

An extensive range of gastronomic courses providing training in regional or classical cuisine is available. These courses are often combined with visits to markets to learn how to source the best

Beautiful, aromatic lavender fields in Châteauneuf-du-Pape

ingredients. The **Hostellerie Bérard** in La Cadière d'Azur runs excellent cookery courses and workshops.

Olive oil is the lifeblood of Mediterranean cuisine and many olive oil producers offer visits to their *moulins*, such as **Château Virant** in Lançon de Provence. The Olive Tree route in Canton de Levens takes you to see oil presses in action.

For lovers of figs, the family-run specialist, **Les Figuières du Mas de Luquet**, is the perfect place to learn about this delicious delicacy.

Lavender Fields and Vineyards

The regions of Provence most associated with the growing and processing of lavender are around Le Mont Ventoux, the Lubéron and the Provençal Drôme. **Musée de la Lavande**, located in Lagarde d'Apt, organizes guided walking tours of a lavender field on a family-run lavender farm.

There are also plenty of opportunities in the whole of the region for *dégustations*. If you are looking to combine a trip to Les-Baux-de-Provence, Les Alpilles or St Rémy-de-Provence with a visit to vineyards, contact the **Les Vignerons des Baux**. For *dégustations* and tours of the wines of the Luberon, contact **Les Vins Luberon**.

A cookery course in progress at Hostellerie Bérard

Perfumery and Aromatherapy Courses

In Grasse, perfume initiation courses allow perfume lovers to create their own *eau de toilette* with the help of a "master perfumer". These courses are available at **Le Studio des Fragrances** at Galimard. The **Perfume Workshop** at Molinard also offers courses. The other major perfumery is **Fragonard**, where aroma-synergy workshops are on offer. These courses allow participants to learn the virtues and benefits of plants and essential oils. Lessons are given by professional aromatherapists and plant experts.

Extreme Sports

The exciting sport of snow-kiting is skiing with a stunt kite to help with the jumps. Join the best snow-kiters on the Col du Lautaret between the Grave, the Meije peak and Serre Chevalier. For an even more extreme sport, try a different kind of diving – under ice. Other

A game of *pétanque* in full swing, this is still a favourite pastime in the region

favourite sports include paragliding (*parapente*) and hang gliding (*deltaplane*). For more information, contact the **Fédération Française de Vol Libre**. Gliding (*vol à voile*) is popular in the southern regions, where the climate is warm and the thermals are also good. For details of gliding clubs, contact the **Fédération Française de Vol à Voile**.

Bird-Watching

The Camargue is a twitcher's paradise. The information centre at the **Parc Naturel Regional de Camargue** provides detailed information on bird-watching. It also organizes walks within the area and has a glassed-in section, where it is possible to observe birds through binoculars. For more information contact the tourist board in Arles (*see pp148–50*) or the tourist office in Stes-Maries-de-la-Mer (*see p141*).

Petanque/Boules

An emblem of Provençal life, this favourite game of the local men is rarely played by women. Somewhat similar to bowls, it is played with small metal balls on any dusty ground surface. Although the rules are simple, it can be very competitive with a touch of ferocity, making it interesting to watch.

Canoeing

Canoeing is popular in the huge Lac de Ste-Croix in the National Regional Park of Verdon. The most famous route is the 24 km (15 miles) paddle down the Gorges du Verdon from Carrejuan Bridge to Lac de Ste Croix, which usually takes two days to cover. La Palud sur Verdon is the best base for whitewater rafting and kayaking on the rapids. For less challenging canoeing, try the River Sorgue, starting from the base of the high cliffs of Fontaine-de-Vaucluse. For more information, contact the **Fédération Française de Canoë-Kayak**.

Canyoning

The Grand Canyon du Verdon, Europe's largest canyon, can be visited by raft or on foot. It has now become a centre for adventure sports. The **Castellane Tourist Office** provides lists of companies offering canyoning, rafting and other outdoor trails.

Fishing

Fishing is a highly popular sport on permitted lakes and rivers. Local tourist offices and fishing shops can help you obtain a licence. You can experience bountiful sea-fishing in the Mediterranean, with catches that include bass, sardines, grey mullet, and crustaceans, such as crayfish and lobster. Night-fishing is becoming increasingly popular too.

Bee-eater, common in Provence

Golf and Tennis

There's a great variety of golf in the area, from high-altitude courses to links facing the sea, or clinging to the fringes of cliffs. Overall, there are around 30 courses, mainly in the Bouches-du-Rhône and the Var and of these, over 20 are 18-hole courses. Some of the best are located at the Frégate course, St Cyr, St Raphaël's Golf de l'Esterel and, close to Avignon, the Golf De Châteteaublanc. Most offer lessons provided by resident experts.

The Provence Golf Pass gives access to 13 courses in the five departments, including five green fees. For golf addicts and occasional golfers alike, this is an excellent way to sample the courses available. For comprehensive information, contact the **Provence-Alpes-Côte d'Azur Regional Tourist Board** or the **Fédération Française de Golf**, which can supply a list of courses in France.

Most of the resorts and towns have their own tennis courts that are open to the public. Many of these are traditional Mediterranean clay courts.

Tennis lovers converge at Monte-Carlo in April, when the International Tennis Championships come here for the Monte-Carlo Open tournament for male players.

Canoeing in the Gorges du Verdon, an exhilarating experience

Horse Riding

Although the wetland area of Camargue is famous for its hardy white horses, said to be direct descendants of prehistoric horses (see p140), the whole region – from coast to mountain to rural areas – is extremely popular with horse lovers. For a detailed list of pony-trekking and riding opportunities, contact the **Ligue Régionale de Provence de Sports Equestres**.

Naturism

The largest and oldest naturist colony in the region is the easternmost of the Hyères islands, the Ile du Levant. It covers half the stretch of the 8-km (5-miles) long island. For more information on other locations where you can bare it all, contact the **Fédération Française de Naturisme**.

Skiing

The most important skiing areas are in the Maritime Alps, at the meeting point of the Alps and Provence. The main resorts, Auron, Isola 2000 and Valberg (see p100) are only a few hours from the coast, making it entirely possible to combine skiing and beach pleasures in a single day. In the north of the region in the Alpes de Haute-Provence are the ski resorts of Pra Loup and Chabanon. For more information, contact the **Fédération Française de Ski** in Annecy or the **Fédération Française de la Montagne et de l'Escalade**.

Spa Breaks

Set in the hilltop village of Gordes, one of France's prettiest villages, is the Daniel Jouvance spa, **La Bastide de Gordes**. It is undoubtedly an ideal spot for relaxing breaks.

In the picturesque, gastronomic village of Mougins, **Le Mas Candille** is an elegant, individual hotel, complemented by a Japanese-style Shiseido spa. For the ultimate in luxury, visit the **Thalazur** spa in Antibes.

Walking, Climbing and Cycling

Long-distance walking and climbing trails are known as Grandes Randonées (GR) and shorter trails as Petites Randonées (PR). Some trails are also open to mountain bikes and horses.

Parc Naturel Régional du Luberon offers some excellent cycling and walking trails. The information centre, **Maison du Parc**, provides a list of hikers' accommodation and details of two dozen walking trails. The Camargue has many trails and walking paths. "Sentier Littoral", a splendid coastal path from St-Tropez, covers 35 km (22 miles) to Cavalaire. You can even break the journey at Ramatuelle. An excellent French book, *Promenez-vous à Pied – Le Golfe de St-Tropez* has details of 26 walks in the area.

Perhaps the most spectacular trail in the whole of Provence is the GR 9, which crosses the Luberon range and the Monts du Vaucluse.

For tough rock climbing, try the Buoux cliffs in the Luberon, or one of the 933 routes in the Gorges du Verdon. The creeks, *calanques*, between Cassis and Marseille are utterly picturesque. Easier ascents can be found in the Dentelles de Montmirail, despite the craggy rock faces. The area boasts excellent vineyards, such as Gigondas, Vacqueyras and Beaumes-de-Venise in which to enjoy a *dégustation* after a climb.

The **Comité Departemental de la Randonnée Pédestre** located in Cagnes-sur-Mer, is equipped with detailed information. For details of trails in the region, contact the **Fédération Française de Randonnée Pédestre**.

Cycling tours of the lush green Luberon in Vaucluse are great for people of all ages. In the upper Var, Figanières is famous for mountain-biking, while the Alps of Haute-Provence boast around 1,500 km (900 miles) of marked tracks. For detailed information, contact the **Fédération Française de Cyclisme**.

Water Sports

Most coastal resorts have excellent facilities for both experienced and amateur sailors. Iles d'Hyères has some top-class sailing schools, in the tiny island of Bendor and the Porquerolles, the largest of the French Riviera islands.

For windsurfing, the reliable winds of the Bouches-du-Rhône and the Var make for favourable conditions. Other good locations include the Camargue, where the lively Mistral wind blows, at Port St-Louis and Les Saintes-Maries-de-la-Mer. The wind-surfing regatta in St-Tropez in July is a particularly glamorous event, which is always exciting and very well attended.

Scuba diving is popular, thanks to sparkling water, an ample sprinkling of underwater wrecks and a wealth of marine life. It is especially good in Marseille and the Iles d'Hyères and Cavalaire. The little island of Port-Cros has a special underwater "Discovery Trail". St-Raphaël is also a leading diving centre, with several World War II shipwrecks off the coast.

For more on scuba diving, contact the **Fédération Française d'Etudes et de Sports Sous-Marins** in Marseille.

The most picturesque stretch of the Rhône passes through Avignon and Arles, otherwise known as the "Cities of Art and History", and the Camargue – home to wild horses, bulls and flamingos. Several companies organize boat trips or river cruises in floating hotels. For details, contact the tourist information centres in Arles, Avignon, Les Stes-Maries-de-la-Mer or Port St Louis du Rhône.

The *calanques* can be visited by boats from Marseille and Cassis. Contact **Les Amis de Calanques** for more details.

Many beaches are privately owned and entry is by fee. Catamarans, dinghies, water-skiing and surfing equipment are all on offer.

For detailed information, contact the national sailing school, **Fédération Française de Voile**.

DIRECTORY

Arts and Crafts

French Institute
17 Queensberry Place,
London SW7 2DT.
Tel 020 7073 1350.
W institut-francais.
org.uk

Maison de la France
Lincoln House, 300 High
Holborn, London WC1V
7JH. **Tel** 090 68 244 123.
W uk.rendezvous
enfrance.com

Provence Verte
Office de Tourisme, 83170
Brignoles.
Tel 04 94 72 04 21.
W la-provence-
verte.net

Union Rempart
1 rue des Guillemites,
75004 Paris. **Tel** 01 42 71
96 55. **W** rempart.com

Cookery

Château Virant
Route de St Chamas, 13680
Lançon de Provence.
Tel 04 90 42 44 47.
W chateauvirant.com

Hostellerie Bérard
83740 la Cadière d'Azur.
Tel 04 94 90 11 43.
W hotel-berard.com

**Les Figuières du
Mas de Luquet**
Chemin du Mas de la
Musique, Mas de Luquet,
13690 Graveson.
Tel 04 90 95 72 03.
W lesfiguieres.com

Lavender Fields and Vineyards

**Les Vignerons
des Baux**
Tel 04 90 92 25 01.
W lesvinsdesbaux.com

Les Vins Luberon
Blvd de Rayol, 84160
Lourmarin.
Tel 04 90 07 34 40.
W vins-luberon.fr

Musée de la Lavande
Route de Gordes,
84220 Coustellet.
Tel 04 90 76 91 23.
W museedela
lavande.com

Perfumery and Aromatherapy

Fragonard
Blvd Fragonard, 06130
Grasse.
Tel 04 92 42 34 34.
W fragonard.com

**Le Studio des
Fragrances**
5 rte de Pegomas,
06131 Grasse.
Tel 04 93 09 20 00.
W galimard.com

Perfume Workshop
60 blvd Victor Hugo,
06130 Grasse.
Tel 04 92 42 33 21.
W molinard.com

Extreme Sports

**Fédération
Française de
Vol Libre**
4 rue de Suisse,
06000 Nice.
Tel 04 97 03 82 82.
W federation.ffvl.fr

**Fédération
Française de
Vol à Voile**
55 rue des petites Ecuries,
75010 Paris.
Tel 01 45 44 04 78.
W ffvv.org

Bird-Watching

**Parc Naturel
Régional de
Camargue**
Mas du Pont de Rousty,
13200 Arles.
Tel 04 90 97 10 82.
W parc-camargue.fr

Canoeing

**Fédération Française
de Canoë-Kayak**
87 quai de la Marne,
94340 Joinville-le-Point.
Tel 01 45 11 08 50.
W ffck.org

Canyoning

**Castellane Tourist
Office**
Rue Nationale, Castellane.
Tel 04 92 83 61 14.
W castellane.org

Golf and Tennis

**Fédération
Française de Golf**
68 rue Anatole France,
92300, Levallois Perret.
Tel 01 41 49 77 00.
W ffgolf.org

**Provence-Alpes-Côte
d'Azur Regional
Tourist Board**
61 le Canabière, Marseille.
Tel 04 91 56 47 00.
W crt-paca.fr

Horse Riding

**Ligue Régionale de
Provence de Sports
Equestres**
298 avenue du Club
Hippique, 13090 Aix-en-
Provence. **Tel** 04 42 20 88 02.
W provence-
equitation.com

Naturism

**Fédération
Française de
Naturisme**
5 rue Regnault, 93500
Pantin. **Tel** 01 48 10 31 00.
W ffn-naturisme.com

Skiing

**Fédération Française
de la Montagne et de
l'Escalade**
8 quai de la Marne, 75019
Paris. **Tel** 01 40 18 75 50.
W ffme.fr

**Fédération Française
de Ski**
50 avenue des Marquisats,
Annecy. **Tel** 04 50 51 40 34.
W ffs.fr

Spa Breaks

Hôtel Thalazur
770 chemin des Moyennes
Bréguières, 06600 Antibes.
Tel 04 92 91 82 00.
W thalazur.fr

La Bastide de Gordes
Le Village, 84220 Gordes.
W bastide-de-
gordes.com

Le Mas Candille
Boulevard Clément
Rebuffet, 06250 Mougins.
Tel 04 92 28 43 43.
W lemascandille.com

Walking, Climbing and Cycling

**Comité
Departemental
de la Randonnée
Pédestre**
7 rue de l'Hotel de Ville,
Cagnes-sur-Mer.
Tel 04 93 20 74 73.
W cdrp06.org

**Fédération
Française de
Cyclisme**
1 rue Laurent Fignon,
78180 Montigny les
Brettonneux.
Tel 08 11 04 05 55.
W ffc.fr

**Fédération
Française de
Randonnée Pédestre**
64 rue du Dessous des
Berges, 75013 Paris.
Tel 01 44 89 93 93.
W ffrandonnee.fr

**Maison du Parc
Naturel Régional
du Luberon**
60 place Jean Jaurès,
84404 Apt.
Tel 04 90 04 42 00.
W parcduluberon.fr

Water Sports

**Fédération Française
d'Etudes et de Sports
Sous-Marins**
24 quai Rive-Neuve,
13284 Marseille.
Tel 04 91 33 99 31.
W ffessm.fr

**Fédération
Française de Voile**
17 rue Henri Bocquillon,
75015 Paris.
Tel 01 40 60 37 00.
W ffvoile.com

**Les Amis de
Calanques**
4 quai Amiral Canteaume,
La Ciotat.
Tel 06 09 33 54 98.
W visite-calanques.fr

SURVIVAL GUIDE

PRACTICAL INFORMATION

The peak holiday period for Provence runs from the middle of June until the end of August. During this time, the coastal areas in particular are very crowded. However, the region offers a range of activities throughout the year to suit all tastes: skiing slopes in the winter, golden beaches in the summer, excellent modern art museums, fine Roman ruins, traditional festivals and superb food and wine. Tourist offices are excellent sources of general information and accommodation advice (see also pp194–5). The main branches in Provence are listed opposite. Shops and banks tend to close between noon and 3pm, so take advantage of this to enjoy a long, leisurely lunch, bearing in mind an old local saying: "Slow in the mornings, and not too fast in the afternoons."

Enjoying a relaxed lunch on a vine-shaded terrace

When to Go

During high season in Provence, local businesses in tourist areas hope to make their whole year's profit, and set their prices higher accordingly. The coast in particular can get very busy so to avoid the crowds, head for the wilds of upper Provence or the hills of the Var and Vaucluse.

Provence is at its best in May and September when the weather is still warm, but there are fewer visitors. The winter months can offer some sunny days, but beware of the cold mistral wind that can sweep through the area. A few festivals, such as the Nice Carnival and the Lemon Festival in Menton, are cleverly timed so as to attract off-season tourists, and skiing is usually possible between mid-November and April (see p100).

What to Take

Apart from prescription drugs, you should find everything you need in local shops. People dress quite casually, but you should take care to be respectful when visiting churches, and some restaurants have a more formal dress code.

Visas and Passports

Currently there are no visa requirements for EU nationals or for tourists from the US, Canada, Australia or New Zealand staying in France for under three months. After that a residency permit (carte de séjour) is required. Visitors from other countries should ask for visa information from their local French authorities prior to departure. Like most EU countries (but not the UK and Ireland) France is part of the Schengen agreement for shared border controls. When you enter the Schengen area through any of the member states, your 90-day stay will be valid for all of them, even if you travel between several countries during your trip.

Customs Information

Visitors from outside the European Union can claim back the sales tax (TVA) levied on French goods if they spend more than €175 in one shop on the same day. To claim your refund, you must obtain an export sales form (bordereau de vente à l'exportation) and take your goods out of the EU within three months of the date of purchase. The form should be signed by both the retailer and yourself. Hand it in to customs officials when you leave the EU, and they will give you a set of forms that you should send back to the shop. The refund will then be sent on to you or credited to your bank card. Exceptions for this détaxe rebate are food and drink, medicines, tobacco, cars and motorbikes.

There are no restrictions on the quantities of duty-paid and VAT-paid goods one is allowed to take from one EU country to another as long as they are for personal use and not for resale. However, you may be asked to prove that goods are for your own use if they exceed the recommended amounts: 10 litres of spirits, 90 litres of wine, 110 litres of beer and 800 cigarettes.

Non-EU nationals arriving in the European Union may bring in the following: up to 2 litres of wine and 1 litre of spirits (or 2 litres of drink less than 22° proof); up to €430 worth of perfume, coffee or tea and up to 200 cigarettes. Visitors under 17 may not import or export duty-free alcohol or tobacco, even as gifts. In general, personal goods (such as a car or a bicycle) may be imported to France free of duty and without any paperwork as long as they

The tourist office at Monieux, Vaucluse

are for personal use and not for resale. A brochure called *Voyagez en Toute Liberté*, available from the **Centre des Renseignements des Douanes**, has further details on this.

Special rules apply for the import and export of plants, medicines, animals, weapons and art objects. Be sure to consult your own or French customs before travelling.

Tourist Information

Most large towns have a tourist office *(Office de Tourisme* or *Syndicat d'Initiative)*; in smaller villages, it is the town hall *(mairie)* that provides information. Tourist offices will supply free maps and details of local events and accommodation; they will also book hotel rooms on your behalf.

Etiquette

The French rituals of politeness apply in Provence too. When introduced to a new person, it is correct to shake hands. In shops, say *bonjour* before asking what you want, then *merci* when you receive your change and *au*

revoir when you depart. In supermarkets, the cashier will not say *bonjour* to you until they have finished with the previous customer. The usual greeting among friends of both sexes is generally two or three kisses on the cheeks.

In smaller communities, any efforts made by English speakers to communicate in French and show a real interest in the area will be met with encouragement.

Opening Times

Opening hours for museums are usually 9am–noon and 2–5:30pm, but they vary according to the season, with longer hours being kept from May to September. Most museums close one day a week: national museums on Mondays and municipal ones on Tuesdays. Be advised that many museums close for the entire month of November.

Most businesses open from 8 or 9am until noon and from 2 or 3pm to 6 or 7pm. Banks are open 8:30am–noon and 1:30–4:30pm Monday to Friday and sometimes on Saturday

The beautifully decorated façade of the Musée Matisse in Nice

mornings. Department stores, supermarkets, tourist offices and some sights may remain open during the lunch break.

Restaurants often close one day a week, usually Monday; many will also close on Sunday evenings.

In winter, much of seaside Provence shuts down. Phone ahead to check what is open, because some establishments may be closed for months. Transport services may also be restricted out of season.

DIRECTORY

French Tourist Offices Abroad

Australia
25 Bligh St, Level 13, Sydney, NSW 2000.
Tel (2) 9210 5400.
 au.rendezvous enfrance.com

Canada
1800 Ave MacGill College, Suite 1010, Montreal H3A 3J6.
Tel (514) 288 2026.
 ca.rendezvous enfrance.com

United Kingdom
300 High Holborn, London WC1 VJH.
Tel (0207) 061 6600.
 uk.rendezvous enfrance.com

USA
825 Third Ave 29th Floor, New York, NY 10022.

Tel (212) 838 7800.
 us.rendezvous enfrance.com

Tourist Offices in Provence

Aix-en-Provence
300 ave Giuseppe Verdi.
Tel 04 42 16 11 61.
 aixenprovence tourism.com

Arles
Blvd des Lices.
Tel 04 90 18 41 20.
 arlestourisme.com

Avignon
41 cours Jean-Jaurès.
Tel 04 32 74 32 74.
 avignon- tourisme.com

Cannes
Palais des Festivals, La Croisette.

Tel 04 92 99 84 22.
 cannes- destination.com

Draguignan
2 ave Lazare Carnot.
Tel 04 98 10 51 05.
 tourisme- dracenie.com

Marseille
4 La Canebière.
Tel 08 26 50 05 00.
 marseille- tourisme.com

Monte-Carlo
2A blvd des Moulins.
Tel 00 377 92 16 61 16.
 visitmonaco.com

Nice
5 promenade des Anglais.
Tel 08 92 70 74 07.
 nicetourism.com

Nîmes
6 rue Auguste.
Tel 04 66 58 38 00.
 ot-nimes.fr

St-Tropez
Quai Jean-Jaurès.
Tel 08 92 68 48 28.
 sainttropez tourisme.com

Customs Information

Centre des Renseignements des Douanes
23 rue de l'Université, 75007 Paris. **Tel** 08 11 20 44 44. **douane.gouv.fr**

Marseille
48 ave R Schuman.
Tel 09 70 27 83 83.

Useful Websites

Anglo Info
 riviera.angloinfo.com

Provence Web
 provenceweb.fr

Provence & Beyond
 beyond.fr

The striking Hôtel de Ville of Aix-en-Provence

Admission Prices

Museum admission prices range from around €3 to €12. National museums are free the first Sunday of the month, and nearly all municipal museums offer free or discounted entry on Sundays.

The Carte Musée Côte d'Azur, which allows unlimited access to more than 50 museums in the region, can be purchased from participating museums, FNAC stores (see p226) and certain tourist offices (see p237). There is also the Nice Riviera Pass, which offers free access to many sights and has various discounts available; see www.nicerivierapass.com for more information.

Churches normally offer free admission, but a small charge may be levied to visit cloisters and chapels.

Tipping and Taxes

Most restaurants include a service charge of 10–15 per cent as part of the bill, so there is no need to tip. In a bar or café, leave some small change. A small amount is usually given to taxi drivers, despite service being included. Hotel porters, hairdressers and tour guides will expect a tip of around €3.

Travellers with Special Needs

Provence's narrow streets can make it a difficult area for travellers with limited mobility. On the plus side, disabled parking spaces are plentiful (remember to bring your international orange disc with you), and wheelchairs and other useful equipment can be hired at pharmacies. Wheelchair access is still rather limited, although newer buildings will have ramps and other facilities.

The train company SNCF has carriages designed to accommodate wheelchair users (see pp246–7), and taxi drivers are also obliged to take disabled people and guide dogs.

For more information, visit Access-Able Travel Source (www.access-able.com).

International Student Identity Card

Travelling with Children

Many hotels have family rooms, but if they don't you can ask them to add a cot or an extra bed. There may be an additional charge for this. If you are hiring a car and need child seats, be sure to book them in advance and ask for them to be fitted for you. Children are eligible for discounted train travel.

Gay and Lesbian Travellers

There is a strong network of gay and lesbian venues in Provence; this includes bars, discos and beaches. For listings of gay-friendly hotels and activities, visit the websites listed in the directory on the opposite page.

Travelling on a Budget

Provence is not the cheapest region in France, but prices are much more reasonable out of season. Staying inland rather than in a seaside resort will also save money. Ask the local tourist office for advice on affordable accommodation, such as hostels and campsites. Travelling by public transport is cheaper than hiring a car, and along the coast this is a perfectly adequate option (see pp246–8 and p252). Buying carnets of tickets for travel on public transport in major towns will also save money. Visiting attractions doesn't have to be costly either, as most museums have free days. Check to see if there are cheaper family tickets too. However, most of the real pleasure of Provence can be experienced for free and consists of admiring the spectacular views of the Mediterranean and mountains, swimming in the sea, walking on the beach and hiking in the hills and national parks.

Student Travellers

Students carrying a valid International Student Identification Card (ISIC) benefit from discounts of between 25 and 50 per cent at museums, theatres, cinemas and many of the public monuments.

The region's main university is split between Aix-en-Provence and Marseille; other large universities are located in Avignon and Nice. You will find the **Bureau Information Jeunesse** (BIJ) and the **Centre Régional Information Jeunesse** (CRIJ) in all university towns. These organizations can provide a great deal of information about student life and a list of inexpensive accommodation options. For information on hostels in the main towns see page 196.

Provence Time

Provence is one hour ahead of Greenwich Mean Time (GMT). It is in the same time zone as Italy, Spain and other western European countries. Standard time differences between Provence and other areas of the world may vary according to local summer alterations to the time.

The French use the 24-hour military clock rather than "am" and "pm".

Electrical Adaptors

The voltage in France is 220 volts. British appliances of 240 volts can be used with an adaptor, while American 110 volts appliances will need a transformer *(transformateur)*.

Plugs have two small round pins; heavier-duty installations have two large round pins. Some of the more upmarket hotels offer built-in adaptors for shavers. Multi-adaptors, useful because they have both large and small pins, can be bought at most airports before departure; standard adaptors can be purchased from department stores.

Façade of the Russian Orthodox church in Nice

Religious Services

Provence is a strong Catholic region, with many religious services and festivals dating back 500 years. In recent decades, immigrants have brought increasing religious

diversification. Regular services in English are held at the Anglican churches in Nice and Marseille.

Responsible Travel

Throughout France there has been a rapid growth in environmental awareness. **Echoway** is one of the leading French ecotourism organizations, which encourages responsible travel. Provence has a long-running rural tourism network, with farmhouse accommodation available through the central **Gîtes de France**. There are also smaller organizations with a more defined ecological stance such as **Accueil Paysan**, which is a network of small-scale farmers practising low-impact, sustainable agriculture. Finally there are hundreds of fully equipped campsites through-out Provence *(see pp196–7)*.

Information on local green tourism *(tourisme vert* or *eco)* initiatives and activities can be found through *département* and local tourist offices. Many towns have weekly markets selling only organic and traditional produce (usually called a *marché bio)*, which allow visitors to give back to the local community. If a town does not have a separate market dedicated to organic produce, there are often stalls within the main market that are exclusively *bio*, as is the case at Nice's market on the cours Saleya. Market days have been provided throughout the guide.

Conversion Chart

Imperial to metric
1 inch = 2.54 centimetres
1 foot = 30 centimetres
1 mile = 1.6 kilometres
1 ounce = 28 grams
1 pound = 454 grams
1 pint (UK) = 0.6 litre
1 gallon (UK) = 4.6 litres

Metric to imperial
1 millimetre = 0.04 inch
1 centimetre = 0.4 inch
1 metre = 3 feet 3 inches
1 kilometre = 0.6 mile
1 gram = 0.04 ounce
1 kilogram = 2.2 pounds

Personal Security and Health

On the whole Provence is a fairly safe place for visitors, however, it is wise to take a few precautions. Extra caution is required in the larger cities and along the Côte d'Azur, especially in Nice, which has a higher crime rate than Marseille. Car crime is prevalent along the coast, so make sure you never leave your valuables in a vehicle. You should also avoid groups of innocent-looking children who may, in fact, be skilled in the art of pickpocketing. Consular offices can be good sources of help in the event of an emergency (see the directory box opposite). Rural areas are usually very safe.

Policeman   Fireman

Personal Property

Pickpockets are common in the tourist areas of the Côte d'Azur and in larger towns. In Nice, bag snatching is on the rise, but fortunately muggings are still rare. Take care of your belongings at all times. Do not carry much cash at any one time, and avoid carrying valuables with you when sightseeing.

Try not to park your car in remote areas, and use multi-storey car parks if you can. These are monitored by video cameras, and parking there will also remove the risk of being towed away, which is a greater everyday issue than most car crime.

It is not advisable to sleep on the beach, since robberies and attacks have been known to take place there at night.

In the event of a theft, go to the nearest police station (*gendarmerie*) with your identity papers (and vehicle papers, if relevant). The report process (*procès-verbal*, or *PV*) may take time, but you will need a police statement for any

Police car

Fire engine

Ambulance

insurance claim you make. If your passport is stolen, contact the police and your nearest consulate (see opposite).

Personal Safety

Certain train routes – for example the Marseille-Barcelona and Marseille-Ventimiglia (Italy) lines – have dubious reputations. Stay alert and keep the compartment door shut and your valuables close to you, especially if you are travelling at night.

Some tourists visiting the area during the summer, have been victims of road piracy, with their vehicle being rammed on the motorway to force them to stop. There are police stations at most motorway exits, so if you encounter any trouble, try to stay calm and keep going until the next exit.

Legal Assistance

If your insurance policy is comprehensive (including a legal service in France), they will be able to help with legal advice on claims, such as accident procedure. If you are not insured, call your nearest consulate office.

Women Travellers

Women should take the usual precautions: wearing their bag strapped across the body; being careful after dark; avoiding quiet, unfamiliar areas; locking the car doors when driving; and taking care on trains, especially sleepers.

For contraceptive advice, go to a GP or a gynaecologist (no referral is necessary); to find one, ask at a pharmacy or look in the Yellow Pages *(Pages Jaunes)*. Pharmacies are also excellent sources of advice and can dispense the morning-after pill without a prescription.

Outdoor Hazards

Forest fires are a major risk in Provence. High winds and dry forests mean that fire spreads rapidly, so be vigilant about putting out cigarette butts. Camp fires are banned in the region. If you witness a fire, contact the emergency services at once and keep well away.

The Mediterranean Sea is safe for swimming, although there can be strong currents off the Cap d'Antibes and the Camargue. Public beaches usually have a lifeguard and indicate safe areas for swimming; some display European blue flags as a sign of cleanliness. If you are stung by a jellyfish or sea urchin, seek advice from a pharmacy. If you are sailing, keep up to date with the weather reports, and carry ID and a radio or mobile phone.

Weather conditions in the mountains can change very quickly and without warning. In winter, be sure to advise the local authorities of your projected route; in summer, pack warm clothes and some provisions in case of sudden storms. Altitude sickness can occur in the southern Alps, so climb slowly, pausing regularly to acclimatize.

In the mountains behind Nice and Cannes, you may encounter the grey-brown Montpellier snake. Despite its size (up to 1.5 m/5 ft), it is very shy and will likely flee. Vipers also live in the region. Mosquitoes are common, and repellents and antidotes can be bought from supermarkets or pharmacies. The local lavender oil is an excellent repellent and a good

antiseptic treatment for mosquito bites and wasp stings if applied immediately. Occasionally hornets and scorpions can be a problem, so get into the habit of always checking shoes and clothing before getting dressed. Also check your bedding before going to sleep. Beware of the heat, especially with children, and seek immediate medical advice for heat stroke.

During the hunting season (Sep–Feb, especially on Sundays), wear brightly coloured clothes when out walking. Signs on trees usually denote hunting areas *(reserve du chasse)*.

Fire-hazard poster

Travel and Health Insurance

Check that your travel insurance is valid in France, and note that you will need extra insurance to cover winter sports. EU residents are entitled to medical treatment with the European Health Insurance Card. You will need the doctor's and pharmacy receipts *(feuille de soins)* to apply for reimbursements.

Medical Treatment

Pharmacists can diagnose and suggest treatments for simple conditions; they can be recognized by the green cross outside. There is usually one pharmacy open at night and at weekends. Hospital accident-and-emergency units will deal with accidents and unexpected illnesses. In rural areas, the *pompiers* (firefighters) are also trained paramedics and can be called in an emergency. In major cities, a 24-hour doctor service *(médecin de garde)* is available.

Public Toilets

Modern automatic toilets are widely available in cities. You may also come across public toilets of the squat variety, in which case you might prefer to use the services in a café or department store.

DIRECTORY

Consulates

Australia
4 rue Jean Rey, 75015 Paris.
Tel 01 40 59 33 00.
W france.embassy.gov.au

Ireland
69 ave Roi Albert, La Californie, 06400 Cannes.
Tel 06 77 69 14 36.
W embassyofireland.fr

UK
24 ave du Prado, Marseille
Tel 04 91 15 72 10.
W ukinfrance.fco.gov.uk

USA
12 place Varian Fry, Marseille.
Tel 04 91 54 92 00.
W marseille.usconsulate.gov

Emergency Numbers

AIDS Helpline
Tel 0800 84 08 00.

Ambulance (SAMU)
Tel 15.

Centre Anti-Poison (Marseille)
Tel 04 91 75 25 25.

Drugs/Tobacco/Alcohol Hotline
Tel 113.

Fire (Sapeurs Pompiers)
Tel 18.

Police (Gendarmerie)
Tel 17.

Rape Hotline
Tel 0800 05 95 95.

SOS Médecins
Nice. **Tel** 08 10 85 01 01.

Hospital Emergencies

Avignon
Hôpital Général Henri Duffaut, 305 rue Raoul Follereau.
Tel 04 32 75 33 33.
W ch-avignon.fr

Marseille
La Conception, 147 blvd Baille.
Tel 04 91 38 30 00.
W fr.ap-hm.fr

Nice
Hôpital St-Roch, 5 rue Pierre-Devoluy.
Tel 04 92 03 77 77.

Banks and Local Currency

Visitors to Provence may change currency in a variety of locations, but it is always wise to arrive with at least a few euros. Credit cards are widely accepted for purchases and in restaurants, but if in doubt, ask in advance. Credit cards and bank cards can also be used to withdraw money, but check the charges levied by the credit card company first.

Banks and Currency Exchange

Banks in big towns usually open from 8:30am to noon and from 1:30 to 4:30pm Monday to Friday and Saturday morning. They are closed during public holidays.

There is no limit to the amount of money you may bring into France, but if you wish to take more than €10,000 back to the UK, you should declare it on arrival. It is wise to carry large sums of money as travellers' cheques.

You will need your four-digit PIN code (code confidentiel) to withdraw money from ATMs (but check the charges levied for this service) and for payment in shops and restaurants. ATM instructions are usually given in French, English and Italian. Note that ATMs may run out of notes just before the weekend.

Travellers' cheques can be obtained from American Express, Thomas Cook or your bank. It is recommended that you have them issued in euros. American Express cheques are widely accepted in France; if they are exchanged at an AmEx office, no commission is charged. In the event of theft, travellers' cheques are replaced at once.

The most common credit cards in France, accepted even at motorway tolls, are Carte Bleue/Visa and Eurocard/MasterCard. Because of the high commissions charged, some Provençal businesses do not accept American Express.

Foreign Banks

Cannes
Barclays, 8 rue Frédéric Amouretti.
Tel 04 92 99 68 00.
 barclays.fr

Marseille
Barclays, 112–114 rue de Rome
Tel 04 91 13 98 13.
w barclays.fr

Nice
American Express, Aeroport terminal 1.
Tel 04 93 215 979.
Barclays, 2 rue Alphonse Karr.
Tel 04 93 82 68 00.

Nimes
Barclays, 20 blvd Gambetta.
Tel 04 91 13 98 31

Lost Cards and Travellers' Cheques

Visa
Tel 0800 90 1179.

MasterCard
Tel 0800 901 387.

American Express Cards and Cheques
Tel 0800 832 820.

Banknotes and Coins

Euro bank notes have seven denominations. The €5 note is grey, the €10 is pink, the €20 is blue, the €50 is orange, the €100 is green, the €200 is yellow and the €500 is purple. There are eight coin denominations: €1 and €2 coins are silver and gold; those worth 50 cents, 20 cents and 10 cents are gold, while the 5-, 2- and 1- coins are bronze.

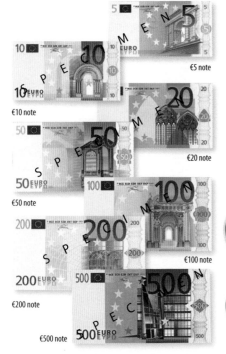

€5 note

€10 note

€20 note

€50 note

€100 note

€200 note

€500 note

€2 coin

€1 coin

50 cents

20 cents

10 cents

5 cents

2 cents

1 cent

Communications and Media

The main telephone company is France Télécom, while postal services are run by La Poste. Post offices *(bureaux de postes)* are identified by the blue-on-yellow "La Poste" sign. In small villages, the post office may be in the town hall *(mairie)*. Internet access is readily available via Internet cafés, hotels and Wi-Fi.

Mail boxes throughout France are a distinctive yellow

Telephone Calls

Public phone boxes can be found throughout Provence, and they take telephone cards *(télécartes)* and credit cards. Telephone cards can be bought at post offices, *tabacs* and some newsagents; they come in units of 50 or 120.

Home Direct calling service (or *pays direct*) lets you make the call via an operator in your country, paying with a credit card or by reversing charges. Reverse-charge calls are known as *PCV*. Main post offices offer long-distance calling facilities from booths *(cabines)*.

Mobile Phones

A mobile phone from another European country can be used in France, though you may need to inform your network in advance so that it can be enabled. US-based mobiles need to be tri-band to work in France.

International calls on mobile phones are expensive. As an alternative, replace your SIM card with a French card and number. Note, however, that French top-up vouchers have strict expiry periods.

Internet Access

Internet facilities are readily available, and many hotels also offer Wi-Fi. The larger towns will have several Internet cafés, lists of which can be obtained from local tourist offices. The major ports in Provence are all equipped with Wi-Fi.

Postal Services

Postage stamps *(timbres)* can be purchased singly or in books *(carnets)* of ten from post offices or *tabacs*.

Post office hours vary. The maximum hours are around 9am–5pm on weekdays, with a lunch break (noon–2pm), and 9am–noon on Saturdays.

To send letters from France, drop them into the yellow mail boxes. These often have two slots: one for the town you are in; the other for the surrounding *département* and other destinations.

Newspapers and Magazines

In main cities and airports, international papers can often be bought on the day of publication. *The Connexion* is a monthly newspaper devoted to France, and Provence also has its own English-language publications. Most major towns have an English bookshop *(see p221)*, often an invaluable source of information.

Television and Radio

The subscription channel Canal+ broadcasts ABC American evening news at 7am daily. Sky News and CNN are available in many hotels. The Franco-German channel ARTE broadcasts programmes and films from all over the world, often in the original language with French subtitles. Listings indicate *VO* or *VF (Version Originale* or *Version Française)* for non-French films.

Riviera Radio broadcasts in English throughout the South of France on 106.3 and 106.5 FM stereo from Monte-Carlo. The station offers music and current affairs, including BBC World Service programmes. *France Musique* (92.2 FM in Nice and 94.7 in Marseille) specializes in classical music, while *France Info* (105.2–105.8 FM) is a national rolling-news station.

TRAVEL INFORMATION

Situated at the crossroads between France, Spain and Italy, Provence is well served by international motorway and rail links. Nice airport is the most modern and the busiest of French airports outside Paris, handling 4 million visitors from all over the world annually. Marseille airport also welcomes daily direct flights from most major European cities. For travelling across France, the TGV train is swift *(see p246)*, while the motorail journey from channel ports takes 12 hours, but is effortless and dispenses with motorway tolls. The autoroutes are excellent, but do become crowded in mid-summer.

Arriving by Air

The two main airports in Provence – Marseille and Nice, Côte d'Azur, which is the second biggest airport in France – are comfortable and modern. **Marseille Provence** (or **Marseille-Marignane**) has national and international flights serving mainly business travellers, and a low-cost air terminal, MP2. It is useful for destinations in western Provence, such as Avignon and Aix-en-Provence.

Airport taxis to the centre of Marseille cost around €40 (€50 at night and on Sundays). There is also an airport bus to the main train station in Marseille (St-Charles), which leaves every 20 minutes. Car hire companies at the airport include Avis, Budget, Citer, Ada, Europcar and Hertz.

Nice, Côte d'Azur has two terminals. The east terminal (one) takes international flights and some domestic flights on

French carriers (Air Littoral and TAT). The west terminal (two) serves domestic flights only. There is a shuttle bus between the buildings, but it is best to make sure you know which terminal you will be using. Taxis to the centre of town cost €25–€30. Airport buses run to the Gare Routière station every 10 minutes, and bus No. 99 goes to Gare SNCF every 30 minutes. There are buses to Cannes every half hour and to Monaco and Menton every hour. **Héli-Air Monaco** offers regular helicopter transits to Monaco, St-Tropez and Cannes, while **Nice Helicoptères** also has many daily flights to Cannes. There are several car hire companies at Nice airport, including Avis, Budget, Europcar and Hertz.

There are three other airports in or near Provence which operate international flights; these are Montpellier, Nîmes and Toulon.

Airline Details

Provence is the most easily accessible place by air in France after Paris. The vast majority of major European cities have daily direct flights to Provence. The British carriers – **British Airways**, **easyJet**, **Ryanair** and **BMI** – all run daily flights from London Heathrow, London Gatwick, Luton, Stansted or Manchester to Nice, Nimes, Marseille, Montpellier or Toulon. A good option among low-cost airlines is **Flybe**, which flies to Nice from Southampton and Exeter. The French national airline, **Air France**, has daily flights to and from Nice to Britain, Spain, Germany, Italy and North Africa.

There is a **Delta** flight from Nice to New York several times a week, and **Emirates** also flies to Nice from Dubai five times a week. From all other international departure

The main international terminal at Nice, Côte d'Azur airport

Departure hall at Marseille airport

points you will be required to change planes in Paris to reach Provence.

Fares and Deals

The large number of low-cost airlines flying to Provence mean that there is a wide range of prices on offer. Fares are at their highest over the Easter period and in July and August. Make sure you check which airport you are flying to when booking, as some low-cost airlines use smaller airports that may be some distance from the city centre.

Fly-Drive and Fly-Rail Package Holidays

Air France and SNCF offer combined fares for flight and train. You fly into Paris and then catch the train south. Good deals are available for the main destinations such as Avignon, Arles, Nice and Marseille. For notes on fly-drive packages see page 250.

There are also a wide variety of companies offering tailor-made package holidays in Provence, with flight, car hire and accommodation included in the cost.

Green Travel

Travelling in France without using high-impact flights or long car drives is easier than in many countries thanks primarily to the high quality of public transport, and above all the SNCF rail network.

The French government has introduced an "Ecomobility" programme, which aims to encourage a reduction in car use by making it easier to transfer from SNCF trains to local buses, bikes or other transport (for more details, see www.sncf.com). This includes free-cycle schemes like the *LeVélo* in Marseille, *V'hello* in Aixen-Provence and *Vélopop* in Avignon. There are cycle-hire shops in many towns and local tourist offices will be able to provide more information on cycle hire and routes in their area. There are also facilities for taking your bikes on SNCF trains *(see p248)*. If you don't hike or cycle, however, exploring the country-side will still be difficult without a car, as local buses are often slow and infrequent.

DIRECTORY

Airport Information

Avignon-Provence
Tel 04 90 81 51 51.
Airport to city 10 km (6 miles). Taxi €24.
W avignon-aeroport.fr

Marseille Provence
Tel 04 42 14 14 14.
Airport to city 25 km (17 miles). Shuttle bus €10, taxi €40.
W marseille-aeroport.fr

Montpellier Méditerranée
Tel 04 67 20 85 00.
Airport to city 7 km (4 miles). Shuttle bus €8, taxi €15–€20.
W montpellier. aeroport.fr

Nice, Côte d'Azur
Tel 0820 423 333.
Airport to city 6 km (4 miles). Shuttle bus €4, taxi €25–€30.
W nice.aeroport.fr

Nîmes/Arles/ Camargue/ Cevennes
Tel 04 66 70 49 49.
Airport to city 15 km (9 miles).
Shuttle bus €5, taxi €25.
W aeroport-nimes.fr

Toulon-Hyères
Tel 08 25 01 83 87.
Airport to city 23 km (15 miles).
Shuttle bus €1.40, taxi €40.
W toulon-hyeres. aeroport.fr

Airline Details

Air France
UK **Tel** 0871 66 33 777.
France **Tel** 3654.
W airfrance.com

British Airways
France **Tel** 0825 825 400.
UK **Tel** 0844 493 0787.
W britishairways.com

(BMI) British Midland
UK **Tel** 0870 6070555.
W bmiregional.com

Delta
France **Tel** 0811 640 005.
US **Tel** 0800 221 1212.
W delta.com

easyJet
France **Tel** 0826 103 320.
UK **Tel** 0871 244 2366.
W easyjet.com

Emirates
France **Tel** 0157 32 49 99.
UK **Tel** 844 800 2777.
W emirates.com

Flybe
UK **Tel** 0871 700 2000.
W flybe.com

Ryanair
France **Tel** 0892 780 210.
UK **Tel** 0871 246 0000.
W ryanair.com

Helicopter Services

Héli-Air Monaco
Tel 00 377 92 05 00 50.
W heliairmonaco.com

Nice Helicoptères
Tel 04 93 90 42 04.
W nicehelicopteres.com

Discount Travel Agencies

Jancarthier Voyages
7 cours Sextius.
Tel 04 42 93 48 48.
W aixvoyages-jancarthier.fr

Thomas Cook Canebiere
9 rue du jeune.
Tel 04 96 11 26 26.
W thomascook.fr

Trailfinders
194 Kensington High St, London W8 7RG.
Tel 020 7938 3939.
W trailfinders.com

Getting Around by Train

Travelling to Provence by train is fast and efficient. The French state railway, Société Nationale des Chemins de Fer (**SNCF**), is one of Europe's best equipped and most comfortable. The train journey from Paris to Avignon is almost as quick as by air – the TGV *(Train à Grande Vitesse)* takes only four hours. The Channel Tunnel provides a fast rail link via Calais between Provence and the UK, although not all of the route is high-speed.

Within Provence and the Côte d'Azur, the coastal route between Nice and Marseille is often crowded, so it is best to reserve tickets in advance on this and other *Grandes Lignes*. In the Var and Haute Provence, railway lines are scarce, but SNCF runs bus services. The private rail service **Chemins de Fer de Provence** runs the Train des Pignes *(see p185)*.

When purchasing a rail ticket – whether in France or abroad – it is also possible to pre-book a car *(Train + Auto)*, bike *(Train + Vélo)* or hotel *(Train + Hôtel)* to await you at your destination.

Further information on rail travel is provided on the main SNCF website.

The interior of Avignon TGV train station

Train Stations

The main stations in the region are Marseille Gare St-Charles, Nîmes and Nice (Nice Ville av Thiers). All offer a range of facilities, including restaurants, shops, Wi-Fi and secure left luggage lockers. Keep in mind that trains in France are punctual and very rarely leave late.

Main Routes

The main train routes to Provence from Northern Europe pass through Lille and Paris. In Paris you have to transfer to the Gare de Lyon – the main Paris station serving the south of France. Tickets from London to Nice, Avignon and Marseille, via **Eurostar**, hovercraft or ferry, are all available from the **Rail Europe** office in New York or on their website. The Eurostar connects at Lille or Paris with TGVs to the rest of France. Passengers arriving by sea at Calais can catch the train to Paris and transfer on to the Corail Lunéa overnight sleeper service to Nice.

From southern Europe, trains run to Marseille from Barcelona in Spain (6½ hours) and Genoa in Italy (3 hours).

Booking from Abroad

Tickets to and within France can be booked in the UK and US through Rail Europe and via www.voyages-sncf.com. Rail Europe also has information on prices and departure times. Reservations made abroad can be difficult to change once in France – you may have to pay for another reservation, or claim for a refund on your return.

Booking in France

Ticket counters at all stations are computerized. There are also automatic ticket and

The TGV Train

Trains à Grande Vitesse, or high-speed trains, travel at up to 300 km/hr (185 mph). There are five versions of TGV serving all areas of France and some European destinations. The Eurostar links Paris and London, the Thalys runs to Brussels. The TGV Méditerranée to Provence leaves from Paris Gare de Lyon. Other TGVs leave from Grenoble, Geneva and Lausanne. The trains' speed, comfort and reliability make them relatively expensive. Always reserve a seat.

Paris to Marseille now takes just three hours by TGV

reservation machines (with English instructions) on the concourse of main stations. For travel by TGV, Corail and Motorail a reservation is essential but can be made as little as five minutes before the train leaves, and up to 90 days in advance. Costs rise considerably at peak times. The international ticket and reservation system at Lille Europe station allows direct booking on services throughout the continent and the UK.

Fares

TGVs have two price levels for 2nd class, normal and peak, and a single level for 1st class. The cost of the obligatory seat reservation is included in the ticket price. Tickets for other trains can be subject to a supplement and do not include the reservation charge of €3.

Discounts of 25 per cent are available for people travelling with children *(Découverte Enfant+)*, for young people *(Découverte 12–25)*, for the over-60s *(Découverte Senior)*, for two people travelling together *(Découverte à Deux)*, for return trips including a Saturday night *(Découverte Sejour)* and for advance booking *(Découverte J8 and Découverte J30)*.

For those spending a bit more time on French railways, the SNCF issues a *Carte Enfant+* and a *Carte Senior* giving reductions of up to 50 per cent. Rail Europe can supply these cards.

Inter-Rail cards allow unlimited travel in European countries excluding the one of issue. (See the Inter-Rail website for more information.) **Eurail** passes are available to non-European residents and, in North America, France Railpass is another option.

Types of Train

SNCF trains are divided into several different types. TGV trains are the flagships of the network, travelling on specially built track at around 300 kph (185 mph). The classic Intercités trains running from city to city can be a good travelling option. Both TGVs and Intercités can be overnight sleepers. Reservations are obligatory for all services and can be made through Rail Europe or SNCF.

Motorail-Rider trains allow drivers to travel overnight with their car. The service runs from Calais to Nice via Avignon. Reservations are essential.

TER trains are regional services that usually stop at every station. Reservations are not required, and tickets are not normally available in advance. Route maps and information (in French only) are available at stations and on the TER website, see the directory box for details.

Picturesque view from the Train des Pignes

Scenic Rail Routes

The private rail service **Chemins de Fer de Provence** runs the Train des Pignes, a 151-km (90-mile) ride from Nice to Dignes-les-Bains. This is a dramatic journey through tunnels and over viaducts, with magnificent views. The single-track railway from Nice to Cuneo in Italy via Peille, Sospel and Tende is also a spectacular ride through mountainous terrain. The Alpazur service runs in summer between Nice and Grenoble with a tourist steam train on the Puget-Théniers section; hikers can leave and rejoin the train after a day's walking. For more information see www.trainstouristiques-ter.com.

DIRECTORY

Information and Reservations

Autotrain
W autotrain.voyages-sncf.com

Eurail
W eurail.com

Eurostar
St Pancras International
Pancras Road,
London NW1.
Tel 08432 186 186.

Paris Gare du Nord,
rue de Dunkerque,
75010 Paris.
Tel 08 92 35 35 39.
W eurostar.com

Eurotunnel
(Off junction 11a, M20,
Folkestone).
Tel 08443 353 535 (France).
Tel 08 10 63 03 04.
W eurotunnel.com

Inter-Rail
W interrail.eu

Motorail-Rider
W motorail-rider.com

Rail Europe USA
44 S. Broadway, White Plains,
NY 10604, US.
Tel 1-800-622-8600
(freephone in US).
W raileurope.com

SNCF
Tel 3635 (France).
Tel 00 33 892 35 35 35
(Outside France).
W voyages-sncf.com
W tgv.voyages-sncf.com

TER
W ter-sncf.com

Private Railway

Chemins de Fer de Provence
Tel 04 97 03 80 80.
W trainprovence.com

Bicycles on Trains

Bicycles can be transported on the Eurostar, either as personal luggage if they fold to the size of a normal suitcase, or by advance reservation. You can transport your bike on nearly every single SNCF train, including the TGV. However, this service must be booked in advance, and in some cases your bicycle will be transported separately, and can take up to four days to arrive. Bikes may also be transported on local trains (indicated by a bicycle symbol in the timetable). The SNCF *train + velo* scheme allows you to reserve a rental bike at your destination station when you book your ticket, although be aware this option is only available on certain routes.

Times and Penalties

Timetables change twice a year in May and September. Leaflets for the main routes are free, and can also be checked on the SNCF website. The Provence Alpes Côte d'Azur region has an all-inclusive TER timetable, which includes coach travel.

You must time-punch your ticket in the yellow *composteur* machine at the platform entrance or pay a penalty on the train. This is very easy to do, simply insert your ticket and (if you have one) separate seat reservation face up and the machine will date-stamp them.

Motorail

Eurotunnel rail shuttles vehicles between Folkstone and Calais in around 35 minutes. **Motorail** carries cars, motorbikes and passengers overnight from Calais to Provence. The journey is not cheap, but it is a practical, stress-free way to avoid the long drive south. You can reserve sleeping compartments exclusively for the people in your car. The service runs to Avignon, Nice and Fréjus/St-Raphaël between May and September. There is also the option to travel separately from your car. **Autotrain** will

Composteur machines are found at the platform entrance

transport your car overnight from Paris to either Fréjus/St-Raphaël, Marseille, Nice or Toulon, while you relax on a passenger train. Tickets must be booked at least five days in advance.

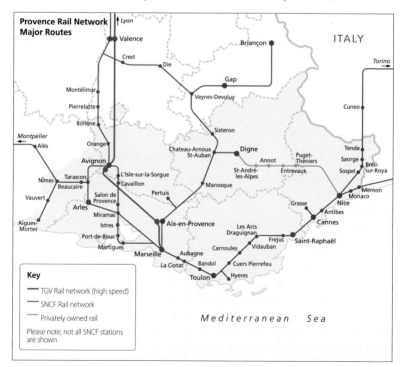

Provence Rail Network Major Routes

ITALY

↑ Lyon

Valence
Crest
Die
Briançon
Torino
Gap
Montélimar
Veynes-Devoluy
Cuneo
Pierrelatte
Bollène
Sisteron
Montpelier
Orange
Chateau-Arnoux St-Auban
Digne
Tende
Alès
Annot
Puget-Théniers
Saorge
Breil-sur-Roya
Avignon
St-André-les-Alpes
Entrevaux
Sospel
Nîmes
Tarascon
L'Isle-sur-la-Sorgue
Monaco
Beaucaire
Cavaillon
Manosque
Menton
Vauvert
Salon de Provence
Pertuis
Grasse
Nice
Arles
Miramas
Antibes
Aigues-Mortes
Istres
Aix-en-Provence
Les Arcs Draguignan
Cannes
Port-de-Bouc
Fréjus
Saint-Raphaël
Martigues
Carnoules
Vidauban
Marseille
Aubagne
La Ciotat
Bandol
Cuers Pierrefeu
Toulon
Hyeres

Key

— TGV Rail network (high speed)
— SNCF Rail network
— Privately owned rail
Please note, not all SNCF stations are shown

Mediterranean Sea

Travelling by Boat

There are few more enticing sights than the glittering Mediterranean of the southern Provençal coast. Almost every city along this stretch of water has a port with boats for hire. Ferry and boat companies operating to offshore islands are easy to find, and there are trips to Corsica from Marseille and Nice throughout the year. The other main waterways in Provence are the Rhône and Durance rivers, and the beautiful Camargue wetland. It is worth noting that the best way to get to St-Tropez in summer is by boat from Ste-Maxime or St-Raphaël. The town has no train station and the roads are usually very busy.

Sailing out of a rocky inlet on the Provençal coast

Mediterranean Ports

Car ferries depart all year round from Marseille and Nice to Corsica (Bastia, Ajaccio and Ile Rousse), operated by **SNCM Ferryterranée**. Summer ferries run from Marseille to Propriano, and from Toulon to Ajaccio, Bastia and Propriano, often crossing overnight.

SNCM has one or two weekly sailings from Marseille and Toulon to Sardinia. There are crossings to North Africa every week from Marseille to Tunis or Algiers, and to Oran weekly in high season.

Regular ferries and boats to nearby islands operate from Bandol to the Ile de Bendor; from Tour Fondu to Porquerolles; from Port d'Hyères and Le Lavandou to Le Levant and Port-Cros; and from Cannes to the Iles de Lérins.

Cruises and River Trips

The Mediterranean is famous as a cruise destination, and numerous companies operate on the south coast of France,

Some of the smaller, local boats moored in St-Tropez

stopping at St-Tropez, Villefranche, Marseille and Monaco. **Grand Bleu** has a good range of boats for hire for weekly river trips.

River travel is also an option in Provence with several cruise lines operating luxury river trips on the Rhône between Avignon and Lyon. **Croisieres Avignon-Mireio** offers lunch, dinner or sightseeing cruises from Avignon to a range of destinations. Or you can take daily cruises through the Camargue in a converted *péniche* – a traditional river cargo boat.

Sailing

Over 70 ports along the Provence coastline welcome yachts, and mooring charges vary. The Côte d'Azur ports are particularly expensive. Contact the **Fédération Française de Voile** for information on sailing clubs and where to hire boats.

DIRECTORY

Car Ferry

SNCM Ferryterranée
Marseille.
Tel 3260 (France).
Tel 00 33 825 88 80 88
(Outside France).
W sncm.fr

Cruises & River Trips

Croisieres Avignon-Mireio
Allée de l'Oulle, Avignon.
Tel 04 90 85 62 25.
W mireio.net

Grand Bleu
Tel 09 50 81 95 78 or
06 69 16 24 24.
W grandbleuyatching.fr

Les Péniches Isles de Stel
12 rue Amiral Courbet, 30220
Aigues-Mortes.
Tel 04 66 53 60 70.
W islesdestel.camargue.fr

Sailing

**Fédération Française
de Voile**
Tel 01 40 60 37 00.
W ffvoile.org

A privately owned motorboat from Cannes

Getting Around by Road

France is a motorist's paradise and the main route to Provence is via an excellent, if expensive, autoroute (motorway) network. Provence is ideal for touring, with some of the most beautiful road routes in the world, including the stunning Grande Corniche above Nice, and the hilltop lanes of the Luberon *(see pp174–5)*. Popular routes, especially the motorway and coastal roads along the Côte d'Azur, are always busy in high season.

Getting to Provence

The quickest route south from Paris is the Autoroute du Soleil, the A6 motorway to Lyon, followed by the A7 to Marseille. Travellers from the UK and northern Europe should try to avoid driving through Paris, especially during the rush hour. The A26 runs from Calais to Troyes, where you can join the A5, which leads into the A6.

From Spain, the A8 motorway leads directly to Marseille and goes on to Nice and Italy.

In high season, the motorways get very crowded and if you have time it may be worth taking more minor (and attractive) roads. Try turning off the main road at Montélimar to travel to the Luberon via Nyons and Vaison-la-Romaine. Or exit at Avignon, and head into the Luberon and on to Var.

For the adventurous, the Route Napoléon (N85) leads from Grenoble south across the Alps to Digne, and continues to Grasse. From Grasse, take the scenic D3 to Cannes, or the Route de Nice, which leads to Nice and its environs.

Car Rental

Car rental in France can be expensive so it is worth checking out your options before you go. There are numerous special offers for pre-paid car rentals in the UK and USA.

Fly-drive options work well for small groups. SNCF offers train and car-rental deals with collection from several main stations *(see pp246–7)*.

Insurance and Breakdown Services

All car insurance policies in the EU automatically include third-party insurance cover that is valid in any EU country. However, the extent of cover provided beyond the legal minimum varies between companies, so it is best to check your policy before you travel. If you are bringing your car from outside the EU, you can purchase extra insurance cover from the **AA**, **RAC** and **Europ Assistance**. While driving in France you must carry in the car your driving licence, passport, the vehicle registration document and a certificate of insurance. A sticker showing the country of registration should be displayed near the rear number plate. The headlights of right-hand drive cars must be adjusted – kits are available at most ports.

Taking out breakdown cover is advisable. It can be arranged with your European insurance cover, or through a motoring organization such as the AA or RAC. There are also local services such as **Dépannage Côte d'Azur Transports**.

Using the Autoroute Toll

When you join an autoroute, collect a ticket from the machine. This identifies your starting point on the autoroute. You do not pay until you reach an exit toll. You are charged according to the distance travelled and the type of vehicle used.

Motorway Sign
These signs indicate the name and distance to the next toll booth. They are usually blue and white; some show the tariff rates for cars, motorbikes, trucks and caravans.

Tollbooth with Attendant
When you hand in your ticket at a staffed tollbooth, the attendant will tell you the cost of your journey on the autoroute and the price will be displayed. You can pay with coins, notes or credit cards. A receipt is issued on request.

Automatic Machine
On reaching the exit toll, insert your ticket into the machine and the price of your journey is displayed in euros. You can pay either with coins or by credit card. The machine will give change and can issue a receipt.

Rules of the Road

Remember to drive on the right. The *priorité à droite* rule applies, meaning that you must give way to any vehicle coming out of a side turning on the right, unless otherwise signposted. On main roads a yellow diamond sign indicates where you have right of way. The *priorité à droite* does not apply at roundabouts, meaning you have to give way to cars already on the roundabout. Flashing headlights mean the driver is claiming right of way.

Seatbelts are compulsory for front and back seats. Children under ten are not permitted to travel in front seats apart from in baby seats facing backwards. Overtaking when there is a single solid centre line is heavily penalized. In case of breakdown it is compulsory to carry one red warning triangle and a luminous vest in the car. The autoroutes have emergency telephones every 2 km.

Speed Limits and Fines

Great efforts have been made to reduce road accidents in France, and there are now speed cameras at frequent intervals. Speed limits are:
• Motorways 130 km/hr (80 mph); 110 km/hr (68 mph) in rain.
• Dual carriageways 110 km/hr (68 mph); 50 km/hr (30 mph) in towns.
• Other roads 90 km/hr (56 mph).
Instant fines are issued for speeding and drink-driving. Driving with more than 0.5g of alcohol per litre of blood can also lead to severe fines, confiscation of your license, or even imprisonment.

Fast Through Routes

There are three main motorways in Provence: the A7 from Lyon to Marseille, the A9 from Orange to Barcelona and the A8 from Marseille to Menton. The A54 cuts across the Camargue from Aix-en-Provence to Nîmes. The A8 is the most expensive stretch of toll motorway in France, but allows you to drive from Nice to Aix-en-Provence in under two hours.

The scenic road through the Grand Canyon du Verdon

Country and Scenic Routes

One of the pleasures of touring Provence is turning off the main routes onto small country roads. The RN and D *(Route Nationale* and *Départmentale)* roads are good alternatives to motorways. *Bison futée* ("crafty bison") signs indicate alternative routes to avoid heavy traffic, and are especially helpful during the French holiday periods, known as the *grands départs*. The busiest weekends are in mid-July, and at the beginning and end of August when French holidays start and finish.

Apart from the busy coastal roads, Provence is a wonderful place to drive around. Some of the best scenic routes include the famous Corniche roads between Nice and Menton, with splendid sea views, or a tour of the back country of the Massif des Maures *(see pp120–21)*. The local tourist office should be able to provide you with more information and some maps.

Maps

The best general map of Provence is the Michelin yellow map No. 245, at a scale of 1:200,000. **IGN** (Institut Géographique National) maps are more detailed. Town plans are usually provided free by tourist offices. In large towns you may need a more detailed map, published by Michelin or **Plans-Guides Blay-Foldex/Berlitz**. In the UK, **Stanfords** is famous for its range of maps.

Parking

Parking in the big towns, particularly along the coast, is strictly regulated. If you are illegally parked, you may be towed away instantly to the police pound and face a substantial fine. Most Provençal towns have pay and display machines (*horodateurs*) and parking is often time limited. Many places offer free parking from noon to 2pm – ticket machines automatically allow for this. Ensure you have enough coins for the meter or purchase a parking card, which are available from the *tabacs*.

Petrol

Petrol is relatively expensive in France, especially on autoroutes. Large supermarkets and hypermarkets sell petrol at a discount, however the pay booths may close over lunch and the automatic pumps only accept *carte bleue* (French bank cards). A map issued by French Government Tourist offices (*see p237*) indicates the cheaper petrol stations situated up to 2 km (just over a mile) from motorway exits. Unleaded petrol (*sans plomb*) and diesel fuel are found in all stations. LPG gas is also available, often on motorways. A map of locations stocking this fuel can be obtained from any LPG station in France. Note that in rural areas petrol stations can be hard to find, so ensure you have enough petrol for your journey.

Mountain bikes are ideal for exploring the Provençal countryside

Cycling

Cycling is one of the most pleasant ways to see Provence. Although the French are cycling enthusiasts, there are few cycle lanes in towns in Provence. However, some cities, such as Arles, Avignon and Nîmes, have specified cycle routes. You can take bikes on certain trains – check the timetable first for the bike symbol (*see p248*). You can also reserve bicycles at several stations (*Train + Velo*). Rental shops can be found throughout the region, especially in the Luberon and in towns around the Camargue, which rent out mountain bikes (*VTT*). Bicycle theft is common along the Côte d'Azur – make sure you are fully insured before you go. Best of all, Provence is now following the initiative of Paris in introducing a free bike scheme in cities such as Marseille and Nice. Enquire at the tourist office for bike locations.

Taxis

Prices vary from one part of Provence to another. The charges are predictably highest along the Côte d'Azur, where it's not uncommon to pay €30 for a 20-minute journey. Elsewhere the pick-up charge is usually around €2, and €0.60 or more for every kilometre. An extra charge will be made for any luggage. All taxis must use a meter, or a *compteur*. Hailing a taxi is not customary in Provence – you must go to a taxi rank or book by phone.

Hitchhiking

Hitchhiking is possible in France, although officially it is frowned upon. You are not supposed to hitch on the motorways and if you do you will be cautioned by the police. Allostop can put you in touch with cars heading south from Paris, and for region to region lifts: www.allostop.net.

Coach and Bus Travel

Coach travel used to be the cheapest way of getting to Provence, but reductions in air fares have now made it a less competitive option. It is, however, one of the more environmentally friendly ways to travel and will take you directly from city centre to city centre. **Eurolines** (*see p251*) coaches depart all year round from London to Nimes, Toulon, Marseille, Aix-en-Provence and Avignon. The journey to Marseille takes about 23 hours from London.

Larger towns have a bus station but, otherwise, the bus services are limited. SNCF runs bus lines in northern Provence, and private companies run along the major motorways between towns and on some minor routes, such as the coastal road between Toulon and St-Tropez. Local bus services are notoriously erratic.

Taxis lined up for business at a taxi rank, Marseille

Travelling in Cities

Apart from Marseille, which competes with Lyon for the title of second city of France, the towns and cities of Provence are small. The best way to get around is generally on foot, parking in most towns is strictly regulated, and in the summer months traffic can be very heavy. Marseille and Nice both have excellent public transport systems that are efficient and easy to use. Marseille and Nice also have bike rental schemes that are similar to the *Vélib* in Paris.

Bicycles can be hired through the Le Vélo scheme in Marseille

Metro

The fastest way to get around Marseille is by **Métro**. The system has two lines, which meet at Gare St-Charles and Castellane stations. Métro 1 goes from the hospital La Fourragère in the east to La Rose in the northeast, passing through the Vieux Port on the way. Métro 2 runs roughly north to south, connecting the shipping port with Notre-Dame-de-la-Garde and Ste-Marguerite. Tickets can be bought from Métro stations, on buses or in *tabacs*. Trains run from 5am–10:30pm daily.

Trams

The Marseille tram network consists of three lines, which together link the centre to areas to the north, south, east and west of the city. The lines meet at Noailles near Gare St-Charles. The Marseille fare system is called *Reseau Liberté*. Tickets are valid for Métro, tram and buses with free transfers within a one-hour period.

In Nice some sections of the long-awaited tramway system are operational. The U-shaped Line 1 connects the northern and eastern neighbourhoods to the centre of the city, passing through Place Massena and the main railway station. Tickets can be bought from machines or tram operators.

Buses

Although bus routes between towns in Provence can be slow and inadequate, within the towns the service is usually good. In Marseille an extensive bus network covers all of the city. Long-distance buses and airport shuttle buses leave from the *gare routière* (bus station) behind the main train station Gare St-Charles. There is a useful left-luggage facility *(consigne)* at both stations.

Nice has a good network of city buses including night buses. The Sunbus is a tourist service that runs daily and has multiple stops throughout the city. Tickets can be bought on board buses or from *tabacs*. Check the website of **Lignes d'Azur** for timetables.

Taxis

There are taxi ranks on most main squares in towns and cities. You can also telephone for taxis; enquire at the tourist office or your hotel for local numbers. It is not usual practice to hail a taxi in the street.

Cycling

Whether you bring your own bicycle or rent one, most of Provence's towns are small enough to cycle around. Marseille, Avignon and Aix-en-Provence have introduced bike-sharing schemes. Ask at a tourist office for further details and locations *(see p245)*.

Walking

Explore the towns on foot as much as you can. Apart from Marseille and Nice the main city-centre sights of Nîmes, Avignon or Aix-en-Provence can easily be seen in a walking tour. Even in Marseille with its louche reputation the crime rate is no higher than any other French city, so the usual precautions should be adequate to stay safe.

DIRECTORY

Metro

Métro (RTM) – Marseille
W rtm.fr

Buses

Ligne d'Azur
W lignedazur.com

Taxis

Nice Taxi Riviera
Tel 08 99 70 08 78.

Taxi Radio Marseille
Tel 04 91 02 20 20.

Cycling

Marseille
W levelo-mpm.fr

Nice
W velobleu.org

Marseille tram travelling along the Boulevard Longchamp

General Index

Acknowledgments

Dorling Kindersley would like to thank the following people whose contributions and assistance have made the preparation of this book possible.

Main Contributor
Roger Williams is a writer and editor who was for many years associated with the *Sunday Times* magazine. He has written two novels and a number of guide books, on places ranging from Barcelona to the Baltic States, and was a contributor to *Over Europe*, the first aerial record of the united continent. He visits France regularly, and has been writing about Provence for more than 30 years.

Contributors
Adele Evans, John Flower, Robin Gauldie, Jim Keeble, Anthony Rose, Martin Walters.

Additional Photography
Demetrio Carrasco, Andy Crawford, Lisa Cupolo, Franz Curzon, Philip Freiberger, Nick Goodall, Steve Gorton, Michelle Grant, John Heseltine, Andrew Holligan, Richard McConnell, Neil Mersh, Ian O'Leary, Clive Streeter.

Additional Illustrators
Simon Calder, Paul Guest, Aziz Khan, Tristan Spaargaren, Ann Winterbotham, John Woodcock.

Cartographic Research
Jane Hugill, Samantha James, Jennifer Skelley, Martin Smith (Lovell Johns).

Design and Editorial
Managing Editor Georgina Matthews
Deputy Editorial Director Douglas Amrine
Deputy Art Director Gaye Allen
Production Controller Hilary Stephens
Picture Research Susan Mennell
DTP Designer Salim Qurashi
Map Co-ordinators Simon Farbrother, David Pugh
Maps Uma Bhattacharya, Kunal Singh, Jennifer Skelley, Samantha James (Lovell Johns Ltd, Oxford)
Researcher Philippa Richmond
Revisions Azeem Alam, Vincent Allonier, Michelle Arness Frederic, Rosemary Bailey, Shahnaaz Bakshi, Laetitia Benloulou, Josie Bernard, Marta Bescos Sanchez, Tessa Bindloss, Hilary Bird, Nadia Bonomally, Kevin Brown, Margaret Chang, Cooling Brown Partnership, Guy Dimond, Joy Fitzsimmonds, Lisa Fox-Mullen, Anna Freiberger, Rhiannon Furbear, Vinod Harish, Victoria Heyworth-Dunne, Jackie Grosvenor, Swati Gupta, Annette Jacobs, Stuart James, Laura Jones, Nancy Jones, Rupanki Kaushik, Rahul Kumar, Rakesh Kumar Pal, Cécile Landau, Erika Lang, Delphine Lawrance, Francesca Machiavelli, James Marlow, Sonal Modha, Sachida Nand Pradhan, Claire Naylor, Scarlett O'Hara, Helen Partington, Sangita Patel, Susie Peachey, Katie Peacock, Alice Peebles, Pure Content Ltd, Carolyn Pyrah, Ashwin Raju Adimari, Philippa Richmond, Ellen Root, Zoe Ross, Kavita Saha, Sands Publishing Solutions, Avijit Sengupta, Baishakhee Sengupta, Sailesh Sharma, Bhaswati Singh, Catherine Skipper, Amelia Smith, Priyanka Thakur, Amanda Tomeh, Daphne Trotter, Janis Utton, Conrad van Dyk, Vinita Venugopal, Ajay Verma, Dora Whitaker, Sophie Wright, Irina Zarb.

Special Assistance
Louise Abbott; Anna Brooke, Manade Gilbert Arnaud; Brigitte Charles, Monaco Tourist Board, London; Sabine Giraud, Terres du Sud, Venasque; Emma Heath; Nathalie Lavarenne, Musée Matisse, Nice; Ella Milroy; Marianne Petrou; Andrew Sanger; David Tse.

Photographic Reference
Bernard Beaujard, Vézénobres.

Photography Permissions
Dorling Kindersley would like to thank the following for their assistance and kind permission to photograph at their establishments: Fondation Marguerite et Aimé Maeght, St-Paul de Vence; Hotel Négresco, Nice; Monsieur J-F Campana, Mairie de Nice; Monsieur Froumessol, Mairie de Cagnes-sur-Mer; Musée Ephrussi de Rothschild, St-Jean-Cap-Ferrat; Musée Jean Cocteau, Menton; Musée International de la Parfumerie, Grasse; Musée Matisse, Nice; Musée National Message Biblique Marc Chagall, Nice; Musée Océanographique, Monaco; Musée Picasso/Château Grimaldi, Antibes; Salle des Mariages, Hôtel de Ville, Menton, and all other churches, museums, hotels, restaurants, shops and sights too numerous to thank individually.

Picture Credits
a = above; b = below/bottom; c = centre; f = far; l = left; r = right; t = top.

Works of art have been reproduced with the permission of the following copyright holders:

© ADAGP, Paris and DACS, London 2011: 30tr, 31tr, 31bl, 34tr, 78tl, 80tr, 80cla, 80clb, 81tl, 81cr, 81br, 82cb, 82crb, 89bl, 103tr, 111br, 123crb, 124ca, 124bc, 125cra, 125crb, 148ca; ©ARS, NY and DACS, London 2006: 63tl, 80clb; © DACS, London 2006: 136tl; © Estate of Francis Bacon/DACS, London: 225bl; © Succession H.Matisse/DACS, London 2006: 31cr, 86tr, 86cla, 86bl, 87tc, 87cr, 87br; © Succession Miro/ADAGP, Paris and DACS, London 2006: 81cra; © Succession Picasso/DACS, London 2006: 30br, 77cl, 77cr, 77clb, 77bc, 77br.

The publisher would like to thank the following individuals, companies and picture libraries for permission to reproduce their photographs:

Alamy Images: AA World Travel Library 155clb; Peter Bowater 178; Tor Eigeland 14cl; Derek Harris 149br; Chris Hellier; Hemis 13tl, 158, 200, Neil Juggins 240clb; Justin Kase zeightz 240cl; Justin Kase zfourz 58tl; Melvyn Longhurst 203bc; Barry Mason 247c; Megapress 109crb; Pictures Colour Library 246cla, 251tc; Pixonnet.com/Goran Strandsten 240cl; Travelshots.com 238tl; Travel Pictures 122clb; Dave Watts 231c; Gregory Wrona 12br, 236br; **Restaurant Alexandre**: Michel Kayser/Alain Guilhot/Fédéphoto 214tc; **Alvey & Towers**: 246br; **Ancient Art and Architecture Collection**: 43t and cb, 44bl, 47tl; **Archives de l'Automobile Club de Monaco**: 56cla; **Artephot, Paris**: Plassart 31c.

La Bastide de Voulonne: 195tr; **La Belle Aurore FRCAM**: 229tl; **Hostellerie Berard**: 230cra, 211tl; **La Bonne Etape**: 197cr, 217bc; **Bridgeman Art Library**: Christie's, London 51crb, 54–55; Giraudon 51tl, 52bl; Schloss Charlottenburg, Berlin 183tr.

Campagne, Campagne!, Paris: Jolyot 96br; JL Julien 35bc; Meissonnier 163cla; Meschinet 142cl; Moirenc 245tl; Pambour 175tl, 176t; Picard 163tr; **Cephas**: Mick Rock 206br, 207cra and br; **Jean-loup Charmet, Paris**: 32cl; © Antoine de Saint-Exupéry/Gallimard 33cla; 41b, 46bl, 50cla and cb, 53t and c, 54tr, 56t, 57tl, 136cl, 144tl, 157tc, 164clb; **Bruce Coleman**: Adrian Davies 118bl; JLG Grande 140cl; George McCarthy 23tl; Andrew J Purcell 119c and bl; Hans Reinhard 141tc, 175bl, bc and br; Dr Frieder Sauer 118cl; Roger Wandscheidt 164cl; K. Wolfe 164bc; **Colombe d'Or**: 203tc; **Corbis**: Sophie Bassouls 33cr; CuboImages srl 15bc; Owen Franken 231tc; Chris Hellier 101tr; Image Source 15tr; Pascal parrot/Sygma 36br; Robert Harding World Imagery/Gavin Hellier 64; **Joe Cornish**: 27tr; **Lisa Cupolo**: 110tc; **Culture Espaces, Paris**: 90tr and cla; Véran 91tl.

Photo Daspet, Avignon: Musée du Petit Palais, Avignon 49bl; Palais des Papes, Avignon 48clb and bl; **Diaf, Paris**: J-P Garcin 37cb; J-C Gérard 228 tl and bc, 155br; Camille Moirenc 166c; Bernard Régent 30tr; Patrick Somelet 162br; **Direction Des Affaires Culturelles, Monaco**: 95cra; **Domaine de Cabasse**: 201bl; **Dreamstime.com**: Chaoss 10cla; Ciuciumama 151tr; Rene Drouyer 234–5; Fotoluminate 12tc; Wieslaw Jarek 1c; Lianem 187br; Evgeny Prokofyev 155tc; Radomír Režný 18; Richard Semik 60–1, 134cr; Luboslav Tiles 2–3; Typhoonski 11tr.

European Commission: 242; **Mary Evans**: 32bl, crb and br, 32crb, 49br and t, 51br; **Jane Ewart**: 26clb, 27crb, 29c, 62cla, 80cla, 131b, 167cra and cr; **Explorer Archives, Paris**: cr; L Bertrand 42cb; Jean-Loup Charmet 128cl, 151crb; Coll. ES 50clb and bl; Coll. G Garde 37cra; J P Hervey 68tl; J & C Lenars 41c; M C Noailles 69br; Peter Willis 44cla; A Wolf 47cb.

La Ferme de la Huppe: 216tr; **Fondation Auguste Escoffier, Villeneuve-Loubet**: 78c; **Fondation Maeght, Saint-Paul-de-Vence, France**: Claude Germain 81tl and cra; Coll. M et Mme Adrien Maeght 81cr; **Frank Lane Picture Agency**: N. Clark 174br; Fritz Polking 22tr; M B Withers 140ca.

Galerie Intemporel, Paris: Les Films Ariane, Paris 58–9; **Editions Gaud, Moisenay**: 74bl, 90br, 91bc and br, 146tl, 185cr; **Getty Images**: Peter Adams 220cla; AFP/Valery Hache 224bl; The Bridgeman Art Library/Gallo-Roman 148cl; DEA/G. Dagli Orti 8–9, 114clb; M. Gebicki 192–3; hemis.fr/Bertrand Gardel 130; Hemis/Bertrand Rieger 20c; Hemis/Jose Nicolas 220br; The Image Bank/Peter Adams 20tl; The Image Bank/Remi Benali 36cl; WireImage/Tony Barson 59br; **Giraudon, Paris**: 31tr, bl and br, 32tr, 40, 44br, 52cla and br, 137b, 176c; Lauros-Giraudon 42cla, 49crb, 50tr (detail), 50–1, 53clb, 55cb, 57cb (all rights reserved), 77tl and tr, 114bl, 129c, 138cla, 148ca, 150tr; Musée de la Vieille Charité, Marseille 42tr; Musée de la Ville de Paris, Musée du Petit Palais/Lauros-Giraudon 30clb; Musée des Beaux-Arts, Marseille 52–3, 53bl, 156cla; Musée du Vieux Marseille, Marseille 52clb, 54cla; **Grand Grottes de St-Cézaire**: 69cl.

Robert Harding Picture Library: 39br; **Hemisphere Images**: Bertrand Gardel 253tr; **Hotel Eden Roc, Cap D'antibes**: 195br; **Hulton-deutsch Collection**: 32ca, 33bl; Keystone 98tr.

Illustrated London News Picture Library: 54b; **Intercontinental Carlton Hotel, Cannes**: 194bc; **ISIC**: 238c.

Le Jardin de la Gare: 215br; **Jardins Secret**: 196tl; **Le Julien**: 213tr.

Catherine Karnow, San Francisco: 114cla; **The Kobal Collection**: United Artists 75tl.

Edouard Loubet Restaurant: 215tc; **Louis XV, Monaco**: Bernard Touillon 209br.

Magnum Photos: Bruno Barbey 228crb; René Burri 58crb; Elliott Erwitt 95br; **Mairie de Nîmes**: Jean-Charles Blais 136t (all rights reserved); Francis Bacon 225bl (all rights reserved); **Mansell Collection**: 43b, 46br, 47bl, 55ca, 56bl; **Le Mas d'Entremont**: 212bc; **Le Mesclun**: 216bl; **Editions Molipor, Monaco**: 98br; courtesy of SBM 55crb, 98cla; **Musée d'Art Classique de Mougins**: 13cr; **Musée De L'Annonciade, St-Tropez**: E Vila Mateu 123crb, 124–5 all; **Musée Archéologique De La Vaison-la-Romaine**: Christine Bézin 45clb; **Musée D'art Moderne Et D'art Contemporain, Nice**: 89bl; **Musée Fabre, Montpellier**: Leenhardt 139b; **Musée De La Photographie, Mougins**: 70br; **Musée Matisse, NICE**: © Service photographique, Ville de Nice 86tr, cla and bl, 87tc, cr, bc and br.

Negresco Hotel, Nice: 198br, 210bc.

L'Olivier Restaurant: 202bl, 217tl; **OSF**: Mike Hill 140c. Tom Leach 164br; Frank Schneider Meyer 140cb. **OTC Marseille**: 253bl. **Palais des Festivals et des Congres**: 72cla, 73tl; **Pastis Hotel**: 194ca, 199tr; **Photolibrary**: 236cla. **Photo Resources**: CM Dixon 45crb. **Planet Earth Pictures**: John Neusch Wander 118br; P. Sloanes 23br; **Popperfoto**: 33cb, tr, 76br.

Retrograph: 34tr. **SA Aeroports**: 244bc; **Service de Presse de la Ville de Cagnes sur Mer**: 83cr; **SNCF**: 59bc, 248tr; **Frank Spooner**: Robin Ekta Orop 71bc; Gamma / C. Viojard 71ca, bc; **Superstock**: Hemis.fr 186tl; Hemis.fr/Camille Moirenc 104; **Sygma**: 79tr; Keystone 57bc. **Editions Tallendier, Paris**: Bibliothèque Nationale 46–7; **Terres du Sud, Venasque**: Philippe Giraud 48cla, 49ca and bl, and br, 68br, 74bc, 85cra, 109br, 171crb, 172b; **Les Terraillers**: 208bl; **La Trattoria, Monaco**: Frédéric Ducout 209tl; **Travel Library**: Philip Enticknap 97t and br.

La Vague d'Or: 212tl.

Wallis Phototheque, Marseille: 38cra, clb and br, 39ca; Bendi 252tr; Clasen 59tl, 71cla; Constant 186br; Di Meglio 119ca; Giani 100tr, 225tr; Huet 189tr; LCI 35br, 180tr; Leroux 20br; Poulet 100c; Royer 100cr and bl; Tarta 196br; **Roger Williams**: 105, 143bl, 169tr, 174c, 185bc, 188cla.

Front endpaper: **Alamy Images**: Peter Bowater Ltr, Hemis Lcla; **Corbis**: Robert Harding World Imagery/Gavin Hellier Rtr; Getty Images: Hemis.fr/Bertrand Gardel Lbc; Superstock: Hemis.fr/Camille Moirenc Rbr.

Jacket: Front and spine - **AWL Images**: Matteo Colombo.

All other images © Dorling Kindersley. For further information see www.dkimages.com

Phrase Book

In Emergency

Help!	**Au secours!**	*oh sekoor*
Stop!	**Arrêtez!**	*aret-ay*
Call a doctor!	**Appelez un médecin!**	*apuh-lay uñ medsañ*
Call an ambulance!	**Appelez une ambulance!**	*apuh-lay oon oñboo-loñs*
Call the police!	**Appelez la police!**	*apuh-lay lah poh-lees*
Call the fire brigade!	**Appelez les pompiers!**	*apuh-lay leh poñ-peeyay*
Where is the nearest telephone?	**Où est le téléphone le plus proche?**	*oo ay luh tehlehfon luh ploo prosh*
Where is the nearest hospital?	**Où est l'hôpital le plus proche?**	*oo ay l'opeetal luh ploo prosh*

Communication Essentials

Yes	**Oui**	*wee*
No	**Non**	*noñ*
Please	**S'il vous plaît**	*seel voo play*
Thank you	**Merci**	*mer-see*
Excuse me	**Excusez-moi**	*exkoo-zay mwah*
Hello	**Bonjour**	*boñzhoor*
Goodbye	**Au revoir**	*oh ruh-vwar*
Good night	**Bonsoir**	*boñ-swar*
Morning	**Le matin**	*matañ*
Afternoon	**L'après-midi**	*l'apreh-meedee*
Evening	**Le soir**	*swar*
Yesterday	**Hier**	*eeyehr*
Today	**Aujourd'hui**	*oh-zhoor-dwee*
Tomorrow	**Demain**	*duhmañ*
Here	**Ici**	*ee-see*
There	**Là**	*lah*
What?	**Quel, quelle?**	*kel, kel*
When?	**Quand?**	*koñ*
Why?	**Pourquoi?**	*poor-kwah*
Where?	**Où?**	*oo*

Useful Phrases

How are you?	**Comment allez-vous?**	*kom-moñ talay voo*
Very well, thank you.	**Très bien, merci.**	*treh byañ, mer-see*
Pleased to meet you.	**Enchanté de faire votre connaissance.**	*oñshoñ-tay duh fehr votr kon-ay-sans*
See you soon.	**A bientôt.**	*a byañ-toh*
That's fine.	**Voilà qui est parfait.**	*vwalah kee ay parfay*
Where is/are…?	**Où est/sont…?**	*oo ay/soñ*
How far is it to…?	**Combien de kilomètres d'ici à…?**	*kom-byañ duh keelo-metr d'ee-see ah*
Which way to…?	**Quelle est la direction pour…?**	*kel ay lah deer-ek-syoñ poor*
Do you speak English?	**Parlez-vous anglais?**	*par-lay voo oñg-lay*
I don't understand.	**Je ne comprends pas.**	*zhuh nuh kom-proñ pah*
Could you speak slowly, please?	**Pouvez-vous parler moins vite, s'il vous plaît?**	*poo-vay voo par-lay mwañ veet seel voo play*
I'm sorry.	**Excusez-moi.**	*exkoo-zay mwah*

Useful Words

big	**grand**	*groñ*
small	**petit**	*puh-tee*
hot	**chaud**	*show*
cold	**froid**	*frwah*
good	**bon**	*boñ*
bad	**mauvais**	*moh-veh*
enough	**assez**	*assay*
well	**bien**	*byañ*
open	**ouvert**	*oo-ver*
closed	**fermé**	*fer-meh*
left	**gauche**	*gohsh*
right	**droite**	*drwaht*
straight on	**tout droit**	*too drwah*
near	**près**	*preh*
far	**loin**	*lwañ*
up	**en haut**	*oñ oh*
down	**en bas**	*oñ bah*
early	**de bonne heure**	*duh bon-urr*
late	**en retard**	*oñ ruh-tar*
entrance	**l'entrée**	*l'on-tray*
exit	**la sortie**	*sor-tee*
toilet	**les toilettes, les WC**	*twah-let, vay-see*
unoccupied	**libre**	*leebr*
no charge	**gratuit**	*grah-twee*

Making a Telephone Call

I'd like to place a long-distance call.	**Je voudrais faire un interurbain.**	*zhuh voo-dreh fehr uñ añter-oorbañ*
I'd like to make a reverse-charge call.	**Je voudrais faire une communication PCV.**	*zhuh voodreh fehr oon kom-oonikah-syoñ peh-seh-veh*
I'll try again later.	**Je rappelerai plus tard.**	*zhuh rapeleray ploo tar*
Can I leave a message?	**Est-ce que je peux laisser un message?**	*es-keh zhuh puh leh-say uñ mehsazh*
Hold on.	**Ne quittez pas, s'il vous plaît.**	*nuh kee-tay pah seel voo play*
Could you speak up a little please?	**Pouvez-vous parler un peu plus fort?**	*poo-vay voo par-lay uñ puh ploo for*
local call	**la communication locale**	*komoonikah-syoñ low-kal*

Shopping

How much does this cost?	**C'est combien s'il vous plaît?**	say kom-byañ seel voo play
Do you take credit cards?	**Est-ce que vous acceptez les cartes de crédit?**	es-keh voo zaksept-ay leh kart duh-kreh dee
Do you take travellers' cheques?	**Est-ce que vous acceptez les chèques de voyage?**	es-kuh voo zaksept-ay leh shek duh vwayazh
I would like …	**Je voudrais…**	zhuh voo-dray
Do you have?	**Est-ce que vous avez?**	es-kuh voo zavay
I'm just looking.	**Je regarde seulement.**	zhuh ruhgar suhlmoñ
What time do you open?	**A quelle heure vous êtes ouvert?**	ah kel urr voo zet oo-ver
What time do you close?	**A quelle heure vous êtes fermé?**	ah kel urr voo zet fer-may
This one	**Celui-ci**	suhl-wee-see
That one	**Celui-là**	suhl-wee-lah
expensive	**cher**	shehr
cheap	**pas cher, bon marché**	pah shehr, boñ mar-shay
size, clothes	**la taille**	tye
size, shoes	**la pointure**	pwañ-tur
white	**blanc**	bloñ
black	**noir**	nwahr
red	**rouge**	roozh
yellow	**jaune**	zhohwn
green	**vert**	vehr
blue	**bleu**	bluh

Types of Shop

antique shop	**le magasin d'antiquités**	maga-zañ d'oñteekee-tay
bakery	**la boulangerie**	booloñ-zhuree
bank	**la banque**	boñk
book shop	**la librairie**	lee-brehree
butcher	**la boucherie**	boo-shehree
cake shop	**la pâtisserie**	patee-sree
cheese shop	**la fromagerie**	fromazh-ree
chemist	**la pharmacie**	farmah-see
dairy	**la crémerie**	krem-ree
department store	**le grand magasin**	groñ maga-zañ
delicatessen	**la charcuterie**	sharkoot-ree
fishmonger	**la poissonnerie**	pwasson-ree
gift shop	**le magasin de cadeaux**	maga-zañ duh kadoh
greengrocer	**le marchand de légumes**	mar-shoñ duh lay-goom
grocery	**l'alimentation**	alee-moñta-syoñ
hairdresser	**le coiffeur**	kwafuhr
market	**le marché**	marsh-ay
newsagent	**le magasin de journaux**	maga-zañ duh zhoor-no
post office	**la poste, le bureau de poste, les PTT**	pohst, booroh duh pohst, peh-teh-teh
shoe shop	**le magasin de chaussures**	duh show-soor
supermarket	**le super-marché**	soo pehr-marshay
tobacconist	**le tabac**	tabah
travel agent	**l'agence de voyages**	l'azhoñs duh vwayazh

Menu Decoder

l'agneau	**l'anyoh**	lamb
l'ail	**l'eye**	garlic
la banane	**banan**	banana
le beurre	**burr**	butter
la bière	**bee-yehr**	beer
le bifteck, le steak	**beef-tek, stek**	steak
le boeuf	**buhf**	beef
bouilli	**boo-yee**	boiled
le café	**kah-fayle**	coffee
le canard	**kanar**	duck
le citron pressé	**see-troñ press-eh**	fresh lemon juice
les crevettes	**kruh-vet**	prawns
les crustacés	**kroos-ta-say**	shellfish
cuit au four	**kweet oh foor**	baked
le dessert	**deh-ser**	dessert
l'eau minérale	**l'oh meeney-ral**	mineral water
les escargots	**leh zes-kar-goh**	snails
les frites	**freet**	chips
le fromage	**from-azh**	cheese
les fruits frais	**frwee freh**	fresh fruit
les fruits de mer	**frwee duh mer**	seafood
le gâteau	**gah-toh**	cake
la glace	**glas**	ice, ice cream
grillé	**gree-yay**	grilled
le homard	**omahr**	lobster
l'huile	**l'weel**	oil
le jambon	**zhoñ-boñ**	ham
le lait	**leh**	milk
les légumes	**lay-goom**	vegetables
la moutarde	**moo-tard**	mustard
l'oeuf	**l'uf**	egg
les oignons	**leh zonyoñ**	onions
les olives	**leh zoleev**	olives
l'orange pressée	**l'oroñzh press-eh**	fresh orange juice
le pain	**pan**	bread
le petit pain	**puh-tee pañ**	roll
poché	**posh-ay**	poached
le poisson	**pwah-ssoñ**	fish
le poivre	**pwavr**	pepper
la pomme	**pom**	apple
les pommes de terre	**pom-duh tehr**	potatoes
le porc	**por**	pork
le potage	**poh-tazh**	soup
le poulet	**poo-lay**	chicken
le riz	**ree**	rice
rôti	**row-tee**	roast
la sauce	**sohs**	sauce
la saucisse	**sohsees**	sausage, fresh
sec	**sek**	dry
le sel	**sel**	salt
le sucre	**sookr**	sugar
le thé	**tay**	tea
le toast	**toast**	toast
la viande	**vee-yand**	meat
le vin blanc	**vañ bloñ**	white wine
le vin rouge	**vañ roozh**	red wine
le vinaigre	**veenaygr**	vinegar

Eating Out

Have you got a table?	**Avez-vous une table libre?**	avay-voo oon tahbl leebr
I want to reserve a table.	**Je voudrais réserver une table.**	zhuh voo-dray rayzehr-vay oon tahbl
The bill, please.	**L'addition, s'il vous plaît.**	l'adee-syoñ seel voo play
I am a vegetarian.	**Je suis végétarien.**	zhuh swee vezhay-tehryañ
Waitress/ waiter	**Madame, Mademoiselle/ Monsieur**	mah-dam, mah-dem wah zel/muh-syuh
menu	**le menu, la carte**	men-oo, kart
fixed-price menu	**le menu à prix fixe**	men-oo ah pree feeks
cover charge	**le couvert**	koo-vehr
wine list	**la carte des vins**	kart-deh vañ
glass	**le verre**	vehr
bottle	**la bouteille**	boo-tay
knife	**le couteau**	koo-toh
fork	**la fourchette**	for-shet
spoon	**la cuillère**	kwee-yehr
breakfast	**le petit déjeuner**	puh-tee deh-zhuh-nay
lunch	**le déjeuner**	deh-zhuh-nay
dinner	**le dîner**	dee-nay
main course	**le plat principal**	plah prañsee-pal
starter, first course	**l'entrée, le hors d'oeuvre**	l'oñ-tray, or-duhvr
dish of the day	**le plat du jour**	plah doo zhoor
wine bar	**le bar à vin**	bar ah vañ
café	**le café**	ka-fay
rare	**saignant**	say-noñ
medium	**à point**	ah pwañ
well done	**bien cuit**	byañ kwee

Staying in a Hotel

Do you have a vacant room?	**Est-ce que vous avez une chambre?**	es-kuh voo-zavay oon shambr
double room	**la chambre pour deux personnes, avec**	shambr ah duh pehr-sonavek
with double bed	**un grand lit**	un gronñ lee
twin room	**la chambre à deux lits**	shambr ah duh lee
single room	**la chambre pour une personne**	shambr ah oon pehr-son
room with a bath, shower	**la chambre avec salle de bains, une douche**	shambr avek sal duh bañ, oon doosh
porter	**le garçon**	gar-soñ
key	**la clef**	klay
I have a reservation.	**J'ai fait une réservation.**	zhay fay oon rayzehrva-syoñ

Sightseeing

abbey	**l'abbaye**	l'abay-ee
art gallery	**la galerie d'art**	galer-ree dart
cathedral	**la cathédrale**	katay-dral
church	**l'église**	l'aygleez
garden	**le jardin**	zhar-dañ
library	**la bibliothèque**	beeblee-o-tek
museum	**le musée**	moo-zay
railway station	**la gare (SNCF)**	gahr (es-en-say-ef)
bus station	**la gare routière**	gahr roo-tee-yehr
tourist information	**les renseignements touristiques, le syndicat d'initiative**	roñsayn-moñ office too-rees-teek, sandee-ka d'eenee-syateev
town hall	**l'hôtel de ville**	l'ohtel duh veel
private mansion	**l'hôtel particulier**	l'ohtel partikoo-lyay
closed for public holiday	**fermeture jour férié**	fehrmeh-tur zhoor fehree-ay

Numbers

0	**zéro**	zeh-roh
1	**un, une**	uñ, oon
2	**deux**	duh
3	**trois**	trwah
4	**quatre**	katr
5	**cinq**	sañk
6	**six**	sees
7	**sept**	set
8	**huit**	weet
9	**neuf**	nerf
10	**dix**	dees
11	**onze**	oñz
12	**douze**	dooz
13	**treize**	trehz
14	**quatorze**	katorz
15	**quinze**	kañz
16	**seize**	sehz
17	**dix-sept**	dees-set
18	**dix-huit**	dees-weet
19	**dix-neuf**	dees-nerf
20	**vingt**	vañ
30	**trente**	tront
40	**quarante**	karoñt
50	**cinquante**	sañkoñt
60	**soixante**	swasoñt
70	**soixante-dix**	swasoñt-dees
80	**quatre-vingts**	katr-vañ
90	**quatre-vingts-dix**	katr-vañ-dees
100	**cent**	soñ
1,000	**mille**	meel

Time

one minute	**une minute**	oon mee-noot
one hour	**une heure**	oon urr
half an hour	**une demi-heure**	oon duh-mee urr
Monday	**lundi**	luñ-dee
Tuesday	**mardi**	mar-dee
Wednesday	**mercredi**	mehrkruh-dee
Thursday	**jeudi**	zhuh-dee
Friday	**vendredi**	voñdruh-dee
Saturday	**samedi**	sam-dee
Sunday	**dimanche**	dee-moñsh